Your Reading

NCTE Committee on the Middle School and Junior High Booklist

James Barton, Rhode Island College, Providence
Jennifer Basile, Gorton Junior High School, Warwick, Rhode Island
Joseph Carroll, Rhode Island College, Providence
Kelly Chandler-Olcott, Syracuse University, Syracuse, New York
Anita E. Childers, Southeast Community College, Middlesboro, Kentucky
Melissa Comer, Cumberland College, Williamsburg, Kentucky
Ruth Copp, Saginaw Valley State University, University Center, Michigan
Marshall A. George, Fordham University, New York City
David Gill, University of North Carolina at Wilmington
Gail Gregg, Florida International University, Miami
Anne Hird, Bridgewater State College, Bridgewater, Massachusetts
Jeffrey Kaplan, University of Central Florida, Orlando
Judith Mitchell, Rhode Island College, Providence
Elizabeth Poe, West Virginia University, Morgantown
David Pugalee, University of North Carolina at Charlotte
Anne Sherrill, East Tennessee State University, Johnson City
Susan Steffel, Central Michigan University, Mount Pleasant
Dee Story, Saginaw Valley State University, University Center, Michigan
Lois Stover, St. Mary's College of Maryland, St. Mary's City
Christa Thompson, Veterans High School, Warwick, Rhode Island
Margaret Watson, Winman Junior High School, Warwick, Rhode Island

Your Reading

An Annotated Booklist for Middle School and Junior High

11th Edition

Jean E. Brown and Elaine C. Stephens, Editors,
and the Committee on the Middle School and Junior High Booklist

Foreword by
Joan Bauer

Afterword by
Joyce Hansen

National Council of Teachers of English
1111 W. Kenyon Road, Urbana, IL 61801-1096

Staff Editor: Bonny Graham
Interior Design: Doug Burnett
Cover Design: Tom Jaczak
Series Cover Design: R. Maul

Cover illustration reprinted with permission of Judith Bloom Fradin, from *Bound for the North Star* by Dennis Brindell Fradin (Clarion, 2000).

NCTE Stock Number: 59443-3050

ISSN: 1051-4740

ISBN: 0-8141-5944-3

To my sister, Mary, who is facing the ultimate challenge with courage, dignity, and hope.

JEB

To my grandchildren, Griffin, Mitchell, and Iza, for their love of reading and adventure.

ECS

About the NCTE Bibliography Series

The National Council of Teachers of English is proud to be part of a tradition that we want to share with you. In our bibliography series are four different booklists, each focused on a particular audience, each updated regularly. These are *Adventuring with Books* (pre–K through grade 6), *Kaleidoscope* (multicultural literature, grades K through 8), *Your Reading* (middle school/junior high), and *Books for You* (senior high). Together, these volumes list thousands of recent children's and young adult trade books. Although the works included cover a wide range of topics, they all have one thing in common: they're good books that students and teachers alike enjoy.

How are these volumes put together? The process begins when educators who know literature and its importance in the lives of students and teachers are chosen by the NCTE Executive Committee to serve as booklist editors. Those editors then work with teachers and librarians who review, select, and annotate hundreds of new trade books sent to them by publishers. It's a complicated process, one that can last three or four years. But because of their dedication and strong belief in the need to let others know about the good literature that's available, these professionals volunteer their time in a way that is commendable and serves as an inspiration to all of us. The members of the committee that compiled this volume are listed in the front of the book, and we are truly grateful for their hard work.

As educators know, no single book is right for every reader or every purpose, so inclusion in this booklist is not necessarily an endorsement from NCTE. But it does indicate that the professionals who make up the booklist committee feel that the work in question is worthy of teachers' and students' attention, whether for its informative or aesthetic qualities. Similarly, exclusion from an NCTE booklist is not necessarily a judgment on the quality of a given book or publisher. Many factors—space, time, availability of certain books, publisher participation—may influence the final shape of the list.

We hope that you'll find this booklist a useful resource in discovering new titles and authors, and we hope that you will want to collect other booklists in the series. Our mission is to help improve the teaching and learning of English and the language arts, and we hope you'll agree that the quality of our booklists contributes substantially toward that goal.

Zarina M. Hock
Senior Editor

Contents

Foreword

I was thirteen years old when I read Harper Lee's *To Kill a Mockingbird.* At the time, I'd never been out of the Midwest. I didn't have any African American friends. I had no desire to live in a sleepy southern town without air conditioning. I'd given lawyers little thought. Some of the words were unfamiliar to me. What was a chifforobe anyway? I looked it up. How could a man face hate and anger and not strike back? Why did the book grab me? Why do I remember where I was when I read it? It's because that story introduced me to people with uncompromising courage and gave me hope that it was possible to stand for what is right and true. It's because I wanted a father like Atticus Finch. The year was 1964. Martin Luther King, Jr.'s "I Have a Dream" speech had mesmerized me. The civil rights movement was in full swing. And now this book set in the thirties seemed to be propelled into the sixties. It was a made-up story, but it was wholly and powerfully true. I can honestly say that book changed my life and continues to challenge me as a reader and a writer.

Good writing should challenge us, teach us, and enlarge us. That's what this important compilation sets out to do. *Your Reading* is a book about challenges—facing them and exploring them through reading and literature.

Challenge involves change, hard truth, and effort. It is both a dare—I *challenge* you to get a better grade—and a call—she was *challenged* every day to become a better student. This is a protein-packed booklist—nothing about these troubled times can be served by filler. The book is full of titles that will dare you to explore new vistas and call you to excellence.

Although I am a fiction writer, I'm a huge fan of nonfiction and the immediacy and historical perspective that it offers. And from poetry flow those just-right phrases that stay with me and help me put the complexities of life into perspective. I don't believe we should read just one type of writing, but rather be exposed to many different styles. I don't believe exposure to fine writing ever leaves us—it attaches to the heart, the mind, the emotions. It presses down to make way for the new material. I sometimes wonder just how many layers I'm made of—perhaps they've become fossilized by now—each one leaving a slight imprint as the years pass. The magic parts of reading keep us coming back for more—to be lost in a book, to be so struck by a poem that we simply have to memorize it, to fully enter the telling of a nonfiction account—it does something to a person. By entering in, we absorb the power of the written word.

What is it about reading and stories that brings people together? If something is made up—like fiction—how can it be living and true? To me, every story begins with the same thing: the writer is creating it to explain something about the world. Stories at their best are mirrors to ourselves. Authors place the mirrors so the reflections that come back are real and relevant.

As a writer, I am unable to create real characters until I understand their challenges at the emotional level. It's one thing to say, I want to write a story about a teenager who doesn't get along with her parents. It's quite another to understand why there is that disconnect in the family. To do that, all kinds of issues must be explored. Rocks must be picked up and looked at in both the light and the shadow. The writer pulls from personal experience, from memory, from truth. All of that is woven together. A novel is a series of challenges presented in book form. Challenges connect to form tunnels and tunnels take us the quickest way through. When a book begins to come together (at least for me), it's not because the writing is flowing, but because the challenges are working together—they're being faced by the characters, who are accepting my dare: "Listen guys, try to work your way through this mess that I've handed you, and please do it in a way that will enhance my career."

Isn't it just like a book to make you learn the overarching lesson again and again?

Life = Challenge.

Your Reading provides a tunnel through.

I began my professional writing career years ago as a journalist. In nonfiction, you have to have your facts right—you can't bend the truth to fit your ending, despite the temptation. I always felt an enormous responsibility to get the facts right, to make them come together, to report with truth and energy. It is more difficult to write like that—at least it was for me—and I respect those who can present the facts alive as real stories that lay down challenges and teach us about the world.

Some challenges are better appreciated once they are behind us and we see the power we've gained from the experience. The process can seem obtuse as we wade through, trip up, get scared, lose our tempers and perspectives, backtrack, and stumble across tough times. That's why stories that show the process are critical. From coming of age to adventure and survival, mystery and suspense, fantasy and science fiction; onward to science and technology; back in time to history and historical fiction, folktales, myths, and legends, the stories in this book show what happens when people of all stripes and circumstances have their backs against a wall.

I continue to be amazed at the elasticity of fiction that reflects the trouble of the day. And what trouble we have now: September 11th, terrorist threats, war, corporate malfeasance, economic doldrums, unemployment, illiteracy, drugs, rampant depression among our youth. I remember my high school years—a big part of them was spent wondering if anyone out there understood me, was like me, thought like I did, was as disenfranchised, as scared, as big a dreamer.

I wondered. And I found many of those answers in books.

How far back does a story go and how far into the present can we take it? A recent *New Yorker* cartoon showed a little girl just put to bed by a parent who is reading her a story. The child asks, "Do you think the Eensy Weensy Spider was obsessive-compulsive?"

Well . . . actually . . . *yes.*

The lovely thing about books is that they are big enough to hold their stories and ours as well. So move in close and explore the challenges we face and the books that will help us meet those challenges now and in the future.

Joan Bauer

Acknowledgments

Your Reading is an exciting and dynamic endeavor made possible through the hard work and dedication of many people. First, we thank the members of our committee for their perseverance and the fine quality of their work. Some committee members were assisted by other teachers and college students, who helped by reading books and writing annotations. These people include Tara Barnett, Andrea DiCicco, Teresa Duffy, and Bonnie Olchowski from Rhode Island; April Blakely, Amy Horton, Terri Knight, Laura Robertson, and Kathy Werline from University School, Johnson City, Tennessee; and Jessica Giesken, Mike Guilbault, Becky Jones, Kelly Mandeville, Cassandra Mazure, Amy Jo McVay, Courtney Putnam, and LaTishia Way, students at Central Michigan University.

Committee member Christa Thompson served as our assistant in compiling the entries and annotations, and we appreciate the numerous hours she spent on this project. Jennifer Basile contributed a great deal of time and good insights as well. Elaine Fluck and Martha Gray, librarians at South Haven Memorial Library in South Haven, Michigan, assisted in tracking down obscure information, and we thank them for their diligence and persistence. We also thank Carol Juchnik and Sandy Sciotti of the Educational Studies Department at Rhode Island College, who handled communications and mailings. A special thanks to Sandy for all the entries she typed for us.

We are most indebted to the publishers who sent us copies of books to review. Without their generous contributions, this project could never have come to fruition. Many committee members donated the books they annotated either to public schools or libraries in their area, and thus young people across the country directly benefit from the publishers' generosity.

As has always been our experience, the staff at NCTE has been unfailingly helpful and supportive. Pete Feely, who was our editor for the first two years of this experience, and Kurt Austin, who succeeded him, have been outstanding to work with. We appreciate their timely responses to our questions and concerns. Bonny Graham, our production editor, epitomizes expertise, professionalism, and efficiency. We are awed by her exacting eye for detail and consistency. The book is immeasurably better because of her talents.

Finally, during the time we have been involved in this project, death has silenced the voices of several major contributors to the field of young adult literature. We are honored to include their last works in this volume and grateful for the legacy they leave for generations of young people: the richness of their words and the power of their stories. We remember Janet Bode, Robert Cormier, Carol Fenner, and Virginia Hamilton.

Introduction

I want to provoke readers, challenge them to think about themselves, how they conduct their lives. . . . And finally, for those who feel most isolated, I want them to come away with a sense of hope, knowing that they are not alone, but also that others have solutions to the same life problems.

Janet Bode

And what better way to help young people gain a sense of connectedness and willingness to meet the challenges of their lives than by encouraging them to read books! One of the pleasures or gifts of books, as Janet Bode says, is that they demonstrate to young people that they aren't isolated. Perhaps even more than the solutions books offer to "the same life problems" is the reassurance they provide readers that others have felt the same way, have raised the same issues, have dreamed the same dreams. In that way, books mirror their lives and challenges while also letting them see themselves in new ways and with new clarity.

We all face many challenges in our lives, especially as events change our world. Students in middle school and junior high face an additional layer—one specific to the world of adolescents—of challenges and new beginnings. We believe in the power of books to help them find both answers and direction.

We structured this eleventh edition of *Your Reading* around the theme of challenges to help teachers, librarians, parents, and students connect with good, recently published books that will make a difference in their lives. Throughout the chapters of this edition, you and your students will find books that can be used for many purposes—for the sheer enjoyment of the story, to pique curiosity or satisfy it, to find new information or confirm old, to complete school assignments, or for the exhilaration of escape.

This book is a valuable resource for you and others who seek to connect young people with books that will answer their questions; provide them with heightened awareness of their world (past and present); engage their imaginations; transport them to different realities and universes; lead them on paths of discovery; and perhaps most important for middle school and junior high school students, demonstrate that the challenges they face others also face.

Given video games, cable television, the Internet, as well as school activities and schoolwork, reading has lots of competition for students' time. This book will help them find books to understand the challenges they face and then help them meet those challenges. *Your Reading* is divided into six sections: Section I addresses relationships; section II focuses on action and activities; section III tackles imagination, suspense, and the arts; section IV deals with science, technology, health, and the environment; section V presents myriad perspectives on worldwide issues of today; and section VI looks at the past through fiction and nonfiction as well as through legend and myth.

The Process

We did an initial screening of the books publishers sent us in order to make a preliminary determination that they were of an appropriate age level for middle school and junior high students. The books were then sent to committee members, who read and reviewed them, making the final determination about age appropriateness, content, and quality. In addition, the members suggested chapter and section placement for their entries. Periodically, they also made suggestions of additional books that were not sent to us but that they felt should be included here. They submitted their entries to us to be edited to conform to the NCTE Guidelines for this volume.

The Content

From 2000 to 2003, we received approximately 1,750 books, and around 1,400 of these were sent to committee members. From this pool of books, we selected and annotated over 1,200 that were published during that time, as well as a number of books that have been reissued in these years. In some cases, we have included books that were published since the last edition of *Your Reading,* which covered books published in 1993 or 1994. Committee members contributed a few annotations of books published from 1997 to 1999 that they felt should be recognized. Certainly, this compilation is not nor could be comprehensive; however, we have sought to provide depth and variety in identifying books that will enrich, enlighten, educate, and excite middle school and junior high school students.

Organization

Using the theme of challenges, we have organized *Your Reading* into six sections: Challenges of Coming of Age, Challenging Our Lives, Challenging Our Imaginations, Challenging Our Minds, Challenges of Today's

World, and Challenges of Yesterday. Each of these sections is subdivided into three chapters. Within each chapter, the books are arranged alphabetically by author's last name; books in a series sharing one annotation are listed at the ends of sections or chapters, alphabetized by series title and then presented chronologically.

The first section, Challenges of Coming of Age, features books that speak to the challenges of growing up. Most are works of fiction, but some are nonfiction that detail the joys, angst, and challenges of growing up and dealing with others. In Chapter 1, "Families," authors explore issues related to family relationships, including disagreements, death, divorce, poverty, grandparents, foster families, and siblings. Chapter 2, "Friends and Peers," focuses on significant relationships beyond families—the friendships, romances, and other interactions with peers that affect us as we grow up. Chapter 3, "Identity," explores the complexities of young people trying to discover who they are or who they want to be.

The overriding focus of section II, Challenging Our Lives, is action oriented. Most of the books in these chapters involve taking action or making choices. The books in Chapter 4 are exciting tales of "Adventure and Survival." Books describing "Obstacles, Barriers, and Opportunities" make up Chapter 5, as well as titles that demonstrate the importance of making choices and decisions. Chapter 6, "Sports and Recreation," explores games, activities, and the players involved in them.

Challenging Our Imaginations, section III, invites readers to seek out books that awaken their curiosity about the known and the unknown, the real and the unreal. Chapter 7, "Mysteries and Suspense," features stories with characters and situations that puzzle, fascinate, and intrigue. Chapter 8 explores the imaginary worlds of "Fantasy and Supernatural," taking us beyond ourselves into new realities. Chapter 9, "The Arts, Architecture, and Other Creative Endeavors," explores a broad range of creative activities from the arts and entertainment, including architecture, photography, literature, and music. While this chapter contains many informational entries, it also features fictional portrayals of talented young people for whom the arts play a significant role. Biographies of authors and artists are also included.

The fourth section, Challenging Our Minds, explores books that stimulate readers' interest in the scientific and natural worlds. Whether for class assignments or personal curiosity, books in this section provide answers to *why* and *what may be.* Chapter 10, "Science and Technology: Fact and Fiction," includes both informational entries and works of science fiction, which look at possible future worlds. Chapter 11 presents books, mostly nonfiction, dealing with "Health, Medicine, and Nutrition."

Chapter 12 concludes with fiction and nonfiction selections about "Nature, Animals, and the Environment."

Challenges of Today's World, the fifth section, engages readers with the rich variety of people and cultures of the present-day world. Chapter 13, "Diversity," presents the stories of people from many cultures, in both the United States and other areas of the world. Chapter 14, "Problems and Issues," looks at nonfiction accounts of today's world and the political, social, and cultural issues that challenge us. Chapter 15, "Geography and Cultures," provides readers with a sense of the geography and the cultures of different areas of the United States and of different countries and regions of the world.

Challenges of Yesterday, the sixth and last section of this volume, explores the richness of the past. Chapter 16, "Historical Fiction," provides a look backward through stories. Factual accounts of the past are presented in Chapter 17, "Historical Nonfiction." We conclude with Chapter 18, "Folktales, Myths, and Legends," the stories and modern variations of the stories that began with oral tradition and survived by being passed down from generation to generation.

I Challenges of Coming of Age

1 Families

1.1 Abelove, Joan. **Saying It Out Loud.** Puffin, 2001. 136 pp. ISBN 0-14-131227-0. Fiction

This is a poignant story about the unexpected death of a parent. Mindy's mother had filled their home with talk and love, but after she is hospitalized, the house is silent and empty. The emptiness worsens when surgery for her brain tumor leaves Mindy's mother in a vegetative state. Mindy must cope with the reality of her mother's condition and her father's unwillingness to face the situation.

1.2 Almond, David. **Counting Stars.** Delacorte, 2002. 205 pp. ISBN 0-385-72946-4. Nonfiction

David Almond has collected previously published autobiographical essays detailing the various life-changing events of his growing up in a devout Catholic family in England in the 1960s. Interestingly, the essays are served up to readers not in chronological order but in the same fluid way that an old friend might recount episodes of his life in a casual conversation. The threads of faith, family bonds, and the hardships of poverty run through the narratives, all of which are tinged with an inescapable sense of loss.

1.3 Antle, Nancy. **Lost in the War.** Puffin, 2000. 137 pp. ISBN 0-14-130836-2. Fiction

Lisa's mom and dad met in Vietnam—and he died there, but her mother never talked much about it. When Lisa's mom begins experiencing depression and nightmares, she is advised to talk about what it was like for her and the other nurses in Vietnam. Lisa and her sister think that talking is just making things worse and want their lives to be normal. But when Lisa's history class studies Vietnam, she comes to a deeper understanding of her family and the Vietnam experience.

1.4 Bauer, Joan. **Backwater.** Putnam, 1999. 185 pp. ISBN 0-399-23141-2. Fiction

Ivy Breedlove resists her father's wish for her to follow the family tradition of becoming a lawyer. Instead, she pursues her love of history by compiling her own family history. To complete the task, she must find her reclusive aunt, whom the family considers to be "stuck in the backwater" in her mountain retreat. Along the way she encounters a cast of interesting characters and experiences the challenges of the wilderness.

1.5 Bauer, Joan. **Stand Tall.** Putnam, 2002. 184 pp. ISBN 0-399-23473-X. Fiction

Tree is the tallest student in the history of Eleanor Roosevelt Middle School, and he wonders if he will ever be able to harness his height and fit in at school. But mostly he's struggling to adjust to all the changes in his life caused by his parents' divorce. The great influence in Tree's life is his grandfather, who is also undergoing changes in his life. An old wound from Vietnam finally necessitates the amputation of his leg.

1.6 Beard, Darleen Bailey. **The Babbs Switch Story.** Farrar, Straus and Giroux, 2002. 166 pp. ISBN 0-374-30475-0. Fiction

Ruthie is excited about singing the solo in the upcoming Christmas concert. But there is trouble in store for Ruthie and her family. Her older sister, Daphne, has always been "different," and now Daphne's love for all soft things, for stroking them and cuddling them, has gotten her—and the entire family—into hot water. But when tragedy occurs during the Christmas celebration, Ruthie learns a great deal about how much Daphne really means to her.

1.7 Clarke, Judith. **Wolf on the Fold.** Front Street, 2002. 176 pp. ISBN 1-886910-79-0. Fiction

This collection of short stories follows the lineage of the Sinclair family through the years 1935 through 2002 and throughout the world, in Australia, Israel, and beyond. Most of the stories deal with simple, everyday moments, magnifying them and their significance in the larger scheme of things. They tell of Kenny Sinclair, his daughters, their children, and finally *their* children. Tying the stories together is the overarching theme of the interconnectedness of family.

1.8 Coman, Carolyn. **Many Stones.** Front Street, 2000. 158 pp. ISBN 1-886910-55-3. Fiction

Sixteen-year-old Berry is angry, bitter, and deeply unhappy. When her beloved sister Laura, a volunteer in South Africa, is murdered, Berry embarks on a journey from Rockville, Maryland, to Cape Town to participate in a memorial service and a dedication in her sister's name. Traveling through South Africa with her estranged father and going to the places her sister loved helps Berry come to terms with the injustices of life. She deals with her difficult relationship with her father and the loss of her sister.

1.9 Connelly, Neil. **St. Michael's Scales.** Arthur A. Levine Books, 2002. 309 pp. ISBN 0-439-19445-8. Fiction

Keegan Flannery is planning to commit suicide on his sixteenth birthday. He is consumed by guilt because his twin brother Michael died in infancy, a death that triggered his mother's breakdown and subsequent years of hospitalization. In a fourteen-day countdown to his birthday, Keegan, a member of the wrestling team, wrestles with both his opponents and his demons. But it is a classmate's suicide that enables him to find his voice, breaking the cycle of denial in his family and allowing him to begin communicating with his father.

1.10 Cormier, Robert. **Frenchtown Summer.** Puffin, 2000. 113 pp. ISBN 0-14-130714-5. Fiction

Robert Cormier, celebrated author of *The Chocolate War*, uses blank verse to tell this story of twelve-year-old Eugene, a French Canadian, in search of "who he really is." An observer rather than a doer, Eugene comments on the world around him—a loving mother, an elusive father, adventurous cousins, a mysterious uncle, and the death of a classmate. Each poem stands alone and yet together they weave the story of a summer in which a young boy begins to understand himself.

1.11 Curtis, Christopher Paul. **Bud, Not Buddy.** Dell Yearling, 2002. 236 pp. ISBN 0-440-41328-1. Fiction

Bud has been living in various foster homes near Flint, Michigan, since his mother died. Now, in 1936, Bud takes his suitcase containing clues to the identity of his father and runs away to find him. What he finds, in addition to danger and adventure, is Herman E. Calloway and his band and a family mystery—eventually revealed. Throughout Bud's adventures and misadventures, his voice is alternately poignant and hilarious. An author's note explains the origin of some of the characters.

1.12 Dahl, Roald. **Danny the Champion of the World.** Illustrated by Quentin Blake. Knopf, 2002 (Originally published in 1975). 205 pp. ISBN 0-375-81425-6. Fiction

After his mother's death, Danny is raised by his loving, poverty-stricken father. By the time Danny is nine, his father has told him countless stories and taught him how to fix cars and make kites and hot air balloons. Most important, he reveals to his son his trade secrets for poaching pheasants. Eventually, Danny comes up with the ultimate scheme for gaining the greatest number of birds in a single outing, a plan that earns Danny the title of Champion of the World.

1.13 Danziger, Paula. **United Tates of America: A Novel with Scrapbook Art.** Scholastic, 2002. 123 pp. ISBN 0-590-69221-6. Fiction

Sixth grader Skate (Sarah Kate) Tate narrates how her life and relationships change the year she moves from elementary school to middle school. Her life is further complicated when her favorite great uncle passes away after a heart attack. Artistic and sensitive, Skate not only survives but also grows and learns during this difficult year, surrounded by her loving family and finding comfort in creating her scrapbook. The novel is illustrated with Skate's scrapbook art.

1.14 Davis, C. L. **The Christmas Barn.** Pleasant Company, 2001. 177 pp. ISBN 1-58485-414-6. Fiction

Every year on Christmas Day, twelve-year-old Roxie and her five brothers and sister receive store-bought candy from their parents and a visit from their grandparents. This year a snowstorm threatens to destroy Christmas for this impoverished Appalachian mountain family. The day is saved, however, when the family exchanges homemade gifts and the grandparents arrive safely despite the heavy snow.

1.15 Delacre, Lulu. **Salsa Stories.** Scholastic, 2000. 112 pp. ISBN 0-590-63118-7. Fiction

Carmen Teresa receives a special notebook as a Christmas gift from her next-door neighbor but is unsure how she wants to use it. Her family and friends recount stories of their childhoods and suggest that Carmen Teresa fill the book with these recollections. Carmen takes note of the exciting tales but decides to use her new notebook in a slightly different way.

1.16 Dowell, Frances O'Roark. **Dovey Coe.** Aladdin, 2001. 181 pp. ISBN 0-689-84667-3. Fiction

Dovey Coe, strong-willed, independent, and unorthodox, worries about the affairs of every member of her family. She takes on this role even though she is the youngest. When Dovey tries to save her sister from a situation, Dovey is the one who needs serious help from those around her. Dovey is on trial for the murder of her sister's jilted suitor, and suddenly the girl who is so used to controlling everything is not in control.

1.17 Doyle, Eugenie. **Stray Voltage.** Front Street, 2002. 136 pp. ISBN 1-886910-86-3. Fiction

Ian, a sixth grader, lives on a Vermont farm with his parents and older brother. The work is demanding, the winters long, and the loneliness unbearable. But the loneliness gets much worse when his mother leaves. Neither his father nor his brother communicates with him. Ian's sense of isolation grows as he hopes and waits for his mother to return.

1.18 Easton, Kelly. **The Life History of a Star.** Margaret K. McElderry Books, 2001. 200 pp. ISBN 0-689-83134-X. Fiction

Witty and wise, fourteen-year-old Kristin navigates through the minefield of high school, the turbulence of the 1960s, and a family altered forever by the return of her wounded brother from Vietnam. Kristin's diary reveals the often humorous observations of her life juxtaposed with her touching responses as she tries to deal with the Ghost, her brother David. David's health, both physically and mentally, was destroyed by the war, and now his family has to deal with the loss.

1.19 Estes, Eleanor. **The Middle Moffat.** Illustrated by Louis Slobodkin. Harcourt, 2001 (Originally published in 1942). 234 pp. ISBN 0-15-202523-5. Fiction

Follow the adventures and misadventures of ten-year-old Jane Moffat, who lives with her widowed mother and three siblings in their new home in Cranbury, Connecticut, during the early twentieth century. Jane is a middle child and decides that the best way to stand out in her family is to become a figure of mystery, the mysterious Middle Moffat. This is the humorous second book in a four-book series about the Moffat family.

1.20 Estes, Eleanor. **The Moffat Museum.** Illustrated by Eleanor Estes. Harcourt, 2001 (Originally published in 1983). 232 pp. ISBN 0-15-202547-2. Fiction

This is the fourth in a four-book series about the Moffats, who live in Cranbury, Connecticut, during the early twentieth century. They are growing up and life is changing. In this story, the Moffats create a museum to hold some of their favorite childhood treasures to remember all the good times. Although Sylvie is getting married and Joey is going to work, daily life is still filled with hilarious fun and daily adventures.

1.21 Estes, Eleanor. **The Moffats.** Illustrated by Louis Slobodkin. Harcourt, 2001 (Originally published in 1941). 211 pp. ISBN 0-15-202535-9. Fiction

This is the story of the four Moffat children who live with their widowed mother on New Dollar Street in the small town of Cranbury, Connecticut. In this first of a four-book series about the family, Sylvie, Joey, Janey, and Rufus frequently experience adventures that combine fun with trouble. Only a Moffat could accidentally lock himself in the breadbox or accidentally hitch a ride out of town on a boxcar during kindergarten recess.

1.22 Estes, Eleanor. **Rufus M.** Illustrated by Louis Slobodkin. Harcourt, 2001 (Originally published in 1943). 233 pp. ISBN 0-15-202571-5. Fiction

This is the story of seven-year-old Rufus Moffat, who lives with his widowed mother and older siblings in early-twentieth-century Connecticut. Rufus isn't quite like other children. He gets things done, but he gets them done his way. He isn't just the youngest Moffat—he is also the cleverest, funniest, and the most unforgettable. This is the third book in a four-book series about the Moffats.

1.23 Grimes, Nikki. **Stepping Out with Grandma Mac.** Illustrated by Angelo. Orchard Books, 2001. 39 pp. ISBN 0-531-30320-9. Poetry

Vignettes in verse gradually reveal the relationship and love between Grandma Mac and her granddaughter. The seemingly aloof and gruff Grandma Mac and her direct, observant granddaughter share insights on shopping, homework, proper manners, and traditions. In addition to Grimes's lyrical words, Angelo's illustrations reveal telling details and the mutual love and respect between Grandma Mac and her granddaughter.

1.24 Gutman, Dan. **The Secret Life of Dr. Demented.** Pocket, 2001. 178 pp. ISBN 0-7434-2704-1. Fiction

Wesley Brown is a normal fourteen-year-old until he discovers the identity of the masked pro wrestler, Dr. Demented. His identity must remain a secret, and this puts pressure on Wesley. Wesley's life becomes more complicated when his mother begins dating Dr. Demented.

1.25 Haddix, Margaret Peterson. **Takeoffs and Landings.** Simon & Schuster, 2001. 201 pp. ISBN 0-689-83299-0. Fiction

Chuck and Lori have been raised primarily by their grandparents after their father died in a tractor accident years earlier and their mother went on tour as a motivational speaker. When their mother invites Chuck and Lori to accompany her on a two-week speaking tour, they are not only transported into the unknown world of air travel and hotels, but they also experience their own forms of emotional takeoffs and landings as they come to know themselves and their mother.

1.26 Hausman, Gerald, and Uton Hinds. **The Jacob Ladder.** Orchard, 2001. 128 pp. ISBN 0-531-30331-4. Fiction

Twelve-year-old Tall T struggles when his father abandons the family, but he has a strong and loving mother. Lacking money for school clothes, he escapes to the library, where the local librarian teaches him to read. Tall T helps his mother keep the family together and climbs Jacob's Ladder, literally and figuratively. Set in Jamaica, this story is based on the childhood of the coauthor and includes an afterword that adds to the reader's understanding of Tall T's courageous struggles.

1.27 Heneghan, James. **Flood.** Frances Foster Books, 2002. 182 pp. ISBN 0-374-35057-4. Fiction

Andy, an Irish Canadian boy, is devastated when he loses his mother and stepfather in a flood. Immediately disliking his strict aunt who comes to take him from his home in Vancouver to Halifax, he is surprised to learn that his father, whom he thought to be dead, is alive and living in Halifax. Luckily, Andy has the mythical Sheehogue, Irish faeries, to look after him as he faces living in a decrepit boardinghouse with his unemployed father.

1.28 Hobbs, Valerie. **Sonny's War.** Farrar, Straus and Giroux, 2002. 224 pp. ISBN 0-374-37136-9. Fiction

Cory depends on her brother Sonny now that their father is dead. Coping with hard truths about the family and Sonny's idea that his father didn't respect him, Cory senses the changes in Sonny through his letters from Vietnam. The novel represents many views of the Vietnam War and portrays Cory as a thinker and reader who gains insight into events and people as she matures.

1.29 Hobbs, Valerie. **Tender.** Frances Foster Books, 2001. 256 pp. ISBN 0-374-37397-3. Fiction

Raised in New York City by her grandmother after her mother died during her birth, fifteen-year-old Liv moves to California to join her estranged father when Gram dies of a sudden heart attack. An abalone diver, her father is a man of few words and fewer comforts and does not make Liv's transition a smooth one. His girlfriend, however, welcomes Liv, and together they weather various crises. When Liv helps her father dive for abalone, their relationship begins to change.

1.30 Horvath, Polly. **Everything on a Waffle.** Farrar, Straus and Giroux, 2001. 160 pp. ISBN 0-374-32236-8. Fiction

Even after the memorial service for her parents, eleven-year-old Primrose Squarp, a lifelong resident of Coal Harbour, British Columbia, is the only person convinced that they did not die in the typhoon. The novel is full of memorable characters (some more helpful than others) and recipes written in Primrose's exuberant voice, including recipes from the local restaurant that serves all food on a waffle. In the end, she discovers that life happens even in the smallest town, a lesson reminiscent of *Our Town.*

1.31 Johnson, Angela. **Running Back to Ludie.** Illustrated by Angelo. Orchard, 2001. 44 pp. ISBN 0-439-29316-2. Poetry

With a powerful, poetic voice, the narrator of these poems recounts her memories of her mother, whom she hasn't seen in years. She remembers her mother through photographs and distant memories. When the narrator gets to spend a few days with her mother, Ludie, she discovers who her mother is while discovering herself as well.

1.32 Johnson, Angela. **When Mules Flew on Magnolia Street.** Illustrated by John Ward. Knopf, 2000. 105 pp. ISBN 0-679-89077-7. Fiction

Charlie and her best friends, Lump and Billy, have grand summertime adventures as they spend their days fishing, solving mysteries, and making a mule fly in order to comfort an elderly friend in the hospital. When Lump and Billy go to camp, Charlie keeps up a hilarious correspondence with them while making a new friend and teaming up with her brother to help a neighbor in need.

1.33 Joseph, Lynn. **The Color of My Words.** Joanna Cotler Books, 2000. 138 pp. ISBN 0-06-028232-0. Fiction

Growing up in a close-knit family in the Dominican Republic, twelve-year-old Ana Rosa values her family, her notebook, and writing above all else, but she lives under a government in which silence is protection. After a rebellion and terrible personal tragedy, the irrepressible Ana Rosa discovers the power of words and the importance of telling people's stories.

1.34 Kimmel, Elizabeth Cody. **Visiting Miss Caples.** Puffin, 2000. 168 pp. ISBN 0-14-230029-2. Fiction

Jenna and her best friend, Liv, are unenthusiastically fulfilling an eight-grade class project by reading to elderly citizens. Jenna's "assignment," Miss Caples, won't talk or react until Jenna stops reading and starts talking to her about problems in her family and with Liv. Because Jenna's experiences with Liv eerily parallel Miss Caples's past, their meetings work to their mutual benefit.

1.35 Lawrence , Iain. **The Lightkeeper's Daughter.** Delacorte, 2002. 246 pp. ISBN 0-385-72925-1. Fiction.

Seventeen-year-old Squid McCrae has been away from home for three years—since the birth of her daughter Tatiana. She returns to introduce her daughter to Lizzie Island, the remote place where Squid grew up with her brother Alastair. Even after her time away from the island, Squid is haunted by her brother's death (a suicide) and is still angry with her father, the lighthouse keeper, for keeping the family on the isolated island for so long. This book may be more appropriate for older readers.

1.36 Littlefield, Bill. **The Circus in the Woods.** Houghton Mifflin, 2001. 199 pp. ISBN 0-618-06642-X. Fiction

Molly tells the story of her summer vacations at a lodge in Vermont, an emphasis on her relationship with her sister and the process of growing up. In the woods, Molly finds a strange circus with interesting performers who lead Molly to examine her life and her childhood.

1.37 Lound, Karen. **Girl Power in the Family: A Book about Girls, Their Rights, and Their Voice.** Lerner, 2000. 80 pp. ISBN 0-8225-2692-1. Nonfiction

Relationships, especially family relationships, are important to girls. In this book, girls are interviewed about the issues they face. The book offers real teenagers' strategies and ideas for dealing with their families and making the most of their time at home. It also discusses prejudices girls face, body image, and development of self-confidence. Resources for parents, teachers, and girls are also provided.

1.38 Lynch, L. M. **How I Wonder What You Are.** Knopf, 2001. 199 pp. ISBN 0-375-80663-6. Nonfiction

A new family moves to town, and when the townspeople suspect that this family is behind the cutting down of the popular "climbing tree," the community is divided. Laurel Shade believes the new boy is an "android" but befriends his sister when others won't. As alliances shift, Laurel discovers what being an outsider means. She develops empathy for others, including her younger sister, and the confidence to confront her fears and stand up for what is right.

1.39 Mackler, Carolyn. **Love and Other Four-Letter Words.** Delacorte, 2000. 247 pp. ISBN 0-385-32743-9. Fiction

Wham! Out of the blue, sixteen-year-old Sammie Davis's life is turned upside down. Her parents separate, and she and her mother leave their upstate New York home for New York City. As her mother attempts to cope with her marital problems, Sammie is forced to play the role of adult as she deals with new responsibilities and experiences. In an attempt to make sense of her life, Sammie learns to evaluate friendships, relationships, and her place in the world.

1.40 Martin, Ann M. **A Corner of the Universe.** Scholastic, 2002. 191 pp. ISBN 0-439-38880-5. Fiction

Hattie has been anticipating an uneventful summer, but when a long-lost "crazed" uncle arrives unexpectedly, life is turned upside down. Trying desperately to connect with this strange and disturbed new relative, Hattie learns a little about his mental illness and much more about becoming a caring and fully realized person.

1.41 Mason, Simon. **The Quigleys.** Illustrated by Helen Stephens. David Fickling Books, 2002. 148 pp. ISBN 0-385-75006-4. Fiction

The Quigleys are a rather unusual English family. At every turn, a new problem arises with yet another member of the family, as when Lucy's sleepover turns into a search party—complete with police—for her missing friend, who turns up asleep under the duvet. The Quigleys, however, face these problems with humor and high spirits.

1.42 Mazer, Anne. **Every Cloud Has a Silver Lining.** Scholastic, 2000. 118 pp. ISBN 0-439-14977-0. Fiction

In this contribution to The Amazing Days of Abby Hayes series, Abby is starting fifth grade. She is concerned about her reputation in school compared with those of her brother and twin sisters, who always seem to be outstanding in all their accomplishments. Abby loves to write and collects calendars for a hobby. The new writing teacher at school helps Abby recognize her own outstanding abilities. The story is told partly through Abby's journal entries and drawings.

1.43 McNichols, Ann. **Falling from Grace.** Walker, 2000. 164 pp. ISBN 0-8027-8750-9. Fiction

Cassie Hill is thirteen and struggling with life in a small Arkansas town in the 1930s. Her sister leaves town without explanation after her boyfriend's suicide; her father is having an affair with the preacher's wife; and her friends and the townspeople seem eager to pronounce judgment. Then Cassie befriends a quiet boy whose family has recently come from Hungary. Together, they help each other deal with the trials of growing up.

1.44 Montgomery, Lucy Maud. **Anne of Green Gables.** Dover, 2000 (Originally published in 1908). 307 pp. ISBN 0-486-41025-0. Fiction

Montgomery, Lucy Maud. **Anne of Green Gables.** Aladdin, 2001 (Originally published in 1908). 446 pp. ISBN 0-689-84622-3. Fiction

In this timeless classic, readers get to know Anne, a redheaded orphan, who insists that her name be spelled with an *e.* Full of energy and imagination, Anne's ardent wish to have a family and friends of her own is granted when Matthew and Marilla Cuthbert, an elderly brother and sister, take her into their home at Green Gables. Throughout her many adventures and misadventures, Anne charms everyone she meets with her irrepressible tongue and delightful nature.

1.45 Mosher, Richard. **Zazoo.** Clarion, 2001. 248 pp. ISBN 0-618-13534-0. Fiction

Born in Vietnam and raised in France, thirteen-year-old Zazoo lives a happy but uneventful life in a stone mill at the canal lock with her adoptive grandfather. Then Marius, the bicycle/binocular boy, appears, and things begin to change. The novel's love and war (World War II and Vietnam) stories, bitter and sweet, kind and cruel, unfold slowly in metaphors, prose, and poems. Many surprising connections are revealed among people in the village and elsewhere.

1.46 Murphy, Rita. **Night Flying.** Delacorte, 2000. 129 pp. ISBN 0-385-32748-X. Fiction

There are two things that set Georgia Hansen apart from her friends: her life is totally controlled by her grandmother, who also legislates life for Georgia's mother and aunts; and she can fly, like all the women in her family. Long ago one aunt rebelled and left home. When that aunt returns to celebrate Georgia's sixteenth birthday, the pieces of her world—horses, family, flying—all need to be realigned and integrated before Georgia can truly soar in this coming-of-age novel.

1.47 Naylor, Phyllis Reynolds. **A Spy among the Girls.** Delacorte, 2000. 134 pp. ISBN 0-385-32336-0. Fiction

First love is never easy, but for Beth Malloy and Josh Hatford it gets more than ordinarily complicated. As Valentine's Day approaches, it seems that Beth's crush on Josh becomes more trouble than it's worth. Beth's sisters and the three Hatford brothers devise a series of hilarious plots ranging from boys spying on girls to a science project involving the town's mysterious night-prowling monster.

1.48 Nelson, Theresa. **The Empress of Elsewhere.** Puffin, 2000. 278 pp. ISBN 0-14-130813-3. Fiction

The Empress is a capuchin monkey left to J. D. (who says her initials stand for Juvenile Delinquent) by her father when he died. J. D. now lives with her wealthy grandmother, who is desperate to find a way to tame her (J. D., not the monkey). Told through the voice of Jim, hired to spend time with J. D., the novel describes the events of a summer in east Texas spent exploring friendship and the effect of a family's secrets from the past on relationships in the present.

1.49 Nolan, Han. **A Face in Every Window.** Puffin, 1999. 264 pp. ISBN 0-14-131218-1. Fiction

Grandma Mary is the glue that holds this dysfunctional family together: mentally challenged Pap, immature Mam, and JP, a teenager who has more sense than both of his parents. When Grandma Mary dies, there is a huge void in all their lives. JP is thrust into the position of being parent and guardian for both of his parents as he deals with his father's limited abilities and his mother's depression.

1.50 O'Connor, Barbara. **Moonpie and Ivy.** Farrar, Straus and Giroux, 2001. 160 pp. ISBN 0-374-35059-0. Fiction

Twelve-year-old Pearl narrates this story of abandonment, love, and hope. After Pearl is abandoned by her mother and left with her aunt, she learns how normal, loving people connect with one another. That lesson offers hope when she is reunited with her mother. Pearls reveals her feelings through a series of unmailed postcards she writes to her mother using cards from her own collection.

1.51 Peck, Richard. **Fair Weather.** Dial, 2001. 140 pp. ISBN 0-803-72516-7. Fiction

Life on the farm is never the same for thirteen-year-old Rosie and her family when a letter arrives from her Aunt Euterpe inviting the family to Chicago to visit the 1893 World's Columbian Exposition. Mama sends Rosie, Buster, and their older sister Lottie on the train to Chicago. They have barely left the station when the train slows to take on another passenger, the irrepressible Granddad. Citification is not easy but it is entertaining as they encounter electricity, the exhibits, Buffalo Bill, and Lillian Russell.

1.52 Peck, Richard. **A Long Way from Chicago: A Novel in Stories.** Puffin, 2000. 160 pp. ISBN 0-141-30352-2. Fiction

Every year for nine years during the Great Depression, Joey and his sister Mary Alice journey from the excitement of their hometown of Chicago to spend time with their Grandma Dowdell in a small town in southern Illinois. Stories of their adventures with Grandma Dowdell, a no-nonsense woman who can only be described as unusual, are never boring and are often laugh-out-loud funny.

1.53 Peck, Richard. **A Year Down Yonder.** Dial, 2000. 130 pp. ISBN 0-803-72518-3. Fiction

This 2001 Newbery Award winner is the sequel to Peck's earlier novel *A Long Way from Chicago.* It is narrated by Mary Alice, a fifteen-year-old girl sent to spend a year with her Grandma Dowdell when her father is laid off during the Great Depression. Faced with the typical problems of adolescence, Mary Alice learns a great deal from her one-of-a-kind grandmother.

1.54 Pevsner, Stella. **Is Everyone Moonburned but Me?** Clarion, 2000. 202 pp. ISBN 0-395-95770-2. Fiction

Hannah, the middle child in her family, is a responsible, dependable, pleasant, gifted young girl. She, however, does not see herself as special at all—in fact, she thinks she is plain. Frustrated at being the middle child, she wants to move in with her father, but the fact that he is dating makes that difficult. Hannah learns that family relationships are complicated.

1.55 Rodowsky, Colby. **Clay.** Farrar, Straus and Giroux, 2001. 176 pp. ISBN 0-374-31338-5. Fiction

Elsie Mcphee lives with her mom and her seven-year-old brother Tommy. Elsie is home tutored, prevented from making friends, and not allowed out of their apartment without her mother. Elise's family is always on the run, and she feels like a prisoner in her own home. Her memories of her father and her past are painful—has it actually been four years since she was abruptly taken from him? Elsie is torn between contacting her father and being loyal to her mother.

1.56 Rushton, Rosie. **Olivia.** Hyperion, 2000. 248 pp. ISBN 0-7868-1392-X. Fiction

Olivia is a fourteen-year-old girl living in England. Her parents are recently separated, and her father has moved in with another woman. While struggling to adjust to her parents' separation, Olivia meets and becomes close friends with a new boy in town, Ryan. Just as Olivia and Ryan move toward a serious relationship, they discover that they are half siblings. Though confused and angry at first, Olivia learns to accept and appreciate her new family structure.

1.57 Rushton, Rosie. **Sophie.** Hyperion, 2000. 241 pp. ISBN 0-7868-0691-5. Fiction

Fourteen-year-old Sophie lives with her mother in England. She doesn't appreciate her mother, whom she finds materialistic in comparison to her missionary father living in Africa. Sophie's father comes for a visit at the same time Sophie meets and befriends Tony. Sophie begins to recognize her mother's love for her and her father's shortcomings. Eventually, she accepts her parents' faults, appreciates their love for her, and finds that she has fallen in love with Tony.

1.58 Rylant, Cynthia. **A Blue-Eyed Daisy.** Aladdin, 2001 (Originally published in 1985). 99 pp. ISBN 0-689-84495-6. Fiction

This is the low-key, poetically told story of Ellie Farley as she moves from eleven to twelve years of age. It's also the story of Ellie and Bullet, the hunting dog her dad unexpectedly brings home. Ellie is glad to have Bullet during this year of odd events, a year when her uncle goes to war, her dad drives his truck off a mountain road, and a boy in her class has a seizure. Yet it's also a year of small, ordinary pleasures of life in rural West Virginia.

1.59 Salisbury, Graham. **Lord of the Deep.** Delacorte, 2001. 182 pp. ISBN 0-385-72918-9. Fiction

Although the lord of the deep in this story is Bill Monks, skipper of the fishing vessel *Crystal-C,* the true hero is Mikey Donovan, his stepson. Mikey sails with Bill every day in order to learn the trade and prepare for his own chance at being skipper. Mikey idolizes Bill and stays with him day in and day out. He's even there the three days the obnoxious clients from Colorado come aboard and everyone is in for a rough ride.

1.60 Shearer, Alex. **The Great Blue Yonder.** Clarion, 2001. 184 pp. ISBN 0-618-21257-4. Fiction

Reminiscent of *Our Town* and *It's a Wonderful Life,* this novel of young Harry's death and moving on to the Great Blue Yonder is in turn hilarious and touching, or "nicely sad," as Harry would say. His authentic ten-year-old voice adds humor to events as Harry discovers how to repair the damage of his last words to his sister, "You'll be sorry when I'm dead," spoken just before he was hit by a truck while riding his bike.

1.61 Shreve, Susan. **Blister.** Arthur A. Levine Books, 2001. 153 pp. ISBN 0-439-19313-3. Fiction

Blister is the name Alyssa gives herself once life begins to turn sour. After "ten ordinary years as an only child," Mom and Dad start having problems, and the baby they've all been waiting for dies during labor. Dad moves out and ignores Alyssa; Mom is too wrapped up in her own worries and depression to notice her; and Grandma is only around when she's not taking part in dance competitions. Finally Alyssa decides she has had enough and proceeds to create some problems of her own.

1.62 Singer, Nicky. **Feather Boy.** Delacorte, 2001. 262 pp. ISBN 0-385-72980-4. Fiction

Robert is the underdog—he's the boy picked on in class and on the playground. Niker, the class bully, even follows him to and from school. When Robert is assigned to Mrs. Sorrell at the retirement home as part of a class project, however, he achieves self-respect and respect from his classmates. His link to Mrs. Sorrell affects his life and hers in a profound way. As Robert becomes feather boy, he transforms many aspects of his life.

1.63 Stone, Phoebe. **All the Blue Moons at the Wallace Hotel.** Little, Brown, 2000. 198 pp. ISBN 0-316-81645-0. Fiction

After the death of her father, Fiona lives with her mother and sister in a neglected mansion. It is Fiona's dream to become a ballet dancer and have a "normal" family, but reality doesn't live up to her dreams. Only after a series of events that put her sister's life at risk does Fiona realize that her family is her best resource to achieving her goals.

1.64 Taylor, Mildred D. **The Land.** Phyllis Fogelman Books, 2001. 373 pp. ISBN 0-803-71950-7. Fiction

This is the story of Paul-Edward Logan, grandfather of Cassie Logan, the protagonist of *Roll of Thunder, Hear My Cry* and its two sequels. Born during the Civil War, Paul-Edward is the son of a white plantation owner and a former slave. Paul-Edward and his sister have many of the privileges their white half brothers enjoy. But at fourteen, Paul-Edward runs away to seek his fortune. His story is filled with excitement and danger, triumph and disappointment, but mostly it is the story of triumph against incredible odds.

1.65 Taylor, Theodore. **A Sailor Returns.** Blue Sky, 2001. 160 pp. ISBN 0-439-24879-5. Fiction

Evan and his mother have no idea how the return of her father, after an absence of thirty years, during which he was thought dead, will change their lives. Evan's grandfather had left Evan's mother when she was three years old and been a carpenter on ships. Now he is dying of a heart condition but returns to bring spontaneity and joy to the Bryant family, gain their forgiveness, and also help Evan deal with a bully at school.

1.66 Thesman, Jean. **Calling the Swan.** Viking, 2000. 147 pp. ISBN 0-670-88874-5. Fiction

Fifteen-year-old Skylar Deacon cannot escape the grip of her overprotective parents or her past. She struggles for independence, yet her past casts shadows on her confidence. Slowly, Skylar begins to rebuild her life as well as come to terms with her older sister's disappearance. As she deals with the past, she finds loyal friends to help her face her fears and uncertainties.

1.67 Thesman, Jean. **The Moonstones.** Puffin, 2000. 166 pp. ISBN 0-14-130809-5. Fiction

Jane and her mother are clearing out grandmother's home to settle the estate. The work is difficult but not nearly as difficult as the emotional strain of battling with selfish Aunt Norma and cousin Rikki, an egocentric slob. Meeting the mysterious, book-loving Carey at the local amusement park adds some color to Jane's otherwise dreary days. But when a jealous Rikki tells Jane's mother that Jane and Carey have been sneaking out at night, family history begins to repeat itself as secrets from the past emerge.

1.68 Wait, Lea. **Stopping to Home.** Margaret K. McElderry Books, 2001. 152 pp. ISBN 0-689-83832-8. Fiction

Abbie and her brother Seth are growing up in Maine—by themselves. Their mother died from the small pox epidemic and their father is away at sea. The siblings end up in the home of Lydia Chase, the widow of a sea captain who also died from small pox. Abbie helps around the house in exchange for room and board, but as Widow Chase's money begins to run out, Abbie needs to find a way to save them all.

1.69 Walker, Pamela. **Pray Hard.** Scholastic, 2001. 172 pp. ISBN 0-439-21586-2. Fiction

Amelia Forrest does not believe in anything—not prayer, not miracles, and certainly not in her father's return. He is gone forever, and it's all her fault. Guilt ridden, twelve-year-old Amelia must learn to accept life for what it is: uncertain. She must also learn to trust again as she attempts to mend her relationship with her mother and accept Brother Mustard Seed's claim of contact with her daddy.

1.70 Warner, Sally. **How to Be a Real Person (in Just One Day).** Knopf, 2001. 123 pp. ISBN 0-375-80434-X. Fiction

When Kara's father leaves town for a new job two hours away, her mother slides deeper into mental illness. Sixth grader Kara hopes that by being a "perfect person" she will blend in at school and prevent the situation at home from getting worse. But it seems that the more Kara tries, the worse her mother's condition becomes and the harder it is for Kara to hide her dysfunctional home life from her friends and teachers.

1.71 Warner, Sally. **Sister Split.** American Girl, 2001. 141 pp. ISBN 1-58485-372-7. Fiction

Sisters Ivy and Lacey are unhappy when their parents announce they are getting a divorce. Ivy, the younger sister, is even more devastated when she finds she can't count on her relationships with Lacey anymore. Sent into a downward spiral by their parents' turmoil, Ivy and Lacey's closeness disappears. When Dad moves out, Lacey goes with him. Tensions escalate and the girls punch, kick, and bite each other when forced to spend the weekend together. Ivy proposes the drastic solution of a "sister spilt."

1.72 Weatherly, Lee. **Child X.** David Fickling Books, 2002. 211 pp. ISBN 0-385-75009-9. Fiction

Jules spends her days as most thirteen-year-olds do. She passes notes in class and tries to avoid talking to Adrian, who has a crush on her. She spends time with her friends and tries to ignore the friction between her parents. But then life turns upside down. Jules's dad, without any explanation, leaves home and refuses to talk to her. Photographers and reporters start hounding her, jumping out from the bushes to steal her picture. What is going on?

1.73 White, Ruth. **Memories of Summer.** Farrar, Straus and Giroux, 2000. 135 pp. ISBN 0-374-34945-2. Fiction

Lyric never really knew her mother, but her older sister Summer has always been there for her. When their father is promised a job in the auto plants of Flint, Michigan, he moves Lyric and Summer to the city from their home in rural Virginia. Summer, whose quirkiness was considered charming in the holler, is frightened and disturbed by the change. She slides rapidly and painfully into full-fledged schizophrenia. When Summer is committed to the state hospital, Lyric loses a loving part of her childhood.

1.74 Wiles, Deborah. **Love, Ruby Lavender.** Harcourt, 2001. 188 pp. ISBN 0-15-202314-3. Fiction

Ruby wrestles with repressed feelings and misconceptions about the previous year's life-changing event, a car accident that killed her grandfather. The letters between Ruby and her grandmother, as well as narration and newspaper articles, reveal a strong intergenerational relationship. Fortunately, Ruby's grandmother's letters and the encouragement of others give Ruby the inner strength to finally deal with the accident. Poignant yet humorous, Ruby's letters reveal an irrepressible character with a southern flavor.

1.75 Wilhelm, Doug. **Raising the Shades.** Farrar, Straus and Giroux, 2001. 167 pp. ISBN 0-374-36178-9. Fiction

Casey is thirteen and lives with his father. The house must be perfect and all chores done just in case Casey's dad is "not feeling well" when he gets home. That leaves little time for Casey to be with friends, and he's starting to resent it. Although he tries to keep it a secret, his friends, relatives, and others assure Casey that despite his fears he must confront his father about his drinking and convince him to get help.

1.76 Williams, Carol Lynch. **A Mother to Embarrass Me.** Delacorte, 2002. 136 pp. ISBN 0-358-72922-7. Fiction

Laura is fed up—her mother is always embarrassing her. She does silly things like wearing slippers in public places just to make Laura crazy. Then her mom drops a bomb: she's pregnant. Laura begins to develop a list of things to change about her mother, and the list is growing longer day by day. Will Laura survive this ultimate embarrassment, or will she realize how wonderful her parents and new little sister truly are?

1.77 Williams, Lori Aurelia. **When Kambia Elaine Flew in from Neptune.** Aladdin, 2000. 246 pp. ISBN 0-689-84593-6. Fiction

Shayla lives with her mom and older sister and is close to her grandmother. She befriends her neighbor Kambia Elaine and eventually learns why Kambia Elaine is so detached from the world. Shayla relays the many conflicts, including sexual abuse, parent-child struggles, and socioeconomic issues, in a touching, straightforward, and compassionate way. Although this is a book for mature reading audiences, at the center of the story is the strong core of Shayla's home and family.

2 Friends and Peers

2.1 Adler, C. S. **One Unhappy Horse.** Clarion, 2001. 156 pp. ISBN 0-618-04912-6. Fiction

Jan is devoted to her horse, especially since her father's death. But it's all her mother can do to earn enough money to make ends meet. When Jan discovers that her horse needs an operation, she knows they can't afford the surgery. Help comes from an unexpected place, however. Jan has befriended Mattie, a lonely elderly woman living next door. Through this unlikely friendship, the two are able to help each other and come up with solutions to both their problems.

2.2 Baker, Julie. **Up Molasses Mountain.** Wendy Lamb Books, 2002. 209 pp. ISBN 0-385-72908-1. Fiction

Fifteen-year-old Elizabeth befriends Clarence, who has been ostracized because of his cleft palate, when they both retreat to the mountain woods for refuge after a mining accident turns the town upside down. Set in West Virginia coal mining country in 1953, the two characters alternate narration of the events as their lives turn violent during the summer the union organizers come to town and pit family members and friends against one another.

2.3 Brashares, Ann. **The Sisterhood of the Traveling Pants.** Delacorte, 2001. 304 pp. ISBN 0-3857-2933-2. Fiction

Four teenage girls from different backgrounds, lifelong friends, agree to mail a pair of thrift-shop jeans back and forth during their first summer away from one another. The pants magically seem to fit each girl even though the girls are very different sizes and builds. The pants give each girl confidence as she experiences various adolescent adventures. Ultimately, the pants come to symbolize their sisterhood as each is faced with difficult decisions and serious consequences.

2.4 Cruise, Robin. **Fiona's Private Pages.** Harcourt, 2000. 195 pp. ISBN 0-15-216572-X. Fiction

Fiona faces a tough decision that could lead to trouble with her best friend, Blanca. She also has to figure out how to stay friends with Natalie, who's moving to a different middle school, how to be friends with a *boy,* and how to juggle loyalty to her friend Katie when keeping Katie's secret could mean Katie is in danger. Pages from Fiona's diary draw readers into her world because of the humor and poignancy with which she chronicles her life.

2.5 Danziger, Paula, and Ann M. Martin. **Snail Mail No More.** Scholastic, 2000. 344 pp. ISBN 0-439-06335-3. Fiction

We first met Tara and Elizabeth in *P.S. Longer Letter Later* following Tara's move to Ohio and a year of writing letters. Now Tara and Elizabeth finally have e-mail, and together they share the intense world of eighth grade in the cyberspace of immediate gratification. Honest and unpredictable, this book addresses many issues today's teenagers face: siblings, dating, drinking, divorce, even death. Through the wonders of e-mail, Tara and Elizabeth learn to broaden their understanding of themselves.

2.6 Dee, Catherine, editor. **The Girls' Book of Friendship: Cool Quotes, True Stories, Secrets, and More.** Little Brown, 2001. 194 pp. ISBN 0-316-16818-1. Nonfiction

Sharing secrets, laughter, and tears is common among girls of all ages. This book celebrates these activities and more. As the subtitle promises, each chapter includes cool quotes, true stories, and sometimes poems or songs written by women such as Oprah Winfrey, Michelle Kwan, and Christina Aguilera. Topics span a wide range of subjects, from slumber party etiquette to flicks to watch with girlfriends. Serious attention is also given to making and maintaining relationships as well as learning to be your own best friend.

2.7 Dessen, Sarah. **Someone Like You.** Puffin, 2000. 272 pp. ISBN 0-141-30269-0. Fiction

Soon after Scarlett's boyfriend is killed in a motorcycle accident, she learns she is pregnant with his child. Never before has she needed her best friend Halley so much. Halley has always been the quiet one and Scarlett the popular one, but now Halley must decide if she can continue to give her friend the emotional support she needs. Scarlett and Halley learn just how difficult teen pregnancy can be and how important and true their friendship is.

2.8 Duffey, Betsy. **Fur-ever Yours, Booker Jones.** Viking, 2001. 100 pp. ISBN 0-670-89287-4. Fiction

Booker Jones enjoys his life with his family and his best friend Germ. His writing and the attention it brings consume him. This all changes when his parents leave and his sister takes charge of the house. His friendship with Germ is tested in Writing Club when Germ's writing draws more attention than his own, and when Grandpa becomes frail, Booker and his sister have to figure out how to bring joy back into his life.

2.9 Farrell, Mame. **And Sometimes Why.** Farrar, Straus and Giroux, 2001. 165 pp. ISBN 0-374-32289-9. Fiction

Jack and Chris have been best friends since first grade. Now in eighth grade, their friendship is tested as Chris blossoms from tomboy into attractive young lady, catching the eyes of other guys while still able to outmaneuver Jack in sports. Jack's feelings for Chris become more complicated until he wonders if he is falling in love with her. But they learn they need the easy and deep friendship they've long had as they move into the strange new world of dating.

2.10 Ferris, Amy Schor. **A Greater Goode.** Houghton Mifflin, 2002. 183 pp. ISBN 0-618-13154-X. Fiction

Addie Goode, who is being raised by her father after her mother abandoned them when Addie was three, always uses her imagination to empathize with and help others. She and her best friend Luke help reunite a pregnant, unwed, abused young woman with her family. At the same time, they learn to cope with Addie's new stepmother and Luke's reunited but contentious parents. Addie's naively wise point of view and practicality help many people and bring a lasting, greater good.

2.11 Fine, Anne. **Up on Cloud Nine.** Delacorte, 2002. 151 pp. ISBN 0-385-73009-8. Fiction

Ian and Stolly have been friends for years—such good friends that Ian's mother has practically raised Stol, whose own parents are often too busy with their high-powered careers to notice him. After Stolly suffers a mysterious fall from an upper-floor window at his home, Ian sits at his hospital bedside and wonders whether the accident was indeed accidental. Hard hitting but tender, this book explores the consequences for young people of being eccentric—"up on cloud nine"—in today's world.

2.12 Frank, Lucy. **Just Ask Iris.** Atheneum, 2001. 214 pp. ISBN 0-689-84406-9. Fiction

Clever and engaging, Iris experiences both the normal trials and tribulations of starting seventh grade (her mom doesn't think she needs a bra, but she *knows* she does) and relationships with strange, eccentric characters like Tattoo Man and Cat Lady. Iris's open heart and friendly nature pull her into many adventures as she offers her services to neighbors who might need help with errands, chores, or shopping. Along the way, she also develops a special friendship with Will.

2.13 Garden, Nancy. **Meeting Melanie.** Farrar, Straus and Giroux, 2002. 199 pp. ISBN 0-374-34943-6. Fiction

Allie never wants to leave the island she calls home. When her family faces a financial struggle, Allie agrees to help out by working in their pie shop. Even though she is busy, Allie longs for a friend her age and is delighted when Melanie turns out to be such a friend. Allie discovers that Melanie is vastly different from her and yet also the same. The two form a fast friendship as they learn about each other, growing up, and the world around them.

2.14 Giff, Patricia Reilly. **All the Way Home.** Delacorte, 2001. 169 pp. ISNB 0-385-32209-7. Fiction

It's 1941 and the Dodgers are on a winning streak. Brick, the son of apple farmers whose orchard has been destroyed by fire, and Mariel, the adopted daughter of an old family friend, develop a friendship around their love of baseball. As the Dodgers fight their way to the pennant, Brick and Mariel fight their way to their goals and, as they help each other, turn out to be as successful as their favorite team.

2.15 Haddad, Charles. **Captain Tweakerbeak's Revenge: A Calliope Day Adventure.** Illustrated by Steve Pica. Delacorte, 2001. 185 pp. ISBN 0-385-32712-9. Fiction

Noreen and Calliope are direct opposites in personality, but they have one thing in common: their love for a mischievous gray parrot named Captain Tweakerbeak. This book chronicles their adventures in and out of school as they develop an unlikely friendship and learn what really counts in life.

2.16 Hansen, Joyce. **One True Friend.** Clarion, 2001. 154 pp. ISBN 0-395-84983-7. Fiction

Amir has been reunited with his little brother, but he still wants to locate his other siblings. As he continues his search, he must adjust to a foster family and the realization that his little brother Ronald doesn't remember him or their parents. Amir sorts out his feelings, frustrations, and choices by writing letters to his friend Doris back in the Bronx. This book, like *The Gift-Giver* and *Yellow Bird and Me,* relates the special friendship between Amir and Doris.

2.17 Hoffman, Alice. **Indigo.** Scholastic, 2002. 84 pp. ISBN 0-439-25635-6. Fiction

After her mother dies, Martha Glimmer, age thirteen, hates her life in Oak Grove, and with two unusual friends she runs away from home. Trevor and Eli McGill, her friends, long to return to the sea, so the three begin a journey that takes several unexpected twists and turns. A fast-paced novella, this story deals with the themes of loss, friendship, self-acceptance, and self-perception.

2.18 Hooper, Mary. **Amy.** Bloomsbury, 2002. 176 pp. ISBN 1-58234-793-X. Fiction

Told in the manner of a police report combining tape-recorded narrative with transcription of conversation, Amy tells her own story of how she turns to the Internet after being dumped by her two best friends. She meets Zed in a chat room and takes him at his word that he is who he says he is. When she sneaks off to meet him, she discovers that he has misrepresented himself. Life gets dangerous very quickly as Amy learns a lot about friendship and trust.

2.19 Howe, James. **The Misfits.** Atheneum, 2001. 274 pp. ISBN 0-689-83955-3. Fiction

Addie, Joe, Bobby, and Skeezie, self-declared misfits in their small town middle school, have been friends forever and figure that together they can survive anything. When Addie refuses to say the Pledge of Allegiance, the quartet challenges the status quo by forming a third political party in the student council elections to serve all the other outsiders and misfits. Through the process of running for election, these four friends learn what their friendship really means and what real courage is all about.

2.20 Hurst, Carol Otis. **Through the Lock.** Houghton Mifflin, 2001. 160 pp. ISBN 0-618-03036-0. Fiction

Etta Prentice is fourteen and an orphan. Separated from her brother and sister, she is determined to reunite her family. Etta discovers another boy, who agrees to take her in. Together these clever teens make a life for themselves, defying all odds. Back in contact with her siblings, Etta is forced to change her dream but comes away stronger for her struggle. In her first novel, Carol Otis Hurst creates an engaging story of adolescents who re-create their family unit.

2.21 Koss, Amy Goldman. **The Girls.** Dial, 2000. 121 pp. ISBN 0-8037-2494-2. Fiction

Being part of the group is often the most important thing in an adolescent's life. Maya, Renee, Darcy, Brianna, and Candace are usually inseparable, until Darcy's sleepover party pulls their clique apart. Written from each girl's point of view, the story reveals their opinions about the importance of being part of the group, their concepts of friendship, and the perils of friendship. Maya learns a valuable lesson about true friendship.

2.22 LaFaye, A. **Strawberry Hill.** Aladdin, 2000. 272 pp. ISBN 0-689-82961-2. Fiction

Raleia Pendle doesn't fit in for many reasons. As her family drives to Tidal, Maine, to spend the summer, she thinks she has finally found a place she can feel comfortable. When she discovers a man who has lived virtually untouched since the tidal wave of 1910, she thinks she's found someone who can understand how she feels. In addition to finding a place of her own, Raleia learns there are friends to be found in unexpected places.

2.23 Levy, Elizabeth. **Seventh-Grade Tango.** Hyperion, 2000. 153 pp. ISBN 0-7868-2427-1. Fiction

Rebecca Luzzaro's newly learned dance steps parallel many of the relation issues common to girls her age. Just as Rebecca learns the steps to the merengue, fox trot, and tango, so she learns the dynamics of relationships with the opposite sex—

ranging from the traumatic "kissing games" her friend Samantha is obsessed with to the finer subtleties of lifelong friends turned romantic dancing partners. Rebecca and her partner, Scott, rise above their thirteen-year-old personas, both on and off the dance floor.

2.24 Moore, Martha. **Matchit.** Delacorte, 2002. 197 pp. ISBN 0-385-72906-5. Fiction

Matchit doesn't know what to think when his father leaves him with Babe, a big-hearted acquaintance who owns a junkyard, so that he can visit Mount Rushmore with his girlfriend. Babe's friends include Sister, a taxidermist who owns a vintage Corvette, and Zebby, a sculptor who lives in an abandoned bus. None of these new people in his life sees Matchit the way he sees himself—fit for the slow-and-dumb class, not gifted and talented—and he gradually begins to change his view of himself.

2.25 Naylor, Phyllis Reynolds. **Alice Alone.** Atheneum, 2001. 229 pp. ISBN 0-689-82634-6. Fiction

Alice is beginning her eighth-grade year with many friends and a boyfriend she is crazy about. She lives with her dad and her brother Lester, who is in graduate school, and her friends think she is cool. Life is good until a new girl comes to town and relationships at school change, making Alice feel alone.

2.26 Naylor, Phyllis Reynolds. **The Boys Return.** Delacorte, 2001. 133 pp. ISBN 0-385-32734-X. Fiction

In this popular series, the Benson boys return to the town of Buckman for spring vacation, concocting a prank involving a nonexistent ghost that continues the war of practical jokes between two local families, the Hartford boys and the Malloy girls. Perfect for middle school students, this book will delight young people with the playfulness of its heroes and their compelling desire to prove to the world that their "boy side" is the best.

2.27 Oates, Joyce Carol. **Big Mouth and Ugly Girl.** HarperCollins, 2002. 264 pp. ISBN 0-06-623756-4. Fiction

Men in white shirts and black suits show up to escort Matt from his high school English class, but before we know what's going on, we're introduced to Ursula, who talks about herself as "Ugly Girl." This novel by Oates, an esteemed author of adult fiction, follows the extraordinary set of events that bring Ugly Girl and Matt together in a story that captures their hurt, anger, and betrayal but also the sense of hope they find in their unlikely friendship.

2.28 Plum-Ucci, Carol. **What Happened to Lani Garver?** Harcourt, 2002. 307 pp. ISBN 0-15-216813-3. Fiction

At sixteen, Claire's life is finally looking up. Her cancer is in remission, she's a cheerleader, and she is sitting at the most popular lunch table. But when she befriends the androgynous Lani, everything changes. Threatened by what they don't understand, Claire's friends spread a web of lies so tangled that even she can't be sure of the truth. The situation spins out of control, and Claire is left wondering: was Lani really just a boy or something much more?

2.29 Powell, Randy. **The Whistling Toilets.** Farrar, Straus and Giroux, 1996. 243 pp. ISBN 0-374-38381-2. Fiction

Finally—a humorous account about love from a boy's perspective. Stan is a teenage boy without a long-term plan. He is content to float through life uncommitted until his best friend Ginny, a tennis phenom, comes home for some rest and relaxation. Stan is chosen to coach her in a local tennis match. Everything, including Ginny's professional career, is at stake. Will Stan help Ginny get her swing back, or would he rather that she stay with him?

2.30 Spinelli, Jerry. **Wringer.** Illustrated by Cliff Nielsen. HarperTrophy, 1998. 246 pp. ISBN 0-06-440578-8. Fiction

In Waymer, ten-year-old boys become wringers at the town's annual Pigeon Day. Their job is to retrieve the pigeons wounded by sharpshooters and wring their necks. Hating the violence of the day and loving his pet pigeon, Palmer LaRue has long dreaded turning ten. But refusing to be a wringer would mean ostracism from his ruthless age-mates. Support from his parents and a girl spurned by the other boys helps Palmer gather the courage to follow his convictions.

2.31 Van Draanen, Wendelin. **Flipped.** Knopf, 2001. 192 pp. ISBN 0-375-81174-5. Fiction

In alternating chapters, Julie Baker and Bryce Loski describe what it's like living next door to each other. Julie always thought Bryce was cool and Bryce always thought Julie was weird, but now in eighth grade everything changes. Bryce discovers that Julie's passion for trees and for the eggs laid by her backyard chickens reveal something much more important about her than just silly craziness. And Julie wonders if Bryce isn't really just a shallow jerk who doesn't care about other people's feelings.

2.32 Voight, Cynthia. **It's Not Easy Being Bad.** Atheneum, 2000. 241 pp. ISBN 0-689-82473-4. Fiction

In their first year of junior high, Margalo and Mikey have a lot in common—they understand each other and they are both unpopular. While they both want to do something about it, they won't relinquish who they are in order to become popular. Both girls have a penchant for being brutally honest; however, this quality is what sets them on the road to popularity while still maintaining their true personalities and their best friendship.

2.33 Wilson, Jacqueline. **Bad Girls.** Illustrated by Nick Sharratt. Delacorte, 2001. 165 pp. ISBN 0-385-72916-2. Fiction

Mandy is pushed into the street in front of an oncoming bus by a pack of older, bad girls. She can't tell her overprotective parents how much these girls pick on her, so she struggles to figure out a way to take care of herself. Fate intervenes when Tanya moves next door. It turns out that though Tanya is an even bigger, badder girl than the bullies at school, she wants Mandy for her friend.

2.34 Winkler, David. **Scotty and the Gypsy Bandit.** Farrar, Straus and Giroux, 2000. 198 pp. ISBN 0-374-36420-6. Fiction

Eleven-year-old Scotty Hansen's life is suddenly complicated when his father dies unexpectedly, leaving Scotty and his mother to deal with their loss. McStew (a.k.a. The Gypsy Bandit) is the next-door neighbor who gives the term "oddball" new meaning. Through a series of comic and tragic events, Scotty learns from McStew the meaning of friendship and growing up.

Winkler combines humor, romance, mystery, and insight in his first novel.

2.35 Zeises, Lara M. **Bringing Up the Bones.** Delacorte, 2002. 214 pp. ISBN 0-385-73001-2. Fiction

Benji and Briget are long-time friends. Bridget persuades the reluctant Benji to take on the role of boyfriend—but then Benji dies, and Bridget is devastated. She decides to take a year off to deal with her grief before going to college. When she meets Jasper, she has to take a good look at herself and at the nature of her relationship with Benji and what it meant, and she eventually learns that she has to take responsibility for her own happiness.

3 Identity

3.1 Adler, C. S. **The No Place Cat.** Clarion, 2002. 153 pp. ISBN 0-618-09644-2. Fiction

No one understands or wants Tess. She is, for all intents and purposes, invisible in her house. At odds with her new stepfamily, Tess knows that life would be better if she lived with her mother. Running away from home and her problems, Tess begins a journey across the desert in search of happiness. Along the way, she befriends a stray cat, whose life is similar to hers. The cat has nowhere to go and neither does Tess.

3.2 Almond, David. **Secret Heart.** Delacorte, 2002. 199 pp. ISBN 0-385-72947-2. Fiction.

Joe Maloney is misunderstood, unwanted, and criticized by the people of Helmouth, who don't see the things Joe sees nor hear the noises he hears. Alone and fearful, Joe spends his days trying to avoid his classmates. The weekend that a pitiful, failing circus comes to town changes Joe forever: he finds friendship and peace inside the tent and a brave tiger inside his own secret heart.

3.3 Alphin, Elaine Marie. **Simon Says.** Harcourt, 2002. 258 pp. ISBN 0-15-216355-7. Fiction

At sixteen, Charles is tired of playing "Simon Says." As an artist, he is not allowed to paint what he sees in his imagination. In his boarding school, he's got to be like everyone else; he can't admit the truth about himself. Charles sets out to seek the one person he believes can help him escape from the game. It turns out, however, that his quest is not an easy one, and the game of "Simon Says" continues anyway—with unforeseen consequences.

3.4 American Girl, editor. **Yikes! A Smart Girl's Guide to Surviving Tricky, Sticky, Icky Situations.** Illustrated by Bonnie Timmons. Pleasant Company, 2002. 87 pp. ISBN 1-58485-530-4. Nonfiction

This book gives tips and advice on solving all sorts of sticky or embarrassing situations that a preteen girl might face in daily life at home and at school. How, for example, can you save face if you fall down the stairs in front of four million people? Can you keep cool in scary situations like getting lost from the group on a hike? Good advice abounds.

3.5 Anderson, Laurie Halse. **Speak.** Puffin, 2001. 208 pp. ISBN 0-141-31088-X. Fiction

After calling the police to bust a summer party, Melinda finds herself an outcast during her first year of high school. Painfully isolated, Melinda eventually quits speaking to anyone. As she engages in a project for her art class, she faces the dangerous events of that terrible night when she was raped. Eventually Melinda speaks out, exposing the boy who violated her and regaining a sense of self.

3.6 Andryszewski, Tricia. **Gay Rights.** Twenty-First Century Books, 2000. 110 pp. ISBN 0-7613-1568-3. Nonfiction

From the 1970s to the present, the gay rights movement has been an increasingly visible presence in U.S. society. Various groups have made their voices heard in an effort to achieve fair treatment for homosexuals. Topics in this book include gays in the military, religious organizations, marriage and family life, hate crimes, and AIDS.

3.7 Bagdasarian, Adam. **First French Kiss and Other Traumas.** Farrar, Straus and Giroux, 2002. 134 pp. ISBN 0-374-32338-0. Fiction

Bagdasarian recounts episodes from his childhood in this collection of loosely interrelated stories that range in topic from a first French kiss, to bullies, to the importance of work, to family relationships, to Little League. The stories are by turns poignant, humorous, and whimsical, covering the author's lived experiences from the age of five to twenty.

3.8 Bauer, Joan. **Hope Was Here.** Putnam, 2000. 186 pp. ISBN 0-399-23142-0. Fiction

In this Newbery Honor Book for 2001, Hope and her Aunt Addie head to Wisconsin where Addie cooks for a restaurant and Hope is a part-time waitress. They become involved in the life and politics of the small town and find a home and love as well as change and even death. This book is classic Bauer, mixing humor with serious life lessons.

3.9 Bauer, Joan. **Rules of the Road.** Puffin, 2000. 201 pp. ISBN 0-698-11828-6. Fiction

High school sophomore Jenna Boller is great at selling shoes at Gladstone's, where she has an after-school job. The store is part of the Gladstone family chain of shoe stores. The company president, crusty, elderly Mrs. Madeline Gladstone, chooses Jenna as her driver on a business trip to visit other Gladstone stores. Jenna agrees to go and begins on a journey, during which she must deal with loss and struggle for understanding.

3.10 Booth, Teena. **Falling from Fire.** Wendy Lamb Books, 2002. 201 pp. ISBN 0-385-72978-2. Fiction

Teri, a first-year high school student, finds her life divided into "before the fire" and "after the fire" that destroyed her home and all its contents. Teri is the daughter of an immature, often divorced local beauty, but she has always been shy and lonely. Before the fire, her only friend was Wesley; after the fire, Teri is the target of new interest. Although her choices seem limited to fitting into one of three groups—the Rowdies, Holy Rollers, or Nobodies—Teri finds the strength to be herself.

3.11 Brooks, Kevin. **Lucas.** Scholastic, 2003. 423 pp. ISBN 0-439-45698-3. Fiction

Caitlin lives on an island connected to the mainland only by a causeway. She encounters Lucas, who seems to know how to live honestly and without the petty vices she sees in herself and her community. When Lucas is accused of a crime he did not commit and is hunted down by the community, with tragic consequences, Caitlin is forced to look into her own heart to find the strength to do what she knows is right.

3.12 Buchanan, Jane. **Hank's Story.** Farrar, Straus and Giroux, 2001. 136 pp. ISBN 0-374-32836-6. Fiction

Hank and his older brother Peter are orphans who ride the Orphan Train from New York City to Nebraska in 1923, hoping to find a family who will love them. Placed with the Olsons, they soon discover that the cruel couple is interested only in how much work the boys can do. Peter runs away and Hank is left alone with the abusive couple. Lonely, angry, and frightened, Hank must find a way to save himself and reclaim his life.

3.13 Cabot, Meg. **The Princess Diaries.** HarperCollins, 2000. 238 pp. ISBN 0-06-029210-5. Fiction

Mia Thermopolis is fourteen years old and in love with Josh Richter, a cool, handsome senior. After measuring her chest size (32A), she knows he will never notice her. But Mia and best friend Lilly are having a good time until Mia learns her true identity: Mia is not just Mia, but Princess Amelia Mignonette Grimaldi Thermopolis Renaldo of Genovia. How does a princess act? Mia is about to find out.

3.14 Cart, Michael, editor. **Love and Sex: Ten Stories of Truth.** Simon & Schuster, 2001. 256 pp. ISBN 0-689-83203-6. Fiction

Sophisticated readers will appreciate this collection of short stories edited by author Michael Cart. With a cast of contributing authors as diverse as Joan Bauer, Laurie Halse Anderson, Angela Johnson, and Chris Lynch, this collection features a wide variety of characters, voices, settings, and relationships—some of them provocative. Adolescent passion, first loves, heterosexual and homosexual attractions, and heartbreaking decisions all have a place in these stories of truth.

3.15 Clifton, Lucille. **The Times They Used to Be.** Illustrated by E.B. Lewis. Delacorte, 2000. 41 pp. ISBN 0-385-32126-0. Fiction

In 1948, twelve-year-old Sookie and her friend Tallahassie learn about coming of age when they confuse religion and physical maturation. As Sookie says, "sin broke all out in [Tassie's] body"—the girls thought that Tassie's starting her period meant she was a sinner. Clifton evokes time and place with her details about the new invention of television, radio shows, and Truman abolishing Jim Crow laws in the army.

3.16 de Guzman, Michael. **Melonhead.** Farrar, Straus and Giroux, 2002. 213 pp. ISBN 0-374-34944-4. Fiction

Tired of living with his uncaring divorced parents, Sidney, a twelve-year-old boy with an unusually large head, takes a bus trip across the United States—from Los Angeles to New York City—that becomes a journey of self-discovery. On this wild adventure, young Sidney tells wild stories about himself and in so doing learns from the strangers he meets, and the experiences he has, that he is indeed "something very special."

3.17 Dessen, Sarah. **Keeping the Moon.** Puffin, 2000. 228 pp. ISBN 0-14-131007-3. Fiction

Having recently lost a great deal of weight, teenage Colie should look forward to spending the summer at the beach with her Aunt Mira. But being a loner, Colie doesn't look forward to the beach and is surprised when she makes two new friends who help her discover her inner and outer beauty.

3.18 Doyle, Malachy. **Who Is Jesse Flood?** Bloomsbury, 2002. 176 pp. ISBN 1-58234-776-X. Fiction

Jesse Flood is a determined fourteen-year-old growing up in Northern Ireland. His poor, dysfunctional family is in conflict, and when Jesse's mother walks out, he has to fend for himself. Though Jesse wants friends, he isn't interested in the normal things other teens are interested in. His one obsession is Sophie Cameron, the most popular girl in school. Seeking Sophie's attention becomes a long process, but one that Jesse eventually completes in his quest to find his place.

3.19 Duncan, Lois, editor. **On the Edge: Stories at the Brink.** Aladdin, 2000. 211 pp. ISBN 0-689-83256-7. Fiction

This collection of twelve short stories centers on the theme of being "on the edge." Topics range from being literally on the edge, which is Vinny's situation in Graham Salisbury's "The Ravine" as he faces the challenge of diving off a cliff into the water far below in the ravine, to being mentally or physically on the edge, as is the case with Bailey, a young woman who, after fainting in math class, awaits test results for a possible brain tumor.

3.20 Ferris, Jean. **Eight Seconds.** Harcourt, 2000. 186 pp. ISBN 0-15-202367-4. Fiction

When his dad signs him up for a week of rodeo school, John figures it will be a good chance to get away during the summer before his senior year of high school. At the school, John learns that his friend and rodeo partner, Kit, is a homosexual. When he finds himself attracted to this good-looking, intelligent, and kind individual, John is forced to face his own sexuality.

3.21 Freymann-Weyr, Garret. **My Heartbeat.** Houghton Mifflin, 2002. 154 pp. ISBN 0-618-14181-2. Fiction

Even as fourteen-year-old Ellen is reading *The Age of Innocence*, the unspoken emotions and hidden social laws of that novel parallel the repressed emotions in her family. Ellen finally asks the unspoken questions: Is her brother, Link, gay? Is his friend James gay? These children of wealthy Manhattanites are sophisticated in their conversations yet naive in their social interactions. This novel, for mature readers, follows Ellen's journey through denial, sexual awakening, and social maturation to an acceptance of herself, her own "heartbeat."

3.22 Frost, Helen. **Keesha's House.** Frances Foster Books, 2003. 116 pp. ISBN 0-374-34064-1. Poetry

Faced with tremendous problems, seven teens each flee their home in search of a place where he or she will find acceptance, reassurance, and a future. Finding refuge is the only hope these adolescents have. They find such a place at Keesha's House. Here they learn about themselves and their places in the world. Each discovers that life is difficult but that difficulties can be overcome. Their stories are told in poetic form.

3.23 Garden, Nancy. **Holly's Secret.** Farrar, Straus and Giroux, 2000. 132 pp. ISBN 0-374-33273-8. Fiction

Twelve-year-old Holly has been adopted by two moms instead of a mother and a father. In addition to figuring out how to handle this unusual household arrangement, Holly must adjust to a new middle school, making new friends, and living in the country. She learns that weaving a web of lies about the relationship of her two moms only brings trouble. She also learns that her real friends care about her and not her family situation.

3.24 Glenn, Mel. **Split Image: A Story in Poems.** HarperCollins, 2000. 159 pp. ISBN 0-688-16249-5. Fiction

Laura Li has it all: beauty, brains, and popularity. She is the image of a model teenager with a perfect job and a perfect life. There is, however, one problem: Laura's perfection is a facade. She has secrets, secrets that prove fatal. Told in verse by various characters, this story demonstrates that the pictures we show the world don't necessarily reveal what lies beneath the lens' reach.

3.25 Gordon, Amy. **When JFK Was My Father.** Puffin, 1999. 202 pp. ISBN 0-14-131279-3. Fiction

Georgia, ignored by her wealthy, preoccupied parents, is sent from Brazil to a boarding school in Connecticut after she moves to the United States with her mother. Georgia finds solace in her fantasy that President John F. Kennedy is her father, in her stamp collection, in her writing for her English teacher, and in her friendship with Tim, whom she had met in Brazil. Seeking acceptance, Georgia ponders the key questions of adolescence: Who am I? and Do I have any control over who I become?

3.26 Graff, Nancy Price. **A Long Way Home.** Clarion, 2001. 199 pp. ISBN 0-618-12042-4. Fiction

Because his father has died, Riley and his mother move to his grandfather's run-down house. Riley dislikes his new home in Vermont. He doesn't like small-town life, and his mother complicates matters by taking up with a social outcast, an old high school sweetheart who is still smitten with his mom. Slowly, Riley comes to accept his new life and come to terms with the strengths and weaknesses of all human beings.

3.27 Grant, Cynthia D. **The Cannibals: Starring Tiffany Spratt.** Roaring Brook, 2002. 148 pp. ISBN 0-7613-2759-2. Fiction

Tiffany tells us she was once the leader of the award-winning cheerleading squad, girlfriend of the best-looking guy in the class, and on her way to making her acting debut in a major movie. But she went from being at the top to being Miss Reject of the Universe. Tiffany survives, however, and in her journal tells us how she finds happiness with the support of her friends, family, and faith—and Campbell, who surprises her when he tells her he's gay.

3.28 Gravelle, Karen. **Five Ways to Know about You.** Illustrated by Mary Lynn Blasutta. Walker, 2001. 166 pp. ISBN 0-8027-8749-5. Nonfiction

This book makes complicated personality analysis systems simple and easy to use. Four ancient systems (astrology, numerology, Chinese horoscopes, and palm reading) and one new system (handwriting analysis) are discussed. For each, a brief history and application is given followed by instructions for learning about the reader's personality traits. Illustrations and charts enhance the book and show readers what traits they possess and what types of people they are likely to befriend.

3.29 Gray, Dianne E. **Holding Up the Earth.** Houghton Mifflin, 2000. 210 pp. ISBN 0-618-00703-2. Fiction

Hope has stayed in more foster homes than she cares to remember in the past eight years. The only feeling of connectedness she has with her dead mother is the backpack she carries with her everywhere. Hope's memories are tied to it, without room for anyone else. She is successful at keeping people out until she meets Sarah and Sarah's mother. These two women open their hearts to Hope, who discovers that allowing others in is part of being human.

3.30 Grove, Vicki. **Destiny.** Illustrated by Kam Mak. Putnam, 2000. 169 pp. ISBN 0-399-23449-7. Fiction

Embarrassed to be selling potatoes with her stepfather, impoverished Destiny takes a job reading to Mrs. Peck, an elderly lady who can no longer see well enough to read. Through her relationship with Mrs. Peck, Destiny learns about ancient Greek mythology and the truth about a family tragedy.

3.31 Hamilton, Virginia. **Time Pieces: The Book of Times.** Blue Sky, 2002. 191 pp. ISBN 0-590-28881-4. Fiction

Heritage, Valena discovers, helps to shape who we are. Throughout the summer, she learns about her family's history and realizes how it plays out in the present while molding her future. Readers glimpse moments of Valena's life in a rural town as she questions who she is and where she belongs. Making sense of her great-grandfather's travels on the Underground Railroad and the time period that supported slavery becomes necessary for Valena to make sense of the present day.

3.32 Hicks, Betty. **I Smell Like Ham.** Roaring Brook, 2002. 133 pp. ISBN 0-7613-2857-2. Fiction

Sixth grader Nick, adjusting to middle school, the death of his mother two years previously, a new stepmother, a new "nerdy" third-grade brother, and sharing his father, responds to the constant question "What did you learn in school today?" in an authentic voice that demonstrates his growth from a somewhat self-centered to a caring person. His genuine middle school voice is delightful and interesting as he copes with peer pressure, girls, growing up, and his new family.

3.33 Hidier, Tanuja Desai. **Born Confused.** Scholastic, 2002. 432 pp. ISBN 0-439-35762-4. Fiction

Growing up and attempting to find oneself is never easy; in fact, it's confusing. Just ask Dimple Lala. She was born confused. On the brink of adulthood, Dimple begins to question her role in life, her parents' traditions, and her own culture. In search of herself, her heritage, and her happiness, Dimple discovers the true meaning of living when she realizes that friendship, family, love, and ancestry make her who she is.

3.34 Holyoke, Nancy. **A Smart Girl's Guide to Boys: Surviving Crushes, Staying True to Yourself, and Other Stuff.** Illustrated by Bonnie Timmons. American Girl, 2001. 112 pp. ISBN 1-58485-368-9. Nonfiction

If you're a girl about to wade into the water of dating, you might find this book helpful (or at least entertaining). With plenty of quizzes, tips, and cartoons about boy-girl relationships, it includes sections on surviving crushes, talking to boys online, and dealing with breakups, among other things. One of the book's messages is to not take yourself too seriously; do the same with this book, as everything in it might not apply to you.

3.35 Jennings, Patrick. **The Beastly Arms.** Scholastic, 2001. 314 pp. ISBN 0-439-16589-X. Fiction

Nicholas is a shy, dreamy boy who photographs clouds and has an unusual pet. He and his recently divorced mother search for a new place to live when their landlord raises the rent. Their search leads them to an unfamiliar part of the city where they encounter a peculiar old gentleman named Mr. Beastly, who offers them a wonderful deal on an apartment in his unusual building. Strange events transpire, leading Nicholas to an amazing discovery about the world he inhabits.

3.36 Johnson, Angela. **Heaven.** Aladdin, 2000. 138 pp. ISBN 0-689-82290-1. Fiction

Marley's family resides in the town of Heaven, a word that accurately describes Marley's feelings about her life there—until her parents reveal a secret about her past. Suddenly, Marley doesn't feel so secure in the world anymore, and she is forced to reassess her feelings about Jack, the ever-traveling man she believed to be her uncle and whose letters and postcards from various destinations she has treasured.

3.37 Kennedy, X. J. **Exploding Gravy: Poems to Make You Laugh.** Illustrated by Joy Allen. Little, Brown, 2002. 117 pp. ISBN 0-316-38423-2. Poetry

Poet X. J. Kennedy brings to life his amusing poems, designed for reading aloud so each word and rhyme can be savored. Rejoice in the likes of "Stevie the Internet Addict," who must be rescued from a fire while he sits glued to his computer screen. Divided into eight sections, this whimsical collection of poetry about bubbling and bumbling adolescents will delight readers of all ages.

3.38 LeMieux, Anne C. **All the Answers.** Avon Camelot, 2000. 149 pp. ISBN 0-380-97771-0. Fiction

Jason's life seems to be falling apart. He is failing algebra, he is bullied by the brother of a girl who has caught his eye, and his relationship with his father is experiencing turbulence. Snafus with friends lead to embarrassment and lost confidence. LeMieux provides a poignant and entertaining story of Jason's personal and academic struggles, which could be those of any adolescent. Conflicts are resolved in convincing ways that make all of Jason's dilemmas seem real.

3.39 McDonald, Joyce. **Shadow People.** Delacorte, 2000. 281 pp. ISBN 0-385-32662-9. Fiction

Four desperate souls who, on the surface, have nothing in common find one another. One is a loner, another a juvenile delinquent, the third a genius, and the last an average teenage boy. On a deeper level, however, the four share rage, loneliness, and a tendency toward violence. They embark on a spree of destruction and find themselves addicted to the havoc they create. As teenage pranks escalate into serious offenses, lives and one small town will never be the same.

3.40 Murphy, Claire Rudolf. **Free Radical.** Clarion, 2002. 198 pp. ISBN 0-618-11134-4. Fiction

Summer has finally come to Alaska and Luke is focusing on making the all-star baseball team. His life is turned upside down suddenly when his mother reveals a thirty-year-old secret: she has been in hiding since her days as a radical during the Vietnam War. Luke's life is in turmoil; he faces losing his mother while he learns of an entire family he never knew.

3.41 Namioka, Lensey. **An Ocean Apart, a World Away.** Delacorte, 2002. 197 pp. ISBN 0-385-73002-0. Fiction

In 1921, sixteen-year-old Yanyan meets Baoshu, a young revolutionary intent on restoring the Manchu dynasty in China. When Baoshu asks her to marry him, a choice that would require Yanyan to give up her dream of becoming a doctor, she chooses her career, traveling to the United States to enroll at Cornell University. There she faces prejudice because of her cultural background and gender, but she also makes new friends, including the brilliant and attentive Chinese student L. H.

3.42 Naylor, Phyllis Reynolds. **The Grooming of Alice.** Aladdin, 2001. 215 pp. ISBN 0-689-84618-5. Fiction

Fourteen-year-old Alice is ready for the best summer of her life. Her dad is going to Europe, leaving her home alone with her brother. She has decided to work as a volunteer and spend the summer getting into shape. But Alice's many plans are put on hold, and she must prepare herself to deal with important issues such as anorexia, romance, and domestic violence. She learns lessons about death and relationships in a humorous but realistic way.

3.43 O'Connell, Rebecca. **Myrtle of Willendorf.** Front Street, 2000. 116 pp. ISBN 1-886910-52-9. Fiction

Myrtle thought that college would be more fun than high school, but it isn't turning out that way. As an art student, she has only food and her sense of humor to rely on. Her beautiful roommate Jada, with her boyfriend and healthy eating habits, is no help. During one painful summer, Myrtle discovers, through her painting and a prehistoric stone figure known as the Venus of Willendorf, a new sense of self and a different kind of beauty.

3.44 Paulsen, Gary. **The Beet Fields: Memories of a Sixteenth Summer.** Delacorte, 2000. 160 pp. ISBN 0-385-32647-5. Nonfiction

Paulson calls on his own experiences as a sixteen-year-old as he describes the summer he ran away from home and survived on his own while learning important truths about himself, other people, and the world. First he works in the beet fields with the migrant workers and experiences the boredom and physically numbing difficulties of field labor. Eventually he joins a traveling carnival and then, underage and without parental consent, the armed forces.

3.45 Pearson, Mary E. **Scribbler of Dreams.** Harcourt, 2001. 223 pp. ISBN 0-15-202320-8. Fiction

Kaitlin Malone's family has always hated the Crutchfields, and that hatred has intensified now that Kaitlin's father has been imprisoned for murdering Robert Crutchfield. But Kaitlin, a poet and "scribbler of dreams," finds herself falling for artist Bram Crutchfield, Robert's son, whom she meets during her senior year. She quickly finds herself enmeshed in a web of lies as she tries to hide her identity in order to maintain her deepening love for this gentle soul.

3.46 Poupeney, Mollie. **Her Father's Daughter.** Delacorte, 2000. 245 pp. ISBN 0-385-32760-9. Fiction

Maggie lives near the Oregon coastline with her two brothers and her parents during the Great Depression. Her adolescent growing pains are complicated by the poverty that causes her family to move from place to place in search of financial stability. Maggie feels "like somebody else gets to be the boss of my life all the time." Her father's drinking gradually takes its toll on the family, and Maggie struggles to deal with her father's absence when her parents divorce.

3.47 Powell, Randy. **Run If You Dare.** Farrar, Straus and Giroux, 2001. 185 pp. ISBN 0-374-39981-6. Fiction

Gardner Dickinson realizes at age fourteen that life is a lot trickier than he had ever expected. He gradually becomes aware that his father is not the heroic figure he once seemed, and this hard truth raises some difficult questions for Gardner about his own identity. These questions include confusion about his sister's budding sexuality and his family's social class. Along with resentment about the changes in his father, Gardner discovers previously hidden talents and strengths within himself.

3.48 Proimos, James. **If I Were in Charge, the Rules Would Be Different.** Scholastic, 2002. 80 pp. ISBN 0-439-20864-5. Poetry

The title of this book, which appears on the cover upside down, will give readers a clue about what sort of adventure they're in for as they read. Those who like Roald Dahl's stories or Jack Prelutsky's humor will appreciate these rhyming poems. The titles are particularly unusual (for example, "The True Story of How I Blew a Bubble as Big as My Head"), and Proimos's whimsical drawings make the poems even more fun to read.

3.49 *Read* Magazine, editor. **Read in a Different Light: Stories of Loners, Outcasts, and Rebels.** Millbrook, 2000. 160 pp. ISBN 0-7613-1615-9. Fiction

From the editors of *Read* magazine comes a collection of ten short stories and excerpts by contemporary and classic authors. Organized into themes such as "The Loners," "The Rebels," and "The Outcasts," these pieces all explore in some way the idea of being unique in society—a familiar feeling for most adolescents. Authors included are Shirley Jackson, H.G. Wells, Ted Hoey, and William Shakespeare, among others.

3.50 Rennison, Louise. **Angus, Thongs and Full-Frontal Snogging: Confessions of Georgia Nicolson.** HarperCollins, 2000. 247 pp. ISBN 0-06-028814-0. Fiction

Georgia Nicolson knows what it means to give in to peer pressure and to be in love with an "older man." She knows too what she looks like without eyebrows and both the connotative and literal meaning of full-frontal snogging. Georgia thinks her parents are clueless, that she is ugly, and that her sister has peed somewhere in her room. Thank goodness for her journal, in which she is free to observe and comment on life (hers, her parents, and her friends).

3.51 Ritter, John H. **Over the Wall.** Philomel, 2000. 312 pp. ISBN 0-399-23489-6. Fiction.

Spending the summer in New York with his aunt and her family, Tyler's focus is on baseball and making the all-star team. While he has plenty of opportunities to show his talent on the field, it is his behavior as a hothead and fighter that earn him a reputation. His coach and his family help him understand his anger and deal with the ongoing impact his grandfather's death in Vietnam has on the family.

3.52 Rushton, Rosie. **Melissa.** Hyperion, 2002. 228 pp. ISBN 0-7868-1502-7. Fiction

Melissa is a British teenager struggling through several major issues. Besides the fact that her mother is a priest, Melissa also has to move to the country, which she finds boring. Forced to make new friends, she resorts to breaking the school dress code to look cool in front of the popular girls. She also meets Kristy, an outcast, and then catches her dad having an affair. Will Melissa survive this new life?

3.53 Rushton, Rosie. **Poppy.** Hyperion, 1996. 224 pp. ISBN 0-7868-1391-1. Fiction

Poppy can make anyone's problems go away, including her friend Livi's problems with boys. This British teenage novel depicts the realities of life no one can escape. Soon Poppy realizes that she may need to spend some time solving her own family's problems, including her own relationship problems. Lately, Poppy's dad has been acting in a suspect manner. Poppy learns about major changes that will soon affect her life, and just when she seems to be adjusting, more bad news comes her way.

3.54 Selznick, Brian. **The Boy of a Thousand Faces.** Laura Geringer Books, 2000. 40 pp. ISBN 0-06-026265-6. Fiction

Ten-year-old Alonzo King was born on Halloween and is fascinated by horror movies and the actor Lon Chaney, called the Man of a Thousand Faces. Alonzo takes photographs of himself in monster costumes but so far has only twenty-three. When a rumored "Beast" comes to town, one of Alonzo's photographs accidentally ends up in the paper. A trusted neighbor helps him set things straight and also achieve his goal of becoming the Boy of a Thousand Faces.

3.55 Slade, Arthur. **Tribes.** Wendy Lamb Books, 2002. 134 pp. ISBN 0-385-73003-9. Fiction

Percivel Montmount (a.k.a. Percy) knows that he is different from most of his classmates who are about to graduate from high school. Ever since his anthropologist father "disappeared," Percy has recorded his extensive observations of the "tribes," or cliques, that exist in his Canadian high school. As Percy and his friend Elissa experience the rituals of graduation, he must come to terms with his past so that he can face the future.

3.56 Smith, Sherri L. **Lucy the Giant.** Delacorte, 2002. 217 pp. ISBN 0-385-72940-5. Fiction

Everyone in Sitka, Alaska, knows about Lucy: her mother's departure years ago, her father's drunkenness, her amazing height that earned her the nickname "Giant." No one has ever *really* gotten to know her, though. At fifteen, with nothing holding her in Sitka and no more strength to face her father, Lucy travels to the strange world of crab fishing in Kodiak, where she eventually finds the home she's never had. Here, Lucy doesn't stick out; she fits in.

3.57 Spinelli, Jerry. **Stargirl.** Knopf, 2000. 192 pp. ISBN 0-679-88637-0. Fiction

Being different at any age is difficult, especially for Mica High students, who think and dress alike and pride themselves on their sameness. No one, in fact, is unique. Until Stargirl, that is. She is color and mystique, caring and feeling—everything the Mica High students are not. When faced with fitting in, Stargirl must decide if she will ignore conformity and remain true to herself or become what others think she should be: normal.

3.58 Torres, Laura. **November Ever After.** Holiday House, 1999. 171 pp. ISBN 0-8234-1464-7. Fiction

Following her mother's death, sixteen-year-old Amy finds support in the company of her best friend Sara. Their rapport becomes strained when Sara begins spending more and more time in the company of another girl. Confused by the secrets her friend seems to be keeping, Amy soon discovers that Sara is romantically involved with the other girl. Both girls must struggle with their personal beliefs to overcome differences and maintain their friendship.

3.59 Vande Velde, Vivian. **Allison, Who Went Away.** Houghton Mifflin, 2001. 211 pp. ISBN 0-618-04585-6. Fiction

Susan is fourteen and trying to recreate herself. Going by the name Sybil, she muddles through life at her new school. Her older sister Alison has left home but though Alison's disappearance is affecting everyone in the family, no one is talking about it. Sybil's parents are now overprotective, but her friend Connie helps convince them to allow Sybil to sign up for the school play. Sybil comes to terms with her sister's disappearance and begins to move on.

3.60 Walker, Kate. **Peter.** Sandpiper, 2001 (Originally published in Australia in 1991). 229 pp. ISBN 0-618-11130-1. Fiction

Peter is an ordinary Australian fifteen-year-old. He loves to ride his dirt bike and wants to be a photographer. But Peter finds himself attracted to the gay friend of his older brother. Realistic conversations between guys about what's "normal," about the problems with labels such as straight and gay, and about Peter's feelings, coupled with carefully crafted scenes about Peter's explorations, make this an engaging book, similar to Blume's *Forever,* but perhaps too direct for many middle school readers.

3.61 Wallace, Karen. **Raspberries on the Yangtze.** Delacorte, 2002. 134 pp. ISBN 0-385-72963-4. Fiction

Set in rural Canada in the 1950s, this novel describes growing up and learning that people aren't always as they seem. The story is told through the hilarious, naive voice of Nancy, a young girl a bit like Tom Sawyer, who is influenced by reading about adventure and by her active imagination. The old wire fence, which makes a "yang" sound when Nancy bounces on it, *could be* the Yangtze River in China, and Nancy could cross it to the wider world as she comes to understand her own world better.

3.62 Wayland, April Halprin. **Girl Coming in for a Landing: A Novel in Poems.** Illustrated by Elaine Clayton. Knopf, 2002. 124 pp. ISBN 0-375-80158-8. Fiction

Effectively illustrated by Elaine Clayton, this novel in poems leads the reader tantalizingly through a year in the life of a high school girl, aspiring writer, daughter, girlfriend, friend, student, sister, and grandniece. The various types of poems precisely and honestly find the heart of language and the heart of a young girl "coming in for a landing."

3.63 Williams, Lori Aurelia. **Shayla's Double Brown Baby Blues.** Simon & Schuster, 2001. 300 pp. ISBN 0-689-82469-6. Fiction

A companion book to *When Kambia Elaine Flew in from Neptune,* this novel takes us further into the world of thirteen-year-old Shayla. We once again meet the strong women who surround and support her, her father comes back into the picture for a short time, and Shayla befriends a young man new to the neighborhood. Shayla is still the incredibly strong and independent young woman she was in the first book, but she faces new challenges as she approaches young adulthood.

3.64 Wilson, Jacqueline. **Girls in Love.** Delacorte, 2002 (Originally published in Great Britain in 1997). 181 pp. ISBN 0-385-72974-X. Fiction

Ellie and her ninth-grade friends seem to be dealing with normal teen issues when those issues become more complex thanks to the London club scene, older boys, and alcohol and other drugs. Fortunately, Ellie and her friends find safety through their support and rescue of one another and their realization that Seventh Heaven, a local club, isn't so heavenly. Ellie's interests in art and writing are revealed through her journal and lists that include her heroes and heroines, major resolutions, and dreams.

3.65 Wittlinger, Ellen. **What's in a Name?** Illustrated by John Mathias. Simon & Schuster, 2000. 160 pp. ISBN 0-689-82551-X. Fiction

The community is divided; the newcomers want to change the town name to Folly Bay, but others are content with the name Scrub Harbor. This story is told from multiple points of view. Juxtaposed with the community's identity crisis are ten teenagers trying to sort out their own identities with an insight and humor that demonstrate that no one should rush to judge others.

3.66 Wooding, Chris. **Kerosene.** Scholastic, 2002. 195 pp. ISBN 0-439-09013-X. Fiction

Shy to the point of being antisocial, Cal attempts to hide in the crowds at school, in the streets of his London suburban town, and even in his own home, where his mostly absent parents rarely venture. The one thing he finds solace in is fire. At first he contents himself with just striking matches, but as the social pressures increase, Cal finds himself setting fires, becoming a danger to himself as well as others. This book uses British dialect.

3.67 Yep, Laurence. **Angelfish.** Putnam, 2001. 216 pp. ISBN 0-399-23041-6. Fiction

A sequel to *The Cook's Family,* this novel continues Robin's story as she struggles with her portrayal of Beauty in the ballet *Beauty and The Beast* and works for a seeming "beast," Mr. Tsow, in a pet fish store. Parallels are drawn between the ballet, Robin, and Mr. Tsow, with his past in the Cultural Revolution in China. Born in the United States, Robin is torn between her Chinese and American backgrounds.

3.68 Young, Ronder Thomas. **Objects in Mirror.** Roaring Brook, 2002. 168 pp. ISBN 0-7613-2600-6. Fiction

Seventeen-year-old Grace, subject to low expectations from her parents and most of her teachers, struggles with family changes after her father's stroke. Most of the novel centers on Grace's planning the "surprise" party her friend Allison has asked her to throw for her and Grace's discoveries about herself and her friends as a result of that planning. She finds her individuality and strength where it always was, within herself, and moves out from beneath the shadow of the past into greater expectations for her future.

II Challenging Our Lives

4 Adventure and Survival

4.1 Allende, Isabel. **City of the Beasts.** Translated from the Spanish by Margaret Sayers Peden. HarperCollins, 2002. 416 pp. ISBN 0-06-050918-X. Fiction

In this ecological and biological mystery, fifteen-year-old Alexander Cold travels on a simultaneously realistic and mystical adventure into the Amazon with his grandmother, who is an author, to search for Yeti-like beasts. Overcoming many fears by necessity, Alexander eventually contacts his mother in his dreams as he evolves from child to young adult and hopes he has found a cure for her cancer.

4.2 Alvarez, Julia. **Before We Were Free.** Knopf, 2002. 166 pp. ISBN 0-375-81544-9. Fiction

Despite the oppressive conditions under the dictatorship in her homeland, twelve-year-old Anita is busy with her life, until the secret police come to her family compound. Suddenly the political situation is real for her family as Anita realizes that her father is involved in a plot to kill El Jefe, the dictator. When her father is arrested, Anita and her mother go into hiding.

4.3 Armstrong, Jennifer, editor. **Shattered: Stories of Children and War.** Knopf, 2002. 163 pp. ISBN 0-375-81112-5. Fiction

This powerful anthology of short stories, collected by noted author Jennifer Armstrong, gives voice to the countless children and young people all over the globe who have found themselves victims of war. From the battlefields of the American Civil War to the Afghanistan minefields of the early eighties, the narratives are linked, not by any political agenda or bias but by one powerful thread—young people caught in a conflict they did not create.

4.4 Arrington, Frances. **Bluestem.** Philomel, 2000. 140 pp. ISBN 0-399-23564-7. Fiction

Two young pioneer sisters are left alone to survive on their isolated prairie homestead. Their only neighbors offer little support as the girls struggle to cope with their father's absence and their mother's mental illness. Despite a series of hardships, the sisters maintain their deep love for the land and each another.

4.5 Avi. **Captain Grey.** HarperTrophy, 2000 (Originally published in 1977). 141 pp. ISBN 0-380-73244-0. Fiction

Set in the days immediately after the American Revolution, an eleven-year-old boy becomes the captive of a ruthless pirate king who has set up his own "nation," supported by thievery, on a remote part of the New Jersey coast. Young readers will revel in the story of a youngster caught up in swashbuckling adventure, and older readers will walk away with a better historical understanding of America's early history.

4.6 Avi. **The Christmas Rat.** Atheneum, 2000. 135 pp. ISBN 0-689-83842-5. Fiction

Bored during Christmas vacation, Eric is at loose ends until the exterminator appears to take care of the rats in the basement. Anje Gabriel is passionate about his war against rats, and when Eric tells him about the huge rodent nibbling away on the Christmas decorations, Anje goes into overdrive. Soon Eric finds himself in the midst of an incredible battle—but neither he nor the reader is certain whether Eric is one of the hunters or one of the hunted.

4.7 Ayres, Katherine. **Silver Dollar Girl.** Delacorte, 2000. 197 pp. ISBN 0-385-32763-3. Fiction

While her father prospects for gold in Colorado, Valentine Harper stays with her aunt and uncle in Pittsburgh and endures her cousin's tormenting. When she discovers five gold pieces sewn into her doll's body, however, she disguises herself as a boy and heads west to find her father. Along the way, Valentine encounters hardship while making a number of new friends. A fast-moving adventure story, this novel also provides plenty of detail about westward expansion and the mining boom.

4.8 Bo, Ben. **Skullcrack.** LernerSports, 2000. 161 pp. ISBN 0-8225-3308-1. Fiction

Irish teenager Jonah Ebbers surfs a dangerous reef named Skullcrack to find a space away from the demons that haunt his dreams. Things begin to unravel when the mysterious Bone Man begins to follow him. When his alcoholic father reveals a long-kept family secret, Jonah must travel to the United States, where he saves someone he has never met but whom he has been missing all his life. On his board, Jonah also faces a storm unlike any other he has seen.

4.9 Briggs, Raymond. **Ug: Boy Genius of the Stone Age and His Search for Soft Trousers.** Knopf, 2001. 32 pp. ISBN 0-375-81611-9. Fiction

This colorful cartoon depicts a prehistoric caveboy genius who questions the limitations of his world. Both funny and sad, the story captures the inquisitive spirit of youth. Ug's conflicts with his parents give a humorous spin to a familiar story about growing up. Readers will enjoy following Ug's explorations with fire, the invention of the wheel, and his primary goal of making a warm pair of trousers.

4.10 Burks, Brian. **Walks Alone.** Harcourt Brace, 2000. 124 pp. ISBN 0-152-02472-7. Fiction

Fifteen-year-old Walks Alone and her younger brother are separated from their Apache tribe when a surprise attack by a rival Apache tribe leaves her wounded and unable to flee. In her efforts to reach her family in Mexico, Walks Alone uses instinct, guile, and her many survival skills to triumph over the challenges she faces along the way.

4.11 Casanova, Mary. **When Eagles Fall.** Hyperion, 2002. 149 pp. ISBN 0-7868-0665-6. Fiction

Alex Castille-Reed, a teenager who got involved in the wrong crowd, is sent to spend time with her father in Minnesota. Her father is an eagle expert and has great passion for his work. Alex resents her father, and their time together is strained. Out of spite, she decides to rescue an eaglet and finds herself in a survival situation. Through her adventure, Alex discovers she is resourceful and courageous.

4.12 Clements, Bruce. **A Chapel of Thieves.** Farrar, Straus and Giroux, 2002. 210 pp. ISBN 0-374-37701-4. Fiction

When Clayton Clements runs off to Paris and begins preaching at a chapel, his brother Henry is convinced he must go to Paris to save his brother from a den of thieves. Henry also feels partially responsible for Clayton's leaving their home in St. Louis. Thus begins Henry's hilarious journey to Paris. The plan seems simple, but Henry encounters some wild situations, such as finding himself in the middle of a revolution and having to care for a dead body.

4.13 Creech, Sharon. **The Wanderer.** Illustrated by David Diaz. HarperCollins, 2000. 305 pp. ISBN 0-06-027730-0. Fiction

Thirteen-year-old Sophie joins her uncles and male cousins on a sailing voyage from Connecticut to England to visit her grandfather. During the journey, Sophie proves herself both to her relatives and to herself and learns the family secrets about her adoption. Alternating chapters from the journals of Sophie and her cousin Cody give readers multiple perspectives on the family dynamics. This book combines a high sense of adventure and suspense with lyrical language and striking illustrations to create a compelling experience.

4.14 Cunningham, Julia. **Dorp Dead.** Illustrated by James Spanfeller. Knopf, 2002 (Originally published in 1965). 92 pp. ISBN 0-375-82255-0. Fiction

Eleven-year-old Gilly Ground lives in an orphanage where he copes by keeping to himself. Because he doesn't fit in, he is placed in a foster home and becomes the helper of Kobalt, the ladder maker and town eccentric. Gilly appreciates his new residence, his own clothes, food, and a dog, Mash. But after Mash's strange disappearance, Gilly realizes Kobalt has other plans for him and now fears for his life!

4.15 Dyer, T. A. **A Way of His Own.** Houghton Mifflin, 2001. 154 pp. ISBN 0-613-35589-X. Fiction

Slowed by a physical handicap, young Shutok is abandoned by his family because he can no longer keep up with his nomadic community. He is forced to survive on his own. Facing an upcoming winter and the threat of wild animals, he manages to fashion a life for himself with the help of an unlikely friend from another prehistoric tribe. Returning in the spring, Shutock's family is surprised to find him alive and eventually awards him the respect he deserves.

4.16 Eckert, Allen W. **Return to Hawk's Hill.** Little, Brown, 2000. 192 pp. ISBN 0-316-00689-0. Fiction

We first met the McDonald family in the novel *Incident at Hawk's Hill.* In this sequel, the McDonalds are celebrating life. Young Ben is home safe, and their enemy George Burton has made himself scarce. The joy turns to despair, however, when Ben disappears. In an attempt to escape Burton, Ben is rescued by the

Metis Indians, who teach the McDonald family that the color of one's skin does not reveal what is in a person's heart.

4.17 Fenner, Carol. **The King of Dragons.** Margaret K. McElderry Books, 1998. 216 pp. ISBN 0-689-82217-0. Fiction

Homeless, Ian and his father take up residence in an unused courthouse, where the heating and plumbing are maintained because the building is on the historical registry. When his father fails to return, Ian must fend for himself. Eventually the courthouse is turned into an art exhibit for decorative kites from around the world. The kites captivate Ian, who becomes an expert on them and helps with the exhibit. The story is an interesting variation on the theme of survival.

4.18 Garfield, Leon. **The Strange Affair of Adelaide Harris.** Farrar, Straus and Giroux, 2001 (Originally published in 1971). 177 pp. ISBN 0-374-37277-2. Fiction

Harris and Bostock, eighteenth-century English schoolboys, are always up to some mischief. Thinking they will become famous, they expose Harris's infant sister, Adelaide, to the elements to test the truth of the ancient Spartan tale in which a wolf adopts an abandon baby. But the baby is found by a young woman rather than a wolf and taken to an orphanage. Adventure, romance, wit, and humor abound in this book filled with eccentric characters and zany action.

4.19 George, Jean Craighead. **My Side of the Mountain.** Puffin, 2001 (Originally published in 1959). 177 pp. ISBN 0-14-131242-4. Fiction

Preferring the simple life over life in New York City, young Sam Gribley runs away to live off the land in the Catskill Mountains. Armed with a penknife, a thin rope, some flint and steel, and forty dollars, Sam learns how to survive many dangerous adventures while living alone in the wilderness. Originally published in 1959 and reissued in 1991, this current edition contains an author's preface.

4.20 George, Jean Craighead. **On the Far Side of the Mountain.** Puffin, 2001 (Originally published in 1990). 170 pp. ISBN 0-14-131241-6. Fiction

In this sequel to *My Side of the Mountain,* Sam Gribley's sister, Alice, joins him in the Catskill Mountains. Sam's life drastically changes when his falcon is confiscated and Alice mysteriously disappears. This novel continues the chronicles of Sam's wilderness adventures.

4.21 Goldsmith, Connie. **Lost in Death Valley: The True Story of Four Families in California's Gold Rush.** Twenty-First Century Books, 2001. 144 pp. ISBN 0-7613-1915-8. Nonfiction

This illustrated biography tells the true story of four families of brave pioneers who were lured across California's Death Valley by hopes of striking it rich during the gold rush. Each person who made the trip endured great hardship, and no family survived intact. The author uses primary texts and historical research to recreate this harrowing tale of exploration and heroism.

4.22 Hesse, Karen. **Out of the Dust.** Scholastic, 1999. 227 pp. ISBN 0-590-37125-8. Fiction

Fifteen-year-old Billy Jo tells her story of suffering, endurance, forgiveness, healing, solace, and hope through a series of poems dating from January 1934 to December 1935. The Great Depression, the Oklahoma dust bowl, her severely burned hands, the death of her mother, and her father's accusations of blame all converge to make Billy Jo's life seem unbearable. But the piano and her new stepmother hear her pain, and Billy Jo digs deep within herself to find the strength she needs.

4.23 Hiçyilmaz, Gaye. **Smiling for Strangers.** Farrar, Straus and Giroux, 2000. 151 pp. ISBN 0-374-37081-8. Fiction

The Yugoslav War of 1991–1995 is raging. Armed only with some letters and an old picture, Nina flees from her home and heads to England where she hopes to find an old friend of her mother's. As a stowaway, Nina has to develop survival skills and learn to trust strangers. The descriptions of war and its effects on its victims make this a provocative and important novel about both the devastation of conflict and the need for hope in its wake.

4.24 Hite, Sid. **Stick and Whittle.** Scholastic, 2000. 202 pp. ISBN 0-439-09828-9. Fiction

Melvin "Stick" Fitchett is a Civil War veteran down on his luck and searching for his long-lost sweetheart. Melvin "Whittle" Smyte is an orphan who narrowly escaped the Great Chicago Fire and is determined to do something important with his life.

When Stick and Whittle meet on the Great Plains, they become partners in a gambling adventure that includes a kidnapping and a dramatic rescue. This funny adventure story explores the mysteries of luck and the power of friendship.

4.25 Hobbs, Valerie. **Charlie's Run.** Frances Foster Books, 2000. 166 pp. ISBN 0-374-34994-0. Fiction

Eleven-year-old Charlie is shocked when his parents tell him and his brothers and sister that they are getting a divorce. Desperate to keep the family together, Charlie formulates a plan to run away from home, hoping that this will shock his parents into staying together. On the road, he meets Doo, a teenage girl who is also running away. The two discover that living on the streets in Los Angeles is not only difficult but also quite dangerous.

4.26 Hobbs, Will. **Jason's Gold.** HarperTrophy, 2000. 221 pp. ISBN 0-380-72914-8. Fiction

In this adventure/survival story, Jason returns to Seattle from New York when he hears of the gold strikes in Alaska. When he learns that his brothers have already headed to the gold fields, Jason sets off to find them as well as gold. From rancid meat to the severity of the early onset of winter, Jason's will, courage, and ingenuity are repeatedly challenged. Winter brings increasing challenges and hardships.

4.27 Hobbs, Will. **The Maze.** Avon Camelot, 1999. 248 pp. ISBN 0-380-72913-X. Fiction

A modern-day Icarus, fourteen-year-old Rick Wallace dreams of flying. His life is a maze of problems: his parents abandoned him; the grandmother who raised him died; he is shuffled among foster homes and finally a detention center, from which he runs away. He ends up with a biologist who is releasing condors back into the wild. The biologist is also in danger, and Rick uses his sleuthing ability and hang-gliding skills to save both their lives.

4.28 Hoffman, Alice. **Green Angel.** Scholastic, 2003. 116 pp. ISBN 0-439-44384-9. Fiction

Fifteen-year-old Green is struggling with grief after having lost her entire family. Taking solace in the natural world, she gradually moves out of darkness and into the light, demonstrating the power of hope and courage and friendship from unusual sources even when the world is turned upside down. In an author's letter, Hoffman says, "*Green Angel* was the first story I was able to tell after the devastating events of September 11—she made me believe in the healing power of storytelling."

4.29 Honey, Elizabeth. **Fiddleback.** Knopf. 2001. 203 pp. ISBN 0-375-90579-0. Fiction

Henni Octon and her family decide to take a camping trip to the mountains of Australia with several of their neighbors. What might have been a typical camping trip turns out to be an adventure, with a flood, the birth of a baby, and loggers who try to poach some valuable old trees. Henni learns how important family and friends can be in times of trouble and how stressful situations often bring people together.

4.30 Hyde, Dayton O. **Island of the Loons.** Boyds Mills, 2002, 176 pp. ISBN 1-56397-681-1. Fiction

A young boy is held prisoner on an uninhabited island in Lake Superior by an escaped convict. This unstable individual starts out by tormenting the young boy but gradually softens his edges, developing a softer and gentler side. The wild surroundings calm the convict's rough demeanor, and slowly he begins to learn to appreciate the beauty of nature and the wisdom of his young captive.

4.31 Kehret, Peg. **Terror at the Zoo.** Puffin, 2001 (Originally published in 1992). 131 pp. ISBN 0-142-30028-4. Fiction

Ellen and her younger brother get an exciting gift from their grandparents, an overnight campout at the local zoo. Because of a mix-up among their relatives, the two end up in the zoo by themselves. This seems exciting until they encounter a thief hiding in the zoo. Ellen and her brother are captured when they try to protect a baby monkey from the thief, and their adventure becomes a frightening experience.

4.32 LaFaye, A. **Edith Shay.** Aladdin, 2001. 251 pp. ISBN 0-689-84228-7. Fiction

Katherine Lunden longed to travel outside of her small Wisconsin town in 1865. When she discovers a suitcase in a train station belonging to an Edith Shay, her curiosity and strong desire to visit Chicago, a city she has only read about, give her the courage to travel. Katherine's adventures do not turn out exactly as she hopes but her life is changed forever.

4.33 Lawrence, Iain. **The Buccaneers.** Delacorte, 2001. 238 pp. ISBN 0-385-32736-6. Fiction

Young John Spencer has spent most of his life sailing ships like the *Dragon,* a cargo ship. One journey becomes unusual when Horn, a suspicious but talented seaman, is rescued and pulled aboard. Then the *Dragon*'s crew encounters disease and disaster as they try to avoid a pirate ship that begins to stalk them. Horn's secrets about his life in and escape from piracy leak out, and John must control the ship and defeat the pirates if the *Dragon* is to survive.

4.34 Leroe, Ellen. **Disaster! Three Real-Life Stories of Survival.** Hyperion, 2000. 233 pp. ISBN 0-7868-2474-3. Nonfiction

Eyewitness accounts are used to describe three different tragic events. Section 1 discusses the sinking of the *Empress of Ireland* on May 28, 1914, in which 1,012 people lost their lives. Section 2 describes an exploration of the North Pole by the airship *Italia,* whose crash on May 25, 1928, stranded nine men on an ice pack in the Arctic Ocean. Section 3 recounts the destruction of the British airship *R-101* on October 5, 1930, which killed 48 people. Questions surrounding these untimely endings remain unanswered.

4.35 Marsden, John. **Burning for Revenge.** Houghton Mifflin, 2000. 272 pp. ISBN 0-395-96054-1. Fiction

War is dangerous. Five teens, Ellie, Fi, Lee, Homer, and Kevin, whose country was invaded and who are in the middle of the fight, know this too well. Whereas once their days were filled with school and minor dilemmas, their days are now consumed with planning how to kill the enemy and wondering if they will survive to see another tomorrow. In this vivid account, readers witness a coming-of-age story built on one of humanity's harshest realities: war.

4.36 Masefield, John. **Jim Davis: A High-Sea Adventure.** Scholastic, 2002 (Originally published in 1911). 224 pp. ISBN 0-439-404363. Fiction

In this classic tale of high adventure, Jim is just an ordinary twelve-year-old boy when he tumbles into adventure involving bloodthirsty pirates led by Marah, who turns out to be more dangerous than Jim initially realizes. Readers follow Jim as he tries to escape from the pirate crew and avoid being lost at sea.

4.37 Meyer, L. A. **Bloody Jack: Being an Account of the Curious Adventures of Mary "Jacky" Faber, Ship's Boy.** Harcourt, 2002. 278 pp. ISBN 0-15-216731-5. Fiction.

Life is difficult on the streets of London in the eighteenth century, especially for an orphan who must struggle and scrape to survive. So when Jacky Faber hears that warships are taking on boys for crew, there is new hope. As a ship's boy, Jacky will have regular meals and a place to sleep—but there is a catch. Jacky is really Mary, and among the adventures ahead, her greatest challenge is to hide who she is from the crew.

4.38 Morpurgo, Michael. **Kensuke's Kingdom.** Scholastic, 2003. 164 pp. ISBN 0-439-38202-5. Fiction

Michael's life was perfectly normal until his twelfth birthday, when he and his sheepdog Stella are tossed overboard from his family's sailboat into the sea. They wake to find themselves on an island, but Michael discovers they are not alone. Kensuke, an older Japanese man, has been stranded on the island for many years. Michael needs Kensuke to survive, but how is he to build a relationship with the untrusting man? Can he survive in Kensuke's kingdom?

4.39 Murphy, Jim. **Blizzard! The Storm That Changed America.** Scholastic, 2000. 136 pp. ISBN 0-590-67309-2. Nonfiction

Through events in the lives of both victims and survivors, the author provides a chilling and spellbinding account of one of the greatest natural disasters in history—the blizzard of 1888. Battling snow measuring ten feet in some areas, winds topping seventy to eighty miles per hour, and subzero temperatures, people from Virginia to Maine experienced the relentless fury of nature. Illustrations and personal stories allow the reader to understand the gravity of this historical life-threatening event.

4.40 Neale, Jonathan. **Lost at Sea.** Houghton Mifflin, 2002. 101 pp. ISBN 0-618-13920-6. Fiction

A spur-of-the-moment sail across the Atlantic Ocean takes a strange turn when Skip, the boat's captain, is lost at sea. He leaves his emotionally unstable girlfriend and her three children,

Jack, Orrie, and Andy (aged six), to get themselves safely to shore. The task falls to Jack and Orrie, who with perception and humor alternate telling the story of their adventure.

4.41 Nesbit, Edith. **The Railway Children.** Dover, 2000 (Originally published in 1906). 188 pp. ISBN 0-486-41022-6. Fiction

This timeless classic offers readers glimpses into the lives of Bobbie, Peter, and Phyllis, the Railway Children. Excitement mounts as they prevent a train disaster and rescue a young boy from certain death. The trio also goes from riches to rags when their father mysteriously disappears. While waiting for his return, the children find themselves embroiled in adventure as their attachment to the railroad and the people who run it grows.

4.42 Orr, Wendy. **Nim's Island.** Illustrated by Kerry Millard. Dell Yearling, 2002. 125 pp. ISBN 0-440-41868-2. Fiction

Nim loves her island home, which she shares with a number of interesting animal companions and her father, a scientist. When her father, Jack, plans a trip to study plankton, Nim is convinced she'll be fine on her own. But danger looms; Jack's cell phone calls stop coming. Fortunately, Nim has an e-mail friend and a carrier bird, both of whom help her stay in contact with Jack. With wit, humor, and their help, Nim manages to survive in this engaging adventure tale.

4.43 Paulsen, Gary. **Caught by the Sea: My Life on Boats.** Delacorte, 2001. 103 pp. ISBN 0-385-32645-9. Nonfiction

This is the fast-paced story of the author's love for and fascination with the sea and boats. It begins on a troop ship, when as a seven-year-old he witnesses a plane crash and subsequent shark attack, and it concludes with his fervent hope to undertake the ultimate sea voyage around Cape Horn. This is an intense, action-packed story of one man's struggle to learn to sail, his life-threatening mistakes, and the lessons learned.

4.44 Paulsen, Gary. **Guts: The True Stories behind *Hatchet* and the Brian Books.** Delacorte, 2001. 148 pp. ISBN 0-385-32650-5. Nonfiction

This book was written as a response to Paulsen's readers who were curious about the real adventures that were catalysts for his fiction. The chapter headings tell it all, including "Heart

Attacks, Plane Crashes and Flying," "Moose Attacks," "Things That Hurt," and "Killing to Live." Paulsen's discussion of his use of memory and events to create Brian's adventures makes for fascinating, thrilling, and sometimes hilarious reading. Both reluctant and avid readers will eagerly check out Paulsen's books after reading *Guts.*

4.45 Paulsen, Gary. **Tucket's Gold.** Delacourt, 1999. 97 pp. ISBN 0-385-32501-0. Fiction

Fifteen-year-old Francis is in charge of protecting Lottie and Billie. Francis learns his lessons well from Mr. Gimm. He must take Lottie and Billie with him if they are to have a chance of escaping the Comancheros. When Lottie and Billie find a dead Spaniard's gold, Lottie proclaims that now they are rich. Francis, however, recognizes that the gold presents great danger as well as wealth. The three still have many hardships to overcome before they can enjoy their treasure.

4.46 Paulsen, Gary. **Tucket's Home.** Delacourt, 2000. 93 pp. ISBN 0-385-32648-3. Fiction

After recovering from a rattlesnake bite, Francis is ready to continue the quest to find his family. Accompanied by his adopted family, Lottie and Billie, Francis leads them through encounters with many colorful characters. Their trip to Oregon is filled with mishaps and tragedies. Francis, Lottie, and Billie struggle, but their courage, hard work, perseverance, and, most of all, teamwork pay off in the end. Paulsen's afterword tells readers what happens to the characters in following years.

4.47 Pearce, Philippa. **Minnow on the Say.** Illustrated by Edward Ardizzone. Greenwillow, 2000 (Originally published in 1955). 256 pp. ISBN 0-688-17098-6. Fiction

It is summer, and David finds a canoe on the banks of the River Say behind his house in England. Soon the canoe's owner, another young boy, Adam, appears and announces that he is on a mission to find long-lost ancestral jewels that could save his family from financial disaster. The ensuing quest and chase for the legendary British treasure is complete with a bad guy seeking the same fortune. This is a classic tale of boys seeking to save their families.

4.48 Peck, Richard. **Amanda/Miranda.** Dial, 1999 (Originally published in 1980). 169 pp. ISBN 0-803-72489-6. Fiction

Originally published over twenty years ago in an unabridged version, this story has been edited by the author into a thoroughly readable young adult novel. It tells the tale of Amanda, an arrogant British heiress, and her maid, Miranda, who bear an uncanny resemblance to each other. They travel together on the *Titanic* and when Amanda drowns during its sinking, Miranda sees a chance to have the life she's always dreamed of.

4.49 Sachar, Louis. **Holes.** Dell Yearling, 2000. 233 pp. ISBN 0-440-41480-6. Fiction

A pig is stolen from a one-legged gypsy. Kissin' Kate Barlow becomes one of the most feared outlaws in the West. Wrongfully convicted Stanley Yelnats is sentenced to Camp Green Lake, a place for "bad boys" that is neither green nor on a lake. Readers will be surprised by how these stories converge in this dark but hilarious book as Stanley escapes the detention center and embarks on a journey with Zero, another boy from the camp who has his own secrets.

4.50 Snicket, Lemony. **The Austere Academy.** Illustrated by Brett Helquist. HarperCollins, 2000. 221 pp. ISBN 0-06-440863-9. Fiction

In this fifth book in Snicket's A Series of Unfortunate Events series about the adventures and misfortunes of the Baudelaire orphans, the now-famous literary youngsters are shipped off to a miserable boarding school where life becomes unbearable, to say the least. There they befriend the Quagmire triplets and discover to their amazement that they are being followed by the outrageous and dreaded Count Olaf.

4.51 Snicket, Lemony. **The Miserable Mill.** Illustrated by Brett Helquist. HarperCollins, 2000. 194 pp. ISBN 0-06-440769-1. Fiction

The three Baudelaire orphans find themselves in their newest home, the Lucky Smells Lumbermill. It is anything but lucky. Their dormitory at the mill is crowded and damp, and they eat only one meal a day. As in the other books in the A Series of Unfortunate Events series, Count Olaf is out to steal the large fortune the children stand to inherit when they are older. And like the other works, readers will delight in how the wily Baudelaire youngsters outwit their dastardly nemesis.

4.52 Snicket, Lemony. **The Wide Window.** Illustrated by Brett Helquist. HarperCollins, 2000. 214 pp. ISBN 0-06-028314-9. Fiction

This is the third book in the continuing saga of the three Baudelaire orphans' search for a home. Their parents were killed in a fire, and now they find themselves in the home of their Aunt Josephine, a woman who is afraid of everything. She lives in a house perched precariously on a cliff with no heat or other creature comforts because she's afraid of explosions. But when Count Olaf creeps into their life and steals Aunt Josephine's fortune, the Baudelaire orphans battle their way out of danger.

4.53 Stevenson, Robert Louis. **Kidnapped.** Dover, 2000 (Originally published 1886). 230 pp. ISBN 0-486-41026-9. Fiction

In this new edition of Stevenson's classic, readers find David Balfour in the midst of the adventure of a lifetime. He has been sold into bondage and put on a boat for the New World. Just when hope seems lost, David is rescued by Alan Breck Stewart, a Highlander. The two find themselves embroiled in a fight for survival. They face many foes and obstacles and emerge stronger people because of their adventures.

4.54 Thompson, Julian F. **Terry and the Pirates.** Atheneum, 2000. 262 pp. ISBN 0-689-83076-9. Fiction

Terry Talley knows that boarding school is not for her. Instead, she decides to run away, stowing away on a yacht—only to find more adventure than she bargained for! There is another runaway on board; he is cute and even though he is two years younger, a romance develops. Together Terry and Mick face a storm, a shipwreck, pirates searching for buried treasure, a host of interesting critters, and eventually rescue by the U.S. Navy.

4.55 Wyss, Johann D. **The Swiss Family Robinson.** Dover, 2001 (Originally published in 1812). 323 pp. ISBN 0-486-41660-7. Fiction

Set in the early 1800s, a Swiss family is shipwrecked on a deserted island. On their own, they learn to use and appreciate nature to survive. When they are finally rescued, the family is reluctant to leave the lifestyle they have learned to love. This unabridged new edition of Wyss's classic may be appreciated by more advanced readers, but the archaic language and writing style may be challenging.

5 Obstacles, Barriers, and Opportunities

5.1 Ashley, Bernard. **Little Soldier.** Scholastic, 2002. 240 pp. ISBN 0-439-22424-1. Fiction

Kaninda Bulumba, orphaned when his family was massacred during African tribal warfare, now lives in London with a foster family but dreams of returning to Africa to avenge his family's murders. Laura, his rebellious foster sister, dreams of finding forgiveness and redemption for her part in a hit-and-run accident. Both become involved in street gang violence as they struggle to come to terms with their pasts. With mature themes, this novel is more suitable for older middle school and high school teens.

5.2 Atinsky, Steve. **Tyler on Prime Time.** Delacorte, 2002. 168 pp. ISBN 0-385-72917-0. Fiction

When Tyler gets to spend part of his summer with his Uncle Pete, a writer for the current top-rated television sitcom, the twelve-year-old is sure he will land a role on the popular show. His time away from his perennially worried mother and strict father is made even better when he is befriended by Samantha, the twelve-year-old daughter of the show's leading lady.

5.3 Atkins, Catherine. **When Jeff Comes Home.** Penguin, 2001. 231 pp. ISBN 0-698-11915-0. Fiction

At age thirteen, Jeff is kidnapped and just as suddenly released to his family three years later. Dialogue and interior monologue reveal details of Jeff's sexual, emotional, and physical abuse. Jeff realizes that his kidnapper still has him captive emotionally, but professional help, the unconditional love of his family, and the loyalty of a friend give Jeff hope that he can rebuild his life. While there are no graphic descriptions of sexual abuse, the novel has mature themes and some strong language.

5.4 Atkins, Jeannine. **Wings and Rockets: The Story of Women in Air and Space.** Illustrated by Dušan Petricic. Farrar, Straus and Giroux, 2003. 208 pp. ISBN 0-374-38450-9. Nonfiction

Women have played an integral part in the advancement of aviation, and the author describes the critical roles played by these women who broke gender, social, and career barriers. The book highlights the contributions of women such as Katharine Wright, the sister of the Wright brothers, and Eileen Collins, the first woman commander of a spacecraft. Also included are Bessie Coleman, Amelia Earhart, Jackie Cochran, Ann Baumgartner Carl, Jerrie Cobb, Shannon Wells Lucid, and others. Includes a time line and biographical summaries.

5.5 Avi. **The Secret School.** Harcourt, 2001. 153 pp. ISBN 0-15-216375-1. Fiction

Ida Bidson lives in the remote Colorado mountains in 1925. More than anything she wants to be a teacher, but she has to finish eighth grade so she can go on to high school. How can she do this if her one-room school closes? When the school closes, Ida, with the encouragement of her friend Tom, takes charge of her life and those of the other students when she takes on the role of teacher and secretly keeps the school open.

5.6 Bechard, Margaret. **Hanging on to Max.** Roaring Brook, 2002. 142 pp. ISBN 0-7613-2574-3. Fiction

As a senior, Sam Pettigrew should be enjoying his final year of high school with his friends and making plans for college. Instead, he is struggling with the daunting job of raising his newborn son after the baby's mother decides she is not up to the task. Enrolled in a special program for single parents, Sam learns just how difficult raising a child can be.

5.7 Beyond Words Publishing, editor. **Boys Who Rocked the World: From King Tut to Tiger Woods.** Illustrated by Lar Desouza. Beyond Words, 2001. 136 pp. ISBN 1-58270-045-1. Nonfiction

This book is a compilation of two kinds of short biographies: those describing what famous men such as Mozart, Bill Gates, and Sammy Sosa accomplished before they turned twenty, and sketches of current-day young men who are making a difference through their activism, inventions, and music. A form is included to nominate other boys who are "rocking the world" for inclusion in future books in the series.

5.8 Blume, Judy, editor. **Places I Never Meant to Be: Original Stories by Censored Writers.** Aladdin, 2001. 202 pp. ISBN 0-689-84258-9. Fiction

Blume has collected stories from twelve highly regarded authors who have experienced censorship challenges to their work. Among the authors included in the collection are Katherine Paterson, Walter Dean Myers, David Klass, Jacqueline Woodson, and Julius Lester. Following his or her story, each author comments on the impact of censorship. Sales of the book are donated to the National Coalition against Censorship, and the collection is dedicated to Leanne Katz, the coalition's late director.

5.9 Bowen, Nancy. **Ralph Nader: Man with a Mission.** Twenty-First Century, 2002. 144 pp. ISBN 0-7613-2365-1. Nonfiction

Each time you get in a car, you have Ralph Nader to thank for the many safety features in modern automobiles. The son of Lebanese immigrant parents, Nader learned very early from his father that American freedom carries with it civic responsibility. After earning his law degree from Harvard, Nader became the champion of many consumer rights issues. This book chronicles the life of Ralph Nader from his Connecticut childhood through his 1996 presidential campaign.

5.10 Brooks, Bruce. **All That Remains.** Atheneum, 2001. 168 pp. ISBN 0-689-83351-2. Fiction.

In three separate stories, young people deal with loss and the choices they make when a loved one dies. In the first story, cousins conspire to beat the system and honor the request of their aunt, who died of AIDS, to be cremated. In the second, a hockey-playing rock musician is asked by his dying uncle to help his "geeky" cousin if needed. In the third, three strangers help a girl cast off her burden and move forward with her life.

5.11 Bunting, Eve. **Blackwater.** HarperTrophy, 2000. 146 pp. ISBN 0-06-440890-6. Fiction

When Brodie plays a seemingly harmless prank on two classmates on the treacherous Blackwater River, it backfires and causes their deaths. Against his better judgment but out of fear, Brodie lies repeatedly about the events even as he is hailed as a hero for trying to save the two classmates. Consumed by guilt and fearful of the power his scheming cousin (who witnessed the prank) now has over him, Brodie, at the urging of a friend, finally tells the truth.

5.12 Bunting, Eve. **Doll Baby.** Illustrated by Catherine Stock. Clarion, 2000. 47 pp. ISBN 0-395-93094-4. Fiction

Fifteen-year-old Ellie tells her own story about becoming pregnant, deciding to keep the baby, and raising her daughter with no help from the father. Tired all the time and excluded from social activities, she remembers how much simpler her life was when she was younger: "Sometimes in the night I think how easy it all was when I was little and only had a doll." This slim volume about teenage parenting packs a big punch.

5.13 Carter-Scott, Cherie. **If High School Is a Game, Here's How to Break the Rules: A Cutting Edge Guide to Becoming Yourself.** Delacorte, 2001. 164 pp. ISBN 0-385-32796-X. Nonfiction

With humor and realistic stories about kids dealing with the pressures of school, parents, media, and society at large, the author helps readers learn more about how to question authority, how to cope with what can't be changed, how to figure out who to trust and when to do so, and, overall, how to become the people they really want to be. Her advice: Think about school as a game. If you know the rules, you can get through it.

5.14 Caseley, Judith. **Praying to A. L.** Greenwillow, 2000. 181 pp. ISBN 0-688-15934-6. Fiction

Sierra Goodman is just thirteen years old when her father dies. Although her Cuban Jewish family tries to help her deal with his death, she struggles with this tragedy. A few days after the funeral, Sierra receives a book of Abraham Lincoln's speeches and writings. Because Sierra and her father both admired President Lincoln, reading this book helps her remember the good times she shared with her father and move through the grieving process.

5.15 Chen, Da. **China's Son: Growing Up in the Cultural Revolution.** Delacorte, 2001. 213 pp. ISBN 0-385-72929-4. Nonfiction

Adapted for younger readers from *Colors of the Mountain,* this book reflects Da Chen's changing voice and attitude as China changes. The autobiography relates the impact of those changes from 1962 through the Cultural Revolution. After a rough period, Chen and his family emerge from the repression of the Cultural Revolution, and he grasps all educational opportunities with the help of his supportive family and realizes his dream of earning a place at Beijing University.

5.16 Clements, Andrew. **The Landry News.** Illustrated by Brian Selznick. Aladdin, 2000. 131 pp. ISBN 0-689-82868-3. Fiction

When Cara prints the first issue of her own private paper, *The Landry News,* and includes an editorial that says her teacher, Mr. Larson, would rather drink coffee and read the paper than teach, she causes quite a commotion. Other students become intrigued by the idea of a newspaper and its role in school life; Mr. Larson is awakened out of the lethargy into which he has sunk; and the principal decides he should be able to control the press.

5.17 Colman, Penny. **Where the Action Was: Women War Correspondents in World War II.** Crown, 2002. 118 pp. ISBN 0-517-80075-6. Nonfiction

With many photographs to help tell the story, *Where the Action Was* relates the blossoming of women in journalism as they helped cover World War II. As the chapters in the book unfold, so does the war itself. The chronological progression of the war is intertwined with the vignettes of women journalists: their whereabouts, struggles, and successes. The action jumps between the front lines and the home countries of the journalists, marking the strides these journalists are making for women once they return. An informative, interesting narrative gives facts and details, while vivid photographs grace nearly every page.

5.18 Corrigan, Eireann. **You Remind Me of You: A Poetry Memoir.** Push, 2002. 123 pp. ISBN 0-439-29771-0. Poetry

This memoir, shared through a series of poems, tells the story of a young girl's struggle with anorexia nervosa and her intense love for her high school sweetheart. Near death, the young girl begins the recovery process when she discovers that her boyfriend has unsuccessfully attempted suicide and now needs her to help him pull through.

5.19 Couloumbis, Audrey. **Getting Near to Baby.** Puffin, 2001. 211 pp. ISBN 0-698-11892-8. Fiction

The reader spends a day in the life of thirteen-year-old Willa Jo who climbs up onto the roof of her Aunt Patty's house to see the sunrise and to cope with the recent death of her baby sister. Telling her tale in a nonlinear fashion—some of the story is about Willa Jo's stay on the roof and some is about her life just after the baby's death—the author artfully breathes life into all the characters of this compelling and haunting human-interest story.

5.20 Coulter, Laurie. **When John and Caroline Lived in the White House.** Madison Press, 2000. 64 pp. ISBN 0-786-80624-9. Nonfiction

When John F. Kennedy became president of the United States in 1961, the White House was transformed. Caroline and John Kennedy Jr. were about to become the first children to live there in fifty years. Find out how the Kennedys tried to preserve a normal childhood for Caroline and John Jr. in the midst of a staff of hundreds, tight security, visiting foreign dignitaries, and constant media attention. Countless Kennedy family photographs give this book the feel of a private family photo album.

5.21 Dash, Joan. **The World at Her Fingertips: The Story of Helen Keller.** Scholastic, 2001. 225 pp. ISBN 0-590-90715-8. Nonfiction

This is the story of courage beyond words. Born in 1880, Helen Keller conquered blindness and deafness at an age when few people understood or knew how to cope with either of these devastating disabilities, let alone both at once. But fear and ignorance did not rule Helen's life. Instead, she relied on a miracle in the shape of her teacher and surrogate parent, Anne Sullivan. Together, they conquered a world Helen could only imagine.

5.22 Denenberg, Dennis, and Lorraine Roscoe. **50 American Heroes Every Kid Should Meet.** Millbrook, 2001. 128 pp. ISBN 0-7613-1612-4. Nonfiction

Each of the fifty entries tells a story of a U.S. citizen who has enriched our world and made a difference. The stories describe teachers, musicians, journalists, jurists, artists, activists, scientists, inventors, and athletes. Each entry is illustrated with photographs and drawings, a significant quote, and sources for additional reading. The book includes a Hero Hunt, which encourages readers to find information on twenty-four additional heroes related in some way to those described in the book.

5.23 Desetta, Al, and Sybil Wolin, editors. **The Struggle to Be Strong: True Stories by Teens about Overcoming Tough Times.** Free Spirit, 2000. 162 pp. ISBN 1-57542-079-1. Nonfiction

Project Resilience compiled accounts by teens, written in their own words, about tough situations and how they overcame those situations. Seven resiliencies are identified: insight, independence, relationships, initiative, creativity, humor, and morality. The narratives describe situations from coping with AIDS to developing a sense of humor, with advice from teens who have experienced these problems.

5.24 Efaw, Mary. **Battle Dress.** HarperCollins, 2000. 291 pp. ISBN 0-06-027943-5. Fiction

Andi Davis is ready to graduate from high school, leave home, and escape her disorganized and dysfunctional family. She figures she will find solace at the famed military academy, West Point. Once there, however, Andi learns life is anything but idyllic. One of only two girls in her platoon, she suffers not only gender discrimination but also belittlement and grueling training designed to break cadets and rebuild them into soldiers. This is a powerful and gripping account of life inside a harsh, rigorous world.

5.25 Ferris, Jean. **Of Sound Mind.** Farrar, Straus and Giroux, 2001. 224 pp. ISBN 0-374-35580-0. Fiction

Theo, the only hearing member of a deaf family, is the official interpreter and liaison for them all, oftentimes sacrificing his own needs and desires. Just as things reach frustration level in the fall of his senior year, he meets Ivy, who helps him deal with his situation. She introduces him to new people and new perspectives. But Theo has the hardest time ahead of him as he considers colleges and makes plans for the future.

5.26 Flinn, Alex. **Breaking Point.** HarperTempest, 2002. 245 pp. ISBN 0-066-23847-1. Fiction

Paul, age fifteen, is lonely as he enters a new boarding school and wants desperately to belong. The novel taps into the fears of students who sit in a classroom wondering daily whether a fellow student is on the edge of meltdown; at the same time, this book tries to help us understand what pushes a teenager to the point of no return, so angry and fearful that he or she strikes out at the world in whatever way possible.

5.27 Freymann-Weyr, Garret. **When I Was Older.** Houghton Mifflin, 2000. 167 pp. ISBN 0-618-05545-2. Fiction

Two years ago Sophie's younger brother died of leukemia, and she is desperately trying to preserve her memories of him by clinging to the past. When she meets Francis, who has lost his mother, he teaches her the importance of going on with life. Comfortable being his friend, Sophie's not sure she wants to date him. Freymann-Weyr has created a memorable character in her first novel of adolescence and transition.

5.28 Gantos, Jack. **Hole in My Life.** Farrar, Straus and Giroux, 2002. 200 pp. ISBN 0-374-39988-3. Nonfiction

Author Jack Gantos shares the story of his own misguided adventures as a teenage drug runner, which landed him in prison for several years. Gantos also reveals how his experiences played a part in his becoming a successful writer. This true-life story is more appropriate for older adolescents.

5.29 Gantos, Jack. **Joey Pigza Loses Control.** Farrar, Straus and Giroux, 2000. 196 pp. ISBN 0-374-39989-1. Fiction

Joey has his attention deficit hyperactivity disorder under control with his new meds and help from the school's special ed program. His alcoholic father, whom Joey has not seen for many years, has stopped drinking and gotten a job. He invites Joey to spend the summer with him and learn to be a winner. Joey's father is an adult version of Joey, but his definition of *winner* does not include relying on medication to solve problems. The summer is a disaster!

5.30 Gantos, Jack. **What Would Joey Do?** Farrar, Straus and Giroux, 2002. 229 pp. ISBN 0-374-39986-7. Fiction

In the final Joey Pigza book, this unlikely hero has his medication working for him and now he calls himself "Mr. Helpful." His mother has a new boyfriend and the hope of a normal life, but Joey's father turns up and things get crazy between them. While Joey struggles to deal with the situation, his grandmother tries to help him maintain stability. The problem is that she is dying. Ultimately, Joey learns that only he can help himself.

5.31 Garden, Nancy. **The Year They Burned the Books.** Farrar, Straus and Giroux, 1999. 247 pp. ISBN 0-374-38667-6. Fiction

A complex chain of events follows when high school senior Jamie Crawford uses the editorial page of the school newspaper to voice support for a new health curriculum, which includes condom distribution to students. Issues of censorship and homophobia become intertwined as Jamie and her friends come to understand themselves and one another better. This book is more appropriate for older adolescents.

5.32 Gottfried, Ted. **Teen Fathers Today.** Twenty-First Century Books, 2001. 128 pp. ISBN 0-7613-1901-8. Nonfiction

Teenage fathers often get lost in the focus on the infant and mother. This book explores the young fathers' feelings, their worries, and their responsibilities. Using firsthand accounts in addition to clinical and governmental records, the author presents a candid portrait of the dilemma of teen fatherhood. The book includes lists of organizations that provide help and support, informative Internet sites, and further reading.

5.33 Grimes, Nikki. **Jazmin's Notebook.** Puffin, 2000. 102 pp. ISBN 0-14-130702-1. Fiction

Jazmin, raised by her older sister, overcomes her poor and nomadic existence in 1960s Harlem through her sense of humor and determination. Readers are privy to Jazmin's observations and poems through her notebook entries, and her writing, reading, and laughter keep her honest and full of hope. Middle and high school students will appreciate Jazmin's personality and her potential to beat the odds of her upbringing after her father dies and her mother is hospitalized with a mental illness.

5.34 Grove, Vicki. **Reaching Dustin.** Puffin, 2000. 199 pp. ISBN 0-698-11839-1. Fiction

Carly Cameron aspires to be a writer. She gets the ultimate assignment—an interview that will prove her potential and help her become editor of the school newspaper. Carly's excitement is short lived, however, when she learns she must interview her nemesis, Dustin Groat. The Groats are well known for their rebellious acts and left-wing views. But Carly's aggravation turns to curiosity as the assignment progresses. Will the assignment be a success? Will Dustin ruin her project? Will Carly discover the truth?

5.35 Hall, Judi. **What Does My Future Hold? 99 Ways to Plan Your Life.** Penguin Compass, 2001. 191 pp. ISBN 014-019621-8. Nonfiction

The ninety-nine ways to plan your life include tarot cards, astrology, palmistry, and sun signs, providing hours of fun for teenagers and adults of all ages. Anyone can examine and learn ancient prophecy techniques to try out on their friends. Learn tools and techniques of ancient oracles for hours of fun!

5.36 Holt, Kimberly Willis. **When Zachary Beaver Came to Town.** Holt, 1999. 227 pp. ISBN 0-805-06116-9. Fiction

When thirteen-year-old Toby meets Zachary Beaver, the fattest boy in the world, his entire outlook on life changes. Struggling with his mother's decision to leave the family to pursue a career as a country music singer and with the death of his best friend's older brother in Vietnam, Toby learns the importance of respecting other people.

5.37 Honey, Elizabeth. **Don't Pat the Wombat!** Illustrated by Gig. Knopf, 2000. 143 pp. ISBN 0-375-80578-8. Fiction

Through narrative, sketches, and photographs, Mark documents his adventures on an Australian school camping trip. What starts out as a humorous account turns serious when Mr. Cromwell, the students' least favorite teacher, arrives late. The boys grow fearful as Mr. Cromwell repeatedly singles out Jonah, the newest student in the class, as the target of his anger. Readers may need some familiarity with Australian word usage and culture.

5.38 Jemison, Mae. **Find Where the Wind Goes: Moments from My Life.** Scholastic, 2001. 196 pp. ISBN 0-439-13195-2. Nonfiction

The author presents a vibrant self-portrait of how her life experiences and perseverance prepared her to be the world's first woman of color to travel into space. The stories are told in short chapters using wind as a metaphor to symbolize key events in this astounding young girl's growth through childhood, to her studies in chemical engineering at Stanford, to Peace Corps work in West Africa, and finally to her dream of being an astronaut.

5.39 Jordan, Sherryl. **The Raging Quiet.** Aladdin, 2000. 266 pp. ISBN 0-689-82877-2. Fiction

After the death of her husband, Marnie, a teenager who married a man more than twice her age to help her family, is spurned by the people of Torcurra. She becomes even more of an outcast and is accused of witchcraft when she befriends a deaf man and teaches him to communicate.

5.40 Jukes, Mavis. **The Guy Book: An Owner's Manual for Teens: Safety, Maintenance, and Operating Instructions for Teens.** Crown, 2002. 149 pp. ISBN 0-679-89028-9. Nonfiction

Using 1950s era photos of auto repair and maintenance as a way to connect with its target audience, this how-to manual covers questions guys might have about their health, sexuality, dating, manners, chat room dangers, shaving, STDs, and many other topics from the mundane to the controversial. The tone is reassuring and casual, the medical and legal information is factual and direct, and the emphasis is always on communicating with parents and other trusted adults. Helplines are listed and myths dispelled. This book contains mature content.

5.41 Korman, Gordon. **No More Dead Dogs.** Hyperion, 2000. 180 pp. ISBN 0-7868-2462-X. Fiction

Wallace always tells the truth regardless of whom it hurts, even when it is himself. This is the case when he tells Mr. Fogelman, his English teacher and school drama coach, that Mr. Fogelman's favorite book, which also happens to be the play he is directing, is a predictable, boring mess. Enter detention and a daily dose of rehearsals of that same play. Soon Wallace is drawn into the play and starts giving suggestions, much to the chagrin of Mr. Fogelman.

5.42 Levitin, Sonia. **Dream Freedom.** Silver Whistle, 2000. 178 pp. ISBN 0-15-202404-2. Fiction

When Marcus and his classmates in California learn about the atrocities of the civil war in Sudan, they resolve to raise money to buy the freedom of some of those enslaved and to raise the awareness of others about the horrors of the conflict. Chapters alternate between Marcus's story and the individual stories of slaves. Readers will both abhor the sad realities of the Sudanese situation and admire their determination in their quest for freedom.

5.43 Liebowitz, Jay. **Wall Street Wizard: Sound Ideas from a Savvy Teen Investor.** Simon & Schuster, 2000. 143 pp. ISBN 0-689-83401-2. Nonfiction

When Jay Liebowitz was twelve years old, he began investing in the stock market. Although his first purchases turned a loss, he learned from that experience and soon became a successful investor. Leibowitz speaks directly and honestly about how both attitudes and behavior contribute to the acquisition of wealth. He summarizes the key points of his philosophy of both life and business, sharing those insights that have made him, at age eighteen, a competitive figure in the stock market.

5.44 Lynch, Chris. **Freewill.** HarperCollins, 2001. 148 pp. ISBN 0-06-028176-6. Fiction

The author effectively uses dialogue coupled with an ironic tone to follow seventeen-year-old Will through the stages of grief to the acceptance of his father's and stepmother's deaths and the realization that he is not responsible for some local teens' suicides. His skill at woodcarving becomes "wood therapy" for Will as he discovers that his grandparents are also grieving, and he shifts his focus from himself to others. Mature readers will appreciate the journey of healing that Will experiences.

5.45 MacDonald, Janet. **Chill Wind.** Frances Foster Books, 2002. 134 pp. ISBN 0-374-39958-1. Fiction

Aisha has what she thinks is a good life. She dances, listens to music, and chills with her friends. But then she gets notice that her welfare checks will stop in sixty days. How is she going to maintain her good life and support her two children without the government's help? She sees an ad for "BIG MODELS" and decides to apply, knowing she's pretty enough, but eventually Aisha has to figure out what life really means and what she really wants.

5.46 Marsden, John. **Checkers.** Laurel-Leaf, 2000. 122 pp. ISBN 0-440-22860-3. Fiction

Imagine life as perfect. You live in the best neighborhood, wear the best clothes, and attend the best school. You have lots of friends and a picture-perfect family. The perfection, however, is a facade. Your world crumbles and the only real thing in your life, your dog Checkers, is murdered. Welcome to Miss Warner's life. Read her diary. Watch her interact with others in the psychiatric ward of the hospital. And see her learn to get a handle on life again.

5.47 Mead, Alice. **Girl of Kosovo.** Farrar, Straus and Giroux, 2001. 128 pp. ISBN 0-374-32620-7. Fiction

Set in 1998–99 Kosovo, this novel presents a balanced, thorough discussion of the personal issues of the Serbian/Albanian conflict through the eyes of eleven-year-old Zana as she observes the attitudes of family, neighbors, and others. The history of the conflict as well as its effects on daily lives is vividly presented. While there is no happy ending, Mead powerfully demonstrates the role of friendship and of individuals to make a difference.

5.48 Mills, Claudia. **Lizzie at Last.** Farrar, Straus and Giroux, 2000. 152 pp. ISBN 0-374-34659-3. Fiction

Lizzie, who has always been considered a nerd by other kids, begins the seventh grade determined to change her image, relying on the advice of her horoscope. She enjoys the new image she creates and throws away her vintage dresses for jeans. She also puts her poetry writing on hold, until she realizes that some of her old qualities are not worth compromising. Lizzie begins to understand how to be true to herself and becomes Lizzie at last.

5.49 Mochizuki, Ken. **Beacon Hill Boys.** Scholastic, 2002. 199 pp. ISBN 0-439-26749-8. Fiction

Sixteen-year-old Dan Inagaki's parents expect him to be like his brother: a model "minority citizen" with a 4.0 GPA, a scholarship to college, a white girlfriend, and assimilated into the majority culture. But Dan is *not* like his brother. He and his friends feel invisible, rejected by teachers and classmates. These Japanese American youths struggle with their anger and confusion and support one another as they try to figure out how to be themselves within a culture that isn't very accepting.

5.50 Moeyaert, Bart. **Hornet's Nest.** Translated from the Dutch by David Colmer. Front Street, 2000. 127 pp. ISBN 1-886910-48-0. Fiction

Fourteen-year-old Susanna recalls her life from her earliest memories. Her village had both interesting and sometimes vicious neighbors during those years. One squabble had to do with a neighbor's barking dogs. Others had to do with old grudges. Susanna is determined to iron things out so people can live in peace, but then her good intentions backfire with serious consequences.

5.51 Moeyaert, Bart. **It's Love We Don't Understand.** Translated from the Flemish by Wanda Boeke. Front Street, 2001. 128 pp. ISBN 1-886910-71-5. Fiction

Fifteen-year-old Sis, the somewhat naive narrator of this story, relates three events in the lives of a family headed by a frequently absent mother who is in denial about serious events in their lives. This episodic novel deals with mature issues and reveals the changes in Sis as she handles life and takes care of her younger sister.

5.52 Myers, Anna. **When the Bough Breaks.** Walker, 2000. 170 pp. ISBN 0-8027-87225-8. Fiction

Ophelia has a secret she has not told anyone, yet students in her new school seem to know, teasing her and making her life difficult. Having moved from one foster home to another, Ophelia knows she must make this one work. She takes a job reading aloud to Portia, an elderly neighbor, and discovers that she and her new friend have much in common. Together they are able to share secrets and come to terms with their haunting pasts.

5.53 Park, Barbara. **The Graduation of Jake Moon.** Atheneum, 2000. 115 pp. ISBN 0-689-83912-X. Fiction

Bullying, peer pressure, and salvation through the support of good people make up the powerful story of how Jake Moon learns to accept himself with the help of his mother and especially his grandfather. Although Grandfather has Alzheimer's and the support roles are reversed, Jake overcomes his embarrassment to realize that this once vital man has been his touchstone in the past. Sources of information about Alzheimer's disease are listed at the end of the novel.

5.54 Robinson, Sharon. **Jackie's Nine: Jackie Robinson's Values to Live By.** Scholastic, 2001. 182 pp. ISBN 0-439-23764-5. Nonfiction

Sharon Robinson, as director of educational programming for Major League Baseball, has initiated a program to use the stories of her father and others as lessons in overcoming obstacles. The nine values of the school program, called Breaking Barriers, are summarized in this book through the personal stories of the Robinsons and others. These values are courage, determination, teamwork, persistence, integrity, citizenship, justice, commitment, and excellence. The main message—to value oneself—is compellingly exemplified in these short narratives.

5.55 Rodowsky, Colby. **Spindrift.** Farrar, Straus and Giroux, 2000. 136 pp. ISBN 0-374-37155-5. Fiction

Life is hard enough when you're thirteen, but for Cassie Barnhart, who prides herself on fixing things, changes come one after another too fast for her to fix. Cassie's parents divorce and her sister leaves her husband and comes home with her newborn baby. Then Grandmother decides to sell the seaside inn where Cassie and her family have moved and which they now call home. Cassie's uncle throws another curve ball her way. Ultimately, Cassie must deal with the complexities of growing up and accept change as the inevitable end to childhood.

5.56 Roehm, Michelle. **Girls Who Rocked the World 2: From Harriet Tubman to Mia Hamm.** Illustrated by Jerry McCann. Beyond Words, 2000. 160 pp. ISBN 1-58270-025-7. Nonfiction

Profiled in this book are women such as Sonja Henie, Anna Pavlova, and Oprah Winfrey who, in the words of editor Michelle Roehm, "left their mark on history" before the age of twenty. Their areas of expertise range widely, from nursing to physics, rock climbing to songwriting. Interspersed between the biographies are photos and commentaries by present-day young women about their current contributions to the world and their plans for the future.

5.57 Savage, Deborah. **Kotuku.** Houghton Mifflin, 2002. 291 pp. ISBN 0-618-04756-5. Fiction

Named after her most famous ancestor, Captain Charles Williamson Thorpe, Wim (Charlotte) is stricken with grief over the death of her best friend, struggling to finish her senior year, and wants to be left alone in the company of her dogs and horses. But other people have different ideas, and Wim learns the awful truth about her ancestors and their treatment of the Maori of New Zealand. She also learns more about the Maori, forgiveness, and moving on after grief.

5.58 Shreve, Susan. **Trout and Me.** Knopf, 2002. 136 pp. ISBN 0-375-81219-9. Fiction

Ben has always had difficulty keeping out of trouble, but when Trout shows up and decides he wants Ben to be his friend, things get even worse. Ben finds out he's got attention deficit disorder—like Trout—and now he has to take Ritalin, also like Trout. And he soon learns, like Trout, that he enjoys troublemaking schemes. But then Ben and Trout get into a really bad mess, and Ben must convince the principal and all the parents that he and Trout are truly not bad kids.

5.59 Slepian, Jan. **The Alfred Summer.** Puffin, 2001 (Originally published in 1980). 119 pp. ISBN 0-698-11910-X. Fiction

The Alfred Summer is a seemingly simple novel about a strong bond between four misfits who are treated by others based on surface attributes only: Alfred is mentally challenged; Lester (the fourteen-year-old narrator) has cerebral palsy; Claire is a tomboy; and Myron is clumsy and obese. Growing up in 1937 Brooklyn, the four neighbors become friends who cooperate on a creative project, thus learning to focus outside themselves and liberating themselves from the limitations set by their families and society.

5.60 Stark, Lynette. **Escape from Heart.** Harcourt, 2000. 212 pp. ISBN 0-15-202385-2. Fiction

Fourteen-year-old Sarah Ruth Heart lives in a quiet Mennonite community founded by her father's family. She is thrilled to qualify for the countywide spelling bee until her rigid uncle, the community's new leader, forbids her to participate. Angered, Sarah decides to sneak out of the community to compete in the spelling bee. She discovers incriminating information about her uncle that forces him to leave the community, which allows the community to return to the kinder practices of the past.

5.61 Strasser, Todd. **Give a Boy a Gun.** Simon & Schuster, 2000. 146 pp. ISBN 0-689-81112-8. Fiction

Gary Searle and Brendan Lawlor, both heavily armed, write suicide notes and then go on a murderous rampage during a high school dance. Through letters, notes, and interviews, their teachers, friends, classmates, and the two boys themselves recreate the crisis and the events and reasons leading up to it. Although fiction, this book provides additional factual information about school violence.

5.62 Tanzman, Carol M. **The Shadow Place.** Roaring Brook, 2002. 178 pp. ISBN 0-7613-2610-3. Fiction.

Being consumed by hatred is as unhealthy as a person can get. This is exactly the sickness that has engulfed Rodney. He hates his father with every fiber of his being, a hatred that has his neighbor and close friend Lissa concerned. In a simple truth-or-dare game, Rodney reveals how deep the hatred goes. Sworn to secrecy, Lissa is faced with a difficult choice: should she reveal Rodney's hatred and fascination with guns or should she keep his secret?

5.63 Vance, Susanna. **Sights.** Delacorte, 2001. 215 pp. ISBN 0-385-32761-7. Fiction

Baby Girl, a teenager in the 1950s, has the ability to see the future. She survives her father's random and frightening attempts to kill her even after she and her mother leave home, thinking he won't find out where they are. Baby Girl overcomes her unusual appearance and background to triumph over formidable odds, including her father's last attempt at murder. She is an unusual girl in unusual circumstances yet very appealing in her persistence and ability to turn adversity into opportunity.

5.64 Weiss, Ann E. **Easy Credit.** Twenty-First Century Books, 2000. 128 pp. ISBN 0-7613-1503-9. Nonfiction

This book explores the history of credit, from its use in ancient society to the development of today's prestige cards. Card users tell their stories of credit used wisely and unwisely. Some have borrowed to go to college, start a business, or buy a home. Others have ruined their credit ratings and even declared bankruptcy. *Easy Credit* provides useful information to help readers understand credit and the responsible use of credit cards.

5.65 Whitcher, Susan. **The Fool Reversed.** Farrar, Straus and Giroux, 2000. 183 pp. ISBN 0-374-32446-8. Fiction

Anna, fifteen, an aspiring poet, meets Thorn, a twenty-nine-year-old professor of poetry, and becomes infatuated with him. As she struggles to understand her feelings and to write her own poems, she must also deal with her relationship with her mother and her developing interest in Dylan, a young man her own age. But the tarot cards warn that she's becoming involved in dangerous situations. Explicit descriptions of sex may make this book a difficult choice for some middle school students.

5.66 Williams, Terrie, with introduction by Queen Latifah. **Stay Strong: Simple Life Lessons for Teens.** Scholastic, 2001. 226 pp. ISBN 0-439-12971-0. Nonfiction

Terri Williams, head of his own public relations firm catering to sports figures and stars, provides insights and advice for teens. Through real life stories about teenagers, readers are challenged to reconsider attitudes that are accepted in today's world and to accept new attitudes that lead to positive self-esteem and success in life. Teens' experiences with school, grades, family, sex, drugs, and peer demands provide a realistic context for thinking about choices and how those choices can affect life now and later.

5.67 Wittlinger, Ellen. **The Long Night of Leo and Bree.** Simon & Schuster, 2000. 111 pp. ISBN 0-689-83566-7. Fiction.

Leo is angry; Bree is defiant. When Leo sees Bree, he impulsively decides to vent his anger on her by taking her hostage. The next nine hours are filled with horror and revelation. As each tells the other about his or her life, the tension eases, and both Leo and Bree gain insights about themselves and each other.

5.68 Wood, June Rae. **Turtle on a Fence Post.** Puffin, 2001. 264 pp. ISBN 0-698-11783-2. Fiction

Delrita Jensen lost her parents in a car accident and is adjusting to life with her aunt and uncle and her aunt's difficult father, a World War II veteran. If that weren't enough, the popular new girl, Heidi, lives in Delrita's former house. Interactions with a host of quirky characters help Delrita accept her grief and losses and learn that people aren't always who they at first seem to be.

5.69 Woodson, Jacqueline. **Miracle's Boys.** Putnam, 2000. 192 pp. ISBN 0-399-23113-7. Fiction

Lafayette Bailey's life is rough. Orphaned at the age of twelve, Lafayette and his fifteen-year-old brother (who has been in a juvenile detention center) are being raised by their oldest brother, twenty-two-year-old Ty'ree. Struggling against poverty, gang violence, and an overwhelming sadness left by the death of their mother, Milagro (Spanish for "miracle"), the three brothers struggle to survive in New York City.

5.70 Wyeth, Sharon Dennis. **A Piece of Heaven.** Knopf, 2001. 200 pp. ISBN 0-679-88535-8. Fiction

Haley (Mahalia) has all the trouble she can handle when, on her thirteenth birthday, her mother has a breakdown and is hospitalized, her older brother is arrested for selling stolen goods, and Haley is placed in a group foster home. Through her employer, Jackson, and those in the group home, Haley realizes that the pieces of her life, while changed, will come together in a new configuration due to her determination to create a piece of heaven for herself and others.

5.71 Zephaniah, Benjamin. **Face.** Bloomsbury, 2002, 208 pp. ISBN 1-58234-774-3. Fiction

Martin is a smart, able, and handsome sixteen-year-old teen who accepts a ride home from a drunken acquaintance and ends up in a terrible accident. Badly burned, his face is completely disfigured. Feeling as though his life is over, Martin loses his girlfriend, his friends, and his universe as he knew it. As doctors work to reconstruct his face, Martin struggles to reconstruct his life—and in so doing changes his perspective on what it means to be a fully functioning human being.

6 Sports and Recreation

6.1 Anderson, Dave. **The Story of the Olympics.** HarperCollins, 2000. 168 pp. ISBN 0-688-17640-2. Nonfiction

Follow the Olympics from its very beginnings in Greece to the winter games in Nagano, Japan. The book is divided into two parts: Part 1 gives a brief history of the Olympics and highlights many fascinating feats of some of the greatest athletes; Part 2 gives an overview of the major events and reviews what is required to be an Olympian. Many photographs that capture the glory and competition of the games have been included.

6.2 Anderson, Joan. **Rookie: Tamika Whitmore's First Year in the WNBA.** Photographs by Michelle V. Agins. Dutton, 2000. 40 pp. ISBN 0-525-46412-3. Nonfiction

Ever wondered what it would be like to be a professional basketball player? Wonder no more. Anderson takes readers inside the fast-paced world of the WBNA, looking through the eyes of Tamika Whitmore, a rookie player for the New York Liberty. Loaded with photos of Tamika on and off the court and featuring a foreword by veteran player Teresa Weatherspoon, this book is sure to appeal to any sports fan.

6.3 Bragg, Linda Wallenberg. **Play-by-Play: Gymnastics.** Photographs by Andy King. LernerSports, 2000. 79 pp. ISBN 0-8225-9877-9. Nonfiction

Gymnastics is a sport that gained popularity due to its exposure on national television during the 1960 Olympic competitions. This sport requires a lot of practice to develop a gymnast's coordination, flexibility, and balance. There are six events in men's gymnastics and four in women's. Readers will learn training techniques and see detailed photographs of gymnasts' moves for all the events.

6.4 Brooks, Bruce. **Throwing Smoke.** HarperCollins, 2000. 136 pp. ISBN 0-06-028972-4. Fiction.

Whiz and his friends are on the worst Little League team in town. Each team member has a particular strength but also a particular weakness. Whiz accidentally discovers that when he prints a baseball card for an imaginary, perfect player for the team, that player actually appears. But when the team starts winning, the real players stop having fun because the game becomes too serious. Whiz's friend E6 convinces him, for the sake of their friendships, to undo whatever it is he's done.

6.5 Coleman, Lori. **Play-by-Play: Soccer.** Photographs by Andy King. LearnerSports, 2000. 63 pp. ISBN 0-8225-9876-0. Nonfiction

Soccer is quickly becoming a favorite pastime of American youth. This book describes the history of the sport and provides details about the skills and techniques a player and team must demonstrate to be proficient. It also serves as an excellent guide for beginning players and coaches because it outlines rules and regulations as well as providing tips for practice. Photos accompany information about the game. A recommended list for additional reading and sources for information are included.

6.6 Foland, Constance M. **Flying High, Pogo!** Illustrated by Allen Brewer. American Girl, 2002. 138 pp. ISBN 1-58485-624-6. Fiction

Pogo is twelve years old and loves gymnastics. When she is chosen to attend a summer gymnastics camp and must find a way to pay for it, Pogo and her best friends find creative ways to make money to help her pay for the trip. This moneymaking experience comes in handy again when her mother loses her business; Pogo's entrepreneur spirit helps solve the family's financial troubles.

6.7 Foley, Mike. **Play-by-Play: Hockey.** Photographs by Andy King. LearnerSports, 2000. 79 pp. ISBN 0-8225-9878-7. Nonfiction

Ice hockey is the fastest sport in the world. A player must not only be a proficient ice skater but also quick to react to an icy puck traveling more than one hundred miles an hour. This book outlines the basics of the game, complete with pictures. Students wanting to learn more about this sport or to become more proficient in playing it will find this book helpful.

6.8 Fuerst, Jeffrey B. **The Kids' Baseball Workout: A Fun Way to Get in Shape and Improve Your Game.** Illustrated by Anne Canevari Green. Millbrook, 2002. 80 pp. ISBN 0-7613-2307-4. Nonfiction

This book is for anyone who wants to improve his or her baseball skills, whether just for fun or to play in the big leagues. Clear, simple diagrams and directions will help readers with everything from pregame conditioning and warm-ups to batting and stealing bases. Each chapter includes practice drills readers can do on their own or with friends. The Skills 'n Drills Progress Chart will help them keep track of improvement.

6.9 Geng, Don. **Play-by-Play: Baseball.** Illustrated by Andy King. LernerSports, 2001. 80 pp. ISBN: 0-8225-9880-9. Nonfiction

This series provides a how-to orientation to the sport of baseball. This basic introduction includes chapters on how the sport got started, necessary equipment and maintenance, and training tips, as well as a glossary of key terms related to the sport. A variety of color action photographs are included as a resource for the reader.

6.10 Greenberg, Keith Elliot. **Pro Wrestling: From Carnivals to Cable TV.** LernerSports, 2000. 128 pp. ISBN 0-8225-3332-4. Nonfiction

This intriguing book describes the origins of pro wrestling and how it has progressed into a cable television sensation. While professional wrestling was recognized as a sport in the early 1900s, promoters helped create the reputation it now holds. The showmanship that is so much a part of pro wrestling has now become a part of the sport in Japan and Mexico as well. Among the facts readers will pick up from this book are that women have participated in the sport throughout its history, and wrestlers are willing to make many sacrifices to please an audience.

6.11 Gutman, Dan. **Babe & Me: A Baseball Card Adventure.** Avon, 2000. 165 pp. ISBN 0-380-97739-7. Fiction

Through time travel, avid baseball fans Joe and his father follow the amazing career of Babe Ruth, eager to find out whether Ruth called his shot in the legendary game three of the 1932 World Series. Packed with facts and details and wonderfully illustrated with photographs and quotes, this book details the troubling times surrounding the amazing career of Babe Ruth.

6.12 Hirschfeld, Robert. **Football Nightmare.** Little, Brown, 2001. 119 pp. ISBN 0-316-14370-7. Fiction

Keith Stedman loves to play football, but after dropping the winning pass in last year's game, he decides to quit football for good. His friends and family encourage him to keep playing, but Keith must learn for himself how to put the past behind him and continue to play the game he loves. This book is part of the Matt Christopher sports series.

6.13 Jensen, Julie. **Play-by-Play: Volleyball.** Photographs by Andy King. LernerSports, 2001. 63 pp. ISBN 0-8225-9882-5. Nonfiction

Anyone interested in volleyball will enjoy this book, which includes a discussion of how and why the game was invented. Just as in any sport, learning the skills necessary to play takes time and effort. Readers will get basic knowledge of the rules and regulations and enjoy the short vignettes of famous players. Each volleyball move is accompanied by color pictures and descriptions. This book also includes suggestions for further reading and a glossary.

6.14 Karr, Kathleen. **The Boxer.** Farrar, Straus and Giroux, 2000. 144 pp. ISBN 0-374-30921-3. Fiction

Johnny "The Chopper" Woods works in an 1880s New York City sweatshop to help support his mother and siblings. He sees boxing as his way out of the tenements. With coaching from a former boxer, he earns a lightweight championship. Johnny also discovers the importance of finishing high school and must eventually decide what path his life will take.

6.15 King, Andy. **Play-by-Play: Mountain Biking.** LernerSports, 2001. 63 pp. ISBN 0-8225-9879-5. Nonfiction

Like others in this series, this book provides a how-to approach to a specific sport. This basic introduction to mountain biking includes the history of the sport, necessary equipment and maintenance, training tips, and a glossary of key terms related to the sport. Also included are color photos that demonstrate the sport in action.

6.16 Klass, David. **Home of the Braves.** Farrar, Straus and Giroux, 2002. 320 pp. ISBN 0-374-39963-8. Fiction

Through the voice and experiences of Joe Brickman, a senior at Lawndale High in North Jersey, author Klass reveals the effects of peer pressure, school bullying, resistance to change, fears resulting in hatred, and learning from the past generation's mistakes. The arrival of a mysterious soccer phenom from Brazil provides the catalyst for Joe's journey from undirected adolescent to goal-oriented young adult as he discovers how his long-time interests and strengths can help him set realistic goals.

6.17 Lurie, John. **Play-by-Play: Snowboarding.** Photographs by Jimmy Clarke. LernerSports, 2001. 61 pp. ISBN 0-8225-9881-7. Nonfiction

This book begins with a brief history of snowboarding, moves on to a description of the basic maneuvers shown step by step through colorful photographs, and then shares tips on competitive moves and explains the different competitions such as freestyle and slalom. The glossary of snowboarding argot is a valuable resource for anyone wanting to learn the sport.

6.18 Myers, Walter Dean. **The Greatest: Muhammad Ali.** Scholastic, 2001. 192 pp. ISBN 0-590-54342-3. Nonfiction

Muhammad Ali, Cassius Clay, and "The Louisville Lip" are all names of one of the most skilled athletes of the twentieth century. Some people remember Muhammad Ali for his boxing skill, others for his political and religious stand against the Vietnam War. For young African Americans in the 1960s, he represented a role model of strength, talent, and persona never before seen. The world of professional boxing is illuminated along with this biography of Ali.

6.19 Myers, Walter Dean. **The Journal of Biddy Owens: The Negro Leagues.** Scholastic, 2001. 144 pp. ISBN 0-439-09503-4. Fiction

As seventeen-year-old equipment manager for the Birmingham Black Barons, Biddy Owens is a fictional character, but the context of the teams, players, and events is based on real history. Biddy's journals reveal elation at games won, problems with prejudice in traveling, and the great popularity of the teams even as players such as Jackie Robinson are recruited for the white teams, signaling the end of the Negro Leagues and of segregation in baseball. Included in this book from the My Name Is America series are photographs and a historical note.

6.20 Nitz, Kristin Wolden. **Play-by-Play: Softball.** Photographs by Andy King. LearnerSports, 2000. 79 pp. ISBN 0-8225-9875-2. Nonfiction

Fast pitch, slow pitch, even an Olympic event, softball is a popular sport played and enjoyed by players of all ages and genders. Softball's history credits a Minnesota fire fighter for developing the game in hopes of providing his crew with some exercise while waiting for an alarm. Since that time, the game's equipment has changed along with types of pitches and strategies. This is a good reference book for beginning players and coaches.

6.21 Owens, Thomas S. **Basketball Arenas.** Millbrook, 2002. 63 pp. ISBN 0-7613-1766-X. Nonfiction

The author takes us behind the scenes into the planning and development of basketball arenas, including a description of the process involved in deciding when and where to build arenas; their costs; and how to finance the project. The book is illustrated with photographs and quotes from players, fans, managers, and designers and highlights several U.S. basketball sports palaces.

6.22 Owens, Thomas S. **Collecting Baseball Cards: 21st Century Edition.** Millbrook, 2001. 80 pp. ISBN 0-7613-1708-2. Nonfiction

The first baseball card was printed in 1869 for the Cincinnati Red Stockings. It was immediately collectible, and cards have since grown in popularity. Today they are a multimillion-dollar business. This book describes the amazing growth of baseball cards from advertising cards to today's glossy, multiple-exposure action cards. Color photos, along with a detailed index and a glossary, make this an excellent reference book.

6.23 Owens, Thomas S. **Football Stadiums.** Millbrook, 2001. 64 pp. ISBN 0-7613-1764-3. Nonfiction

In this book, readers explore the history behind the construction of football stadiums and learn about the design of scoreboards, seating arrangements, and hidden rooms. Great color pictures of these steel masterpieces are included, and additional informative facts are listed on each page. The last chapter contains a list of Web sites for young athletes.

6.24 Owens, Thomas S., and Diana Star Helmer. **NASCAR.** Twenty-First Century Books, 2000. 64 pp. ISBN 0-7613-1374-5. Nonfiction

Ever dream about being in a fast car and winning a race? Auto racing is a big sport. Many fans consider only the driver important, but auto racing is a team event that involves the owners, crew chief, and seven pit crew members. Auto racing involves many rituals, and one major race requires the team to prepare weeks in advance. Highlights of the history of stock car racing, including today's popular drivers, are described.

6.25 Owens, Thomas S., and Diana Star Helmer. **Soccer.** Twenty-First Century Books, 2000. 64 pp. ISBN 0-7613-1400-8. Nonfiction

Soccer has become an international sport with a huge following. All positions on a soccer team, from the forward to the goalie, play an important role in the game. Various international male and female soccer players are highlighted in this book and their style of play used to emphasize a strategy or game plan. The 1994 and 1998 World Cup competitions are also highlighted.

6.26 Pietrusza, David. **The Baltimore Orioles Baseball Team.** Enslow, 2000. 48 pp. ISBN 0-7660-1283-2. Nonfiction

Pietrusza, David. **The San Francisco Giants Baseball Team.** Enslow, 2000. 48 pp. ISBN 0-7660-1284-0. Fiction

This series introduces readers to professional baseball by providing a look at the players, coaches, and behind-the-scenes stories of two winning teams, the Baltimore Orioles and the San Francisco Giants. The easy-reading text is accompanied by both color and vintage photographs as well as charts highlighting the statistics of the teams' records.

6.27 Powell, Randy. **Three Clams and an Oyster.** Farrar, Straus and Giroux, 2002. 216 pp. ISBN 0-374-37526-7. Fiction

The four-man flag football team that he captains is the most important aspect of Flint McCallister's life. He and two of his best friends and teammates have great hopes for the new season; the fourth team member, however, is more focused on partying than on sports, causing tension between the "three clams" and their "oyster" teammate. As they search for a new team member, the boys have to take a long look at their own behaviors.

6.28 Roberts, Robin. **Basketball the Right Way.** Millbrook, 2000. 48 pp. ISBN 0-7613-1409-1. Nonfiction

If you are interested in learning the basics of basketball, you will enjoy this book. It includes a detailed chapter on the fundamentals of dribbling, passing, shooting, and rebounding, as well as chapters on other important characteristics of a good basketball player, such as relating to teammates and good sportsmanship. Color photographs with detailed captions are included, plus a list of recommended books and Web sites.

6.29 Roberts, Robin. **Basketball Year: What It's Like to Be a Woman Pro.** Millbrook, 2000. 48 pp. ISBN 0-7613-1406-7. Nonfiction

Women's basketball has taken a giant step forward in the last decade. Although women's professional basketball games do not draw the crowds the men's pro teams do, the women are nevertheless highly trained athletes who demand our attention and admiration. Various aspects of the life of women playing on pro basketball teams, including the traveling and training and interacting with fans, are highlighted.

6.30 Roberts, Robin. **Careers for Women Who Love Sports.** Millbrook, 2000. 48 pp. ISBN 0-7613-1408-3. Nonfiction

Do you love sports but know you don't have the athletic ability to make the pros? What other kinds of careers are there for sports-minded women? Seven women discuss their sports-related careers, including referee, sports journalist, athletic trainer, coach, nutritionist, marketing specialist, and broadcaster. Professional and nonprofessional opportunities are described and real women discuss their careers and the skills and educational needs of their jobs.

6.31 Roberts, Robin. **Sports for Life: How Athletes Have More Fun.** Millbrook, 2000. 48 pp. ISBN 0-7613-1407-5. Nonfiction

Robin Roberts, broadcaster and women's sports ambassador, has put together a fact-filled, colorfully photographed text about the benefits of being a lifelong athlete. Written with girls in mind, Roberts encourages youngsters to think beyond sports as simply winning or losing a game, but instead as a "way of life" that can keep them physically, intellectually, and emotionally fit. We can all be athletes forever, reaping awards that are immeasurable.

6.32 Ruth, Amy. **Wilma Rudolph.** Lerner, 2000. 112 pp. ISBN 0-8225-4976-X. Nonfiction

From the acclaimed Arts and Entertainment channel program *Biography,* this book recounts the life of Wilma Rudolph, the African American woman who overcame crippling polio as a child to become the first woman to win three gold medals in a single Olympics. Accompanied by excellent photographs, this is an inspiring book for people of all ages, especially sports-minded adolescents eager for heroes they can aspire to someday be like.

6.33 Rutledge, Rachel. **Marion Jones: Fast and Fearless.** Millbrook, 2000. 48 pp. ISBN 0-7613-1870-4. Nonfiction

Strong, independent, and gifted, Marion Jones has risen to become one of the premier track stars of the twenty-first century. This is the remarkable story of one of America's most gifted athletes. Through simple words and colorful pictures, we see her struggle to achieve, to endure the pain necessary to conquer her chosen sport, only to cheer her triumphs as she prepares for Olympic gold. This is a must-read for all young athletes and future track stars.

6.34 Rutledge, Rachel. **Mia Hamm: Striking Superstar.** Millbrook, 2000. 48 pp. ISBN 0-7613-1802-X. Nonfiction

For shy, quiet Mia Hamm, soccer was a way to make new friends as her military family moved frequently from base to base. By age fourteen, Mia's speed and agility had attracted the attention of Team USA coaches. For the next several years, she balanced high school and college competition with the demands of playing for Team USA. All of Mia's hard work paid off when she starred on the gold medal–winning U.S. Olympic soccer team.

6.35 Savage, Jeff. **Kobe Bryant: Basketball Big Shot.** Lerner, 2000. 64 pp. ISBN 0-8225-3680-3. Nonfiction

A gifted athlete and fan favorite of the Los Angeles Lakers, Kobe Bryant has lived a remarkable life, both on and off the basketball court. Skipping college and heading straight to the pros, Kobe won fan attention through his natural ability, flashy style, and youthful exuberance. As Kobe describes what it's like to be the youngest person ever to play in the NBA, readers come to understand what it takes to make it in the arena of world-class athletes.

6.36 Savage, Jeff, **Sammy Sosa, Home Run Hero.** LernerSports, 2000. 64 pp. ISBN 0-8225-3678-1. Nonfiction

When Sammy Sosa was a child in the Dominican Republic, an older brother went to work full time so that Sammy could spend more time practicing baseball. That sacrifice paid off, as Sosa became one of his sport's brightest stars. This book chronicles his life, devoting an entire chapter to the record-breaking home run race of 1998. Sosa's humanitarian work is also discussed, including his contribution to relief efforts after a hurricane devastated his homeland.

6.37 Schulman, Arlene. **Muhammad Ali.** Lerner, 2000. 128 pp. ISBN 0-8225-9693-8. Nonfiction

Muhammad Ali's status derives not only from winning the heavyweight championship three times but also from his battles outside the boxing ring. To many people, Ali is a symbol of honor for standing up for his beliefs such as refusing to serve in Vietnam. The author gives us fascinating details from Cassius Clay's early days growing up in Louisville to his current struggles with Parkinson's disease. This is a fascinating account of the man who earned the title "Athlete of the Century."

6.38 Steiner, Andy. **Girl Power on the Playing Field: A Book about Girls, Their Goals, and Their Struggles.** Lerner, 2000. 96 pp. ISBN 0-8225-2690-5. Nonfiction

Young female athletes need a strong physical education program that helps them develop the skills necessary to play competitive sports. Unfortunately, research shows that girls often drop out of organized sports because of feelings of inadequacy and discrimination. In addition to a chapter that highlights outstanding female athletes and their accomplishments, this book includes a detailed index and the names and addresses of organizations that support programs for female athletes.

6.39 Stewart, Mark. **Allen Iverson: Motion & Emotion.** Millbrook, 2001. 48 pp. ISBN 0-7613-1958-1. Nonfiction

The title of this book tells it all. Allen Iverson is a man in motion, with deep emotions about where he has been and where he is going. Growing up in the projects of Hampton, Virginia, Iverson became involved in sports as a means of staying out of trouble. This book chronicles his continuing development as a basketball superstar. Included are color photographs, sport and player statistics, and interviews with coaches, family, and friends.

6.40 Stewart, Mark. **Andruw Jones: Love That Glove.** Millbrook, 2001. 48 pp. ISBN 0-7613-1967-0. Nonfiction

Andruw Jones was the first person from his country, Curaçao, a small island nation in the Caribbean, to become a major league baseball player. Sometimes compared to Mickey Mantle, Joe DiMaggio, and Willie Mays, Jones became the youngest player ever to start in a World Series game. He also hit home runs in his first two World Series for the Atlanta Braves. A dream has come true for the young boy from Curaçao.

6.41 Stewart, Mark. **Chamique Holdsclaw.** Millbrook, 2000. 48 pp. ISBN 0-7613-1801-1. Nonfiction

Chamique Holdsclaw is one of the top players in a professional sport that has only recently received national attention—woman's basketball. This photo-filled, informative, and inspiring text tells the story of how one young girl from Queens, New York, conquered the boy-dominated basketball courts of her inner-city neighborhood and rose to become a superstar both on and off the basketball court. Disciplined, determined, and dedicated, Chamique inspires all through her sheer grit and natural talent.

6.42 Stewart, Mark. **Daunte Culpepper: Command and Control.** Millbrook, 2002. 48 pp. ISBN 0-7613-2613-8. Nonfiction

Daunte Culpepper's life is chronicled in this biography about a player who refused to give up his dream of playing professional football. A frank discussion reveals how Daunte's low school grades almost finished his career before it began. Color pictures and quotations from coaches and team players highlight the text. Also included are an index and statistics on Culpepper's football career and the Minnesota Vikings.

6.43 Stewart, Mark. **Ichiro Suzuki: Best in the West.** Millbrook, 2002. 48 pp. ISBN 0-7613-2616-2. Nonfiction

Ichiro Suzuki, the latest pitching sensation in the major leagues, is the subject of this easy-read sports book. From humble beginnings as a baseball player in Japan, Suzuki has become an international success. Thanks to the support of his former manager Shozo Doi and Suzuki's family, he has paid his dues and is now on top of his game. This account describes the life of professional baseball players, and a question-and-answer section adds interest.

6.44 Stewart, Mark. **Jackie Stiles: Gym Dandy.** Millbrook, 2002. 48 pp. ISBN 0-7613-2614-6. Nonfiction

This biography of Jackie Stiles chronicles her growth as a rising superstar in the world of women's sports. A high scorer in high school and in college, she continues her professional career in the Women's National Basketball Association with the Portland Fire team and an endorsement deal with Nike. This book includes color photographs and sport statistics.

6.45 Stewart, Mark. **Kevin Garnett: Shake Up the Game.** Millbrook, 2002. 52 pp. ISBN 0-7613-2615-4. Nonfiction

Kevin Garnett is known in the NBA as Da Kid. This great athlete has many NBA honors and even won a gold medal as a member of the U.S. Olympic team. He achieved all these honors before his twenty-first birthday. Kevin was drafted out of high school and signed a record five-million-dollar contract. He has matured as a leader, but his nickname is still Da Kid. He says, "I'll always have a kid in me."

6.46 Stewart, Mark. **Kobe Bryant: Hard to the Hoop.** Millbrook, 2000. 48 pp. ISBN 0-7613-1800-3. Nonfiction

While his father played Italian professional basketball, young Kobe Bryant was launching a sports career of his own. Kobe wouldn't know how good he was until his family returned to the

United States, where competition is far tougher than in Italy. With his uncanny ability to learn other players' best moves, Kobe proved talented enough to be drafted into the NBA directly out of high school. Kobe's next challenge was to grow into his new role as star player.

6.47 Stewart, Mark. **Kurt Warner: Can't Keep Him Down.** Millbrook, 2001. 48 pp. ISBN 0-7613-1953-0. Nonfiction

Kurt Warner, now a football superstar, spent years working toward his goal of playing for the National Football League. Ignored by the "scouting combines" where potential pro football players are tapped, he created his own path to football history. Warner's life story shows how perseverance and determination made him a winner. Included in the book are color photographs, interviews with family and friends, and player statistics.

6.48 Stewart, Mark. **Mario Lemieux: Own the Ice.** Millbrook, 2002. ISBN 0-7613-2555-7. Nonfiction

Canadian-born ice hockey all-star Mario Lemieux's biography details his colorful past in the National Hockey League. Lemieux's team, the Pittsburgh Penguins, surprised everyone by winning two Stanley Cup National Championships in a row (1990–1992). Now retired, Lemieux is concentrating on his family and new job as owner of the Pittsburgh Penguins. Filled with vivid pictures of Lemieux in action and great writing detail, this easy-read sports guide introduces the game of hockey in a clear, concise manner.

6.49 Stewart, Mark. **Nomar Garciaparra: Non-Stop Shortstop.** Millbrook, 2000. 48 pp. ISBN 0-7613-1520-9. Nonfiction

For Nomar Garciaparra, baseball is life. From the first time young Nomar swung the bat, he aimed to play with perfection. After three years as an outstanding student and star athlete at Georgia Tech, Nomar left college and was drafted by the Boston Red Sox. It was on the minor league teams and not in the college classroom that Nomar felt he would best learn what he needed to know to become one of the American League's best all-around players.

6.50 Stewart, Mark. **One Wild Ride: The Life of Skateboarding Superstar Tony Hawk.** Twenty-First Century Books, 2002. 64 pp. ISBN 0-7613-2666-9. Nonfiction

Tony Hawk is the most publicized professional skateboarder of all time, and this biography traces his roots from childhood to stardom. Interesting facts about Tony's need for personal perfection give insight into the sport and path he has chosen. Personal information about family, friends, and advice from Tony himself is included. Many photographs at different stages of his career make this an easy and enjoyable read for any sports enthusiast.

6.51 Stewart, Mark. **Peyton Manning: Rising Son.** Millbrook, 2000. 48 pp. ISBN 0-7613-1517-9. Nonfiction

Many boys dream of growing up to be just like their fathers. For Peyton Manning, this meant becoming a professional football player. After gaining national attention as star quarterback for his New Orleans high school, Peyton continued to shine at the University of Tennessee. Because Peyton wanted his college experience to include more than football, he took difficult courses and starred in the classroom as well. He chose to complete college before entering the professional draft and starting his NFL career with the Indianapolis Colts.

6.52 Stewart, Mark. **Randy Moss: First in Flight.** Millbrook, 2000. 48 pp. ISBN 0-7613-1518-7. Nonfiction

Life has not always been fun and games for Minnesota Vikings receiver Randy Moss. The victim of racism and his own foolish mistakes, Randy almost missed his opportunity to play college and professional football. Only through the support of coaches who were willing to give him a second chance after an assault conviction and minor drug violation was Randy able to realize his potential on the playing field.

6.53 Stewart, Mark. **Se Ri Pak: Driven to Win.** Millbrook, 2000. 48 pp. ISBN 0-7613-1519-5. Nonfiction

While still a teenager, Korean Se Ri Pak became one of Korea's best golfers and then went on to become a champion on the U.S. professional golf tour. In the process, she discovered that being a sports superhero in her home country has its drawbacks. Only by establishing a new home for herself in the United States has Se Ri been able to escape the constant public pressure she experienced and focus on her personal growth as well as her golf game.

6.54 Stewart, Mark. **Steve McNair: Running & Gunning.** Millbrook, 2001. 48 pp. ISBN 0-7613-1954-9. Nonfiction

Steve McNair made the decision in middle school to become a quarterback in the National Football League. He accomplished his dream with a great deal of patience and determination. This biography details his life from a small town in Mississippi to his position as a superstar quarterback on the Tennessee Titans team. Included are color photographs, football statistics, and interviews with coaches and friends.

6.55 Stewart, Mark. **Sweet Victory: Lance Armstrong's Incredible Journey, the Amazing Story of the Greatest Comeback in Sports.** Millbrook, 2000. 64 pp. ISBN 0-7613-1387-7. Nonfiction

Winning the world's most challenging and prestigious bicycle race is an amazing accomplishment. But before winning the 1999 Tour de France, Lance Armstrong first had to beat life-threatening cancer. In this book, readers get to know Lance Armstrong the person as well as Lance Armstrong, champion cyclist. Through Armstrong's story, the reader also gets a glimpse into the world of competitive cycling.

6.56 Stewart, Mark. **Tiger Woods: Drive to Greatness.** Millbrook, 2001. 64 pp. ISBN 0-7613-1966-2. Nonfiction

Tiger Woods has become a household name; even people who aren't golf aficionados know who he is. At the age of four, Tiger appeared on *The Mike Douglas Show* to showcase his talent. The local country club, however, wouldn't allow him to play on its course because of his skin color. Through his own determination and the guidance of his parents, Tiger has prevailed and made golf history. He has set many records, most recently becoming the first player since 1953 to win three majors in the same year.

6.57 Stewart, Mark. **Venus & Serena Williams: Sisters in Arms.** Millbrook, 2000. 47 pp. ISBN 0-7613-1803-8. Nonfiction

Filled with colorful pictures and easy to read, this book is one in the Tennis's New Wave series. The two stars are Venus and Serena Williams, champion tennis players and devoted sisters who are reshaping the landscape of American sports. Told simply and succinctly, this is the tale of two young African American women who stunned the professional tennis world with their rapid rise to the top.

6.58 Stewart, Mark, with Mike Kennedy. **Latino Baseball's Finest Fielders/Más destacados guantes del béisbol latino.** Millbrook, 2002. 64 pp. ISBN 0-7613-2566-2. Nonfiction

The book profiles U.S. baseball players from Latin American countries. Written with parallel Spanish translations, this text describes the pioneers of the first professional baseball league in the United States. It also includes individual biographies of current star fielders such as Javy Lopez and future players to watch such as Marlins outfielder Abraham Nunez. Interspersed with photos, quotes, and interesting facts, this biography is a good choice for baseball fans.

6.59 Stewart, Mark, with Mike Kennedy. **Latino Baseball's Hottest Hitters/Los mejores bateadores del béisbol latino.** Twenty-First Century Books, 2002. 64 pp. ISBN 0-7613-2567-0. Nonfiction

This book profiles U.S. baseball players from Latin American countries. Written with parallel Spanish translations, this text describes the pioneers of the first professional baseball league in the United States. It also includes individual biographies of current star hitters such as Sammy Sosa and future players to watch such as Carlos Pena of the Texas Rangers. Interspersed with photos and interesting descriptions of each player, this book will appeal to a wide variety of sports fans.

6.60 Stewart, Mark, and Mike Kennedy. **Michelle Kwan: Quest for Gold.** Millbrook, 2002. 64 pp. ISBN 0-7613-2622-7. Nonfiction

Michelle Kwan's skating ability is world famous. This book describes her career and her life on and off the ice. She began skating as a young child and had to make many sacrifices to attain the level of skating that allowed her to get to the world championships and finally make it to the Olympics. Color photographs and quotations from experts in the field are included throughout the book.

6.61 Stout, Glenn. **On the Halfpipe with . . . Tony Hawk.** Little, Brown, 2001. 87 pp. ISBN 0-316-14223-9. Nonfiction

Tony Hawk can ride a skateboard as easily as he can walk down the street. This biography traces his early rides through his domination of the skateboarding world. Descriptions of his skating sessions and statistics of his competitive history are also included in this Matt Christopher sports biography.

6.62 Stout, Glenn. **On the Track with . . . Jeff Gordon.** Little, Brown, 2000. 111 pp. ISBN 0-316-13469-4. Nonfiction

This Matt Christopher series biography traces the life of one of today's top NASCAR drivers, Jeff Gordon. Born in California in 1971, this dynamic driver worked his way from go-carts to stock cars on a career pace that in 1995 made him the youngest Winston Cup champion of the modern era. Incredibly, after only five years as a Winston Cup driver, Jeff Gordon is already considered a veteran driver and ranks among the top twenty NASCAR drivers of all time.

6.63 Sullivan, George. **Any Number Can Play: The Numbers Athletes Wear.** Illustrated by Anne Canevari Green. Millbrook, 2000. 62 pp. ISBN 0-7613-1557-8. Nonfiction

Illustrated with humorous pen-and-ink cartoons, this book tells the story of athletes' attachments to their uniform numbers. Many players consider their number lucky or at least traditional. Some have had the same number at every level they've played their sport. The book discusses the assignment of numbers, how they are retired, even occasions when they've been banned. A glossary of teams and athletes is included.

6.64 Sullivan, George. **Don't Step on the Foul Line: Sports Superstitions.** Illustrated by Anne Canevari Green. Millbrook, 2000. 62 pp. ISBN 0-7613-1558-6. Nonfiction

Many famous athletes and sports teams have rituals or superstitions that are a part of their preparation for play. This book describes some of these behaviors in a variety of sports, such as wearing only a particular ball cap, always eating the same food before a game, and wearing lucky charms. The pen-and-ink cartoons add a humorous touch. A glossary of teams and athletes is included.

6.65 Sweeney, Joyce. **Players.** Winslow, 2000. 222 pp. ISBN 1-890817-54-6. Fiction

Part of a cohesive team, Corey Brennan and his basketball buddies are on the cusp of an all-city championship for St. Phillips School. It is their senior year and it seems that good things are coming their way—that is, until Noah Travers shows up. Noah is determined to get the one spot left on the team at all costs. All of a sudden, the team's magic is broken. Threats to health, reputations, and friendships follow.

6.66 Tagliaferro, Linda. **Bruce Lee.** Lerner, 2000. 112 pp. ISBN 0-8225-9688-1. Nonfiction

Considered a troublemaker for getting in fights with British students in his native Hong Kong, Bruce Lee was expelled from high school and sent to the United States to live with family friends. An expert in kung fu, Lee helped to popularize this ancient martial art and became the first Asian American to be featured in an American film. His film exploits paved the way for later action-movie stars such as Jean-Claude Van Damme, Steven Segal, and Arnold Schwarzenegger.

6.67 Testa, Maria. **Some Kind of Pride.** Delacorte, 2001. 117 pp. ISBN 0-385-32782-X. Fiction

Named after the greatest baseball player of all time, Ruth dreams of becoming a major league baseball player until she overhears her father lamenting the fact that she is a girl. Crestfallen, Ruth turns to friends—her mother died long ago—for solace, comfort, and renewed spirit to pursue her dream of making the majors. This is an excellent story for discussing the notion of gender prejudice and its place in both literature and the real word.

6.68 Wallace, Rich. **Playing without the Ball: A Novel in Four Quarters.** Knopf, 2000. 213 pp. ISBN 0-679-88672-9. Fiction

Jay is on his own after his alcoholic mother leaves and his father moves to California. A high school senior, Jay lives above the bar where he works washing dishes and devotes himself to his passion in life: basketball. The sport provides a structure for Jay's life although he is not a great player. Cut from the school team, Jay joins a church-sponsored youth league. He also tries to work out his feelings about girls. This book is for mature students.

6.69 Zusak, Markus. **Fighting Ruben Wolfe.** Arthur A. Levine Books, 2001. 217 pp. ISBN 0-439-24188-X. Fiction

As they search for identity and dignity, brothers Cameron and Ruben Wolfe agree to become boxers in an underground fight circuit. Ruben discovers he is a champion fighter, while his more sensitive younger brother lives up to his fight nickname, "Underdog." The boys' already strong relationship grows even stronger as they try to conceal their activities from their parents, who are busy struggling to make ends meet.

III Challenging Our Imaginations

7 Mysteries and Suspense

7.1 Alexander, Lloyd. **The Drackenberg Adventure.** Puffin, 2001 (Originally published in 1988). 152 pp. ISBN 0-14-130471-5. Fiction

Alexander, Lloyd. **The Jedera Adventure.** Puffin, 2001 (Originally published in 1989). 152 pp. ISBN 0-14-131238-6. Fiction

Move over Nancy Drew. Vesper Holly, an adventurous young woman living in Victorian England under the protection of her long-suffering guardian, constantly finds herself facing mystery, intrigue, and difficulties ranging from kidnapping to slave traders and art thieves. As the dauntless Vesper travels throughout the world, readers not only learn about other cultures and times, but they also enjoy fast-paced plots filled with beautiful costumes, bizarre situations, and, of course, hairbreadth escapes.

7.2 Alphin, Elaine Marie. **Counterfeit Son.** Harcourt, 2000. 180 pp. ISBN 0-15-202645-2. Fiction

Fourteen-year-old Cameron Miller has always dreamed of sailboats, for sailing represents freedom from his abusive, criminal father and the life on the run he's endured for years. When his father is killed in a shoot-out with police, Cameron finds his chance and assumes the identity of one of his father's kidnapping victims. He is reunited with the family he has only studied through newspaper clippings. The family is both thrilled and suspicious. Can Cameron pass the test?

7.3 Blackwood, Gary. **Shakespeare's Scribe.** Dutton, 2000. 265 pp. ISBN 0-525-46444-1. Fiction

When Shakespeare breaks his arm and needs someone to take rapid dictation, he is rescued by Widge's knowledge of shorthand. Their relationship is strengthened but also put to the test when sickness ravages London and the theater players head for the provinces, accompanied by a newcomer. Challenged by this newcomer's knowledge, Widge throws himself into his acting while trying to determine the identity of the mysterious man who claims to be his father.

7.4 Blackwood, Gary. **The Shakespeare Stealer.** Puffin, 2000. 216 pp. ISBN 0-14-13595-9. Fiction

Widge, the one and only apprentice of Dr. Timothy Bright, has been taught a sort of shorthand and is recruited to insinuate himself among the boys who play Shakespeare's female characters—and, unknown to the company, pirate *Hamlet* so that less talented playwrights can add it to their repertoire. Unused to fair treatment, let alone kindness, Widge resents the easy camaraderie of the other boys and tries to ignore his gnawing fascination with the actor's craft.

7.5 Brooks, Kevin. **Martyn Pig.** Scholastic, 2002. 240 pp. ISBN 0-439-29595-5. Fiction

When his drunken father dies in an accident, fourteen-year-old Martyn Pig decides to cover up the death, afraid the police will suspect foul play. Enlisting the help of his neighbor and friend, Alexandra, Martyn disposes of his father's body, planning to go on with his life, finally free of his alcoholic father's abuse. His plans go awry, however, and Martyn is suspected of murder.

7.6 Chandler, Elizabeth. **Dark Secrets: No Time to Die.** Pocket, 2001. 210 pp. ISBN 0-7434-0030-5. Fiction

After her sister's murder at drama camp, Jenny finds herself at the same camp looking for answers to the questions surrounding her sister's death. Jenny is a gymnast, not an actress, and she has been plagued by bouts of stage fright since she was a young child. While at camp, she must face her worst fears. Told to trust no one, she must race against time to use her psychic powers to find the true murderer before the murderer finds her.

7.7 Cheaney, J. B. **The Playmaker.** Knopf, 2000. 306 pp. ISBN 0-375-90577-4. Fiction

From the moment a bear steals his cap, Richard Malony knows that his quest to find Martin Feather is not going to be easy. A convinced Protestant, young Richard finds himself an at-risk participant in the Catholic plots against Queen Elizabeth. Who is the elusive Martin Feather, and why would Richard's dying mother have commended her son to him? What are Richard's real loyalties and how secure is his distrust of the theater, when it seems to offer his only chance to survive?

7.8 Cheaney, J. B. **The True Prince.** Knopf, 2002. 340 pp. ISBN 0-375-81433-7. Fiction

In this historical tale of suspense, Richard and Kit are actors in a sixteenth-century London play company with Richard Burbage and William Shakespeare. A new player in the company does not get along with Kit, and when Kit is fired, there are rumors of robberies of men from the queen's court. Richard wonders if the mysterious and intimidating Kit is involved and realizes that the new player is not all he seems.

7.9 Collins, Pat Lowery. **Just Imagine.** Houghton Mifflin, 2001. 216 pp. ISBN 0-618-05603-3. Fiction

During the Great Depression of the 1930s, Mary Francis discovers she has the ability to have out-of-body experiences and decides to use this gift to deal with the strife in her family and their separate living arrangements. Intrigue, mystery, and the search for self-identity surround this adventure into matters we cannot see—ghosts, the supernatural, the other world—while at the same time challenging our vision of what it means to be truly alone and longing for a family that lives together.

7.10 Cooney, Caroline B. **For All Time.** Delacorte, 2001. 261 pp. ISBN 0-385-32773-0. Fiction

The fourth book in Cooney's Time Travel Quartet, *For All Time* continues Annie Lockwood's adventures through time. In this volume, Annie visits the Metropolitan Museum of Art in hopes of finding some trace of her true love Strat amongst the Egyptian artifacts in a new exhibit. Time sends her a new twist when instead she finds a boy named Lockwood Stratton, supposedly the great-grandson of Strat's sister. Before Annie can unravel the mystery, she is sucked back into time and transported to ancient Egypt—unfortunately, one hundred years before Strat worked as a photographer on archaeological digs. How will she move forward to find him and how will she figure out who Lockwood is, the boy who strangely resembles Strat?

7.11 Cormier, Robert. **The Rag and Bone Shop.** Delacorte, 2001. 154 pp. ISBN 0-385-72962-6. Fiction.

Jason, age twelve, is the last person known to have seen his seven-year-old neighbor Alicia alive before she was battered to death. Jason is eager to help the police solve the murder until he encounters Trent, an interrogator, who is more interested in confessions than the truth. Under intense questioning, the innocent Jason begins to question himself. In this, his last novel, Robert Cormier revisits familiar territory of abuses of power and the shameful manipulation of young people.

7.12 DeFelice, Cynthia. **Death at Devil's Bridge.** Farrer, Straus and Giroux, 2000. 192 pages. ISBN 0-374-31723-2. Fiction

At thirteen, Ben must adjust to his father's death by drowning while his home on Martha's Vineyard is beginning to come to life with the influx of summer people. Ben and his friend Jeff fall under the influence of Tommy, an older teen. They encounter drug trafficking, a Porsche submerged in the ocean, and a mystery about the fate of the car's driver. When a body washes up on the beach at Devil's Bridge, Ben realizes he must take action.

7.13 DeFelice, Cynthia. **The Ghost and Mrs. Hobbs.** Farrar, Straus and Giroux, 2001. 192 pp. ISBN 0374-38046-5. Fiction

This book is a sequel to *The Ghost of Fossil Glen.* The main character, Allie Nichols, a strong and brave heroine, encounters the ghost of a handsome young man who asks for her help in unraveling an old mystery of murder and jealousy. Strange events complicate Allie's life as fires begin to ignite wherever she goes. Soon she is unsure whom to trust as she tries to solve this mystery and put the ghost to rest.

7.14 Easton, Kelly. **Trouble at Betts Pets.** Candlewick, 2002. 133 pp. ISBN 0-7636-1580-3. Fiction

Things are difficult for the Betts family. Business is off in their pet shop; the neighborhood is being plowed under to make way for expensive apartments, leaving neighborhood character Bertha without shelter; and animals are disappearing from their cages in the shop. Aaron forms an uneasy alliance with classmate Sharon Trout, who has been assigned his math tutor. Aaron then takes it on himself (with a little help from his friends) to solve the mystery of the missing animals.

7.15 Ericson, Helen. **Harriet Spies Again.** Delacorte, 2002. 230 pp. ISBN 0-385-32786-2. Fiction

Ericson has written a sequel to Louise Fitzhugh's 1964 novel *Harriet the Spy.* Golly returns to take care of Harriet, who is thrilled to have her friend and mentor back. She soon realizes, however, that Golly has changed and seems distracted and mysterious. Harriet and Sport are joined by a new friend, a mysterious girl. Despite the title, Harriet does very little spying, except in trying to solve the mystery of her friend and Golly's strange behavior.

7.16 Farber, Erica, and J. R. Sansevere. **Islands of the Black Moon.** Delacorte, 2002. 121 pp. ISBN 0-385-32789-7. Fiction

Lila leaves her everyday world in search of her father who disappeared six years earlier. Her search takes her to the Islands of the Black Moon, where terrifying sea creatures, including a beautiful but evil sorceress, are all after one thing—Lila's inheritance from her missing father. Lila refuses to relinquish what is rightfully hers until the evil sorceress says, "I know where your father is." Lila risks everything to save her father and free the world from darkness and evil.

7.17 Feder, Harriet. **Death on Sacred Ground.** Lerner, 2001. 191 pp. ISBN 0-8225-0741-2. Fiction

Vivi Hartman once more finds herself enmeshed in the investigation of a violent death. Mindy Solomon has been found with an arrow through her heart, and Vivi's dad, a rabbi, is called on to do the funeral on a Seneca reservation. Vivi has to use all her skills to solve the case before someone else ends up dead. The mix of Native American and Jewish traditions provides an intriguing backdrop for this fast-paced story.

7.18 Fitzhugh, Louise. **The Long Secret.** Delacorte, 2001 (Originally published in 1965). 277 pp. ISBN 0-385-32784-6. Fiction

In this classic, the irrepressible Harriet and her shy friend Beth Ellen leave Manhattan to summer in Water Mill, on the ocean. Harriet, with her ever-present notebook, is determined to find the source of mysterious notes left all over town—notes that contain appropriate verses about the receivers. With Jessie Mae, the girls create and encounter many unusual situations, including the return of Beth Ellen's long-absent mother, and the culprit is finally found, to Harriet's surprise, right under their noses.

7.19 Fitzhugh, Louise. **Sport.** Delacorte, 2001 (Originally published in 1979). 216 pp. ISBN 0-385-32785-4. Fiction

Eleven-year-old Sport lives with his absent-minded but loving father in New York City. Although Sport manages their meager finances, his absent, greedy, cruel mother is wealthy. When her father dies, he leaves much of his millions to Sport, who fears he will now have to live with his mother. Eventually, her cruelty and scheming are revealed, and Sport stays with his father and new (kind and understanding) stepmother. Harriet plays a minor role in this novel.

7.20 Funk, Cornelia. **The Thief Lord.** Scholastic, 2002. 345 pp. ISBN 0-439-40437-1. Fiction

This suspenseful tale tells of a detective who sets out to find two orphaned boys—twelve-year-old Prosper and five-year-old Bo—who ran away when their aunt decided to adopt Bo but not Prosper. Seeking asylum in the city of Venice—a place their late mother dreamed of—Bo and Prosper take up with a thief, a young boy who steals from the rich to give to the poor. Originally published in Germany in 2000, this book has wacky characters and complex intrigue.

7.21 Gaiman, Neil. **Coraline.** Illustrated by Dave McKean. HarperCollins, 2002. 162 pp. ISBN 0-380-97778-8. Fiction

In this mixture of humor and terror, Coraline saves her own life and that of several other people so that, by the end of the story, as she faces a new school year, Coraline realizes that after all she's been through nothing about school can scare her ever again. Readers will admire Coraline's courage and determination as they enjoy this juicy, creepy tale that, according to the author, children experience as an adventure but adults experience as a nightmare.

7.22 Garfield, Leon. **Black Jack.** Farrar, Straus and Giroux, 2000 (Originally published in 1968). 197 pp. ISBN 0-374-30827-6. Fiction

Black Jack, a seven-foot-tall villain thought to be dead, teams up with Bartholomew Dorking to venture into some of the seamiest places in London, where they meet some unusual characters. One of their adventures takes them to an insane asylum, where they release Belle from her chains and free her from the dungeon she has been condemned to for life.

7.23 Garfield, Leon. **John Diamond.** Farrar, Straus and Giroux, 2001 (Originally published in 1980). 177 pp. ISBN 0-374-32450-6. Fiction

Young William Jones goes on a desperate search through the streets of London to discover the truth of his dying father's secret. Encountering all sorts of strange people and weird happenings, William attempts to locate the man his father once apparently cheated. Young adolescent readers will enjoy the surprise ending of this book that has also been published under the title *Footsteps.*

7.24 Gilbert, Barbara Snow. **Paper Trail.** Front Street, 2000. 161 pp. ISBN 1-886910-44-8. Fiction

Walker, age fifteen, lives with his parents among the Soldiers of God, an antigovernment, extremist militia group in Oklahoma. The novel begins with the soldiers hunting him and his family because, as Walker discovers after they kill his mother, his father is an undercover FBI agent assigned to infiltrate the group. As Walker remembers clues from his past and gets more information, he begins to understand what is happening in this exciting and suspenseful story.

7.25 Harrison, Michael. **Facing the Dark.** Holiday House, 1999. 128 pp. ISBN 0-8234-1491-4. Fiction

Simon and Charley are an unlikely pair who have teamed up to solve a murder in their small British village. Simon's father has been arrested for the murder of Charley's father, but both Simon and Charley are convinced the arrest is a mistake. Together they face great danger to solve the mystery and find the real killer.

7.26 Hoffman, Mary. **Stravaganza: City of Masks.** Bloomsbury, 2002. 344 pp. ISBN 1-58234-791-3. Fiction

This is the story of a character with a hidden life. During the day, Lucien battles cancer, but at night he becomes Stravagante, a time traveler of sorts who finds himself in Belleza, a city that parallels Venice, Italy. Befriended by a local girl and protected by an older Stravagante, Lucien learns of a plot to murder the city's beloved ruler, Duchessa. To save the day, Lucien must decide how much he is willing to risk those he deeply loves.

7.27 Honey, Elizabeth. **Remote Man.** Knopf, 2002. 260 pp. ISBN 0-375-81413-2. Fiction

Ned is a thirteen-year-old Australian boy interested in computers and herpetology. When his depressed mother decides they should move to Massachusetts, Ned keeps in contact with his Australian cousin Kate through the Internet and forms a friendship with his new neighbor Rocky. When they encounter an international wildlife smuggler, Ned, Kate, and Rocky establish a global network of teenagers who use technology to plot against the criminals.

7.28 Hoobler, Dorothy, and Thomas Hoobler. **The Demon in the Teahouse.** Philomel, 2001. 181 pp. ISBN 0-399-23499-3. Fiction

Seikei is desperate to become a samurai. Although common law dictates he become a merchant like his father, he has other plans. A chance meeting with Judge Ooka, the shogun's top advisor, sets Seikei on the path of becoming a true samurai. He is to find a murderer who is responsible for three killings. Seikei must prove himself if he wants to continue his journey and change his future.

7.29 Hoobler, Dorothy, and Thomas Hoobler. **The Ghost in the Tokaido Inn.** Puffin, 2001. 214 pp. ISBN 0-698-11879-0. Fiction

Seikei is the fourteen-year-old son of a merchant in Japan. Although he dreams of becoming a samurai, he knows this is impossible in the Japanese culture that dictates that he follow in his father's footsteps. Through a simple twist of fate, he is given the opportunity to train as a samurai under the tutelage of Judge Ooka. His assignment is to find a thief by working with a kabuki actor in a Japanese theater.

7.30 Horowitz, Anthony. **Stormbreaker.** Philomel, 2001. 192 pp. ISBN 0-399-23620-1. Fiction

Fourteen-year-old Alex Rider suddenly finds himself in a very grown-up world. His uncle and guardian has died, and Alex knows only that his death was an accident. Yet, when he learns that his uncle was a spy who died at the hands of terrorists, there is no turning back. Alex must now outsmart the people who want him dead too. With the help of his uncle's boss, Britain's intelligence agency, Alex sets out to save the children of England from cold-blooded killers.

7.31 Jensen, Dorothea. **The Riddle of Penncroft Farm.** Harcourt, 2001. 254 pp. ISBN 0-15-216441-3. Fiction

Lars Olafson and his parents move in with Great Aunt Cass on the old family farm near Valley Forge, Pennsylvania. Lonely and miserable, Lars has few friends and even fewer things to do until he meets an unconventional friend—a ghost from the eighteenth century named Geordie. Geordie entertains Lars with stories of the American Revolution, and when Aunt Cass dies, Geordie leads Lars on a search for his aunt's missing will, all the way to the Revolutionary War.

7.32 Jones, Elizabeth McDavid. **Mystery on Skull Island.** Pleasant Company, 2001. 173 pp. ISBN 1-58485-342-5. Fiction

Twelve-year-old Rachel's life changes drastically when she moves to South Carolina to live with her father. When Rachel is forbidden to see her best friend Sally, they secretly meet on a deserted island. There they discover a pirate's hiding place filled with mysterious things. Might there be a connection to a woman whom Sally's father is intending to marry?

7.33 Karr, Kathleen. **Playing with Fire.** Farrar, Straus and Giroux, 2001. 192 pp. ISBN 0-374-23453-1. Fiction

Fourteen-year-old Greer Duquesne moves with her fortune-teller mother Madame Camille and Drake Morley, a sinister presence in her mother's life, to Cliff House, owned by a wealthy, grieving widower who longs to contact his wife through a séance. Karr's book uses the fascination with spiritualism of 1920s United States to develop and eventually solve the mysteries surrounding Camille's past so that Greer can come to terms with her extrasensory powers and her own past to move forward with her life.

7.34 Karr, Kathleen. **Skullduggery.** Hyperion, 2000. 227 pp. ISBN 0-786-82439-5. Fiction

In an effort to support himself, Matthew, a twelve-year-old orphan living in the nineteenth century, takes a job working for Dr. ABC, a phrenologist. To facilitate his research in judging character by interpreting bumps in the human skull, Dr. ABC includes Matthew in a quest to find famous and interesting skulls to study. While robbing graves for additional specimens, they meet with violence from professional body snatchers who are paid to provide bodies to medical schools.

7.35 Kehret, Peg. **Don't Tell Anyone.** Puffin, 2000. 137 pp. ISBN 0-525-46388-7. Fiction

Twelve-year-old Megan finds a group of feral cats living in an open field near her house. When she discovers that the land is to be bulldozed for an apartment building, she develops a plan to rescue the cats. Megan's life becomes complicated when she unknowingly gets involved in a criminal scheme that threatens her life. This mystery takes many twists and turns before it is solved.

7.36 King-Smith, Dick. **Mysterious Miss Slade.** Illustrated by Ann Kronheimer. Crown, 2000. 123 pp. ISBN 0-517-80045-4. Fiction

When Jim and Patsy Reader wander onto Miss Slade's Blackberry Bottom property, they discover she is not the witch that most villagers suspect. Instead, they find an eccentric but lovable elderly woman living in a trailer surrounded by farm animals of all sorts. When Jim and Patsy finally convince their mother to visit Miss Slade, Mrs. Reader motivates the lonely heiress to start a new life.

7.37 Konigsburg, E. L. **Silent to the Bone.** Scholastic, 2000. 261 pp. ISBN 0-439-31698-7. Fiction

A call is made to 911 and a scream in the background claims "he dropped her." It is six-month-old Nikki's nanny who makes the claim and grabs the phone to summon the emergency team. Nikki's half brother Branwell placed the call but then goes mute. Since Bran can't or won't explain what happened, he is sent to a behavioral center. Through Bran's signs, pictures, and associations, his best friend sets out to solve the mystery and absolve Bran from blame.

7.38 Lawrence, Caroline. **The Secrets of Vesuvius.** Roaring Brook, 2001. 173 pp. ISBN 0-7613-2603-0. Fiction

Second in the Roman Mysteries series, which will consist of six Roman mysteries, *The Secrets of Vesuvius* follows the adventures of young Flavia, Jonathan, Nubia, and Lupus (introduced in *The Thieves of Ostia*) as they meet Pliny and try to solve Vulcan's riddle. They not only escape from the unexpected eruption of Vesuvius in A.D. 79 but also solve a family's secret. All the children exhibit great bravery and resourcefulness in the face of danger. The book includes a glossary, map, and plans of a farm and villa.

7.39 Lawrence, Caroline. **The Thieves of Ostia.** Roaring Brook, 2002. 151 pp. ISBN 0-7613-2602-2. Fiction

Reminiscent of the Hardy Boys and Nancy Drew series, the Roman Mysteries series involves a group of young teens who get involved in local mysteries. This particular book is set in Ostia, Rome's seaport, in A.D. 79. The group, led by the resourceful Flavia Gemina, solves a mystery of stolen coins and beheaded dogs. The many authentic references to locations and mythology add richness to the mystery, and the topics of religion, slavery, city life, architecture, diet, and shipping conclude with the theme of forgiveness. The map, historical note, and glossary enrich readers' understanding of the period.

7.40 Levin, Betty. **Shadow-Catcher.** Greenwillow, 2000. 152 pp. ISBN 0-688-17862-6. Fiction

Jonathon Capewell is chosen to accompany his grandfather on his annual photographing tour. Grandpa Capewell owns the family farm but has always paid more attention to his burgeoning photographic career. He is also fiercely independent and doesn't exactly make Jonathan feel welcome as they set out on this summer together. Jonathon's relationship with his grandfather pales in comparison to the mystery Jonathan stumbles onto thanks to the "Shadow-Catcher," his grandfather's camera.

7.41 MacPhail, Catherine. **Missing.** Bloomsbury, 2002. 192 pp. ISBN 1-58234-773-5. Fiction

Maxine's older brother Derek has disappeared and is believed to be dead. Overwhelmed with grief, Maxine's family tries desperately to cope, as Maxine suffers in school, loses friends, and slowly loses the interest of her distracted and despondent parents. Then something mysterious happens; a boy claiming to be Derek calls their house, driving everyone involved crazy with fear and anxiety. This is a compelling story of loss and fear as it manifests itself in a young mind.

7.42 Marsden, John. **Winter.** Scholastic, 2002. 147 pp. ISBN 0-439-36849-9. Fiction

Set in Australia, *Winter* is a suspenseful novel about resourceful and independent sixteen-year-old Winter De Salis, who, after an absence of twelve years, has returned to her family's home to solve the mystery of her parents' deaths and the shoddy condition of the estate. Through a great-aunt and other friends, Winter gradually uncovers her family history as she investigates past lies and omissions to find the truth and move toward her future.

7.43 McAllister, Margaret. **Hold My Hand and Run.** Dutton, 2000. 150 pp. ISBN 0-525-46391-7. Fiction

Kazy and Beth had different mothers, but their father, a canon at the cathedral, loves them both. After Beth's mother dies, however, he is unable to reach out to the girls, and sadistic Aunt Latimer moves in to run the house. Kazy watches Beth's growing terror at her aunt's cruelty and, unable to rouse their father from his grief, the two girls flee, thus beginning an adventure in which they will have to prove their resourcefulness and courage.

7.44 McDonald, Joyce. **Shades of Simon Gray.** Delacorte, 2001. 245 pp. ISBN 0-385-32659-9. Fiction

When high school junior Simon Gray crashes his car into the oak people call the Hanging Tree, the secret he shares with three friends threatens to come out and change all of their lives forever. The mystery of his accident unfolds at the same time that Simon, lying in a coma in a hospital bed, makes an eerie connection with the victim of an eighteenth-century crime that occurred at the same tree.

7.45 Montes, Marisa. **A Circle of Time.** Harcourt, 2002. 261 pp. ISBN 0-15-202626-6. Fiction

Allison lies in a hospital in a coma. Although she can't hear the voices of those close to her, the voice of Becky Lee Thompson comes through loud and clear, pleading for help—except Becky's pleas come from 1906. As Becky's spirit keeps Alison's body alive in the present, Alison strives to determine just exactly what it is she's supposed to do in the past to help right a series of terrible wrongs.

7.46 Montes, Marisa. **Something Wicked's in Those Woods.** Harcourt, 2000. 214 pp. ISBN 0-15-202391-7. Fiction

After their parents are killed in a car accident in Puerto Rico, Javier Cisneros and his little brother Nico travel to California to live with their aunt. Strange things begin to happen around the house, and Nico has a new imaginary friend—a ghost. When Javier discovers that the ghost is a young victim of an unsolved crime from many years ago, he must try to solve it to protect his family, despite his aunt, who doesn't believe in ghosts.

7.47 Nixon, Joan Lowery. **Playing for Keeps.** Delacorte, 2001. 197 pp. ISBN 0-385-32759-5. Fiction

Rose and her lawyer grandmother Glory, while on a Caribbean cruise ship, encounter more than relaxation and Glory's bridge tournament when a famous baseball player attempts to seek asylum for his nephew, a rising star in Cuban baseball, by smuggling him onto the ship from Haiti. The novel starts with Rose's complicated relationship with her mother but is mainly about Rose solving various mysteries associated with the young Cuban with the help of two other young friends and, eventually, her grandmother.

7.48 Nixon, Joan Lowery. **The Trap.** Delacorte, 2002. 165 pp. ISBN 0-385-32762-5. Fiction

Julie is furious when her parents send her to spend the summer on a Texas ranch with her elderly aunt and uncle. Her uncle has broken his ankle after mysteriously falling down a set of stairs. Her visit to the ranch is made more interesting when she finds herself involved in a complicated murder mystery. Julie gets help in solving the mystery from her new friends on the ranch, as well as from her best friend back in California, who uses the Internet to keep in touch with Julie.

7.49 Peck, Richard. **Dreamland Lake.** Puffin, 2000 (Originally published in 1973). 147 pp. ISBN 0-14-130812-5. Fiction

Best friends since third grade, Flip and Brian now are thirteen, and their friendship is threatened when they find a dead man lying on the bank of Dreamland Lake and investigate his death. The police think he is a tramp who died of natural causes, but the boys think otherwise. As they collect clues, they are convinced not only that someone is watching them but also that the man may have been involved in some sort of cult activity.

7.50 Peters, Julie Anne. **A Snitch in the Snob Squad.** Little, Brown, 2001. 200 pp. ISBN 0-316-70287-0. Fiction

Money is missing from Mrs. Jonas's room. Several people were in her room at the time it was taken. Who could the thief be? More money is taken and more suspicions arise. The Snob Squad, a group of middle school girls, takes on the task of discovering the thief. But there's a lot more trouble before the culprit is captured.

7.51 Reiss, Kathryn. **Paint by Magic.** Harcourt, 2002. 271 pp. ISBN 0-15-216361-1. Fiction

Conner is worried; his mom is acting *weird,* freezing into trances that overcome her without warning. As he's puzzling over what to do for her, he finds himself whisked back into 1926, where, posing as an orphan, he is able to live with an artist who seems obsessed with Connor's mom. In this suspenseful novel, Conner has to figure out how to save both his mother and himself and return to his proper place in history before it's too late.

7.52 Reiss, Kathryn. **PaperQuake: A Puzzle.** Harcourt, 2002. 274 pp. ISBN 0-15-216782-X. Fiction

Violet, the nonidentical triplet, feels like the third wheel. Her sisters are adventurous and worldly, while she is sickly, frail, and deathly afraid of earthquakes. But when mysterious diary entries, letters, and newspaper clippings from almost one hundred years ago start appearing, some bearing a remarkable resemblance to the triplets, Violet discovers that she has been chosen by some force of nature to save her family from the dangers of the big San Francisco earthquake of 1906.

7.53 Reiss, Kathryn. **The Strange Case of Baby H.** Pleasant Company, 2002. 162 pp. ISBN 1-58485-533-9. Fiction

Clara Curfman is twelve years old when the San Francisco earthquake of 1906 hits. She and her family are fine, but Clara finds a baby on the doorstep of her family's boarding house. They welcome the baby into their home, and Clara hopes it will help them get through the lingering grief over the death of Clara's brother two years earlier. But Clara is also determined to find out more about the infant, even though the search involves more danger.

7.54 Rinaldi, Ann. **The Staircase.** Harcourt, 2000. 230 pp. ISBN 0-15-202430-1. Fiction

When her mother dies on the wagon train from Missouri to Colorado, thirteen-year-old Lizzy Enders is left by her father at a convent in Santa Fe, New Mexico. Hurt and angry, Lizzy struggles to adjust. A mysterious carpenter who becomes her friend solves the problem of the chapel's missing stairway and brings love and hope into Lizzy's life. Rinaldi successfully weaves the Southwestern legend of the miraculous staircase at the Chapel of Loretto into this engaging story.

7.55 Sedgwick, Marcus. **Witch Hill.** Delacorte, 2001. 147 pp. ISBN 0-385-32802-8. Fiction

After his house burns down, twelve-year-old Jamie is sent to stay with relatives in an English village, where a legendary witch begins to pursue him in terrifying nightmares. Haunted houses and bewitching ghosts are the highlights of this young adult novel, which should prove satisfying for readers who enjoy mystery, suspense, and adventure.

7.56 Snyder, Zilpha Keatley. **The Ghosts of Rathburn Park.** Delacorte, 2002. 182 pp. ISBN 0-385-32767-6. Fiction

Matt Hamilton is definitely real. He gets into and out of trouble easily with the help of two friends. One friend, a small dog, leads Matt to safety after he becomes lost in Rathburn Park. The other friend, a young girl, tells Matt stories of long ago. There is one small problem: Matt thinks the two are ghosts. Believing this, Matt learns some important truths about himself and his place in the world.

7.57 Synder, Zilpha Keatley. **Spyhole Secrets.** Delacorte, 2001. 186 pp. ISBN 0-385-32764-1. Fiction

Hallie Meredith is the new kid in town. Everyone's interested in her story, but she doesn't want to answer anyone's questions. Since her father's death, all she wants to do is hide. Hallie's newest hiding place raises some questions. From the attic of her new apartment building she can see straight into the apartment of the adjacent building. An intriguing story unfolds, which leads Hallie to some grueling detective work and, eventually, unexpected friends and answers to her own questions.

7.58 Tolan, Stephanie S. **The Face in the Mirror.** HarperTrophy, 2000. 214 pp. ISBN 0-380-73263-7. Fiction

Jared joins his estranged father in a professional production of Shakespeare's *Richard III.* In the midst of rehearsals, Jared tries to cope with his acting insecurities, his obnoxious television star half brother, and a theater ghost. Young readers interested in the performing arts will enjoy literary character with similar interests, while others will relish the elements of mystery and intrigue that surround this novel about a haunted theater.

7.59 Vande Velde, Vivian. **Companions of the Night.** Magic Carpet, 2002 (Originally published in 1995). 212 pp. ISBN 0-15-216669-6. Fiction

Sixteen-year-old Kerry Nowicki helps a young man escape from the clutches of a group of men who claim the young man is a vampire. Pulled into an intriguing mystery, Kerry must save the day and herself from the lure of vampires and strange twists of fate. This is simultaneously an exciting novel for young people who enjoy a smart thriller, an offbeat love story, an engaging plot twister, and a story filled with moral complexity.

7.60 Van Draanen, Wendelin. **Sammy Keyes and the Hollywood Mummy.** Knopf, 2001. 256 pp. ISBN 0-375-80266-5. Fiction

Sammy Keyes and her friend Marissa hop a bus to Hollywood to visit Sammy's mother, who left her with Grams while she pursues her dream of becoming a movie star. Sammy is worried that her mother, with her dyed hair and fake ID, has finally lost touch with reality. Even worse, Sammy must discover if her mother is a murderer or the murderer's next victim. Other books in this series include *Sammy Keyes and the Hotel Thief; Sammy Keyes and the Skeleton Man; Sammy Keyes and the Sisters of Mercy; Sammy Keyes and the Runaway Elf; Sammy Keyes and the Curse of Moustache Mar; Sammy Keyes and the Search for Snake Eyes.*

7.61 Wilson, Eric. **Spirit in the Rainforest.** Orca, 2001. 142 pp. ISBN 1-55143-224-2. Fiction

Tom and Liz Austen find themselves embroiled in a mystery in the British Columbian rain forest. While on vacation with friends, the Austen siblings encounter murder, deceit, lies, and theft. Believing the secrets of Nearby Island hold the answers, the two are determined to solve the mystery. In an attempt to identify the owner of screams they hear in the night, Tom and Liz face Mosquito Joe, a legendary hermit, as they delve deeper into the island's trees.

7.62 Winterfeld, Henry. **Detectives in Togas.** Illustrated by Charlotte Kleinert. Translated by Richard and Clara Winston. Harcourt, 2002. 249 pp. ISBN 0-15-216280-1. Fiction

Winterfeld, Henry. **Mystery of the Roman Ransom.** Illustrated by Fritz Biermann. Translated by Edith McCormick. Harcourt, 2002. 217 pp. ISBN 0-15-216268-2. Fiction

Originally published in English (translated from the German) in 1956 and 1971 respectively, these mysteries combine elements of Sherlock Holmes-like reasoning, geometric principles (because of their studies of Euclid), and Nancy Drew-like events as seven young, male pupils of the Xanthos School in ancient Rome solve the mysteries of graffiti on the Temple of Minerva *(Detectives in Togas)* and a death warrant issued against a senator, perhaps the father of one of the boys *(Mystery of the Roman Ransom).* Readers learn much about ancient Roman customs, beliefs, and history.

7.63 Woodruff, Elvira. **The Ghost of Lizard Light.** Illustrated by Elaine Clayton. Knopf, 1999. 176 pp. ISBN 0-679-89281-8. Fiction

After leaving Iowa for Maine, Jack and his family move into a lighthouse. But this lighthouse has another occupant, the 150-year-old ghost of Nathaniel Witherspoon. Together, Jack and Nathaniel's ghost unravel the mystery of a shipwreck that happened 150 years before. Along the way, Jack learns important lessons about life and grows closer to his demanding father.

7.64 Wright, Betty Ren. **The Moonlight Man.** Scholastic, 2000. 181 pp. ISBN 0-590-25237-2. Fiction

In the seventh move since their mother's death, fifteen-year-old Jenny and her younger sister Allie think they have finally found the perfect home—until they discover it is haunted. As Jenny unravels the mystery behind the ghosts that visit the houses in their new neighborhood and torment elderly neighbors, she forms a friendship with musically talented April and learns more about her own gifts.

7.65 Wynne-Jones, Tim. **The Boy in the Burning House.** Farrar, Straus and Giroux, 2000. 213 pp. ISBN 0-374-30930-2. Fiction

Jim Hawkins is a young man haunted by his father's mysterious disappearance two years earlier and by a ghostly girl who approaches him in the outreaches of his family's farm. Although mysterious, Ruth Rose is trying to help Jim put together missing pieces of the puzzle. She believes she knows the person responsible for Mr. Hawkins's death, but she needs Jim's help. Both make terrifying discoveries about their families but also worthwhile ones about themselves in this unpredictable thriller.

8 Fantasy and Supernatural

8.1 Aiken, Joan. **The Cuckoo Tree.** Houghton Mifflin, 2000 (Originally published in 1971). 289 pp. ISBN 0-618-07023-0. Fiction

As she travels home, Dido stumbles on adventure. After her coach is hijacked and her escort wounded, the journey must be delayed so the escort can heal. Dido finds a place to stay, which happens to be next door to an evil witch. Along with another crone, the witch plans to steal a young boy's inheritance and overthrow the government. Dido uncovers the plot and, with the help of friends, manages to save the king and the inheritance.

8.2 Aiken, Joan. **The Stolen Lake.** Houghton Mifflin, 2000 (Originally published in 1981). 314 pp. ISBN 0-618-07021-4. Fiction

On her way home from China, Dido, a spunky, tomboyish young girl, is forced to accompany the ship to a South American English colony named Bath. While there, she learns of a secret plot to overthrow Bath's rightful king. The reigning queen has stolen the princess from a neighboring land, and only Dido can save her. Sacrificing her own safety, Dido reveals the queen's plot and discovers that the rightful king is Mr. Holyston—the captain's personal servant!

8.3 Alexander, Lloyd. **The Gawgon and the Boy.** Dutton, 2001. 199 pp. ISBN 0-525-46677-0. Fiction

"The Boy" is David, slowly recovering from "New Monia" during the Great Depression; "The Gawgon" is his Aunt Annie, who volunteers to take over his education during his extended convalescence. It doesn't take David long to spin imaginary scenarios in which the intrepid Gawgon mixes it up with Napoleon, Mona Lisa, and Sherlock Holmes, among others. But Aunt Annie's mental acuity is stronger than her overtired heart; when she dies, David is desolate until she comes back to comment on his first attempts to impress a girl.

8.4 Almond, David. **Heaven Eyes.** Delacorte, 2001. 233 pp. ISBN 0-385-32770-6. Fiction

Whitegates is an English orphanage for abandoned, wounded children. One moonlit night Erin Law, an orphan who still dreams of her mother, and two friends escape on a raft and sail down the river. Before long their joy at being free turns to fear as they get stuck in a mud hole. Rescued by a girl named Heaven Eyes, their lives are changed forever as she takes them on a journey filled with bizarre characters and mystical experiences.

8.5 Almond, David. **Skellig.** Delacorte, 2000. 182 pp. ISBN 0-440-41602-7. Fiction

Michael finds a mysterious and haunting stranger living in his garage. This birdlike creature is unlike anyone or anything he has seen before. This mystery is only part of the recent turmoil in Michael's life, which includes an ill infant sister and a move to a new home. With the help of his new friend Mina, Michael learns about the healing power of love. The book is written in lyrical prose.

8.6 Amato, Mary. **The Word Eater.** Illustrated by Christopher Ryniak. Holiday House, 2000. 151 pp. ISBN 0-8234-1468-X. Fiction

What do a lonely sixth-grade girl and a hungry baby worm have in common? Lerner Chanse struggles with cliques and fitting in at her new school, but then she discovers an unusual ally—Fip, a word-eating worm. With both frightening and hilarious results, Fip eats a word or phrase, causing that "item" to disappear from the world, thus setting off unexpected chains of events. As the consequences of Fip and Lerner's actions take unexpected twists and turns, Lerner faces some important decisions.

8.7 Atwater-Rhodes, Amelia. **Demon in My View.** Delacorte, 2000. 176 pp. ISBN 0-385-32720-X. Fiction

Seventeen-year-old Jessica Allodola doesn't fit in at her high school. Cynical and dressed in dark clothing, she writes vampire tales on her laptop and prefers the company of her imaginary creatures to the real students. But when she discovers that the new guy in school is actually an alluring male vampire from her novel, Jessica goes deeper and deeper into her imaginary world, meeting other supernatural beings, until she must decide what direction she will take with her life.

8.8 Atwater-Rhodes, Amelia. **Midnight Predator.** Delacorte, 2002. 248 pp. ISBN 0-385-32794-3. Fiction

The place is Midnight, the ancient evil sanctuary of vampires and their human slaves that centuries ago was burned to the ground. Now it has risen from the ashes to open its dark doors once more. Only one person can save the world from impending doom—Turquoise Draka, famed human vampire who has the power and will to kill the most malevolent Midnight vampire, Jeshikah. The resulting adventures provide plenty of hair-raising turns and ironic twists.

8.9 Atwater-Rhodes, Amelia. **Shattered Mirror.** Delacorte, 2001. 228 pp. ISBN 0-385-32793-5. Fiction

As seventeen-year-old Sarah, daughter of a powerful line of vampire-hunting witches, continues to pursue the ancient bloodsucking vampire Nikolas, she finds herself in a dangerous friendship with two vampire siblings in her high school. Readers will enjoy the scenes of high school life, the inevitable conflicts of growing up, and the haunting qualities of Sarah's high school friends.

8.10 Bauer, Steven. **A Cat of a Different Color.** Illustrated by Tim Raglin. Delacorte, 2000. 197 pp. ISBN 0-385-32710-2. Fiction

Soon after electing Mayor Hoytie, the townspeople of Felicity-by-the-Lake regret voting for the candidate who gave them free bonbons. The town becomes a somber place when Mayor Hoytie establishes new rules declaring all fun off-limits to everyone except his family. Ulwazzer, a cat unique in his ability to change color, and Mrs. Hoytie's orphaned distant cousin Daria team up to restore the town to its former idyllic state.

8.11 Beaverson, Aiden. **The Hidden Arrow of Maether.** Delacorte, 2000. 177 pp. ISBN 0-385-32750-1. Fiction

Linn's dead father abhorred the worship of Rane, but her abusive stepfather wants to marry her off to a cult leader. Linn's escape is only the first of her tests in a pilgrimage that will consistently force her to choose between good and evil. This is the first novel in a series as Linn joins the ranks of those mythical people who bear the lysemarks.

8.12 Billingsley, Franny. **The Folk Keeper.** Aladdin, 2001. 161 pp. ISBN 0-689-84461-1. Fiction

Corinna, a skinny and awkward orphan, passes herself off as a boy (Corin) and becomes the folk keeper. Corinna/Corin tells her story through journals, from which we learn that the job of folk keeper requires the strength of will and the power to fend off the destructive power of the folk—mysterious, carnivorous creatures that live beneath the earth. If their voracious appetites are not appeased with food left in dark cellars, the folk will plague humankind with horrible mischief or bad luck.

8.13 Browne, N. M. **Warriors of Alavna.** Bloomsbury, 2000. 308 pp. ISBN 1-58234-775-1. Fiction

After wandering into a mysterious mist, contemporary British teenagers Dan and Ursula find themselves in a wild, unfamiliar place. Eventually they realize they have passed into first-century Great Britain, where tribes of Celtic warriors battle Roman legions and magic is taken for granted. Dan discovers he has great prowess as a fighter, and Ursula learns she has power as a priestess. Both are tested as they vow to avenge the village of Alavna, ravaged by Roman soldiers.

8.14 Casanova, Mary. **Curse of a Winter Moon.** Hyperion, 2000. 137 pp. ISBN 0-7868-2475-1. Fiction

Although he longs to pursue his gift for music, Marius must serve as protector for his younger brother, Jean-Pierre, whose Christmas Eve birthday causes the villagers to suspect he is a werewolf. As religious tensions mount and fear spreads in the sixteenth-century France village, endangering his family further, Marius is faced with a terrible choice.

8.15 Colfer, Eoin. **Artemis Fowl.** Hyperion, 2001. 277 pp. ISBN 0-7868-0801-2. Fiction

Artemis may not be everybody's hero: he's smart, rich, and inclined toward crime. This inclination is part of his heritage; the Fowls have been making deals people can't refuse for a long time. For that matter, the leprechauns are hardly typical either, and when Artemis seeks to mend the family fortunes by kidnapping one, his action sets off a chain reaction of bluff and double bluff, all played without much sentimentality or fabled Irish charm.

8.16 Corlett, William. **The Bridge in the Clouds.** Pocket, 2001 (Originally published in 1992). 342 pp. ISBN 0-7434-1004-1. Fiction

William Constant and his younger sisters travel to Golden House in Wales for their holidays. But this seemingly innocent vacation is a turning point in their lives. Something is wrong at Golden House: Morden's evil rats are everywhere and the children can't find the magician. Wondering if he is ill, they decide they must risk their lives traveling back in time to lead the final battle in order to keep Morden from becoming all-powerful while they search for the magician.

8.17 Coville, Bruce, editor. **Half-Human.** Scholastic, 2001. 212 pp. ISBN 0-590-95944-1. Fiction

This collection of ten short stories is aptly titled. Each features a different central character who is half human and half animal and struggling with identity. A story by Gregory Maguire, for example, tells the origin of the scarecrow from *The Wizard of Oz.* Other authors include Jude Mandell, Jane Yolen, Tamora Pierce, and Nancy Springer. The last short story in this collection is a complex tale by Bruce Coville about an old crone who is half snake.

8.18 Coville, Bruce. **Jennifer Murdley's Toad.** Illustrated by Gary A. Lippincott. Harcourt, 2002 (Originally published in 1992). 159 pp. ISBN 0-15-204613-5. Fiction

Jennifer Murdley leaves Mr. Elives's magic shop with Bufo, a talking toad. Soon people she knows are being transformed into toads and then back again with a simple kiss. Convinced she is unattractive, Jennifer is eventually transformed into a toad herself. When a witch offers to transform Jennifer into a beautiful person, Jennifer must decide whether beauty can truly replace happiness. This book is part of A Magic Shop Book series.

8.19 Coville, Bruce. **Jeremy Thatcher, Dragon Hatcher.** Illustrated by Gary A. Lippincott. Harcourt, 2002 (Originally published in 1991). 151 pp. ISBN 0-15-204614-3. Fiction

This hilarious fantasy takes us into the world of twelve-year-old Jeremy Thatcher who unknowingly buys a dragon's egg. The dragon comes alive and leads our hero on a spirited and humorous adventure. Originally published in 1991, this story has been updated with line-drawn illustrations designed to vividly depict Jeremy's magical adventure and escape into a world of make-believe.

8.20 Coville, Bruce. **The Monsters of Morley Manor.** Harcourt, 2001. 224 pp. ISBN 0-15-2163892-4. Fiction

Anthony and his younger sister are intrigued by a neighborhood "supposedly haunted" estate home called Morley Manor. According to legend, Morley Manor is the home of ghosts, and Anthony and Sarah are determined to see for themselves. They stumble across a mysterious box at Morley Manor that yields all sorts of surprises. The result—a whimsical read about two young people who experience fantastical journeys to other worlds in an effort to save planet Earth.

8.21 Coville, Bruce. **The Monster's Ring.** Illustrated by Katherine Coville. Harcourt, 2002 (Originally published in 1982). 100 pp. ISBN 0-15-204618-6. Fiction

When Russell Crannaker stumbles into a mystery magic shop while running from the schoolyard bully, he begins an adventure larger than his monster fantasies. The ring the magician sells Russell prompts a whirlwind of changes involving his relationship with the bully, his self-confidence, and even his appearance. Ultimately, Russell's actions may bring more trouble than he bargained for. This book is part of A Magic Shop Book series.

8.22 Coville, Bruce. **Odder Than Ever.** Hartcourt Brace, 1999. 146 pp. ISBN 0-15-201747-X. Fiction

Bruce Coville does it again with this collection of nine short stories that push the boundaries of imagination. Whether forced to live in the cavity of a giant's tooth or to battle a very real monster under the bed, his characters combine ingenuity, pluck, and a sense of humor to cope with their predicaments and fears. Three of the stories are published in this collection for the first time.

8.23 Coville, Bruce. **The Skull of Truth.** Illustrated by Gary A. Lippincott. Harcourt, 2002 (Originally published in 1997). 194 pp. ISBN 0-15-204612-7. Fiction

Charlie is a sixth grader with a compulsion to tell lies. When Charlie wanders into Mr. Elives's magic shop, he spies a mysterious skull that forces its owner to tell only the truth. Although Charlie is a liar, not a crook, somehow he feels compelled to steal the skull, and having done so, he spends the rest of the story enmeshed in awkward moments before he fully realizes the error of his ways.

8.24 Cowley, Joy. **Starbright and the Dream Eater.** HarperCollins, 2000. 199 pp. ISBN 0-06-02842-0. Fiction

Starbright is twelve years old, yet she is the only one who can save the world. Spindle sickness is infecting people while they sleep. What appears to be a deadly virus, however, is really a Dream Eater, a being of pure energy with a highly formed intelligence. With the help of a stranger who appears to have the information necessary to defeat this energy, Starbright goes into the dream world to fight the villain.

8.25 Curley, Marianne. **The Named.** Bloomsbury, 2002. 333 pp. ISBN 0-7475-5764-0. Fiction

As if being a regular kid in school isn't enough, Ethan is also one of The Named, charged with protecting the present and future from those who wish to change history. His grades begin to suffer as his larger assignment takes more and more of his nonschool time and his two separate roles begin to intersect. Ethan's classmate Isobel becomes his apprentice and helps him as they travel back in time to fight evil, in this first book of a trilogy.

8.26 Dahl, Roald. **Charlie and the Chocolate Factory.** Illustrated by Quentin Blake. Knopf, 2001 (Originally published in 1964). 162 pp. ISBN 0-375-81526-0. Fiction

Five young children—Augustus Gloop, who eats himself sick; Veruca Salt, who is spoiled rotten; Violet Beauregarde, who chews gum day and night; Mike Teeve, a television fiend; and Charlie Bucket, our hero—learn they are the lucky winners of a contest to take a tour of Mr. Willy Wonka's world famous chocolate factory. Problems arise when four of the five children receive their just desserts for taking advantage of this rare and special privilege.

8.27 Dahl, Roald. **Charlie and the Great Glass Elevator.** Illustrated by Quentin Blake. Knopf, 2001 (Originally published in 1972). 167 pp. ISBN 0-375-81525-2. Fiction

This sequel to *Charlie and the Chocolate Factory* finds Mr. Wonka, Charlie, and his grandparents launched into space on the great glass elevator from the Willy Wonka factory. Propelled into the outer regions of the universe, they stumble from one adventure to the next, with Charlie finally saving the day—to the delight of readers everywhere.

8.28 Dahl, Roald. **George's Marvelous Medicine.** Illustrated by Quentin Blake. Knopf, 2002 (Originally published in 1981). 89 pp. ISBN 0-375-82206-2. Fiction

The fun begins when George, left alone with his "grizzly old grunion" of a grandmother, decides to replace her regular medicine with a concoction of his own meant to make her more pleasant. When a mix of ingredients such as hairspray, horseradish sauce, cow pills, and brown paint causes Grandma to outgrow the house, George's father enlists his son to make a new batch for a get-rich-quick scheme. Unfortunately, George can't quite recreate the medicine, and amusing results ensue.

8.29 Dickinson, Peter. **The Ropemaker.** Delacorte, 2001. 375 pp. ISBN 0-385-72921-9. Fiction

For many generations, the valley has been safe from a rapacious empire. But not even magic incantations or spells of protection last forever. As the magic weakens, two young people, each with a grandparent, seek to extend the safety. It is Filja who captures the lion's share of the reader's attention; she finds healing in the relationship with her grandmother, and this intergenerational attachment is one of the most creative aspects of Dickinson's novel.

8.30 Downing, Wick. **Leonardo's Hand.** Houghton Mifflin, 2001. 201 pp. ISBN 0-618-07893-2. Fiction

Orphan Leonard "Nard" Smith ends up in a foster home with a family struggling to keep their farm from developers. Born without one hand, Nard finds a friend in Julie, who understands him and his physical disability. In a narrative that combines realism with magic, Nard is visited by a spirit friend who communicates through writings and drawings. Helped by the "Hand," they enter a contest, hoping to win enough money to keep the farm and pay for surgery that Julie desperately needs.

8.31 Etchemendy, Nancy. **The Power of UN.** Front Street/Cricket Books, 2000. 148 pp. ISBN 0-8126-2850-0. Fiction

Gib Finney is given a device that will allow him to undo what has happened in the past. At first he thinks this is better than winning the lottery, but soon things begin to go wrong. After a terrible traffic accident, Gib must decide which events in the past two days he must change in order to prevent disaster. Gib soon learns that some things are more worthy of an "undo" than others and that some events may be impossible to change.

8.32 Ewing, Lynne. **Goddess of the Night.** Hyperion, 2000. 294 pp. ISBN 0-786-80653-2. Fiction

Ewing, Lynne. **Into the Cold Fire.** Hyperion, 2000. 264 pp. ISBN 0-786-80654-0. Fiction

Vanessa, Catty, Serena, and Jimena are teenagers living in contemporary Los Angeles. All of them possess a gift—the ability to become invisible, for example, or the ability to read minds—because they are Daughters of the Moon, mortals whose mother was Selene, the goddess of the moon. These powers help the friends confront the Atrox, a dark force of evil. Although each book in the Daughters of the Moon series centers on a challenge faced by a different girl, all four teens appear in every story.

8.33 Gliori, Debi. **Pure Dead Magic.** Knopf, 2001. 182 pp. ISBN 0-375-81410-8. Fiction

Pure dead in the dialect of Glasgow, Scotland, means "very fine indeed, verging on the excellent." Here is a story involving a kidnapped father, a witchcraft-preoccupied mother, a shrunk and e-mailed sibling, a gamboling gangster, and one very unusual nanny. The setting for all the strange antics is a Scottish castle. Humor and tongue-in-cheek wit are the hallmarks of this madcap family and its outrageously comical trials and tribulations.

8.34 Gray, Luli. **Falcon and the Charles Street Witch.** Houghton Mifflin, 2002. 138 pp. ISBN 0-618-16410-3. Fiction

Twelve-year-old Falcon longs to see her beloved dragon, Egg, again, but alas it has flown off into the night, never to be seen again. But when Falcon leaps out of a plane after her younger brother Toody (Toody jumps out because he is in a hurry), young Falcon begins a series of magical misadventures that entail a distracted old dragon, a bumbling witch, a saved brother, and a reunion with her favorite dragon.

8.35 Griffin, Peni R. **The Ghost Sitter.** Dutton, 2001. 131 pp. ISBN 0-525-46676-2. Fiction

When Charlotte and her family move into a new house, strange things happen, such as her little brother talking to an invisible presence. The girl next door believes their house is haunted. The pair begins to trace the history of a ten-year-old girl who used to live in Charlotte's house but who died in a firecracker accident fifty years ago. Charlotte must find a way to help the ghost remember her past and accept her death before it is too late.

8.36 Herman, John. **Labryinth.** Philomel, 2001. 188 pp. ISBN 0-399-23571-X. Fiction

Gregory is plagued by two life-altering events: his father's suicide and his mother's possible remarriage. Struggling to cope, Gregory retreats into a dream world, where he battles the question of what is real. Caught between two worlds—one dream and one real—Gregory embarks on a mission to save the world and himself from the fierce Minotaur, a creature that is half bull and half man. The ensuing struggle is compelling and also revealing about coping with real and imagined stress.

8.37 Hirsch, Odo. **Bartlett and the Ice Voyage.** Illustrated by Andrew McLean. Bloomsbury, 2003. 176 pp. ISBN 1-58234-797-2. Fiction

The young queen who rules seven kingdoms has loyal subjects who bring her gifts from far and wide. Still, the one thing the young queen longs for is the elusive melidrop, a highly coveted fruit that has, alas, never reached the queen's home in a state fit to eat. So young Bartlett, an adventurer par excellence, sets out to capture this prized possession in a whimsical and fantasy-laden adventure story filled with clever plot twists and humorous dialogue.

8.38 Hoban, Russell. **The Mouse and His Child.** Illustrated by David Small. Arthur A. Levine Books, 2001 (Originally published in 1967). 244 pp. ISBN 0-439-09826-2. Fiction

Updated with charcoal-and-ink illustrations by David Small, this classic fantasy follows the complicated journey of a mouse and his son, tin windup toys, looking for territory to call their own. Their arch nemesis Manny Rat, a devilish rat from the city dump, seeks to capture and destroy them. Mouse and his son meet a menagerie of characters as they pursue their quest to become self-winding. Funny, sad, and at times violent, this tale appeals to all ages.

8.39 Hughes, Carol. **Jack Black & the Ship of Thieves.** Random House, 2000. 231 pp. ISBN 0-375-90472-7. Fiction

Jack Black sets sail with his father on *Bellerophon*, the largest airship in the world. A freak accident sends Jack tumbling thousands of feet down onto a pirate's ship. Now held captive, he must convince the pirates to search for the *Bellerophon* to save his father. Their wild voyage takes them through many dangerous adventures with sea monsters, a deadly ocean-going war machine, and wild storms.

8.40 Ibbotson, Eva. **Island of the Aunts.** Puffin, 2001. 281 pp. ISBN 0-14-230049-7. Fiction

Somewhere in the middle of the sea is an island from which magic has not fled; indeed, it is all too alive and getting to be too much for the elderly aunts to handle. And so they enlist (kidnap) the aid of certain children. Two of the children know they have found their real home on the island, but a third is unhappy. The unhappy child's father comes looking for him, triggering a series of events.

8.41 Ibbotson, Eva. **The Secret of Platform 13.** Illustrated by Sue Porter. Puffin, 1998 (Originally published in 1994). 231 pp. ISBN 0-14-130286-0. Fiction.

Once every nine years the passage between earth (normal earth) and the island opens. When the baby prince's nurses are overcome by the smell of fish and chips from their long-ago London home, the baby is stolen, and it is up to Odge Gribble, a failure as a hag but a rousing success as a rescuer, to bring the young prince home.

8.42 Ibbotson, Eva. **Which Witch?** Illustrated by Annabel Large. Puffin, 2000 (Originally published in 1979). 249 pp. ISBN 0-14-130427-8. Fiction

The appealing Belladonna is smitten with Arriman the Awful, but the competition for him is fierce, full of comically dreadful magic that can be trusted to go awry. Add to this mixture young Terence, who appears a natural "to extend the frontiers of wizardry and darkness" just as soon as he can manage to escape from the orphanage, and the recipe for mayhem is complete.

8.43 Jarvis, Robin. **The Crystal Prison.** SeaStar, 2001 (Originally published in 1989). 246 pp. ISBN 1-58717-107-4. Fiction

In this sequel to *The Dark Portal,* the Deptford mice come up from the sewers, but Oswald, a young mouse, falls deathly ill. Starwife, the squirrel mystic, declares that Oswald will be saved only if Audrey Brown and her brother accompany the rat, Madame Akkikuyu, to the field mouse society in the countryside. Once there, however, Audrey is accused of horrible murders as menacing evil swirls all around her. At the conclusion, the reader discovers what happens to the Crystal Prison.

8.44 Jarvis, Robin. **The Dark Portal.** SeaStar, 2000 (Originally published in 1989). 243 pp. ISBN 1-58717-021-3. Fiction

The Browns are a family of mice living in Deptford, London. Albert Brown is irresistibly drawn to The Grill, a passage leading to the dangerous sewers below the city. While exploring The Grill, Albert learns that the rats are planning something ominous. Join Albert and his band of mice friends as they fight to save all of London from the evil lurking below. This is the first book in the three-book Deptford Mice Trilogy series.

8.45 Jennings, Richard. **Orwell's Luck.** Houghton Mifflin, 2000. 146 pp. ISBN 0-618-03628-8. Fiction

Orwell, a fortune-teller, comes to live with an average family from the suburbs. There is, however, one small catch: Orwell is a rabbit. An avid reader of the daily horoscopes, Orwell's twelve-year-old caretaker is certain that her life is controlled by fate. When she begins receiving coded messages, she becomes convinced that Orwell has the power to foretell the future. Acting on the messages, this seventh grader learns to look at life from more than one angle.

8.46 King-Smith, Dick. **The Roundhill.** Illustrated by Siân Bailey. Dell Yearling, 2002. 84 pp. ISBN 0-44-041844-5. Fiction

Fourteen-year-old Evan, home on a school holiday, is fascinated with a girl he repeatedly encounters at Roundhill, his special, secret spot. As their relationship progresses, it is characterized by a wistful, old-fashioned charm that emanates from Alice and intrigues Evan. Why does she speak in riddles? Why does she remind him of *Alice in Wonderland*? Like Evan, the reader picks up clues about the mysterious Alice until her true identity is shockingly revealed in this story set in 1936 England.

8.47 Langton, Jane. **The Time Bike.** HarperCollins, 2000. 176 pp. ISBN 0-06-028437-4. Fiction

The Hall family has the most extraordinary adventures, from finding enchanted diamonds to flying with geese. In this sixth book about the Halls, Eddy is given an old-fashioned bicycle for his birthday. While it looks unassuming and unappealing, it possesses the ability to travel through time. Eddy discovers that travel in the fourth dimension offers glimpses into the recent and not-so-recent past. He learns too that his travels are not without consequences.

8.48 Lee, Tanith. **Wolf Star.** Dutton, 2001. 232 pp. ISBN 0-525-46673-8. Fiction

This sequel to *Wolf Tower* in The Claidi Journals series tells, through her diary, Claidi's story of kidnapping and fantasy adventure. She is kidnapped on her wedding day and taken to a castle complete with realistic robots, constantly moving and shifting rooms and staircases, unusual animals, and the fascinating Wolf Star. Prince Venn eerily resembles Argul, Princess Claidi's fiancé, and the mystery is ultimately a story of separation and reconciliation. Claidi's tone and voice are realistic despite the fantasy setting.

8.49 Lee, Tanith. **Wolf Tower.** Dutton, 2000. 223 pp. ISBN 0-525-46394-1. Fiction

Claidi escapes her slave life in the House with a handsome young man from the forbidden Waste. They travel a long journey together, and although she is falling in love with him, Claidi still doesn't understand why. She keeps a detailed journal of their experiences, which allows the reader to learn her secrets. The story begins as a hopeful journey—until they reach their destination of Wolf Tower.

8.50 Levine, Gail Carson. **The Wish.** HarperCollins, 2000. 197 pp. ISBN 0-06-027900-1. Fiction

Wilma Sturtz is an average middle school student. She makes average grades, has average looks, and enjoys average things. This is a problem, however, because Wilma despises being average. She longs to be recognized, to be noticed, to be popular. Armed with the belief that being part of the in-crowd will make her world perfect, Wilma meets a peculiar old lady who grants wishes. Instantly, Wilma has more friends than she can count. Life is perfect, but for how long?

8.51 McCaughrean, Geraldine. **The Stones are Hatching.** HarperCollins, 2000. 230 pp. ISBN 0-06-028765-9. Fiction

The Stoor Worm is waking! An evil and monstrous creature bent on destroying the world, its murderous hatchlings are already terrorizing Britain. Phelim, an ordinary boy of eleven who just happens to believe in ghosts and magic, is the only one who can save the world. On his strange odyssey, Phelim meets mythical creatures, has terrifying adventures, and outwits death several times until he finally learns the lessons he needs to save the world. But will he be in time?

8.52 McCutchen, H. L. **LightLand.** Orchard, 2002. 229 pp. ISBN 0-439-39565-8. Fiction

Lottie Cook is twelve when her father gives her the special memory box in which to store memories of her mother and stories of her past. With her best friend Lewis, Lottie is able to travel to LightLand, a fantasy place created from people's collective memories. Here the evil NightKing preserved his kingdom by stealing the memories of others. To destroy him, the young characters must take ownership of their own painful pasts and confront the challenges of living in the present.

8.53 Molloy, Michael. **The Time Witches.** Scholastic, 2002. 255 pp. ISBN 0-439-42090-3. Fiction

This sequel to *The Witch Trade* exhaustively reviews the previous book before launching the main characters into a back-to-the-future-like plot involving time travel to 1894, coincidences, and questions about the ethics of altering the past and the future. The Night and Light Witches again plot against one another, and the many plot elements finally come together. Abby starts to come into her own as a potentially powerful Light Witch.

8.54 Molloy, Michael. **The Witch Trade.** Scholastic, 2001. 256 pp. ISBN 0-439-29659-5. Fiction

Abby and Spike both discover their unusual powers after they befriend Captain Starlight and join the battle of the Light Witches against the Night Witches for control of the powerful Ice Dust. Ice Dust, a white powder, must be present in the Light Witches' spells, but the Night Witches have discovered a way to mix it with toxic waste, thus creating the dangerous Black Dust. In the struggle of good versus evil, who will possess the Ice Dust?

8.55 Nicholson, William. **The Wind Singer.** Illustrated by Peter Sis. Hyperion, 2000. 358 pp. ISBN 0-78682494-8. Fiction

Hard work, testing, and upward mobility with no time for ideas or dreams is the approved way of life in the city of Aramanth. Teenage twins Kestrel and Bowman, with their friend Mumpo, use their individual strengths to combat this conformist and repressive society by restoring the key to the Wind Singer so that Aramanth can be saved from its rigid leadership. This book combines themes from *The Giver, The Lord of the Rings, Pleasantville, Animal Farm,* and *Gulliver's Travels.*

8.56 Nimmo, Jenny. **Midnight for Charlie Bone.** Orchard, 2002. 401 pp. ISBN 0-439-47429-9. Fiction

Charlie Bone receives the powers of the Red King. Some of these gifts are evil and some are good, but Charlie is not sure he wants any of them. When he realizes he can overhear the thoughts of individuals captured in photographs, his horrible aunts are delighted—now they can send him off to Bloor's Academy for Gifted Children. There, Charlie meets other children like himself who have a wide array of mysterious powers, and together they help their friend Emma.

8.57 Pierce, Tamora. **Shatterglass.** Scholastic, 2003. 361 pp. ISBN 0-590-39683-8. Fiction

A gifted glassmaker makes beautiful art objects until a freak lightning accident destroys his world. Helping him to cope is Tris, a young magician-in-training, who helps the glassmaker recapture his talent by using a strange new magic—one of the pieces of shattered glass that now reflects the past—and in so doing expose a murderer. Together, Tris and the glassmaker race against time to identify a killer who is in plain sight.

8.58 Pierce, Tamora. **Squire.** Random House, 2001. 399 pp. ISBN 0-679-88916-7. Fiction

Kel faces the same obstacle many women and girls face: survival in a man's world. There is, however, one major difference. The man's world she is attempting to enter is that of knighthood. Throughout her training, Kel's gift of communicating with animals enables her to excel in her role in the king and queen's realm. Unfortunately, this communication means nothing as she faces her last hurdle: surviving the Ordeal in the magical chamber, a place where she must confront her innermost fears.

8.59 Pierce, Tamora. **Street Magic.** Scholastic, 2001. 293 pp. ISBN 0-590-39628-5. Fiction

Former child thief and gang member Briar Moss, now mostly rehabilitated and a powerful magi, spots a street waif whose magical gift is with stones. The teenaged Briar accepts responsibility for the little girl, but in a corrupt and ancient city it's not long before both come to the attention of a vicious manipulator of child gangs. Can Briar put his past behind him and find a way to protect both of them?

8.60 Pullman, Philip. **The Amber Spy Glass**. Knopf, 2000. 518 pp. ISBN 0-679-87926-9. Fiction

In this startling and provocative conclusion to the His Dark Materials trilogy, Lyra is at the center of the struggle either to conserve or to jettison the mysterious energy, called dust, at the heart of the universe. Because it is defined as the consequence of original sin, this energy has launched a religious crusade to purge it from all worlds. Will, Lyra, and their friends, however, suspect that dust is connected to the essence of joy and thus undertake a sacred pilgrimage of their own as a counteroffensive.

8.61 Reiss, Kathryn. **Time Windows.** Harcourt, 2000 (Originally published in 1991). 260 pp. ISBN 0-15-202399-2. Fiction

Moving to Massachusetts with her parents, Miranda is intrigued by an old dollhouse in the attic that is an exact replica of her new home. She is also troubled by her mother's mysterious behavior change. Peering in the dollhouse windows, Miranda can see the past and discovers a girl whose angry mother locked her in the attic. As her own mother becomes more abusive, Miranda must find a way to release the women of the house from its evil spell.

8.62 Roberts, Katherine. **Song Quest.** Chicken House/Scholastic, 2002. 256 pp. ISBN 0-439-33892-1. Fiction

The Isle of Echoes is a fantasy world held together by magical creatures called the Singers. The Singers, who have the ability to heal with their beautiful songs, live harmoniously with their half-creature friends, the water and the waves. This magical world is challenged when Singers Rialle and Kherron are forced to travel afar to face an enemy. They must work together to overcome the darkness that may destroy their world.

8.63 Roberts, Katherine. **Spellfall.** Scholastic, 2000. 250 pp. ISBN 0-439-29653-6. Fiction

Natalie discovers a strange candy wrapper floating in a parking lot puddle. Accompanying the wrapper is an ominous yellow-eyed man who promptly informs Natalie that the wrapper is a witch's spell. What unfolds next is a bewitching tale of kidnapping and sorcery, sure to delight readers intrigued with fantasy and adventure, that includes a message of care and concern for the natural world.

8.64 Rowling, J. K. ["Newt Scamander"]. **Fantastic Beasts and Where to Find Them.** Arthur A. Levine books, 2001. 42 pp. ISBN 0-439-29501-7. Fiction

Many readers will find that the real lure of this compilation is its marginal notes, which consist of Harry's and Ron's comments on the text. Given all of the beasts, insects, and so forth mentioned here, the scope is wide. Some of these creatures will be familiar to Harry Potter addicts; we can only hope to make the acquaintance of the rest of this fantastic menagerie in future additions to the series. This slim collection is one of the two works Rowling wrote for a British charity.

8.65 Rowling, J. K. ["Kennilworthy Whisp"]. **Quidditch through the Ages.** Arthur A. Levine Books. 2001. 56 pp. ISBN 0-439-29502-5. Fiction

When Rita Skeeter of *The Daily Prophet* is quoted as saying, "I've read worse," and with a foreword by Albus Dumbledore, Harry Potter fans can be confident that this collection of interesting facts about the genesis of Hogwarts School's favorite game will add to their appreciation of all things magical. The early versions of quidditch are meticulously researched, including a poignant description of the near-extinction of the birds who were the original golden snitches.

8.66 Shan, Darren. **Tunnels of Blood.** Little, Brown, 2002. 224 pp. ISBN 0-316-607630-0. Fiction

Teenage vampire Darren Shan is just becoming familiar with his new powers when his mentor, Mr. Crepsley, demands that Darren and his friend Evra, otherwise known as Snake Boy, leave the circus they have called home. When they settle in a new city, however, Crepsley's enemy Murlough abducts Evra and threatens to kill him on Christmas, forcing Darren to make a terrible choice between friendship and a new romance. This is the third book in the ongoing Cirque du Freak series.

8.67 Shan, Darren. **The Vampire's Assistant.** Little, Brown, 2001. 241 pp. ISBN 0-316-60610-3. Fiction

This is the second book in the Cirque du Freak series about the eponymous Darren Shan, who becomes a half vampire to save his friend's life. Darren is not going gently into vampiredom; he insists on making friends and being loyal to them, and he is appalled by the compulsions of his new nature.

8.68 Taylor, Theodore. **The Boy Who Could Fly without a Motor.** Harcourt, 2002. 144 pp. ISBN 0-15-216529-0. Fiction

Jon Jeffers thinks he might be the loneliest boy on earth. He lives on a tiny rocky island off the coast of San Francisco with his mother and father, who is the lighthouse keeper for the coast guard. Jon's greatest dream, being able to fly, becomes a reality when a mysterious, ancient man appears and teaches him the secret of levitation. Unfortunately, Jon's new gift of flight gets him into a bit of trouble.

8.69 Thesman, Jean. **The Other Ones.** Puffin, 2001. 181 pp. ISBN 0-670-88594-0. Fiction

Bridget recently discovered that she is a witch, but the only person she can talk to about it is her aunt, who is also a practicing witch. At the same time, Bridget is struggling with being a normal teenager. Trouble with friends, teachers, and parents seem to be overpowering her when a strange new girl comes to town. Bridget must solve the mystery of the new girl and her family before it is too late.

8.70 Thompson, Kate. **Wild Blood.** Hyperion, 2002. 261 pp. ISBN 0-786-81422-5. Fiction

Tess, a fourteen-year-old girl who can switch from human form to animal form at will until her fifteenth birthday, agonizes over her dilemma—should she remain a human forever, or take on an animal form. Before deciding, Tess switches to animal form and locates her missing cousins who have mysteriously disappeared in a forest where their uncle had disappeared years earlier.

8.71 Tolkein, J. R. R. **Bilbo's Last Song.** Knopf, 2002. 31 pp. ISBN 0-375-82373-5. Fiction/poetry

This beautifully illustrated poem is an epilogue to Tolkein's masterpiece, *The Lord of the Rings.* Saying goodbye to Middle-earth,

Bilbo Baggins takes his final voyage, to the Undying Lands. This poem is Bilbo's farewell to his friends and the beginning of a new journey.

8.72 Tolkien, J. R. R. **The Hobbit, or, There and Back Again.** Houghton Mifflin, 2001 (Originally published in 1937). 330 pp. ISBN 0-618-15082-X. Fiction

Tolkien's masterpiece of fantasy has been reissued with corrections made from previous texts to conform to what is perceived as the author's intended form. This is the story of Bilbo Baggins, a hobbit, and his wondrous adventures with wizards, dragons, elves, and dwarfs in a world of magic and fantasy. It is a journey from the safe confines of home and self to the unknown land of adventure and discovery and back again.

8.73 Turner, Megan Whalen. **The Queen of Attolia.** Greenwillow, 2000. 279 pp. ISBN 0-688-17423-X. Fiction

Trapped in the enemy castle of Attolia, Eugenides, the Royal Thief of Eddis, finds himself awaiting a death sentence. But instead the queen of Attolia orders Eugenides' right hand to be cut off, which humiliates him and renders him unable to pilfer items for the queen of Eddis. In order to save Eddis from being overtaken by her enemies, Eugenides is asked to rise above his shame and steal the unthinkable: the heart of Attolia's queen.

8.74 Vande Velde, Vivian. **Being Dead.** Harcourt, 2001. 203 pp. ISBN 0-15-216320-4. Fiction

These ghost stories will keep readers on the edge of their seats. The collection of stories is set up in a conventional manner, and the characters interact with one another through conversation more than situation. Readers are lulled into thinking these will be regular stories about people much like themselves. But the author always manages to sneak in the twist and turn expectations upside down until the realization sets in: the clues have been present all along.

8.75 Venokur, Ross. **The Autobiography of Meatball Finkelstein.** Delacorte, 2001. 153 pp. ISBN 0-385-32798-6. Fiction

Meatball Finkelstein is big. He was born big—twenty-seven pounds of big. Unlike his sister Precious, Meatball has no accomplishments. Instead he spends his days trying to be invisible, hoping to avoid the "session" with Rufus Delaney, a really bad-smelling bully at school. Meatball has accepted his role in life as one of humongous size and unimportance. He soon discovers, however, that he possesses a unique, magical power and that it is up to him to save all kids.

8.76 Voight, Cynthia. **Elske.** Aladdin, 2001. 245 pp. ISBN 0-689-84444-1. Fiction

Elske, the death maiden of the Volkaric people, is saved from death by her grandmother's sacrifice. Trusting in fate, she wanders to Trastad and becomes servant to Beriel, a future warrior queen of the kingdom. Both young women gain strength and courage from each other. This is a richly detailed, complex fantasy novel of betrayal, greed, loyalty, and triumph set in some past time when black powder (for weapons) was to that world what oil is today to our world.

8.77 Wilson, Jacqueline. **Vicky Angel.** Illustrated by Nick Sharratt. Delacorte, 2001. 172 pp. ISBN 0-385-72920-0. Fiction

After her lifelong best friend Vicky dies, Jade struggles with grief, guilt, and the domineering personality of Vicky's ghost. Turning up everywhere, Vicky's ghost soon upsets Jade, who despite her obvious sadness longs to live her life free of constant intrusions. Readers will relate both to the central character's struggle to come to terms with the death of her friend and to the haunting and perilous world of dealing with imaginary beings such as ghosts.

8.78 Winter, Laurel. **Growing Wings.** Houghton Mifflin, 2000. 195 pp. ISBN 0-618-07405-8. Fiction.

Linnett attends school and lives alone with her mother. For the most part, Linnett's life is a normal one until the excruciating itch and weird bumps form on her shoulders. And so begins the unraveling of her mother's secret. Linnett is not normal and her life never will be. She must learn to accept herself and try to find her place in a world that may not embrace her for who she is: a person with wings.

8.79 Wrede, Patricia C. **Dealing with Dragons.** Magic Carpet, 2002 (Originally published in 1990). 212 pp. ISBN 0-15-204566-X. Fiction

Wrede, Patricia C. **Searching for Dragons.** Magic Carpet, 2002 (Originally published in 1991). 242 pp. ISBN 0-15-204565-1. Fiction

The Enchanted Forest Chronicles feature Princess Cimorene, who constantly rebels against admonishments to be "proper." An outdoorsy type, intelligent, and strong-willed, Cimorene is also very *bored.* So she does what many bored young people do—she runs away, into the enchanted forest, where she eventually meets Kazul, the most dangerous of dragons, and a host of other magical creatures. Dashes of humor and romance are added to these tales of high adventure about a likable young woman and her enchanted stomping grounds.

8.80 Yolen, Jane. **The Bagpiper's Ghost.** Harcourt, 2002. 125 pp. ISBN 0-15-202310-0. Fiction

In this third book of the Tartan Magic Trilogy, twins Peter and Jennifer are in Scotland visiting relatives when they become entwined in the lives of ghost twins Mary and Andrew McFadden. The present-day thirteen-year-olds need to reunite Mary with her love, the ghostly bagpipe player, all the while seeking to free Peter from Andrew's possession. Weaving the past with the present, humor and adventure abound in this magical tale of love and deception.

8.81 Yolen, Jane. **Boots and the Seven Leaguers: A Rock-and-Troll Novel.** Harcourt, 2000. 159 pp. ISBN 0-15-202557-X. Fiction

Gog and his best friend are desperate to attend the sold-out concert of the most popular rock-and-troll band in the entire kingdom. When you're a troll, you resort to magic, so the two teens pass themselves off as roadies and get hired to work in return for free concert passes. When his little brother is kidnapped, however, Gog risks missing the concert to rescue Magog. He discovers that life's real rewards come in the form of family and friends.

8.82 Yolen, Jane. **The Pictish Child.** Magic Carpet, 2002. 135 pp. ISBN 0-15-216359-X. Fiction

Book two of the Tartan Magic Trilogy is the continuing story of three children from Connecticut who become involved with magic while visiting relatives in Scotland. This adventure finds Molly and twins Peter and Jennifer coming to the aid of a young Pictish lass, Ninia, who has escaped a massacre in the distant past but who is pursued by evil in the present. Can they come to the rescue of Ninia and help her return to her own era?

8.83 Yolen, Jane. **The Wizard's Map.** Magic Carpet, 2002. 146 pp. ISBN 0-15-216365-4. Fiction

Book one of the Tartan Magic Trilogy finds the American twins Jennifer and Peter, along with their younger sister Molly, visiting their mother's elderly relatives in Fife, Scotland, and becoming involved in magic. A rainy day in the attic becomes an adventure with a wizard's map, a disappearing sibling, and a talking dragon. This is a fanciful, fast-paced story in which virtue battles vice.

Fantasy Series

Green Knowe Chronicles

8.84 Boston, L. M. **The Children of Green Knowe.** Harcourt, 2002 (Originally published in 1955). 183 pp. ISBN 0-15-202468-9. Fiction

Boston, L. M. **Treasure of Green Knowe.** Harcourt, 2002 (Originally published in 1958). 214 pp. ISBN 0-15-202601-0. Fiction

Boston, L. M. **The River at Green Knowe.** Harcourt, 2002 (Originally published in 1959). 161 pp. ISBN 0-15-202607-X. Fiction

Boston, L. M. **The Stranger at Green Knowe.** Harcourt, 2002 (Originally published in 1961). 199 pp. ISBN 0-15-202589-8. Fiction

Boston, L. M. **An Enemy at Green Knowe.** Harcourt, 2002 (Originally published in 1964). 171 pp. ISBN 0-15-202481-6. Fiction

The first novel, *The Children of Green Knowe,* introduces the reader to Tolly, who comes to the manor to live with his great-grandmother and befriends its ghostly inhabitants. *Treasure of Green Knowe* finds Tolly returning to the manor only to discover that great-grandmother is in financial trouble and the possession of the estate in jeopardy. In *The River at Green Knowe,* we meet the children and wards of an eccentric anthropologist who rents the estate for the summer. The children discover a canoe and find enchantment and mystery along the numerous nearby waterways. *The Stranger at Green Knowe* finds the young Asian refugee Ping, one of the anthropologist's wards from the previous novel, living on the estate with Tolly's great-grandmother and befriending an escaped gorilla that makes the forest around the manor his new home. The final volume, the creepy *An Enemy at Green Knowe,* tells of a mad magician's search for the dark secrets of an old alchemist. The heart of all these novels is the centuries-old manor estate Green Knowe in England. Its rooms, halls, gardens, and general environs as well as inhabitants drift from era to era and from spiritual world to actual world with a subtle and comfortable ease. Indeed, the one character who provides a crucial link through almost all the novels (though she is absent in *The River at Greene Know*) is great-grandmother Oldknow. As her name suggests, her intimate knowledge of the events of the past hints at something secret about her nature.

Harry Potter series

8.85 Rowling, J. K. **Harry Potter and the Sorcerer's Stone.** Scholastic, 1999. 312 pp. ISBN 0-590-35342-X. Fiction

Rowling, J. K. **Harry Potter and the Chamber of Secrets.** Scholastic, 2000. 341 pp. ISBN 0-439-06487-2. Fiction

Rowling, J. K. **Harry Potter and the Prisoner of Azkaban.** Scholastic Trade, 2001. 435 pp. ISBN 0-439-13636-9. Fiction

Rowling, J. K. **Harry Potter and the Goblet of Fire.** Scholastic, 2002. 734 pp. ISBN 0-439-13960-0. Fiction

The basic plots, characters, and situations of all four novels are immediately familiar. Harry is the down-and-out-of-luck orphan who discovers his secret powers and identity and continually uses them to battle the forces of evil. What makes the novels more than retreads of tired plots, however, is Rowling's amazing ability to construct an intricate and enchanting parallel magical world that is just the right blend of historical, mythical, and current cultural references. Rounding out this mix is a wonderful sense of humor and playfulness with language. With each successive narrative, the conflict and characters become more complex as mysteries are unraveled, only to be replaced by newer, deeper ones.

Sweep series

8.86 Tiernan, Cate. **Blood Witch.** Puffin, 2001. 202 pp. ISBN 0-14-131111-8. Fiction

Tiernan, Cate. **Dark Magick.** Puffin, 2001. 186 pp. ISBN 0-14-131112-6. Fiction

Tiernan, Cate. **Awakening.** Puffin, 2001. 188 pp. ISBN 0-14-230045-4. Fiction

Tiernan, Cate. **Spellbound.** Puffin, 2001. 190 pp. ISBN 0-14-230046-2. Fiction

Filled with suspense, danger, and struggles between good and evil, this series chronicles the life and adventures of Morgan, a teenage blood witch. Trying to be just another teenager, Morgan discovers that her birth parents, now dead, were powerful witches and that she too has magical powers. Morgan struggles with what to do with her powers and who to trust. She knows witchcraft can be dangerous, but then she discovers that someone is trying to destroy her. Can she trust her boyfriend, or is he leading her into danger? Unsure who she can trust, Morgan must use her most powerful magic to survive and in doing so confront some unpleasant truths.

Young Wizards series

8.87 Duane, Diane. **So You Want to Be a Wizard.** Harcourt, 2001 (Originally published in 1983). 385 pp. ISBN 0-15-216250-X. Fiction

Duane, Diane. **Deep Wizardry.** Harcourt, 2001 (Originally published in 1985). 371 pp. ISBN 0-15-216257-7. Fiction

Duane, Diane. **High Wizardry.** Harcourt, 2001 (Originally published in 1990). 353 pp. ISBN 0-15-216244-5. Fiction

These three titles come as a boxed set, *Diane Duane's Box of Wizardry,* and constitute the first part of her Young Wizards series. This high fantasy series focuses on Nita, who is thirteen and living in Manhattan at the time she discovers she is going to be a wizard—a discovery that helps her deal with the bullies who have been tormenting her. The second book finds Nita and her friend Kit turning into whales during summer vacation as they help the whale-wizard combat the Master Shark. In the third installment, Nita and Kit face the challenge of finding Nita's little sister Dairine, whose wizard software sends her off across the galaxy. Even though Dairine is a smart young wizard with almost limitless wizard powers, Nita and Kit know that Dairine is facing trouble too deep to fight alone.

8.88 Duane, Diane. **The Wizard's Dilemma.** Harcourt, 2001. 403 pp. ISBN 0-15-202551-0. Fiction

Nina Callehan's mother has brain cancer, and Nina, a fledgling wizard, is determined to save her. In this fifth book in the Young Wizard series, we follow Nina in her travels as she struggles with good and evil, forced to learn wizard's knowledge along the way. She enlists the help of friends and mentors but ultimately discovers the secret herself and saves her mother.

8.89 Duane, Diane. **A Wizard Alone.** Harcourt, 2002. 320 pp. ISBN 0-15-204562-7. Fiction

Distraught over her mother's death, Nita is besieged by mysterious, disturbing dreams and unable to help her friend Kit search for Darryl, a young autistic wizard trapped for over three months in the middle of his Ordeal. With his dog Ponch's assistance, Kit desperately searches for Darryl before he is destroyed by the Lone Power. In this sixth book in the Young Wizards series, Nita must try to solve her own problems in time to help Kit and Ponch save Darryl.

9 The Arts, Architecture, and Other Creative Endeavors

9.1 Agee, Jon. **John Agee's Palindromania.** Farrar, Straus and Giroux, 2002. 62 pp. ISBN 0-374-35730-7. Nonfiction.

Palindromania is the excessive fascination with palindromes, the play with words and numbers that are exactly the same when read forward and backward. Agee's word pursuits use dialogues and monologues in amusing comic strip illustrations. This journey with words entertains readers while allowing them to develop an appreciation for palindromes.

9.2 Aller, Susan Bivin. **Mark Twain.** Lerner, 2001. 128 pp. ISBN 0-8225-4994-8. Nonfiction

Samuel Langhorne Clemens was a man who yearned for adventure. He found it—or it found him. Clemens, better known as Mark Twain, explored the Mississippi River, Hawaii, and Europe in search of stories he could share with his readers. Spellbound by the tales Twain told in newspaper articles, books, and lectures, listeners and readers clamored for more. Twain's life is detailed from early childhood through his death.

9.3 Ashabranner, Brent. **Badge of Valor: The National Law Enforcement Officers Memorial.** Photographs by Jennifer Ashabranner. Twenty-First Century Books, 2000. 64 pp. ISBN 0-7613-1522-5. Nonfiction

In 1984, President Ronald Reagan signed a new law that authorized the creation of the National Law Enforcement Memorial, a memorial that honors law enforcement officers who give their lives in the line of duty. Through both words and photographs, this book shares the seven-year process of the design and construction of this memorial. It also tells the story of some of the officers who have given their lives to keep this country safe for its citizens.

9.4 Ashabranner, Brent. **A Date with Destiny: The Women in Military Service for America Memorial.** Photographs by Jennifer Ashabranner. Twenty-First Century Books, 2000. 64 pp. ISBN 0-7613-1472-5. Nonfiction

In 1997 the first U.S. memorial in honor of American military women opened at the entrance of Arlington National Cemetery. In words and photographs, this book tells the story of the establishment of the monument and the behind-the-scenes work of creating it. It includes a brief history of women's involvement in the military, as well as stories of individuals whose sacrifices served as inspiration for the memorial.

9.5 Ashabranner, Brent. **No Better Hope: What the Lincoln Memorial Means to America.** Twenty-First Century Books, 2001. 64 pp. ISBN 0-7613-1523-3. Nonfiction

The conception and construction of the Lincoln Memorial from its inception after Lincoln's death through current preservation efforts are described in this book, which also provides a context for understanding Lincoln's place in American history and contemporary life. The author explains how the project was initially funded, describes how the actual structure was designed and built, and examines the completed monument's role in significant political and social events during the past century.

9.6 Ashabranner, Brent. **On the Mall in Washington, D.C.: A Visit to America's Front Yard.** Photographs by Jennifer Ashabranner. Twenty-First Century Books, 2002. 64 pp. ISBN 0-7613-2351-1. Nonfiction

This tour of the Mall in Washington, D.C., describes the many museums, galleries, and memorials located on this great lawn. Splendid sights such as the Washington Monument, Lincoln Memorial, and the Capitol are described in great detail. Historical snapshots of these special buildings and notes about the architects are included. The text is easy reading and can be used as an excellent classroom or personal resource.

9.7 Ashabranner, Brent. **The Washington Monument: A Beacon for America.** Photographs by Jennifer Ashabranner. Twenty-First Century Books, 2002. 64 pp. ISBN 0-7613-1524-1. Nonfiction

The glory of one of America's most recognized memorials comes alive through careful attention to facts and details. Colorful photographs, historical prints, and meticulous illustrations chronicle the history of this symbol of American freedom. The author discusses the history of the monument from development through design and construction and has included a fact sheet, visitor information, bibliography, and index.

9.8 Augustyn, Frank, and Shelley Tanaka. **Footnotes: Dancing the World's Best-Loved Ballets.** Millbrook, 2001. 94 pp. ISBN 0-7613-2323-6. Nonfiction

Did you ever wonder what ballet is all about? Frank Augustyn, former principal dancer for the National Ballet of Canada, describes the history of ballet since the introduction of the pointed toe shoe in the early nineteenth century. Although the pointed toe that has come to characterize modern ballet is a painful and unnatural weight-bearing position even for experienced dancers, these artists are willing to suffer as they present the best-loved stories of ballet through perfect body movement.

9.9 Benson, Michael. **Gloria Estefan.** Lerner, 2000. 112 pp. ISBN 0-8225-4982-4. Nonfiction

Arriving in this country from Cuba at the age of two, Gloria Estefan overcomes poverty, the tragic death of her father, and a serious back injury to become a world-renowned singer and entertainer. Believing that she can be anything she wants to be, this compassionate superstar becomes a successful wife, mother, singer, and songwriter. In recognition of her contributions, Estefan is awarded the Ellis Island Congressional Medal of Honor—the highest award given to a citizen born outside this country.

9.10 Bentley, Nancy, and Donna Guthrie. **Writing Mysteries, Movies, Monster Stories, and More.** Illustrated by Jeremy Tugeau. Millbrook, 2001. 75 pp. ISBN 0-7613-1452-0. Nonfiction

This book is designed to help the young author begin to write stories and get them published. Detailed descriptions of different genres are included along with guidelines for writing mysteries, speculative fiction, screenplays, and more. In the chapter on speculative fiction, for example, comic fantasy is defined as a genre that includes talking animals, tiny people, and humorous characters. Examples of book titles and authors for each genre are given, and a list of Web sites is also included.

9.11 Berenstain, Stan, and Berenstain, Jan. **Down a Sunny Dirt Road: An Autobiography.** Random House, 2002. 202 pp. ISBN 0-375-81403-5. Nonfiction

You don't need to be a fan of the Berenstain Bears to enjoy Stan and Jan Berenstain's autobiography, which is less about cute little bears and more about growing up during the Great Depression and World War II. The Berenstains learned early on that artistic talent rarely leads to instant fame and fortune. But their persistence paid off and took them from painting numbers on trash barrels and teaching children's art classes to worldwide fame as author-illustrators.

9.12 Branch, Muriel Miller. **Fine Arts and Crafts.** Twenty-First Century Books, 2001. 96 pp. ISBN 0-7613-1868-2. Nonfiction

In this fourth book in the African-American Arts series, a brief but pithy overview of three hundred years of African American art is richly enhanced by photographs, illustrations, a short glossary, and an excellent "further reading" section. History and biography are integrated effectively as the reader encounters artists in many fields including photography, pottery, sculpture, primitive art, basketry, clothing, metalwork, murals, and painting. Information on museums and art restoration is also included.

9.13 Carter, Don. **Heaven's All-Star Jazz Band.** Knopf, 2002. 32 pp. ISBN 0-375-81571-6. Fiction

You can almost hear the music as the young boy in this book describes all of his grandfather's favorite jazz musicians. The characters in each illustration seem to come off the page, leading readers into the Cotton Club, home of many jazz greats. The final page includes a short biographical sketch of each jazz musician mentioned in this picture book.

9.14 Christensen, Bonnie. **Woody Guthrie, Poet of the People.** Illustrated by Bonnie Christensen. Knopf, 2001. 32 pp. ISBN 0-375-81113-3. Nonfiction

This picture book biography recounts the events of Woody Guthrie's life through wonderful illustrations by the author and Guthrie's own words. Throughout the book, the lyrics of "This Land Is Your Land" frames the times and events of Guthrie's life, and both illustrations and text capture the era of the Great Depression.

9.15 Cooper, Michael L. **Slave Spirituals and the Jubilee Singers.** Clarion, 2001. 86 pp. ISBN 0-395-97829-7. Nonfiction

One way to truly understand a time and people is to hear their songs and music. Slave spirituals provide glimpses into the pre–Civil War world by telling the tale of unjust treatment while showing how oppressed people coped with what life dealt them. In this unique chronicle, readers gain valuable insight into America's dark history by discovering the richness of spirituals as they follow the Jubilee Singers around the world and recognize the importance of their songs.

9.16 Cox, Clinton. **Houdini.** Scholastic, 2001. 194 pp. ISBN 0-590-94960-8. Nonfiction

Ehrich Weiss, who became known as Harry Houdini, appeared to achieve the impossible. Master of suspense, Houdini went from an impoverished childhood to the status of greatest magician of all times. His early interest in magic and tricks led to the fulfillment of a dream—performing amazing and puzzling feats.

9.17 Creech, Sharon. **Love That Dog.** HarperCollins, 2001. 112 pp. ISBN 0-06-029287-3. Fiction

Jack isn't very interested when his class begins a poetry study and reluctantly completes his writing assignments in his journal. Slowly, however, Jack realizes he can explore his feelings and experiences by writing poetry, and he embarks on a journey of discovery. In this novel in verse, Jack models a poem about his dog Sky after Walter Dean Myers's poem "Love That Boy."

9.18 Dahlberg, Maurine F. **Play to the Angel.** Farrar, Straus and Giroux, 2000. 186 pp. ISBN 0-374-35994-6. Fiction

Greta wants to be a concert pianist and is determined to become the best. When her mother plans to sell their piano, Greta turns to the mysterious Herr Hummel for help. He agrees to teach

Greta and offers the encouragement she needs. Struggling to learn the music of the great composers, Greta realizes her dream of playing a recital at the Vienna Academy of Music and Performing Arts. Her success is marred, however, when the Nazis invade Austria.

9.19 Denenberg, Barry. **All Shook Up! The Life and Death of Elvis Presley.** Scholastic, 2001. 176 pp. ISBN 0-439-09504-2. Nonfiction

This biography of Elvis Presley is divided into two parts, first covering his early life and rise to fame and then the crest and fall of that fame. Woven into the description of Elvis's professional life are personal details revealing the motivations and desires behind his career. The cultural and social milieu of the times that created Elvis is also described. His personal life, relationships, and the public persona all tell the story of the rock-and-roll legend.

9.20 Doucet, Sharon Arms. **Fiddle Fever.** Clarion, 2000. 166 pp. ISBN 0-618-04324-1. Fiction

Felix LeBlanc has music in his soul and desperately wants to learn to play the fiddle. Felix's parents forbid him even to mention the word *fiddle* in the house because they associate his uncle's free style of living with his love for the fiddle. Felix struggles with honoring his parents and obeying his own needs and desires. His struggle to express himself is set within the context of the normal dilemmas and decisions that are part of growing up, facing responsibility, and discovering personal identity.

9.21 Emberley, Ed. **Ed Emberley's Drawing Book of Trucks and Trains.** Little, Brown, 2002. 31 pp. ISBN 0-316-23898-8. Nonfiction

This drawing book allows anyone to be an artist. Using just a few basic shapes, young artists can create a wide variety of truck and train scenes. The illustrations take readers step by step through the drawing series. Color illustrations enhance this book.

9.22 Emberley, Ed. **Ed Emberley's Fingerprint Drawing Book.** Little, Brown, 2000. 46 pp. ISBN 0-316-23638-1. Nonfiction

This fingerprint sketchbook shows readers how to create all kinds of pictures using their own fingerprints, some dots, and lines. Using the step-by-step directions, anyone can hand stamp different figures of animals and people. One section, for example, illustrates how to create over a hundred different funny faces. Another focuses on how to create unusual animal scenes. This hand stamp book will keep fingers inked with fun.

9.23 Freedman, Russell. **Martha Graham: A Dancer's Life.** Clarion, 1998. 175 pp. ISBN 0-395-74655-8. Nonfiction

Exquisite photographs and lively prose illuminate the life of groundbreaking American dancer, choreographer, and teacher Martha Graham. Born in 1894 in Pittsburgh, Graham created eighty-one dances, many in which she danced the leading role. She performed until she was seventy-five and choreographed and taught until she was ninety-six. The life of this legendary American artist, whose genius revolutionized the world of dance, will fascinate as well as inspire readers of all ages.

9.24 Giff, Particia Reilly. **Pictures of Hollis Woods.** Wendy Lamb Books, 2002. 166 pp. ISBN 0-385-32655-6. Fiction

Hollis Woods is a twelve-year-old foster child who is moved from placement to placement, her drawing her only solace. She is placed with a retired art teacher who encourages Hollis's talent as an artist. Although her relationship with Josie is positive, Hollis keeps flashing back to the family she almost had. When Josie has a problem, Hollis takes charge and in the process finds both herself and a family.

9.25 Glover, Savion, and Bruce Weber. **Savion! My Life in Tap.** Morrow, 2000. 79 pp. ISBN 0-688-15629-0. Nonfiction

The varying fonts and print sizes, exciting photos, alternating colors, and alternating voices of Glover and Weber come as close as a book can to recreating the dynamic tap dancing style of Savion Glover. The reader learns not only about Glover's career and philosophy but also about the history of tap. The influences of various dancers and musical styles helped develop Glover's natural kinesthetic and musical abilities, and readers can almost hear and feel the dance and music on the page.

9.26 Haskins, James. **One Nation under a Groove: Rap Music and Its Roots.** Jump at the Sun/Hyperion, 2000. 166 pp. ISBN 0-786-82414-X. Nonfiction

Focusing on the evolution of rap music in the United States, including its African origins, this book contains information on the different styles of rap music and the social statements communicated through rap lyrics. In addition, brief biographies of various rap artists and a glossary of terms common to rap music have been included.

9.27 Hettinga, Donald. **The Brothers Grimm: Two Lives, One Legacy.** Clarion, 2001. 180 pp. ISBN 0-618-05599-1. Nonfiction

While they are best known for the fairy tales they collected and preserved for generations to come, Jacob and Wilhelm Grimm left a far greater legacy of scholarship in a number of areas. This book chronicles the interrelationship between the lives and the work of the brothers. Their legacy includes work in the history of language, a linguistic explanation of consonant sounds called Grimm's Law, two volumes of a dictionary, and numerous translations and collections of medieval poems and tales.

9.28 Hirsch, Robin. **FEG: Ridiculous Poems for Intelligent Children.** Illustrated by Ha. Megan Tingley Books, 2002. 48 pp. ISBN 0-316-36344-8. Poetry

You can tell this book of poetry is different from most when the first page confesses that some of the poems are really "stupid," followed by the "brotherly rebuttal" from another narrator that they are "*not* stupid. They may be ridiculous, but they are not stupid." On some pages, the humorous footnotes explaining aspects of the poems take up more space than the poems themselves. If you like puns, puzzles, and silly rhymes, this book is for you.

9.29 Hirschfelder, Arlene B. **Photo Odyssey: Solomon Carvalho's Remarkable Western Adventure, 1853–54.** Clarion, 2001. 128 pp. ISBN 0-395-89123-X. Nonfiction

Solomon Nunes Carvalho accompanied Colonel John Charles Fremont on his 1853 expedition of the western United States. Carvalho was a professional photographer, and it was his job to photograph the terrain and any inhabitants. Taken from Carvalho's journal, this narrative details the life of frontier explorers who braved rugged conditions, disease, and starvation. The book contains many photographs, including the only one of Carvalho's originals in existence.

9.30 Isaccson, Philip. **Round Buildings, Square Buildings, & Buildings That Wiggle Like a Fish.** Knopf, 2001(Originally published in 1988). 121 pp. ISBN 0-394-89382-4. Nonfiction

Art critic Isaacson traveled the world photographing notable buildings, from the Taj Mahal to Rhode Island's Wilkinson Cotton Mill to Monticello. As a primer on architecture, the book focuses on the unique characteristics of buildings and their environments. Chapters focus on aspects of the form, ornament, lighting, and the impact of building materials on the structure.

9.31 King-Smith, Dick. **Chewing the Cud.** Illustrated by Harry Horse. Knopf, 2001. 197 pp. ISBN 0-375-81459-0. Nonfiction

Dick King-Smith, creator of the acclaimed novel *Babe,* writes his account of life, love, family, and his beloved farm. King-Smith recalls the Second World War, his marriage to Myrtle, and the affectionate relationships he has developed with farm animals and family pets. From poor soldier to family farmer, King-Smith gives the reader insight into farm life, why animals are so important, and what led him to a career in writing.

9.32 Krohn, Katherine. **Ella Fitzgerald: First Lady of Song.** Lerner, 2001. 112 pp. ISBN 0-8225-4933-6. Nonfiction

From homelessness at age seventeen to retirement after a fifty-eight-year career, Ella Fitzgerald's odyssey through song is a history of music in the twentieth century. Her appearance wasn't "right," but she was so impressive, determined, and talented that opportunities came her way. She persevered through racial prejudice and other obstacles to become world famous for her clear voice and improvisation. Included are a brief biography of Louis Armstrong, a time line, jazz terms, and Harlem slang.

9.33 Lawlor, Laurie. **Window on the West: The Frontier Photography of William Henry Jackson.** Holliday House, 1999. 132 pp. ISBN 0-8234-1380-2. Nonfiction

Many of our mental images of the American West come from the work of frontier photographer William Henry Jackson (1843–1942). Often shot at great personal risk, his pictures (sixty-five of which are included in this book about his life and times) documented the Yellowstone region, the growth of mining towns, the slaughter of the buffalo, and the displacement of Native Americans. Anyone interested in photography, westward expansion, or the history of the railroad will like this book.

9.34 Macaulay, David. **Building Big.** Houghton Mifflin, 2000. 192 pp. ISBN 0-395-96331-1. Nonfiction

David Macaulay, author and host of the television show *Building Big,* creatively gets readers thinking about structures they see and use daily. From bridges to skyscrapers, he discusses the connections between planning and design problems and their solutions. Digging beneath the grandeur of imposing structures, Macaulay shows the reader that common sense and logic play just as important a part in architecture as imagination and technology.

9.35 Mack, Tracy. **Drawing Lessons.** Scholastic, 2000. 168 pp. ISBN 0-439-11202-8. Fiction

A sketchpad, paints, and charcoal are more than tools for drawing; they are what connect Aurora (Rory for short) and her father. Art is their common bond and passion—it is, in essence, who they are. Rory revels in the art lessons her father gives her and treasures her time spent with him. All of this changes, however, when she sees her father with another woman. Life as Rory knows it will never be the same.

9.36 Markel, Rita J. **Jimi Hendrix.** Lerner, 2001. 112 pp. ISBN 0-8225-4990-5. Nonfiction

This book describes the life of Jimi Hendrix as he grows from a child living in poverty and playing an old one-string ukulele to an overnight international rock music sensation. It provides an inside view of Hendrix's struggle to balance his own need for creative freedom with his fans' expectations. Drug abuse, difficulty working with managers and other musicians, high costs associated with producing an album, and other obstacles plagued Hendrix throughout his short career, which ended with his death at age twenty-eight.

9.37 Márquez, Herón. **Latin Sensations.** Lerner, 2001. 112 pp. ISBN 0-8225-4993-X. Nonfiction

Just as the young Latin American singer Selena was about to break into the American pop music industry, she was murdered by a deranged fan. Although Selena's death brought her career to an early end, it marked the beginning of a new wave of popularity for Latino music. This book describes the lives and music of five American-born Latino music stars: Selena, Ricky Martin, Jennifer Lopez, Marc Anthony, and Enrique Iglesias.

9.38 Mason, Antony. **In the Time of Picasso.** Copper Beech, 2002. 48 pp. ISBN 0-7613-1628-0. Nonfiction

The 1900s was marked by a generation of new artists who challenged the conventional artistic approach in which art mirrored the real world. Through the use of color and shape, artists such as Picasso, Matisse, Klee, and Miró opened art to expressions of imagination and emotion. Colorful illustrations depict artistic contributions from around the world. The book includes a chronology of early-twentieth-century art, a glossary, and an index.

9.39 Mason, Antony. **In the Time of Warhol.** Copper Beech, 2002. 48 pp. ISBN 0-7613-1629-9. Nonfiction

The end of World War II marked a shift in art emphasis from Europe to the United States. The author details the development of abstract expressionism, minimalism, pop art, superrealism, and land art, spurring an international movement that challenged traditional art by breaking away from conventional ideas and materials. Colorfully illustrated, this book includes a chronology of late-twentieth-century art, glossary, and index.

9.40 McGowen, Tom. **Giant Stones and Earth Mounds.** Millbrook, 2000. 80 pp. ISBN 0-7613-1372-9. Nonfiction

The building of things other than dwellings to live in marks the New Stone Age. Since stone was the hardest and most plentiful source, people began to create great stone structures that were the world's first buildings. Scientists have named these structures *megaliths,* from two Greek words meaning "great stone." This book gives the legends and the scientific meanings behind these great structures. Photographs aid the reader in understanding these artistic puzzles.

9.41 McMahon, Patricia. **Dancing Wheels.** Photographs by John Godt. Houghton Mifflin, 2000. 48 pp. ISBN 0-395-88889-1. Nonfiction

Mary Verdi-Fletcher always dreamed of being a dancer, but she was born with spina bifida and is confined to a wheelchair. To fulfill her dream, she created a dance company for two kinds of dancers: "stand up dancers," those who use their legs, arms, backs, necks, and faces for expression, and "sit down dancers," those who use the same but also use wheelchairs. The book focuses on several members of this amazing dance troupe.

9.42 Meltzer, Milton. **Walt Whitman: A Biography.** Twenty-First Century Books, 2002. 160 pp. ISBN 0-7613-2272-8. Nonfiction

Meltzer describes the life and work of American poet Walt Whitman, but he also reflects on the trying and difficult political times during which Whitman lived and wrote. As his poetry demonstrates, Whitman was a man of his times, nursing the wounded in the Civil War and taking on the roles of carpenter, teacher, and shopkeeper, among others. While he was not considered a success by his society, he was a man of the people whose life experiences influenced the poetry he wrote and the rich legacy of his poetry.

9.43 Murphy, Jim. **Pick & Shovel Poet: The Journeys of Pascal D'Angelo.** Clarion, 2000. 162 pp. ISBN 0-395-77610-4. Nonfiction

Imagine being sixteen years old and leaving the only home you have ever known. You have little money and no knowledge of the land, the culture, or the language of the place you are traveling to. Welcome to Pascal D'Angelo's life. This biography follows the immigration of noted poet D'Angelo and others from southern Italy to the United States in 1910, examining the hardships they suffered as well as their steadfast search for a better life.

9.44 Myers, Walter Dean. **Bad Boy: A Memoir.** HarperTempest, 2001. 214 pp. ISBN 0-06-447288-4. Nonfiction.

In this memoir of his family history and of growing up in Harlem in the 1940s and 1950s, author Myers relates his experiences in school, on the streets, and at home, presenting a vivid view of the times and life in Harlem. While he found, with the help of some of his teachers, an entirely different world through reading, he was astute enough to realize that he needed to be a "bad boy" in order to fit in with his peers.

9.45 Nixon, Joan Lowery. **The Making of a Writer.** Delacorte, 2002. 97 pp. ISBN 0-385-73000-4. Nonfiction

Nixon relates the experiences of her life that contributed to her becoming a writer. In addition to describing growing up, her family, and her early awareness that she would be a writer, Nixon relates happy memories of her family and her interest in the world around her that led her to be a people watcher, a skill that contributes to her skill as a writer. This memoir includes photos from Nixon's childhood. She concludes the book with her own "Top 10 Writing Tips."

9.46 Nye, Naomi Shihab, selector. **Salting the Ocean: 100 Poems by Young Poets.** Illustrated by Ashley Bryan. Greenwillow, 2000. 103 pp. ISBN 0-688-16193-6. Poetry

Poetry is often humorous, reflective, and representative of who we are and where we live. It can make us laugh and make us cry. This anthology of poems does all that. Composed of works by one hundred poets ranging in grade level from 1 through 12, the text is arranged around four topics: the self and the inner world, where we live, anybody's family, and the wide imagination. Some poems are simple, others complex, and all of them speak to the reader.

9.47 O'Connor, Barbara. **Katherine Dunham: Pioneer of Black Dance.** Carolrhoda, 2000. 103 pp. ISBN 1-57505-353-5. Nonfiction

This biography tells the story of dancer Katherine Dunham, a pioneer in the art of African American dance during the first part of the twentieth century. Readers will learn not only about the challenges faced by this young dancer but also about traditional Caribbean and African dance traditions.

9.48 Park, Linda Sue. **A Single Shard.** Clarion, 2001. 152 pp. ISBN 0-395-97827-0. Fiction

Thirteen years old and orphaned, Tree-ear lives under a bridge with his elderly friend outside a potter's village in medieval Korea. He becomes infatuated with the process of creating the unique celadon pottery of the area. When his friend dies, Tree-ear must make his own way in life. Through persistence and cleverness, Tree-ear is able to follow his dream, and from apprentice to master potter, he finds success.

9.49 Partridge, Elizabeth. **Restless Spirit: The Life and Work of Dorothea Lange.** Puffin, 2001. 117 pp. ISBN 0-14-230024-1. Nonfiction

Dorothea Lange, one of America's most celebrated photographers, devoted her life to capturing the essence of people in visual images. She discovered the power of individual stories, revealed through photographs, to cause social change. Included are Lange's portraits of migratory workers on the West Coast during the Great Depression and of Japanese Americans in internment camps during World War II. This biography provides insight into the difficulties she encountered trying to balance an artistic career with family responsibilities.

9.50 Powers, Tom. **Steven Spielberg.** Lerner, 2000. 128 pp. ISBN 0-8225-9694-6. Nonfiction

Spielberg's fascination with moviemaking began as a child, from commissioning family members to perform roles in his homemade movies to experiments he conducted as part of high school theater arts. This biography chronicles Spielberg's growth into one of the industry's most awarded directors and provides an absorbing look at events that shaped him. His growth as a director has taken him from adventurous movies such as *Jaws* and *E. T.* to serious endeavors such as *Schindler's List* and *Minority Report.*

9.51 Priceman, Marjorie. **It's Me, Marva! A Story about Color & Optical Illusions.** Knopf, 2001. 32 pp. ISBN 0-679-88993-0. Nonfiction

In this brightly illustrated book, mishaps involving color and optical illusions befall Marva as a result of her new invention, the Ketch-o-matic, a device intended to make Marva's hair turn red. Caldecott Honor Book award–winning artist Marjorie Priceman has created a disarmingly clever book that will both amaze and amuse readers. Told in boldly colored fonts and propelled by optical effects, this book provides a good introduction to color theory.

9.52 Reef, Catherine. **Paul Laurence Dunbar: Portrait of a Poet.** Enslow, 2000. 128 pp. ISBN 0-7660-1350-2. Nonfiction

This engaging biography paints a portrait of Paul Laurence Dunbar, the son of slaves and the first African American to earn his living as a writer. His poetry broke ground with its examination of themes of concern to black Americans and his use of dialect. In addition to providing fascinating anecdotes from Dunbar's life, the book introduces the reader to the beautiful poetry of this African American literary master.

9.53 Severence, John B. **Skyscrapers: How America Grew Up.** Holiday House, 2000. 110 pp. ISBN 0-8234-1492-2. Nonfiction

This informative and engaging book provides a fascinating look into the historical development of tall buildings that seem to "scrape the sky." Readers will discover various innovations that have allowed buildings to grow higher and higher over the years and explore the history of several of the most well-known skyscrapers.

9.54 Sills, Leslie. **In Real Life: Six Women Photographers.** Holiday House, 2000. 80 pp. ISBN 0-8234-1498-1. Nonfiction

Six biographical sketches—of Imogene Cunningham, Dorothea Lange, Lola Alvarez Bravo, Carrie Mae Weems, Elsa Dorfman, and Cindy Sherman—profile the creativity, compassion, and courage of women photographers whose work spans the twentieth century. In addition, Sills presents a primer on how to view and assess photographs, This book includes camera basics, a bibliography, and an index.

9.55 Silverman, Jerry. **Songs and Stories of the Civil War.** Twenty-First Century Books, 2002. 96 pp. ISBN 0-7613-2305-8. Nonfiction

Exploring the issues, personalities, and politics of the Civil War by analyzing the songs, poems, and stories through which they were expressed, Silverman accomplishes his goal of opening that window on the past in a readable, informative, and useful text filled with scores for melodies, illustrations, and recommendations for further listening.

9.56 Sortland, Bjørn. **The Dream Factory Starring Henry and Anna.** Illustrated by Lars Elling. Translated by Emily Virginia Christianson and Robert Hedin. Carolrhoda, 2001. Unpaged. ISBN 0-87614-009-6. Fiction

Uncle Paul tells Henry and his sister Anna that their Christmas present can be found by answering a riddle. Their quest leads them to the Dream Factory, where they become a part of some of the most famous films of all time and meet with famous actors. This wonderful picture book is a primer on film history.

9.57 Sortland, Bjørn. **The Story of the Search for the Story.** Illustrated by Lars Elling. Carolrhoda, 2000. Unpaged. ISBN 1-57505-375-6. Fiction

This wonderfully innovative picture book is the story of Henry in search of a story to read to his uncle. His journey leads him into fanciful encounters in which he meets major writers, from Shakespeare and Cervantes to Hemingway and Rushdie. Ultimately, Henry learns that his encounters are the story he has been seeking and that stories must be told. The book has an anti-censorship message.

9.58 Staples, Suzanne Fisher. **Shiva's Fire.** HarperTrophy, 2001. 276 pp. ISBN 0-064-40979-1. Fiction

Even as a toddler, when Parvati danced unusual things happened, and those around her come to believe this talented young woman has supernatural powers. Eventually, one of India's greatest gurus of Indian classical dance observes the girl and verifies her extraordinary abilities. When Parvati moves to Madras to study with the master, she meets a boy with rare gifts of his own. As the two become closer, Parvati questions her destiny and learns what she most values in her life.

9.59 Streissguth, Tom. **Edgar Allan Poe.** Lerner, 2001. 112 pp. ISBN 0-8225-4991-3. Nonfiction

This biography outlines the major events in the personal and professional life of writer Edgar Allan Poe, chronicling the influences and major events in Poe's life, from the arrival of his mother in the United States to his death at age forty-five, alone and confused, in Baltimore. The text is supplemented with black-and-white photographs, sidebars outlining important concepts such as "transcendentalism," and copies of covers of Poe's works. The useful bibliography and detailed index add to the book's appeal.

9.60 Thoreau, Henry David. **New Suns Will Arise: From the Journals of Henry David Thoreau.** Edited by Frank Crocitto. Photographs by John Dugdale. Hyperion, 2000. 86 pp. ISBN 0-7868-0539-0. Nonfiction

Using a photographic printing process called cyanotype, photographer Dugdale echoes earlier times as he combines his remarkable photos with selections from Thoreau's journal entries. Some of the entries have not previously been published. Editor Frank Crocitto begins the book with two short essays, one about the artistry of Dugdale and the other about the artistry of Thoreau. This book serves as a wonderful introduction to help new readers discover Thoreau's world.

9.61 Vaz, Mark Cotta. ***Alias* Declassified: The Official Companion.** Bantam, 2002. 210 pp. ISBN 0-553-37597-0. Nonfiction

For a look inside the hit television show *Alias,* treat yourself to this tell-all book about the inner workings and makings of the spy thriller. Read about cast members, script ideas, gadget construction, special effects, and much more, as the author reveals everything you could want to know about a show that combines wit and intelligence with intrigue and suspense.

9.62 Wittlinger, Ellen. **Razzle.** Simon & Schuster, 2001. 247 pp. ISBN 0-689-83565-5. Fiction

When his parents buy a motel on Cape Cod, Kenyon meets Razzle at the local dump's Swap Shop, where she works. Razzle is a unique individual who intrigues Kenyon, and he asks her to let him photograph her. As their friendship grows, he develops a portfolio of her pictures. Their relationship is complicated by Kenyon's mother's disapproval, by Razzle's odd family, and by the boy-crazy Harley, who decides to add Ken to her collection of boys.

IV Challenging Our Minds

10 Science and Technology: Fact and Fiction

Fact

10.1 Adkins, Jan. **Bridges: From My Side to Yours.** Illustrated by Jan Adkins. Roaring Brook, 2002. 96 pp. ISBN 0-7613-1542-X. Nonfiction

Through illustrations, diagrams, and interesting stories, the author-illustrator presents a remarkable narrative of a common, everyday structure—the bridge. From Roman engineering to the marvels of the world's famous bridges such as the London Bridge and the Golden Gate Bridge, the reader is taken on a journey of engineering inventiveness and artistic triumph that notes some of the missteps and failures along the way.

10.2 Allan, Jerry, and Georgiana Allan. **The Horse and the Iron Ball: A Journey through Time, Space, and Technology.** Illustrated by Jerry Allan. Lerner, 2000. 50 pp. ISBN 0-8225-2158-X. Nonfiction

The authors present a colorfully illustrated history of the universe, complete with foldouts. Exploring age-old questions about how the universe and life began, they examine the composition of the cosmos and the interrelationship of all things. The book is full of intriguing and informative scientific ideas and includes a glossary and a selected bibliography.

10.3 Ashby, Ruth. **Steve Case: America Online Pioneer.** Twenty-First Century Books, 2002. 80 pp. ISBN 0-7613-2655-3. Nonfiction

Steve Case saw the potential of computers to transform lives in a way no one else had envisioned, and he sold that potential of transformation by providing a means for individuals to get online—to become part of the Internet revolution. Case combined his interest in marketing and advertising with the power of technology to create Internet access through a friendly and nonthreatening interface. America Online is now part of one of the world's largest multimedia corporations, AOL-Time Warner.

10.4 Baker, Christopher W. **Robots among Us: The Challenges and Promises of Robotics.** Millbrook, 2002. 48 pp. ISBN 0-7613-1969-7. Nonfiction

As the author speculates about how robots will become an increasingly common part of our lives, readers learn the basics of how robots work and are challenged to consider important questions about the future development of robotics. Photographs and illustrations aid descriptions of how robots are currently used in science and industry. The book includes a list of Internet resources.

10.5 Baker, Christopher W. **Scientific Visualization: The New Eyes of Science.** Millbrook, 2000. 48 pp. ISBN 0-7613-1351-6. Nonfiction

Colorful photos illustrate the power of technology to allow humans to see scientific phenomena never before witnessed. Whether it is astronomers gazing into the solar system, doctors imaging the human body, geologists and hydrologists studying Earth formations, or environmentalists modeling climatic changes, technology provides the eyes that allow scientists to create images of previously unseen domains, as well as the power to simulate various events. The book includes a listing of Internet resources and a subject index.

10.6 Baker, Christopher W. **Virtual Reality: Experiencing Illusion.** Millbrook, 2000. 48 pp. ISBN 0-7613-1350-8. Nonfiction

Baker takes readers on an adventure through the world of virtual reality. Stops along the way include comprehensible descriptions of the technical difficulties involved in making a virtual world, including creating illusions of touch, sight, hearing, and motion. The tour includes glimpses into such applications as safety testing of automobiles, surgical-related systems, and telerobotics. The generous use of photographs helps illustrate abstract technical material. Included are a list of Internet resources and a subject index.

10.7 Bortz, Fred. **Collision Course! Cosmic Impacts and Life on Earth.** Millbrook, 2001. 72 pp. ISBN 0-7613-1403-2. Nonfiction

The book presents a colorfully illustrated story of past cosmic collisions between Earth and rocks from space. Building on knowledge of the solar system and evidence from past impacts, the author argues that future collisions are inevitable and that programs such as Spacewatch may hold the key to preparing for such events. Informative accounts of Asteroid 1977 XF11, the Tunguska event, and Comet Shoemaker-Levy 9 are included. Readers particularly interested in the subject will appreciate the lists of books and Internet resources for further information.

10.8 Bortz, Fred. **Techno-Matter: The Materials behind the Marvels.** Twenty-First Century Books, 2001. 96 pp. ISBN 0-7613-1469-5. Nonfiction

Have you ever considered what it might take to sustain a human colony on Mars? The field of materials science and engineering offers possible answers to that question as well as to many other wonders of technology. Through rich illustrations and examples, the author describes how explorations with materials have led to fascinating breakthroughs in science and technology. The author links the past with the future in a journey that follows mankind's fascination and progress in working with materials.

10.9 Brashares, Ann. **Linus Torvalds: Software Rebel.** Twenty-First Century Books, 2001. 80 pp. ISBN 0-7613-1960-3. Nonfiction

Everyone likes something for free. Torvalds provides free software to anyone who has the capability of downloading it from the Internet. The software is an operating system called Linux, which competes with Microsoft's Windows. While not as user-friendly as Windows, Linux is used by tech savvy businesses and government divisions. The creator maintains a job as a programmer for a software company.

10.10 Brashares, Ann. **Steve Jobs: Thinks Different.** Twenty-First Century Books, 2001. 80 pp. ISBN 0-7613-1959-X. Nonfiction

This book tells the intriguing story of Steve Jobs, founder of Apple Computer, detailing how his and others' ingenuity and fascination led to a revolution in technology through the design of the personal computer. The author provides a candid portrait of the advent of the Macintosh computer and the business practices and events that shaped Apple's successes and setbacks. Readers get an insider's look at an industry that has forever changed our technology landscape.

10.11 Butts, Ellen R., and Joyce R. Schwartz. **Carl Sagan.** Lerner, 2001. 112 pp. ISBN 0-8225-4986-7. Nonfiction

Fascinated by planets and stars at an early age, Carl Sagan grew up to become "America' s most effective salesman of science," in addition to making major contributions to NASA space exploration programs. Using his talents to teach science to nonscientists, Sagan created *Cosmos,* a television series that explored the origins of Earth and the search for life on other planets, and wrote *Contact,* a book (which became a major motion picture) about contact between humans and extraterrestrial civilization, in order to bring science to millions of ordinary people.

10.12 Campbell, Peter A. **Alien Encounters.** Illustrated by Peter A. Campbell. Millbrook, 2000. 48 pp. ISBN 0-7613-1402-4. Nonfiction

Have aliens really visited Earth? Campbell summarizes eight reported "close encounters" with alien beings. Each of the summaries features a narrative of the encounter, attractive paintings and sketches of the aliens and their spaceships, as well as detailed information about the time, place, and date of the sighting; names of witnesses; descriptions of the extraterrestrials; and details about the spaceships. A bibliography and list of recommended reading are also included.

10.13 Cobb, Vicki. **Sources of Forces: Science Fun with Force Fields.** Illustrated by Steve Haefele. Millbrook, 2002. 48 pp. ISBN 0-7613-1574-8. Nonfiction

Some of the most important and powerful forces in the universe are invisible. The author uses colorful cartoonlike illustrations to describe how the invisible forces of magnetism, electricity, and gravity operate. Characters V. C. and Igor show the reader how to engage in simple demonstrations that display some of the properties of these forces. This easy-to-read work is full of important vocabulary, definitions, and scientific concepts.

10.14 Cooper, Margaret. **Exploring the Ice Age.** Atheneum, 2001. 93 pp. ISBN 0-689-82556-0. Nonfiction

Cooper uses cultural artifacts and bones to piece together a fascinating story of how human beings might have lived 35,000 years ago, taking the reader back in time to learn about the activities and inventions that characterize the cave-dwelling people during this cold period in history. Photographs and drawings illustrate key ideas. A bibliography is included.

10.15 DuTemple, Lesley A. **Jacques Cousteau.** Lerner, 2000. 112 pp. ISBN 0-8225-4979-4. Nonfiction

After discovering the amazing world under the ocean, at first through the use of aviator goggles, Jacques Cousteau, a young French naval officer, invented scuba equipment and underwater cameras to further his underwater explorations. Leaving the navy, Cousteau traveled with a small crew on his ship the *Calypso,* giving voice to the "silent seas" by writing the book *The Silent World* and filming an underwater documentary that later became the basis for a popular television series.

10.16 Dyson, Marianne J. **Space Station Science: Life in Free Fall.** Scholastic, 1999. 128 pp. ISBN 0-590-05889-4. Nonfiction

If you've ever been curious about daily life on the International Space Station, this book is for you. Find out how astronauts and other scientists are transported to the station, as well as how they deal with aspects of daily living such as eating, sleeping, and going to the bathroom in zero-gravity conditions. The book includes numerous color photographs taken from the station and a series of experiments you can try at home to learn more about space.

10.17 Ehrenhaft, Daniel. **Larry Ellison: Sheer Nerve.** Twenty-First Century Books, 2001. 80 pp. ISBN 0-7613-1962-X. Nonfiction

The Internet has provided many opportunities for success and failure. The story of Larry Ellison is one of success. He learned computer programming as a way to earn extra money while a student at the University of Chicago. Both dropping out of college and strained family relationships influenced him to move to Berkley with a drive to accomplish something. Eventually, he founded Oracle, the multibillion-dollar Internet software giant.

10.18 Ehrenhaft, Daniel. **Marc Andreessen: Web Warrior.** Twenty-First Century Books, 2001. 80 pp. ISBN 0-7613-1964-6. Nonfiction

The author captures the way in which brilliant ideas and hard work pay off in this biography of Marc Andreessen, founder of Netscape. This enterprise helped transform the Internet into an easily accessible communications network that has fueled a revolution, changing how people communicate with one another. Andreessen's financial and personal success was influenced by his goal to make computer technology that everyone could use. This story chronicles the origins of Netscape and provides insights into the man behind it.

10.19 Fleisher, Paul. **Liquids and Gases: Principles of Fluid Mechanics.** Lerner, 2002. 56 pp. ISBN 0-8225-2988-2. Nonfiction

From the ideas of Archimedes emerged the science of mechanics, or the study of how objects move. Scientific studies of the laws that govern the behavior of liquids and gases have contributed to many advances in science and technology. Archimedes' Principles, Pascal's Law, Boyle's and Charle's laws, and the Bernoulli Principle are clarified through experiments and illustrations. This book includes a time line and short biographies of scientists.

10.20 Fleisher, Paul. **Matter and Energy: Principles of Matter and Thermodynamics.** Lerner, 2002. 64 pp. ISBN 0-8225-2986-6. Nonfiction

The author provides fascinating illustrations of natural laws that describe how matter and energy behave. Conservation of matter, how elements combine, the periodic law, conservation of energy, and entropy are masterfully clarified through concrete examples and informative graphics. Readers are encouraged to engage in several experiments that show the laws in action. The narrative is reinforced through a time line of important scientific events related to matter and energy and short biographic entries of important scientists.

10.21 Fleisher, Paul. **Objects in Motion: Principles of Classical Mechanics.** Lerner, 2002. 80 pp. ISBN 0-8225-2985-8. Nonfiction

Fleisher provides clear and engaging descriptions of universal laws, laws that apply throughout the universe as well as on Earth. Planetary motion, pendulums and falling objects, universal gravitation, conservation of momentum, and Newton's three laws of motion are illuminated through practical examples. Readers are encouraged to engage in several demonstrations that further exhibit the laws in action. The book includes a time line of scientific milestones in science and a section containing short biographic notes of important scientists.

10.22 Fleisher, Paul. **Relativity and Quantum Mechanics: Principles of Modern Physics.** Lerner, 2002. 64 pp. ISBN 0-8225-29890. Nonfiction

The laws of relativity and quantum mechanics provide a basis for answering important questions about the behavior of electronics and other atomic particles. Illustrations and examples illuminate complex ideas, such as Einstein's famous equation $E = mc^2$. Conservation of mass/energy and the uncertainty principle round out a well-conceptualized discussion of this important branch of modern physics. Included are a time line of important scientific events and short biographies of scientists who have contributed to our understanding of quantum mechanics.

10.23 Fleisher, Paul. **Waves: Principles of Light, Electricity, and Magnetism.** Lerner, 2002. 64 pp. ISBN 0-8225-2987-4. Nonfiction

Light has long fascinated mankind, and great scientists such as Newton and Einstein tried to understand the laws of light. Optics is the branch of physics devoted to the study of light. In this book, the author explores the behavior of light and electromagnetism through experiments and the use of illustrations. Electric current is clarified through concise descriptions of Ohm's Law and Joule's Law. The book includes a time line and short biographies of scientists.

10.24 Jablonski, Carla. **Esther Dyson: Web Guru.** Twenty-First Century Books, 2002. 80 pp. ISBN 0-7613-2657-X. Nonfiction

This biography highlights the events that have made Esther Dyson one of the most sought-after voices in the world of high tech. Named by *Fortune* magazine as one of the fifty most powerful women in American business, Dyson has developed a knack for predicting who and what will shape this technological revolution. She continues to break preconceptions about how technology will affect our lives.

10.25 Jackson, Donna M. **The Bone Detectives: How Forensic Anthropologists Solve Crimes and Uncover Mysteries of the Dead.** Photographs by Charlie Fellenbaum. Little, Brown, 1996. 48 pp. ISBN 0-316-82961-7. Nonfiction

Whether three weeks or three million years old, human bones hold clues to many mysteries. Find out how highly trained anthropologists can determine a person's age, sex, race, size, and other physical characteristics from a single bone. The book discusses how this information is used to solve crimes and provides information about prehistoric humans.

10.26 Katz, Jon. **Geeks: How Two Lost Boys Rode the Internet out of Idaho.** Broadway, 2000. 208 pp. ISBN 0-7679-0699-3. Nonfiction

Jon Katz tells the true story of Jesse and Eric, two young adults who have always seen themselves as outsiders, as they struggle to escape the oppression of their small town in Idaho and as they move to Chicago to find careers in the booming technology industry. Katz also explores the societal causes of and reaction to school violence, such as that experienced at a high school in Columbine, Colorado.

10.27 Kranmer, Stephen. **Hidden Worlds: Looking through a Scientist's Microscope.** Photographs by Dennis Kunkel. Houghton Mifflin, 2001. 57 pp. ISBN 0-618-05546-0. Nonfiction

When Dennis Kunkel's parents gave their ten-year-old son a microscope for Christmas, his curiosity quickly developed into a passion for exploring life too small to be seen by the naked eye. Fascinating full-color photographs invite the reader to follow microscopist Kunkel on his explorations of Mount Saint Helens' volcano, Hawaii, and other sites. The book includes information on different types of microscopes, tips on becoming a scientist, and a link to Kunkel's Web site.

10.28 Lesinski, Jeanne M. **Bill Gates.** Lerner, 2000. 112 pp. ISBN 0-8225-4949-2. Nonfiction

A math and science whiz and Harvard dropout becomes a tycoon when he turns his fascination with computer technology into a multibillion-dollar corporation. Growing up in a family that encouraged reading and games, Bill Gates discovered his life's work when he encountered his first computer at thirteen years of age. Shortly thereafter he began writing programs for computers, and in his early twenties he started a company named Microsoft, the corporate leader in today's technology revolution.

10.29 Majoor, Mireille. **Inside the *Hindenburg*.** Illustrated by Ken Marschall. Little, Brown, 2000. 32 pp. ISBN 0-316-12386-2. Nonfiction

This oversized special scholastic edition provides rich illustrations of the *Hindenburg*'s majesty as seen through the eyes of two young people on its inaugural flight. Inserts, illustrations, and photographs depict the airship's amazing technological accomplishments, from its enormous size to the grandeur of the inside levels, including the various decks, the control car, and the gallery. With clarity and descriptiveness, the author tells the story of how this amazing vehicle ended in a terrible tragedy that shocked the world.

10.30 Marshall, Elizabeth L. **A Student's Guide to the Internet.** Twenty-First Century Books, 2001. 144 pp. ISBN 0-7613-1661-2. Nonfiction

The Internet has transformed our lives by advancing our access to information and communication. This book describes the Internet and presents clear guidelines on how to use the Internet for fun and research, from searching with directories and search engines to creating and publishing Web pages. It includes an appendix of search engines and directories.

10.31 McGowan, Eileen Nixon, and Nancy Lagow Dumas. **Stock Market Smart.** Millbrook, 2002. 64 pp. ISBN 0-7613-2113-6. Nonfiction

Everyone wants to make money, and investing provides a means of meeting financial goals. This book is written from the perspective of a financial advisor providing basic information about money and the stock market: What is the stock market? How does the stock market work? What can the stock market do for individuals? These questions and basic approaches to investing are explored in clear, understandable language accentuated through sidebars, illustrations, a listing of additional resources, and a glossary of terms.

10.32 Meltzer, Milton. **Case Closed: The Real Scoop on Detective Work.** Orchard, 2001. 88 pp. ISBN 0-439-29315-4. Nonfiction

If you've ever wondered how crimes get solved with DNA evidence, ballistics reports, and fingerprint results, this book will help satisfy your curiosity. Divided into three sections—What It's Like to Be a Detective, Behind the Scenes in the Lab, and Detective Work—Not on the Police Force—it provides some historical background on detective work as well as an interesting look at today's methods.

10.33 Miller, Ron. **Extrasolar Planets.** Twenty-First Century Books, 2002. 96 pp. ISBN 0-7613-2354-6. Nonfiction

Before moving on to the world beyond our own solar system, the author describes the exploration of our solar system and the discovery of new planets, providing in addition a biography of how our solar system came into existence. Beyond our solar system lie fascinating worlds that come alive through the author's vivid descriptions and colorful illustrations. A glossary and sources for additional information are included.

10.34 Miller, Ron. **Jupiter.** Twenty-First Century Books, 2002. 65 pp. ISBN 0-7613-2356-2. Nonfiction

Beginning with a general information overview that includes a description of how the planet Jupiter was formed, this book provides a history of the discovery of Jupiter by Galileo. The greatest portion of the book is devoted to the moons of Jupiter. Each moon is described with numerous illustrations, including NASA photographs. The final chapters describe the composition of the planet and the space missions that have gathered data from Jupiter.

10.35 Miller, Ron. **The Sun.** Twenty-First Century Books, 2002. 64 pp. ISBN 0-7613-2355-4. Nonfiction

Our existence depends on the sun, the Earth's nearest star. The author provides concise information about the history of the sun, how the sun works, the relationship between the sun and Earth, and the sun's future. The mysteries of the sun come alive through colorful illustrations and NASA photographs. The book includes a glossary of terms and sources for additional information.

10.36 Miller, Ron. **Venus.** Twenty-First Century Books, 2002. 58 pp. ISBN 0-7613-2359-7. Nonfiction

This book describes the history, formation, exploration, and defining characteristics of the planet Venus. It begins with an overview of the impact Venus had on the early Greeks, on Galileo's theories, and on science fiction writers, and is followed by a detailed description of the planet's formation and atmosphere. Subsequent chapters detail space missions to Venus and include numerous NASA photographs. Venus and Earth are also compared and contrasted as similar planets.

10.37 Mitten, Christopher. **Shawn Fanning: Napster and the Music Revolution.** Twenty-First Century Books, 2002. 80 pp. ISBN 0-7613-2656-1. Nonfiction

Shawn Fanning's contributions to the technology revolution go beyond development of a computer software system allowing individuals to download music via the Internet. His model has given scientists and other researchers a way to handle vast amounts of data through a peer-to-peer software model. This contribution will likely long outlive his notoriety as the controversial provider of free music.

10.38 Reef, Catherine. **Sigmund Freud: Pioneer of the Mind.** Clarion, 2001. 152 pp. ISBN 0-618-01762-3. Nonfiction

Sigmund Freud's controversial theories and methods clearly serve as the foundation for today's psychology. Reef has managed to present his life and complex contributions in a completely engaging and understandable way. As we read about Freud's early childhood through his difficult adult life, we see what we now take for granted in the context of history. Text merged with wonderful photographs present an overall picture of Freud—the doctor, the scientist, and the man.

10.39 Ross, Michael Elsohn. **Exploring the Earth with John Wesley Powell.** Illustrated by Wendy Smith. Carolrhoda, 2000. 48 pp. ISBN 1-57505-254-7. Nonfiction

This book allows the young science student to study the puzzles of the earth's history along with nineteenth-century geologist John Wesley Powell. It provides a historical and biographical glimpse into the life of this noted scientist as well as a wealth of knowledge about the scientific study of the earth.

10.40 Ross, Michael Elsohn. **Pond Watching with Ann Morgan.** Illustrated by Wendy Smith. Carolrhoda, 2000. 48 pp. ISBN 1-57505-385-3. Nonfiction

This book allows the young scientist to study the aquatic life of a pond along with nineteenth-century naturalist Anna Haven Morgan. It provides a historical and biographical glimpse into the life of this aquatic biologist as well as a wealth of knowledge about the scientific aquatic life found in ponds.

10.41 Sayre, April Pulley. **El Niño and La Niña: Weather in the Headlines.** Twenty-First Century Books, 2000. 80 pp. ISBN 0-7613-1405-9. Nonfiction

Global weather patterns affect the lives of people all over the world. Both El Niño and La Niña have drastically altered weather patterns. Meteorologists can now track and predict how and when these phenomena will occur, allowing communities to prepare for weather-related disasters. Color photographs show examples of the damage incurred by catastrophic hurricanes, tornadoes, and droughts. There is also a glossary and a listing of additional references at the end of the book.

10.42 Searle, Bobbi. **Electricity and Magnetism.** Copper Beech, 2002. 48 pp. ISBN 0-7613-1630-2. Nonfiction

The properties of magnetism and electricity become clear through the projects and experiments presented in simple and concise language. Each of the ten chapters deals with a different topic and contains a major project supported by simple experiments along with a list of necessary materials. Each chapter also contains a simply stated explanation of what happened in the investigation and what it means. The book includes an index and a glossary of terms.

10.43 Sherman, Josepha. **Jeff Bezos: King of Amazon.** Twenty-First Century Books, 2001. 80 pp. ISBN 0-7613-1963-8. Nonfiction

This biography of Jeff Bezos illustrates the power of curiosity in overcoming obstacles to realize dreams. The author provides an interesting and informative account of Amazon.com from challenging beginnings in a garage in Seattle to one of the largest Internet start-up companies in history. The story gives the reader a glimpse into the fascinating world of online retail and the life of a young man who realized the potential of an electronic shopping center.

10.44 Silverstein, Alvin, Virginia Silverstein, and Laura Silverstein Nunn. **Hearing.** Twenty-First Century Books, 2001. 64 pp. ISBN 0-7613-1666-3. Nonfiction

The complex nature of the sense of hearing is explicated in this work in a concise fashion. The authors provide a glimpse into the biological, mechanical, and neurological influences that affect our ability to hear sounds. The book includes discussions on the relationship between hearing and speech, hearing loss, and the role of technology in making sounds visible.

10.45 Silverstein, Alvin, Virginia Silverstein, and Laura Silverstein Nunn. **Seeing.** Twenty-First Century Books, 2001. 64 pp. ISBN 0-7613-1663-9. Nonfiction

Humans use their sense of sight more than any of the other senses. The authors explain and illustrate the mechanics of sight, including what allows humans to see colors and motions and how the brain processes the vast amount of information that comes through the eyes. The book also highlights how technology overcomes limitations, permitting us to see in 3-D and explore that which is by nature invisible.

10.46 Silverstein, Alvin, Virginia Silverstein, and Laura Silverstein Nunn. **Smelling and Tasting.** Twenty-First Century Books, 2002. 64 pp. ISBN 0-7613-1667-1. Nonfiction

The authors describe the neurological and biological foundations of smelling and tasting in easily comprehended language, taking interesting informational expeditions into the role of smell in other species as well as discussing why humans produce different personal smells. The closing chapter delves into the technology behind artificial chemosensors. Illustrations and interesting sidebars further clarify ideas, and a glossary and suggested additional resources have been included.

10.47 Silverstein, Alvin, Virginia Silverstein, and Laura Silverstein Nunn. **Touching and Feeling.** Twenty-First Century Books, 2002. 64 pp. ISBN 0-7613-1668-X. Nonfiction

After describing the neurological and biological foundations of touching and feeling in easily comprehended language, the authors take interesting informational voyages into the effectiveness of touching and feeling in some animal species. They also explore the development of artificial sensors that provide support for individuals with disabilities and technologies that make our lives simpler and safer. Illustrations and interesting sidebars further clarify ideas. A glossary and suggested additional resources are included.

10.48 Singh, Simon. **The Code Book: How to Make It, Break It, Hack It, Crack It.** Delacorte, 2002. 263 pp. ISBN 0-385-72913-8. Nonfiction

For the serious code enthusiast, this book starts by explaining the difference between a code and a cipher. Each chapter details a different technical feature of coding and provides famous examples in which the course of history has been affected by coding. The final chapter looks ahead to applications of cryptography to protect privacy in the digital age. Appendixes include classic codes as well as a list of additional resources.

10.49 Thomas, Peggy. **Marine Mammal Preservation.** Twenty-First Century Books, 2000. 64 pp. ISBN 0-7613-1458-X. Nonfiction

This book is one of a series about conservation and preservation efforts with marine animals. Readers learn about whales, dolphins, otters, and other endangered marine mammals. Instead of letting these animals perish, dedicated scientists, volunteers, and government agencies have taken a proactive role in protecting these animals' environments. Color photographs have detailed captions. Also included are a glossary, an index, Internet information, and a list of further recommended reading.

10.50 Trumbauer, Lisa. **Cool Sites: Homework Help for Kids on the Net.** Millbrook, 2000. 80 pp. ISBN 0-7613-1655-8. Nonfiction

This book provides Internet sites helpful for science, math, history, geography, and language arts/English homework and projects and also lists general reference sites. It includes a glossary of Internet terms, an index of sites by name, and Web addresses and notice of any fees required for each site. Readers should be aware that some of the information on these sites may no longer be current, given the rapidly changing nature of the Internet.

10.51 Vogt, Gregory L. **Space Mission Patches.** Millbrook, 2001. 78 pp. ISBN 0-7613-1613-2. Nonfiction

This book tells the history of NASA through the unique patches worn by astronauts on each space mission. Each space crew works with a professional graphic artist to design a flight patch symbolizing the goals of that particular mission. The book provides helpful hints and resources for collecting patches and includes a glossary, an index, and illustrations.

10.52 Weitzman, David. **Model T: How Henry Ford Built a Legend.** Crown, 2002. Unpaged. ISBN 0-375-81107-9. Nonfiction

This well-illustrated work takes the reader onto an automobile assembly line for the United States' first cars, capturing the thrill of the invention that revolutionized travel and industry. The easy-to-read narrative, including quotes from workers, provides a colorful story of the manufacturing process of the Tin Lizzie and of Henry Ford's enterprising spirit.

10.53 Wilcox, Charlotte. **Mummies, Bones, & Body Parts.** Carolrhoda, 2000. 64 pp. ISBN 1-57505-428-0. Nonfiction

So you think mummies were made only in Egypt? Author Wilcox debunks that notion with these stories of preserved human remains from Peru, England, China, and Italy. She explains how mummification works and discusses some of the enigmas that have been solved by forensic anthropologists using clues from human remains. Featuring many color photos and a useful glossary, this book will appeal to mystery lovers, history buffs, and future scientists alike.

10.54 Wulffson, Don L. **The Kid Who Invented the Trampoline: More Surprising Stories about Inventions.** Dutton, 2001. 120 pp. ISBN 0-525-46654-1. Nonfiction

The last millennium was a period of countless inventions, many of which were the result of accidents and others the result of tireless pursuit. Wulffson tells the incredible story of fifty inventions, including those of the Iowa teenager who invented the trampoline and Walt Disney, who invented animated cartoons. The stories reveal the successes and failures of humanity's resourcefulness.

Science Series

Planet Library Series

10.55 Kerrod, Robin. **Asteroids, Comets, and Meteors.** Lerner, 2000. 32 pp. ISBN 0-8225-3905-5. Nonfiction

Kerrod, Robin. **Jupiter.** Lerner, 2000. 32 pp. ISBN 0-8225-3907-1. Nonfiction

Kerrod, Robin. **Mars.** Lerner, 2000. 32 pp. ISBN 0-8225-3906-3. Nonfiction

Kerrod, Robin. **Mercury and Venus.** Lerner, 2000. 32 pp. ISBN 0-8225-3904-7. Nonfiction

Kerrod, Robin. **The Moon.** Lerner, 2000. 32 pp. ISBN 0-8225-3900-4. Nonfiction

Kerrod, Robin. **Planet Earth.** Lerner, 2000. 32 pp. ISBN 0-8225-3902-0. Nonfiction

Kerrod, Robin. **Saturn.** Lerner, 2000. 32 pp. ISBN 0-8225-3909-8. Nonfiction

Kerrod, Robin. **The Solar System.** Lerner, 2000. 32 pp. ISBN 0-8225-3903-9. Nonfiction

Kerrod, Robin. **The Sun.** Lerner, 2000. 32 pp. ISBN 0-8225-3901-2. Nonfiction

Kerrod, Robin. **Uranus, Neptune, and Pluto.** Lerner, 2000. 32 pp. ISBN 0-8225-3908-X. Nonfiction

This series is replete with color photographs, drawings, and diagrams complementing text that explores aspects of the solar system. A separate book is devoted to each planet; the sun; the moon; and asteroids, comets, and meteors, as well as the solar system as a whole. These books benefit from information and pictures provided by our space program's explorations. Each book also provides a glossary of terms.

Fiction

10.56 Engdahl, Sylvia Louise. **Enchantress from the Stars.** Illustrated by Leo Dillon and Diane Dillon. Walker, 2001 (Originally published in 1970). 286 pp. ISBN 0-8027-8764-9. Fiction

Elana sneaks aboard her father's spaceship, joining him on a mission to study another planet for possible colonization. They discover two other civilizations that are doing the same thing but not with the same peaceful intentions. Though her society is based on advanced technology and the native society is based on magic and superstition, Elana helps to bridge the gap between civilizations and preserve the lives of the natives in this thoroughly delightful rerelease of Engdahl's award-winning book.

10.57 Haddix, Margaret Peterson. **Among the Impostors.** Simon & Schuster, 2001. 172 pp. ISBN 0-689-83904-9. Fiction

Luke Garner, a.k.a. Lee Grant, has been in hiding all his life as a forbidden third child in a society dictating population control as a result of previous famines. Illegally and unwillingly taking on the identity of a deceased second child, Luke/Lee is separated from his family and sent to a school where he is encouraged to blend in. Luke discovers the plans of his chief tormentor, Jason, to reveal the identities of the many third children in hiding at the school.

10.58 Haddix, Margaret Peterson. **Turnabout.** Simon & Schuster, 2000. 240 pp. ISBN 0-689-82187-5. Fiction

In 2001, hundred-year-old nursing home resident Melly Hazelwood participates in Project Turnabout, an experiment meant to reverse aging. When scientists find they cannot stop the process, Melly and her friend Anny Beth leave the facility to begin new lives, growing younger each year. Suspense builds as the chapters alternate between 2001, when the experiment takes place, and 2085, when the teenage pair seeks a caregiver for the inevitable day when they will be too young to fend for themselves.

10.59 Halam, Ann. **Dr. Franklin's Island.** Wendy Lamb Books, 2002. 247 pp. ISBN 0-385-73008-X. Fiction

Three science students are forced to work together after their plane crashes and they are stranded on a deserted island. Survival becomes more difficult when they are captured and imprisoned by a doctor intent on using them as part of his experiments with human genetic transfer with animals. Bravery, knowledge, and sheer determination help these students form the unlikely bond that allows them to succeed as the reader travels with them beyond the limits of human life and back.

10.60 Hautman, Pete. **Hole in the Sky.** Simon & Schuster, 2001. 179 pp. ISBN 0-689-83118-8. Fiction

The year is 2028 and a killer flu has swept across the globe, killing most of the world's population. The few humans who remain form into groups—Survivors, who have had the flu and lived, and others, who try to live in isolation to keep from getting it. Add to the mix marauding Survivors intent on infecting or killing others. This novel's plot lines are many and lead to an intriguing climax.

10.61 Lassiter, Rhiannon. **Hex.** Archway, 2001. 244 pp. ISBN 0-7434-2211-2. Fiction

It is London in the late twenty-fourth century, and people with a mutant gene for computer proficiency are called Hexes. The government experiments on these supercomputer minds and then exterminates them. Aided by several other teenagers, Raven, a fifteen-year-old Hex with untested but remarkable powers, seeks to find and free her sister from the sinister Center for Paranormal Studies. This book is the first in a series published first in England.

10.62 Levitin, Sonia. **The Cure.** HarperTrophy, 2000. 258 pp. ISBN 0-380-73298-X. Fiction

Imagine an emotionless "utopian" society set in the future that values conformity above all else. When Gemm exhibits signs of deviance through his love of music, he has to take the cure. He is sent back in time to Germany as a sixteen-year-old Jewish boy in the era of the Black Death plague. Later, remembering his experiences of love and pain, Gemm declares to his mate Gemma that they will secretly start the transformation of their society.

10.63 Logue, Mary. **Dancing with an Alien.** HarperCollins, 2000. 144 pp. ISBN 0-06-028318-1. Fiction

What would it be like to meet an alien, someone who is really, as they say, "out of this world"? Tonia, our teenage heroine, does just that when she unexpectedly meets Branko, an alien who is visiting Earth on a special mission. Branko must bring home a female earthling. Bemused and confused, Tania and her new-found alien friend set off on a mission filled with great mystery, excitement, and passion.

10.64 Lowry, Lois. **Gathering Blue.** Houghton Mifflin, 2000. 215 pp. ISBN 0-618-05581-9. Fiction

Orphaned and physically flawed, Kira isn't sure how she will survive in a world that doesn't accept weakness of any kind. In this harsh futuristic society, only the strong live. Governed by The Council of Guardians, Kira's world is consumed with fear. Will her artistic gifts help her find a way to survive? Faced with an uncertain future, Kira discovers things about her civilization that cause her to reexamine her world.

10.65 Osterweil, Adam. **The Comic Book Kid.** Illustrated by Craig Smith. Front Street, 2001. 151 pp. ISBN 1-886910-62-6. Fiction

Five years ago Brian accidentally spilled punch all over his father's prized 1939 *Superman #1* comic book. When Mr. Somerset, the general store owner, gives twelve-year-old Brian and his friend Paul a blank *TimeQuest* comic book, the boys set out to replace the ruined treasure. It should be simple to use *TimeQuest*'s mysterious powers to travel back to 1939, purchase another copy of *Superman #1,* and bring it into the present. But when the boys return home in time, they find that home is not quite as they had left it.

10.66 Paulsen, Gary. **The White Fox Chronicles.** Delacorte, 2000. 281 pp. ISBN 0-385-32254-2. Fiction

Set in the year 2057, this fast-paced adventure story chronicles fourteen-year-old Cody Pierce's efforts to rescue a group of children from a concentration camp. Nicknamed White Fox for his ability to outsmart military officials from the Confederation of Consolidated Republics, which has taken over the

United States, Cody learns to balance self-reliance and teamwork as he faces a succession of life-threatening challenges.

10.67 Philbrick, Rodman. **The Last Book in the Universe.** Blue Sky, 2000. 223 pp. ISBN 0-439-08758-9. Fiction

Set in the future, when a great earthquake has destroyed modern civilization, this book tells the story of a young epileptic boy called Spaz. Relegated to the part of the world where people are plagued by genetic defects and a toxic environment, Spaz ventures to the other side, Eden, where people have been genetically altered to be perfect, and he learns just how unequal the world can be.

10.68 Philbrick, Rodman. **REM World.** Blue Sky, 2000. 192 pp. ISBN 0-439-08362-1. Fiction

Tired of being the butt of fat-boy jokes, eleven-year-old Arthur Woodbury purchases an REM Sleep Device that promises he will go to sleep fat and wake up thin. Unfortunately, he fails to follow the instructions exactly and breaks an essential law of the universe by being in two places at once. Arthur has many exciting adventures in the world of REM as he tries to save the universe from destruction. Maybe, he decides, he's not such a loser after all.

10.69 Rector, Rebecca Kraft. **Tria and the Great Star Rescue.** Delacorte, 2002. 184 pp. ISBN 0-385-72941-3. Fiction

Tria and her best friend Star like to go on adventures. But Tria actually never leaves the safety of home, and Star, like all of their adventures, is merely a holographic illusion. All changes, however, when Tria receives a cryptic message from her archaeologist mother on a faraway excavation. With Star saved to disc, Tria ventures forth into the real world for the first time in an attempt to rescue her kidnapped mother from the clutches of the evil Dr. Roparian.

10.70 Sedgwick, Marcus. **Floodland.** Delacorte, 2001. 148 pp. ISBN 0-385-32801-X. Fiction

In a future that may be closer than we would like, the polar ice caps have melted and whole cities have disappeared under water. Zoe, separated from her parents, has been trying to survive in the midst of escalating anarchy. When she finds a little rowboat, she decides to put to sea in search of her parents. Before the happy resolution, Zoe is captured by a group of feral children.

10.71 Spinner, Stephanie, and Terry Bisson. **Expiration Date: Never.** Delacorte, 2001. 118 pp. ISBN 0-385-32690-4. Fiction

In this sequel to *Be First in the Universe*, Gemini Jack asks Tod and Tessa for help once again. His planet is in danger of being invaded by the Vorons, vacationing tourists who find impoliteness appealing. But Tod and Tessa have problems of their own. Nigel Throbber, a famous drummer, is living at their grandparents' house and shows no indication of leaving. The duo needs Gemini Jack's help as much as he needs theirs.

10.72 Vande Velde, Vivian. **User Unfriendly.** Harcourt, 2001 (Originally published in 1991). 256 pp. ISBN 0-15-216353-0. Fiction

Arvin and his friends enter into a computer-generated role-playing game, taking on the roles of fantasy characters; the game plugs directly into their brains without requiring keyboard, monitor, or modem. But the computer program has been pirated and contains errors that, in the end, turn deadly, and Arvin's mom may be the one who pays the price. In a world grown ever dependent on computers, this book provides a cautionary tale, part science fiction, part swashbuckling adventure.

10.73 Verne, Jules. **20,000 Leagues under the Sea.** Illustrated by Diane Dillon and Leo Dillon. Translated by Anthony Bonner. HarperCollins, 2000 (Originally published in 1869–1870). 394 pp. ISBN 0-688-10535-1. Fiction

An excellently illustrated edition of a reissued classic first published beginning in 1869, this science fiction masterpiece captures the adventures of Professor Aronnax, Conseil, and Ned Land as they contend with all sorts of fantastic creatures and inventions—i.e., a giant octopus and the amazing submarine *Nautilus.* A beautiful translation captures the majesty and grandeur of the sea and its environs, but it also delineates the demonic genius of Captain Nemo, which keeps the reader in suspense about what will happen next.

Poetry

10.74 Sidman, Joyce. **Eureka! Poems about Inventors.** Illustrated by K. Bennett Chavez. Millbrook, 2002. 48 pp. ISBN 0-7613-1665-5. Poetry

In this slim volume, readers learn about familiar individuals, such as Marie Curie, and those less well known, such as George D. Mestral, inventor of Velcro; Walter Morrison, who gave us the Frisbee; Dr. Sara Josephine Baker, who founded the first government agency devoted to children's health; and Francois-Louis Cailler, who created the first chocolate bar. What these individuals have in common is their ability to see beyond the obvious and to pursue a dream.

11 Health, Medicine, and Nutrition

Nonfiction

11.1 Billitteri, Thomas J. **Alternative Medicine.** Twenty-First Century Books, 2001. 112 pp. ISBN 0-7613-0965-9. Nonfiction

Alternative medicine includes therapies such as herbs, acupuncture, hypnosis, and special diets that are believed to influence health. Through the use of ten hypothetical cases representing situations in which alternative medicine might be considered, the author describes some of the more popular types of therapies. This book includes source notes, a glossary, an index, and a list of alternative medicine resources.

11.2 Bisignano, Alphonse. **Cooking the Italian Way: Revised and Expanded to Include New Low-Fat and Vegetarian Recipes.** Lerner, 2002. 72 pp. ISBN 0-8225-4113-0. Nonfiction

A revised and expanded edition, this cookbook not only gives ideas on what and how to cook for dinner but also provides information on the culture behind these Italian recipes. The entire first half of the book introduces readers to the land of Italy, its agriculture, and its cultural traditions, and then offers practical and useful information on preparing for and ensuring safety during cooking. This book does a nice job of making traditional Italian fare accessible without removing it from its rich culture and heritage.

11.3 Brill, Marlene Targ. **Tourette Syndrome.** Twenty-First Century Books, 2002. 92 pp. ISBN 0-7613-2101-2. Nonfiction

Tourette syndrome is a physical disorder that affects millions of people. Those who have it experience movements and sounds, called tics, that are beyond their control. This book is a good resource that provides an extensive definition and discusses causes and latest treatments available for persons living with this disorder. The effects of Tourette syndrome extend to family members, friends, and teachers of the sufferer.

Helpful information for those in a relationship with a person with Tourette is included.

11.4 Brynie, Faith Hickman. **101 Questions about Blood and Circulation, with Answers Straight from the Heart.** Twenty-First Century Books, 2001. 176 pp. ISBN 0-7613-1455-5. Nonfiction

The author presents straightforward responses to hundreds of questions raised by students about blood and circulation. In concise and clear language, and through the generous use of illustrations, complex questions are answered about how blood prevents entropy through an elaborate mechanical system of pumps, pipes, and valves. Details about the circulatory system's ability to transport food and water, as well as serve as a corridor for chemical communication, offer a fascinating picture of the human body's intricate transportation system.

11.5 Brynie, Faith Hickman. **101 Questions about Food and Digestion That Have Been Eating at You . . . Until Now.** Twenty-First Century Books, 2002. 176 pp. ISBN 0-7613-2309-0. Nonfiction

Food provides us with the energy for growth and activity. The author uses various questions, many submitted by students and teachers, to explore fundamental concepts about the process food undergoes to provide the human body with necessary nutrients and energy. Also included are questions related to health and digestion, food safety, and the use of foods as medicine. Illustrated with photographs, diagrams, and informative tables, this book also includes a glossary of terms.

11.6 Brynie, Faith Hickman. **101 Questions about Your Immune System You Felt Defenseless to Answer . . . Until Now.** Twenty-First Century Books, 2000. 176 pp. ISBN 0-7613-1569-1. Nonfiction

This book provides up-to-date answers to more than a hundred questions asked by hundreds of students about the human immune system. Many are questions related to HIV and AIDS, but readers will also gain a complete understanding of the complexities of the human immune system through this valuable resource.

11.7 Gottfried, Ted. **Should Drugs Be Legalized?** Twenty-First Century Books, 2000. 128 pp. ISBN 0-7613-1314-1. Nonfiction

Heroin, crack cocaine, marijuana, nicotine, and even caffeine are among the wide range of substances classified as drugs. This book examines U.S. policy, past and present, governing the use of many different drugs. It includes a description of how different drugs affect the mind and the body, the potential risks and benefits associated with each, and the distinction between addictive and habitual use. The reader must weigh the evidence and decide whether the War on Drugs should continue.

11.8 Gottlieb, Lori. **Stick Figure: A Diary of My Former Self.** Berkley, 2001. 240 pp. ISBN 0-425-17890-0. Nonfiction

According to statistics cited in this diary that reads like a novel, 50 percent of today's *fourth-grade* girls diet because they think they are too fat. At age eleven, the author experienced anorexia, and she chronicles, with humor and compassion, how she managed to traverse that perilous time in her life. The book provides useful insight for all young girls—particularly for those with an eating disorder—and for the adults who care about them and who need to care for them.

11.9 Harris, Jacqueline L. **Sickle Cell Disease.** Twenty-First Century Books, 2001. 96 pp. ISBN 0-7613-1459-8. Nonfiction

This easily read informational resource about sickle-cell anemia provides interesting stories of victims and survivors as well as inspiration and education about this heredity disease. The author provides up-to-date material, including causes and symptoms, as well as information about celebrities living with this illness. Illustrations further aid understanding.

11.10 Hughes, Meredith Sayles. **Flavor Foods: Spices and Herbs.** Lerner, 2000. 88 pp. ISBN 0-8225-2835-5. Nonfiction

With numerous diagrams and maps, this book from the Plants We Eat series describes how spices and herbs are grown and used, as well as providing some fascinating facts about the history of particular plants. Did you know that wars were fought over spices, or that peppercorns sometimes substituted for money during the Middle Ages? Recipes for fare such as chicken curry, ginger beer, and cinnamon-almond snails are included in case readers would like to experiment in the kitchen.

11.11 Hughes, Meredith Sayles. **Green Power: Leaf & Flower Vegetables.** Lerner, 2001. 80 pp. ISBN 0-8225-2839-8. Nonfiction

This book provides a historical perspective on green plants that contain powerful nutrients: cabbage, broccoli, artichokes, spinach, and endive. Among the interesting facts the author offers about the plants is the information that the creator of the cartoon *Popeye* loved spinach and ate it regularly for the nutrients. The book also provides a recipe for each plant and explains why it's so nutritious. A glossary and colorful photographs enhance the reading.

11.12 Hughes, Meredith Sayles. **Hard to Crack: Nut Trees.** Lerner, 2001. 88 pp. ISBN 0-8225-2838-X. Nonfiction

With its in-depth look at pecans, walnuts, almonds, cashews, macadamias, and pistachios, this book will make readers hungry. It also describes the interesting trees nuts grow on and gives some unusual and little-known facts about the healing properties of the nuts. Included are excellent recipes using nuts, as well as a variety of illustrations.

11.13 Hyde, Margaret O., and John F. Setaro. **Medicine's Brave New World: Bioengineering and the New Genetics.** Twenty-First Century Books, 2001. 143 pp. ISBN 0-7613-1706-6. Nonfiction

If you needed an organ or bone marrow transplant, would it be acceptable for your parents to have another child for the purpose of providing a donor? Or for cells from a human embryo to be used to grow the necessary tissue? New developments in bioengineering and genetics research hold great promise for the medical world, but each new development comes with ethical questions. This book provides clear, simple explanations and also explores the ethical issues associated with bioengineering.

11.14 Ichord, Loretta Frances. **Toothworms & Spider Juice: An Illustrated History of Dentistry.** Millbrook, 2000. 94 pp. ISBN 0-7613-1465-2. Nonfiction

Starting with ancient misconceptions about the origins of toothaches (toothworms), this book describes the history of dental care from ancient Egyptians to modern times. It includes a rogues' gallery of herbal remedies (garlic inserted into the nose), superstitious treatments (kissing a donkey), and gory procedures ("tooth drawers"—pulling teeth with blacksmith's tongs), as well as commentary on inventions such as the dentist's chair and modern drills and the advent of the use of anesthesia.

11.15 Jackson, Donna M. **Twin Tales: The Magic and the Mystery of Multiple Birth.** Little, Brown, 2001. 48 pp. ISBN 0-316-45431-1. Nonfiction

What is it like to be a twin? Twins born months apart, twins married to twins, and twins separated at birth are only a few of the fascinating stories included in this book. The author, whose mother was a twin, explains the biological phenomena of identical, fraternal, and conjoined twins and multiple births. Many stories about and photos of real life twins are used to help readers understand the special relationships twins have with each other.

11.16 Kramer, Barbara. **The Founders of Famous Food Companies.** Enslow, 2001. 100 pp. ISBN 0-7660-1537-8. Nonfiction

Ten biographical sketches of founders of famous food companies include Milton S. Hershey, pioneer of the chocolate bar; Colonel Harland Sanders, who developed a secret chicken recipe; and Ben Cohen and Jerry Greenfield, who make ice cream. Another, Dave Thomas, founder of Wendy's, dropped out of school at age fifteen. After a few unsuccessful attempts at opening a restaurant, Thomas came up with the idea of offering hamburgers made fresh rather than frozen.

11.17 Madison, Lynda. **The Feelings Book: The Care & Keeping of Your Emotions.** Illustrated by Norm Bendell. Pleasant Company, 2002. 104 pp. ISBN 1-58485-528-2. Nonfiction

A companion book to *The Care & Keeping of You: The Body Book for Girls* and part of the American Girl Library series, this book provides an inside look at our emotions. Starting with an explanation of feelings and why they ebb and flow, the book then gives insight into specific feelings, explaining why we have these feelings. It also provides sections on "what happens" and "what to do" that give helpful advice for anyone overwhelmed by emotion.

11.18 McClafferty, Clara Killough. **The Head Bone's Connected to the Neck Bone: The Weird, Wacky, and Wonderful X-Ray.** Farrar, Straus and Giroux, 2001. 132 pp. ISBN 0-374-32908-7. Nonfiction

X rays have revolutionized the study of medicine and also influenced art, music, science, industry, television, advertising, and many other facets of everyday life. The author traces the history of the mysterious X-ray beginning with the work of Roentgen in Germany during the late 1800s. Illustrations and photographs contribute to this story filled with amazement and tragedy.

11.19 Moragne, Wendy. **Depression.** Twenty-First Century Books, 2001. 112 pp. ISBN 0-7613-1774-0. Nonfiction

This book is designed to address any questions and concerns adolescents may have about depression. It examines case studies of teenagers experiencing various forms of depression, diagnoses, symptoms, and treatments. This is a real life look into adolescent depression from the perspective of actual teenagers and is written with an audience of other teenagers in mind.

11.20 Murphy, Wendy B. **Spare Parts: From Peg Legs to Gene Splices.** Twenty-First Century Books, 2001. 160 pp. ISBN 0-7613-1355-9. Nonfiction

Medical device technology has entered a new era. This book traces the development of medical science in dealing with the replacement of damaged or missing human body parts. In explicit terms, the author contrasts antiquated and modern developments in organ transplants, genetic engineering, and replacement limbs. The book includes illustrations and photographs and incorporates a discussion of ethical and social issues related to humanity's ability to alter the natural order of things.

11.21 Silverstein, Alvin, Virginia Silverstein, and Laura Silverstein Nunn. **Cells.** Twenty-First Century Books, 2002. 64 pp. ISBN 0-7613-2254-X. Nonfiction

Cells are the building blocks of life, and the authors take the reader on a microscopic journey exploring the components of a cell and their functions, including specialization. The complex nature of cell division is illuminated through clear tables, diagrams, and illustrations. Controversial topics including cloning and stem cell research are included in a discussion on the future of the cell in science and research. The book includes a glossary of terms and listings of resources.

11.22 Silverstein, Alvin, Virginia Silverstein, and Laura Silverstein Nunn. **DNA.** Twenty-First Century Books, 2002. 64 pp. ISBN 0-7613-2257-4. Nonfiction

DNA is the working part of genetic material, providing the code that determines the characteristics of new cells and the instructions for forming new cells. The authors describe this complex process of heredity in succinct detail. Illustrations and sidebars guide the reader through an investigation of heredity, genetic mutations, the Human Genome Project, and life-changing applications of DNA research. The book includes a glossary, index, and lists of additional resources.

11.23 Smith, Linda Wasmer. **Depression: What It Is, How to Beat It.** Enslow, 2000. 64 pp. ISBN 0-7660-1357-X. Nonfiction

What is the difference between feeling sad and dealing with true depression? Why are so many more females likely to experience depression than males? What are the warning signs, where can you go for support, and what kinds of help are the most useful? These and other questions are addressed in a concise manner, providing an easy-to-follow introduction to this important health topic.

11.24 Sperekas, Nicole B. **SuicideWise: Taking Steps against Teen Suicide.** Enslow, 2000. 64 pp. ISBN 0-7660-1360-X. Nonfiction

In the past two decades, suicide rates among teenagers ages fifteen to nineteen have tripled. Written by a child psychologist, this book provides current thinking that relates suicide to drug and alcohol abuse and depression, outlines the warning signs, and explains why so many teens experience suicidal tendencies. The book provides ways to help prevent such tragedies and discusses how friends and family members of a loved one who commits suicide can cope with the feelings and emotional tensions they experience.

11.25 Tull, Mary Herd. **Dreams: Mind Movies of the Night.** Illustrated by Amy Ning. Millbrook, 2000. 64 pp. ISBN 0-7613-1512-8. Nonfiction

This book addresses the scientific and cultural explanations of dreams through a question-and-answer format. It discusses the significance of dreams in the ancient world and in world religions such as Islam, Judaism, and Christianity. Dreams have inspired and changed the world. Albert Einstein's teenage dreams about sledding, for instance, led to his discovery of the theory of relativity. This book has a list of dream definitions, bibliographical references, and an index.

11.26 Vogel, Carole Garbuny. **Breast Cancer: Questions and Answers for Young Women.** Twenty-First Century Books, 2001. 176 pp. ISBN 0-7613-1855-0. Nonfiction

For many girls, puberty brings with it questions and concerns about breast cancer. This book uses a question-and-answer format to provide teens with information on topics ranging from how cells become cancerous to what to expect if your mother has breast cancer. Offering clear, direct answers to pressing questions that readers may be afraid to ask, this book also includes diagrams and photographs, glossary, resource list, and index.

11.27 Whitman, Sylvia. **What's Cooking? The History of American Food.** Lerner, 2001. 88 pp. ISBN 0-8225-1732-9. Nonfiction

From seventeenth-century settlers' fare to modern fast food, author and restaurant critic Sylvia Whitman describes the history of food in America. She discusses foods of various generations and includes sections on planting, harvesting, packaging, and cooking. Also included are chapters about America's fascination with oysters, early food packaging, and the unique demands of feeding U.S. soldiers.

11.28 Yancey, Diane. **STDs: What You Don't Know Can Hurt You.** Twenty-First Century Books, 2002. 128 pp. ISBN 0-7613-1957-3. Nonfiction

Did you know that you don't have to "go all the way" to contract sexually transmitted diseases (STDs)? If you think only other people get STDs, this book will make you think twice. The personal stories of teens who contracted STDs help readers understand the short- and long-term risks associated with casual sex. The book includes information on the transmission, symptoms, and treatment of diseases, including chlamydia, genital herpes, and HIV/AIDS, along with advice on how to reduce the risk.

11.29 Yancey, Diane. **Tuberculosis.** Twenty-First Century Books, 2001. 128 pp. ISBN 0-7613-1624-8. Nonfiction

Contrary to popular belief, tuberculosis is *not* a disease of the past. This book chronicles the lives of nineteenth-century and present-day victims and provides scientific information about how this airborne bacterial infection attacks the lungs. In addition, the book describes the efforts of public health agencies worldwide to combat the disease.

Fiction

11.30 Cole, Babette. **Hair in Funny Places: A Book about Puberty.** Hyperion, 2000. Unpaged. ISBN 0-7868-0590-0. Fiction

When the little girl in this picture book asks her teddy bear about growing up, the bear tells her all about Mr. and Mrs. Hormone. The book provides a clear, simple introduction to puberty for young children and many laughs for those who are already familiar with Mr. and Mrs. Hormone. It is also appropriate for junior high and middle school students seeking basic information.

11.31 Ellis, Ella Thorp. **The Year of My Indian Prince.** Delacourt, 2001. 212 pp. ISBN 0-385-32779-X. Fiction

April Thorp is in high school with everything going her way. She is on a swim team with her boyfriend Mike when she suddenly becomes tired and sick. The news is startling: April has tuberculosis. When April is sent to a hospital for tuberculosis patients, her boyfriend bolts. April must face this disease with the help of the staff, Dr. Shipman, her father, and new friends, including a handsome Indian prince who courts her. This novel is based on the author's personal experiences.

11.32 Hamilton, Virginia. **Bluish.** Scholastic, 2002. 127 pp. ISBN 0-439-36786-7. Fiction

Dreenie is stunned to discover a new girl sitting in a wheelchair and clutching a puppy in her class. How should she act? Can she catch the girl's disease? Weaving excerpts from Dreenie's diary into the main narrative, this poignant novel describes Dreenie's growing friendship with the newcomer, Natalie, whom everyone calls Bluish because her life-threatening illness makes her skin so pale. Although the overall tone is serious, the antics of Dreenie's dramatic friend Tuli provide some laughter too.

11.33 Kerner, Charlotte. **Blueprint.** Translated from the German by Elizabeth D. Crawford. Lerner, 2000. 187 pp. ISBN 0-8225-0080-9. Fiction

Iris Sellen, famous concert pianist, is desperate to sustain her legacy when she is diagnosed with multiple sclerosis at the age of thirty. Convincing a genetic scientist to clone her, she succeeds, giving birth to Siri, her genetic twin. Told as a memoir from Siri's point of view, this absorbing novel engages the reader in the unhappy struggle of the daughter/clone's attempts to find her own identity and come to terms with her genetic past.

11.34 McCormick, Patricia. **Cut.** Front Street, 2000. 168 pp. ISBN 1-886910-61-8. Fiction

This novel portrays one teenager's attempt to maintain her mental stability, detailing the maladaptive coping mechanisms she uses as a way to stay alive. Readers join Callie during her first day at Sea Pines, a residential treatment facility for troubled teens, and follow her on the path she takes to recovery.

11.35 McDaniel, Lurlene. **How Do I Love Thee? Three Stories.** Bantam, 2001. 258 pp. ISBN 0-553-57154-0. Fiction

Three stories feature a diverse set of couples all facing serious odds that test the limits of their love. Brett, in remission from leukemia, falls for Shayla, suffering from a rare genetic disorder that makes her terribly sensitive to light. Dana has to decide which of two brothers should receive her heart, a choice made more complicated because one is dying of cancer. Laura, waiting for a heart transplant, learns about the importance of love in facing whatever life deals her.

11.36 Pennebaker, Ruth. **Both Sides Now.** Laurel-Leaf, 2002. 202 pp. ISBN 0-440-22933-2. Fiction

Told in two voices, Lisa's, a high school junior, and Rebecca's, her mother, we hear the story of how cancer disrupts lives once felt to be safe and how, through the struggle, courage, strength, and hope come to be differently defined. With Rebecca and Lisa, readers come to recognize the importance of not counting on an endless future and of letting people you love know how you feel about them.

11.37 Trueman, Terry. **Stuck in Neutral**. HarperCollins, 2000. 114 pp. ISBN 0-06-028519-2. Fiction

At age fourteen, Shawn McDaniel exists imprisoned in his body, unable to speak or move since birth. Unknown to all those around him, Shawn's mind is vital, and he observes and remembers everything he experiences. Only through his seizures does he feel that he experiences a world beyond the confines of his body, especially since the medication makes them painless. But his father, an award-winning poet, believes that Shawn suffers during these episodes and wants his son to be free from pain—but at the price of death.

11.38 Wilson, Jacqueline. **Girls under Pressure.** Delacorte, 2002. 160 pp. ISBN 0-385-72975-8. Fiction

When Ellie's friends enter a modeling contest, Ellie's insecurities about her body intensify. Although her teacher and stepmother assure her that her weight is normal, she begins a strict regimen of starving herself and exercising, occasionally making herself throw up when she can't help binging. Soon food is all she can think about, distracting her from her talent as an artist and her place in her family. Will an acquaintance's similar plight help Ellie reassess her actions?

12 Nature, Animals, and the Environment

12.1 Aaseng, Nathan. **Wildshots: The World of the Wildlife Photographer.** Millbrook, 2001. 80 pp. ISBN 0-7613-1551-9. Nonfiction

The world of wildlife photographers as depicted through media leaves the impression of a glamorous and exciting career. While this is at times true, the author draws readers into interesting anecdotes demonstrating the demanding skills, patience, and extensive knowledge of wildlife necessary to be successful in a crowded career field. The book is illustrated with colorful photographs and vivid anecdotes. It also includes additional readings and steps to finding out more about this fascinating career.

12.2 Baker, Beth. **Sylvia Earle, Guardian of the Sea.** Lerner, 2001. 112 pp. ISBN 0-8225-4961-1. Nonfiction

This biography recounts the adventures of one of the world's foremost defenders of the sea and its creatures. The story of Sylvia Earle, one of the first female marine biologists, is full of excitement and adventure, including walking the bottom of the Pacific Ocean, swimming with whales, and living under the sea for two weeks.

12.3 Bishop, Nic. **Digging for Bird-Dinosaurs: An Expedition to Madagascar.** Houghton Mifflin, 2000. 48 pp. ISBN 0-395-96056-8. Nonfiction

The link between birds and dinosaurs has fascinated paleontologists for more than a century. This link obtains credibility through the fossil discovery of a primitive bird that lived alongside dinosaurs about seventy million years ago. The author uses photographs to illustrate the story of this important discovery on the island of Madagascar and its contribution to our understanding of bird evolution.

12.4 Bright, Michael. **Storms at Sea.** Copper Beech, 2002. 32 pp. ISBN 0-7613-2724-X. Nonfiction

Though beautiful when calm, the ocean can quickly turn deadly. Powerful ocean storms pose a serious threat to humans worldwide. Full of photographs and diagrams, this book describes the forces that come together to create hurricanes, tsunamis, rogue waves, and many other ocean storms. The author also tells about ocean weather forecasting and chronicles the devastating damage caused by the ocean. This book in the Awesome Oceans series includes a glossary and an index.

12.5 Conniff, Richard. **Rats! The Good, the Bad, and the Ugly.** Crown, 2002. 36 pp. ISBN 0-375-81207-5. Nonfiction

The author uses wit and scientific fact to describe the world of Earth's most successful animal—the rat. Colorfully illustrated with vivid photographs, this book includes discussions on the biology of these rodents, their behavior, their role in spreading disease, and their intelligence. The reader learns fascinating and impressive information about the rat's successful survival and amazing capabilities. An index is included.

12.6 Downs, Sandra. **Earth's Fiery Fury.** Twenty-First Century Books, 2000. 64 pp. ISBN 0-7613-1413-X. Nonfiction

Volcanoes, fumaroles, lava landscapes, and geysers are just a few of the explosive forces of nature explored in this book. Especially interesting are examples of worldwide thermal displays. These "hot" geologic topics are explained in detail and accompanied by colorful, captioned photographs. A detailed glossary, index, recommended resource guide, and list of Web sites are included in the back of the book.

12.7 Downs, Sandra. **Shaping the Earth: Erosion.** Twenty-First Century Books, 2000. 64 pp. ISBN 0-7613-1414-8. Nonfiction

Looking for a clear, easy to read, and well-illustrated book about how Earth's surfaces came to be? This smart picture book highlights what young scientists need to know about Earth's formations and how they affect the world we live in. In this excellent resource for budding researchers who want to know more about the complex and ever-changing world of our environment, the pictures are smartly labeled and key terms are well defined.

12.8 Downs, Sandra. **When the Earth Moves.** Twenty-First Century Books, 2000. 64 pp. ISBN 0-7613-1412-1. Nonfiction

This informative and nicely illustrated book introduces readers to the many ways that our planet is always in motion. Earthquakes, landslides, rockslides, mudflows, and avalanches are some of the many ways in which the volatile planet shows us that it is always changing.

12.9 Facklam, Margery. **Spiders and Their Web Sites.** Illustrated by Alan Male. Little, Brown, 2001. 32 pp. ISBN 0-316-27329-5. Nonfiction.

Long before the Internet, spiders were weaving webs to attract their prey. This book describes how twelve different kinds of spiders, along with the daddy longlegs (which only looks like a spider), build and use their webs to survive. Readers will learn more about how dangerous the feared tarantula really is, why spiders are important for insect control, and even which spider can survive under water. The book begins with an introduction to spiders and includes a glossary and a list of additional resources.

12.10 Feldman, Jane. **I Am a Rider.** Random House, 2000. Unpaged. ISBN 0-679-88664-8. Nonfiction

Thirteen-year-old Eve Shinerock possesses a special relationship with Lightning, her horse since she was five years old. Featuring more than seventy-five photographs and told in Eve's own words, this visually appealing book shows Eve at home, at school, and at work, where she helps her mother with riding lessons for other children. It also includes some suspense: what will happen to Eve and Lightning when Eve's parents announce they are moving to a house with no horse barn?

12.11 Friend, Sandra. **Earth's Wild Winds.** Twenty-First Century Books, 2002, 64 pp. ISBN 0-7613-2673-1. Nonfiction

Wind is an invisible force, yet its effects can be observed. From gentle breezes to ferocious attacks, winds shape the world around us. The author explores both the beneficial and the terrifying impact of wind. This text is illustrated with colorful photographs and informative tables and charts and includes a glossary, recommended resources, and an index.

12.12 Hehner, Barbara. **Ice Age Cave Bear: The Giant Beast That Terrified Ancient Humans.** Illustrated by Mark Hallett. Crown, 2002. 32 pp. ISBN 0-375-81329-2. Nonfiction.

Travel back in time to the days of early man and Ice Age creatures, when the cave bear was revered and feared by ancient man. The author describes these creatures in striking detail, exploring questions about their place in the culture of early man and their extinction. Included are color photographs and maps, a glossary, and sources for additional information.

12.13 Hehner, Barbara. **Ice Age Mammoth: Will This Ancient Creature Come Back to Life?** Illustrated by Mark Hallett. Crown, 2001. 32 pp. ISBN 0-375-82192-9. Nonfiction

Colorful illustrations and photographs tell the story of this magnificent prehistoric creature and how it has been frozen in time. This book chronicles the mammoth's travels from Africa to Siberia, where remains, including those of a baby, have been found, and explores whether the modern technologies of cloning will allow the woolly mammoth to live again. A glossary, suggested further readings, Web resources, and an index are included.

12.14 Hehner, Barbara. **Ice Age Sabertooth: The Most Ferocious Cat That Ever Lived.** Illustrated by Mark Hallett. Crown, 2002. 32 pp. ISBN 0-375-81328-4. Nonfiction

The saber-toothed tiger's trademark is perhaps its seven-inch-long teeth, razor sharp with serrated inner edges. These and other fascinating characteristics of this ferocious animal come alive through powerful illustrations and descriptions. The book discusses what the creature looked like, how and what it hunted, and the causes of its extinction. Included are a glossary, additional resource lists, and an index.

12.15 Helfer, Ralph. **Mosey: The Remarkable Friendship of a Boy and His Elephant.** Orchard, 2002. 133 pp. ISBN 0-439-29313-8. Nonfiction

Bram Gunterstein and the elephant he calls Mosey live in a small German town where Bram's father trains elephants. The boy and the animal have a unique relationship. When the circus is sold, Bram stows away on a ship to stay with his special friend. The story is a true one; the author has taken factual information and added dialogue and a plot line.

12.16 Hirschi, Ron. **Salmon.** Carolrhoda, 2001. 48 pp. ISBN 1-57505-482-5. Nonfiction

Smart, crisp, and *informative* are all words to describe this nature book about an American delicacy—Pacific Northwest salmon. This book examines the anatomy, habitat, behavior, life cycle, and legends of this torpedo-shaped fish. With handsome color photographs, this book is a perfect fit for the young person who loves science—particularly marine life—and wants a quick and easy read about this venerable and nutritious fish.

12.17 Jackson, Donna M. **The Wildlife Detectives: How Forensic Scientists Fight Crimes against Nature.** Photographs by Wendy Shattil and Bob Rozinski. Houghton Mifflin, 2000. 48 pp. ISBN 0-395-86976-5. Nonfiction

More than 90 percent of crimes against wildlife go unpunished. Through photographs, illustrations, and tragic accounts, the author chronicles the work of the wildlife detectives at the National Fish and Wildlife Forensics Laboratory in Oregon. These detectives use forensic clues such as DNA, bone fragments, bloodstains, footprints, firearms, and other evidence to fight crimes against animals. The author shows how the work of these men and women helps protect endangered species and our natural wildlife resources from human destruction.

12.18 Johnson, Sylvia A. **Songbirds: The Language of Song.** Carolrhoda, 2001. 48 pp. ISBN 1-57505-483-3. Nonfiction

For naturalists and the merely curious, this book introduces the phenomenon of birdsong, explaining how and why birds sing, how scientists learn about bird communication, and the dangers to songbirds due to changes in their habitats. Bird lovers, bird watchers, and just plain bird observers will enjoy the chance to learn more about a species that inhabits our daily lives without much fanfare or recognition.

12.19 Kurth, Linda Moore. **Keiko's Story: A Killer Whale Goes Home.** Twenty-First Century Books, 2000. 72 pp. ISBN 0-7613-1500-4. Nonfiction

In 1996, Keiko, a killer whale, began a journey from a small pool in Mexico City to his current home in Iceland. This book recounts in photographs and facts a wealth of information about Keiko and his orca roots, combining the story of Keiko's journey, fascinating details about killer whales, and the logistics involved in transporting a mammoth sea creature across many continents. The reader's journey concludes with plenty of references.

12.20 Maze, Stephanie, and Catherine O'Neill Grace. **I Want to Be an Environmentalist.** Harcourt, 2000. 47 pp. ISBN 0-15-201862-X. Nonfiction

Readers are given a thorough overview of environmentalism, from its history to current research in the field. Colorful photographs help present the many careers that focus on the environment and the individuals who have made significant contributions to its preservation. Topics covered include rain forests, recycling, pollution, endangered species, and other issues that have attracted global attention and effort. Additional resources include a basic glossary and a listing of environmental organizations.

12.21 Montgomery, Sy. **Encantado: Pink Dolphin of the Amazon.** Photographs by Dianne Taylor-Snow. Houghton Mifflin, 2002. 73 pp. ISBN 0-618-13103-5. Nonfiction

Experience the magic of the Amazon through vivid descriptions and luxuriant photographs. The author guides the reader on an adventure with scientists and researchers in search of the bufeo Colorado—the astonishing river-dwelling dolphins ranging in color from white to vivid pink called *encantados,* or enchanted ones, by the local people. The book includes notes on how it was researched, information sources on the Amazon, statistics on the Amazon and whales, questions to which scientists don't yet have answers, and suggestions for further reading.

12.22 Norell, Mark A., and Lowell Dingus. **A Nest of Dinosaurs: The Story of Oviraptor.** Illustrated by Mark Ellison. Doubleday, 1999. 42 pp. ISBN 0-385-32558-4. Nonfiction

Dinosaur fossils found in the Gobi Desert in 1993 provide new clues about oviraptor, a dinosaur first believed to be an egg-stealing killer. This discovery, including a dinosaur embryo and a parent sitting on its nest of eggs, brought into question conclusions about oviraptor that had been based on fossil records discovered in the 1920s. Sidebars provide information about the work and training of paleontologists, and photographs and illustrations provide information about the fossils and the geography of the Ukhaa Tolgod.

12.23 Orenstein, Ronald, with a foreword by Jane Goodall. **New Animal Discoveries.** Millbrook, 2001. 64 pp. ISBN 0-7613-2274-4. Nonfiction

The author, a zoologist, unveils some of the fascinating new animal discoveries of the last fifteen years. This journey around the world shows how scientists discover, identify, and name new species. Many of these animals are in danger of extinction, creating a race against time to find millions of yet undiscovered species. From microscopic organisms to huge whales, the animals in this work are illustrated with rare photographs.

12.24 Patent, Dorothy Hinshaw. **Shaping the Earth.** Photographs by William Muñoz. Clarion, 2000. 88 pp. ISBN 0-395-85691-4. Nonfiction

The author gives a concise account of Earth's history from its beginnings more than 4.5 billion years ago to the present. She describes, frequently using vivid photographs, some of the forces that have had the most profound effect on our planet. Looking toward a new millennium, she also presents the impact of humans on the environment. The work includes a glossary of terms, a list of books and magazines for further reading, and a list of relevant Web sites.

12.25 Pringle, Laurence. **The Environmental Movement: From Its Roots to the Challenges of a New Century.** HarperCollins, 2000. 144 pp. ISBN 0-688-15626-6. Nonfiction

Outlining the growth of the environmental movement from its early beginnings during the seventeenth century, author Pringle describes the impact of key events such as the first Earth Day, the growth of organizations focused on the environment and conservation, and the responsibility of government in environmental issues. The efforts of writers, philosophers, scientists, politicians, and ordinary citizens on behalf of environmental issues are highlighted. The book includes further readings and a listing of both private and governmental groups and agencies.

12.26 Silverstein, Alvin, Virginia Silverstein, and Laura Silverstein Nunn. **Different Dogs.** Twenty-First Century Books, 2000. 48 pp. ISBN 0-7613-1370-2. Nonfiction

This book provides information about various popular dogs including Akitas, bulldogs, Chihuahuas, dachshunds, shih tzus, and others. The authors discuss pet care, including emotional as well as physical needs. Individual sections provide information on the history of the dog and aspects of the animal's temperament that should be considered before obtaining one as a pet. Each section concludes with a listing of Internet resources that provide additional information.

12.27 Silverstein, Alvin, Virginia Silverstein, and Laura Silverstein Nunn. **Pocket Pets.** Twenty-First Century Books, 2000. 48 pp. ISBN 0-7613-1370-2. Nonfiction

This book provides information about pets typically small enough to fit in a pocket, presenting both pros and cons involved in caring for small pets such as chinchillas, hamsters, guinea pigs, rabbits, and other small exotic pets. Individual sections provide information on the history of the particular pet as well as their physical and emotional needs. Each section concludes with a listing of Internet resources that provide additional information.

12.28 Tagliaferro, Linda. **Galápagos Islands: Nature's Delicate Balance at Risk.** Lerner, 2001. 88 pp. ISBN 0-8225-0648-3. Nonfiction

For centuries, scientists have been fascinated by the Galápagos Islands, a chain of small islands located near the equator in the Pacific Ocean. Still unspoiled, the Galápagos are famous for the vast variety of species found there. Close study of these different species led Charles Darwin to propose his theory of evolution. The book describes research projects on the Galápagos and efforts to protect the islands' biodiversity from natural and human threats. Additional resources include glossary, index, and resource list.

12.29 Thomas, Peggy. **Big Cat Conservation.** Twenty-First Century Books, 2000. 64 pp. ISBN 0-7613-3231-6. Nonfiction

Part of The Science of Saving Animals series, this book begins with a rationale for saving large feline species from the threats to their habitats. Next, author Thomas goes into detail about how scientists track lions, panthers, tigers, and other big cats, as well as the problem of poaching. Details are provided about the use of noninvasive tracking methods and scientific efforts to help cats share their environments with humans, as well as about successful conservation efforts.

12.30 Thomas, Peggy. **Bird Alert.** Twenty-First Century Books, 2000. 57 pp. ISBN 0-7613-1457-1. Nonfiction

This book will appeal to anyone interested in the conservation of birds and their habitats. Readers learn about how ornithologists, scientists who study birds, are working to protect these creatures from extinction and about techniques for studying birds, such as banding and netting. A chapter titled "Citizen Science" explains how volunteers can help collect information for scientific bird counts. The book also includes a glossary, suggestions for further reading, related Internet sites, and beautiful color photographs with detailed captions.

12.31 Thomas, Peggy. **Reptile Rescue.** Twenty-First Century Books, 2000. 64 pp. ISBN 0-7613-3232-4. Nonfiction

Part of the The Science of Saving Animals series, this book begins with a rationale for saving reptiles from the threats to their habitats. Next, author Thomas goes into detail about how scientists track turtles, as well as the problem of poaching that many reptile species face. Details are provided about the use of DNA in genetic tracking of reptilian species and about scientific efforts to save alligators, turtles, and snakes. The closing chapter describes successful conservation efforts.

12.32 Winner, Cherie. **Woodpeckers.** Carolrhoda, 2000. 47 pp. ISBN 1-57505-445-0. Nonfiction

Out of about 182 kinds of woodpeckers in the world, more than half a dozen species are fighting for existence due to human actions and loss of their environment. Far from being the crazy creature many think of from cartoons, the woodpecker's excavations provide other woodland creatures homes and food. But this woodland bird can cause havoc too, as was once proved at the Kennedy Space Center in 1995. This book is a good source for information about and photographs of woodpeckers.

Nonfiction Series

12.33 Biomes of North America Series:

Johnson, Rebecca L. **A Walk in the Boreal Forest.** Illustrated by Phyllis V. Saroff. Carolrhoda, 2001. 48 pp. ISBN 1-57505-156-7. Nonfiction

Johnson, Rebecca L. **A Walk in the Deciduous Forest.** Illustrated by Phyllis V. Saroff. Carolrhoda, 2001. 48 pp. ISBN 1-57505-155-9. Nonfiction

Johnson, Rebecca L. **A Walk in the Desert.** Illustrated by Phyllis V. Saroff. Carolrhoda, 2001. 48 pp. ISBN 1-57505-152-4. Nonfiction

Johnson, Rebecca L. **A Walk in the Prairie.** Illustrated by Phyllis V. Saroff. Carolrhoda, 2001. 48 pp. ISBN 1-57505-153-2. Nonfiction

Johnson, Rebecca L. **A Walk in the Rain Forest.** Illustrated by Phyllis V. Saroff. Carolrhoda, 2001. 48 pp. ISBN 1-57505-154-0. Nonfiction

Johnson, Rebecca L. **A Walk in the Tundra.** Illustrated by Phyllis V. Saroff. Carolrhoda, 2001. 48 pp. ISBN 1-57505-157-5. Nonfiction

Colorful photographs and detailed illustrations propel readers on a journey through the biomes of North America. They can explore the fascinating worlds of the boreal forest, the deciduous forest, the desert, the prairie, the rain forest, and the tundra. Easy-to-read narratives explain how plants and animals depend on each other for survival. Each book includes words to know, a list of books and Web resources, and an index.

Secrets of the Rainforest Series:

12.34 Chinery, Michael. **Partners and Parents.** Crabtree, 2000. 32 pp. ISBN 0-7787-0226-X. Nonfiction

Chinery, Michael. **Plants and Planteaters.** Crabtree, 2000. 32 pp. ISBN 0-7787-0228-6. Nonfiction

Chinery, Michael. **Poisoners and Pretenders.** Crabtree, 2000. 32 pp. ISBN 0-7787-0229-4. Nonfiction

Chinery, Michael. **Predators and Prey.** Crabtree, 2000. 32 pp. ISBN 0-7787-0227-8. Nonfiction

In this series of informational books, a celebrated naturalist introduces readers to the fascinating world of the rain forest. Through colorful pictures and easy-to-read text, readers get a revealing look at the startling array of plant and animal life that is threatened in these fragile wildernesses.

Fiction

12.35 Anderson, Laurie Halse. **Fear of Falling.** American Girl, 2001. 105 pp. ISBN 1-58485-059-0. Fiction

David Hutchinson loves to ride horses and spends his afternoons and evenings working at the stables and helping as a volunteer at the Wild at Heart Veterinary Hospital. When his father returns to the family after a year's absence, David must find a way to bridge the difficulties that have developed between them. David must also find a way to conquer his fear after falling from a horse.

12.36 Anderson, Laurie Halse. **Masks.** Pleasant Company, 2002. 91 pp. ISBN 1-58485-531-2. Fiction

Sunita is one of the young volunteers at a local veterinary clinic. After assisting with her cat's surgery, she questions her aspirations to work with sick animals. She is offered an internship working at an animal research lab and wrestles with hard decisions about using live animals for testing the development of new medicines.

12.37 Anderson, Laurie Halse. **Say Good-Bye.** American Girl, 2001. 125 pp. ISBN 1-58485-051-5. Fiction

This book, from the Wild at Heart series, features Zoe, who comes to live with her veterinarian grandmother and learns some valuable lessons about life through her work with animals. Zoe misses her mother but with the help of a friend becomes involved with dog therapy at the local children's cancer wing. This gives Zoe and her puppy the opportunity to help others.

12.38 Anderson, Laurie Halse. **Time to Fly.** American Girl, 2002. 113 pp. ISBN 1-58485-061-2. Fiction

Zoe lives with her grandmother, a local veterinarian. When she sees flocks of parrots in a tree in her backyard, she knows that something is wrong. Then her mother arrives to announce that she would like to have Zoe move back to California to be with her. With the help of her understanding grandmother, Zoe works to solve the mystery of the parrots and come to a solution about her family situation.

12.39 Anderson, Laurie Halse. **The Trickster.** American Girl, 2000. 126 pp. ISBN 1-58485-047-7. Fiction

When David sees the horse Trickster, it's love at first sight, but Trickster has been hurt, and it will take time and a lot of care before he can run again. David's determined to ride him, but he's got to prove to Mr. Quinn, owner of the stables, that he's responsible enough to be trusted with the horse, and that won't be easy. David and his fellow volunteers at Wild at Heart, Dr. Mac's veterinary clinic, now have another chance to prove themselves.

12.40 Avi. **The Good Dog.** Atheneum, 2001. 243 pp. ISBN 0-689-83824-7. Fiction

This is an adventure story of dogs and wolves narrated by McKinley, a malamute owned by a boy named Jack. When a she-wolf is wounded in a canyon near the edge of town, McKinley, the other dogs, and his "human pup" Jack attempt to save her and lead her to safety. McKinley must also compete for the job of head dog against an Irish setter who is determined to track the wolf and become the next leader of the pack.

12.41 Bell, Hilari. **Songs of Power.** Hyperion, 2000. 219 pp. ISBN 0-786-80561-7. Fiction

Mourning the loss of her Inuit shaman grandmother, Imina struggles to adjust to life in a science station at the bottom of the ocean. When someone sabotages the station, the members of the community are in grave danger. Drawing on her mystical powers and the help of a friend who has his own reasons for wanting to help, Imina races to discover the saboteur's identity. Will she be successful before their underwater habitat collapses?

12.42 Blatchford, Claire H. **Nick's Secret.** Lerner, 2000. 175 pp. ISBN 0-8225-0743-9. Fiction

Seventh grader Nick is self-conscious about being deaf until he discovers that he is not the only one with a problem. When Nick is lured by the school bully to an old abandoned hotel, he discovers Ionie living in hiding there with a pack of prize sheepdogs. In the midst of a blizzard, Nick devises a plan to help Ionie and protect the dogs from a would-be dognapper.

12.43 Brooke, Lauren. **Coming Home.** Scholastic, 2000. 140 pp. ISBN 0-439-13020-4. Fiction

For Amy, Heartland is not only a place of miracles, where horses are healed under the tender loving care of her mother, but also her home, where she feels confident and capable. Amy inherited her mother's gift with horses. When Amy's mom dies in a car accident and Amy's older sister, Lou, returns to the farm from New York City convinced that Heartland should be sold, Amy fears she will lose all that is dear to her.

12.44 Burgess, Melvin. **Kite.** Farrar, Straus and Giroux, 2000. 182 pp. ISBN 0-374-34228-8. Fiction

In 1964 England, kites are an almost extinct bird of prey, yet young Taylor Mase and his friend Alan manage to raise a red kite. Therefore, the boys must confront the conflicting interests of the English gamekeeping system involving killing birds of prey, the environmentalists' desire to save the kites, Taylor's father's job security under the gamekeeping system, and doing the right thing. *Kite* deals with a serious subject by providing information, describing warm family settings, and injecting suspense and humor throughout.

12.45 Choldenko, Gennifer. **Notes from a Liar and her Dog.** Putnam, 2001. 216 pp. ISBN 0-399-23591-4. Fiction

Eleven-year-old Antonia McPherson, better known as Ant, believes that lying is a way of life. At least, it's the only way she can cope. Stuck in a family she doesn't like, Ant copes by pretending that her "real parents" will be arriving any day to rescue her. And when that doesn't work, she copes by showering love on her dog, Pistachio; volunteering at the neighborhood zoo; and telling "whopper lies" to anyone who will listen.

12.46 George, Jean Craighead. **Frightful's Mountain.** Illustrated by Jean Craighead George. Puffin, 2001. 255 pp. ISBN 0-14-131235-1. Fiction

After being raised in captivity, Frightful, an endangered bird, has to learn to live in the wild without knowing how to take care of herself. As she struggles to survive in her newfound freedom, she remains loyal to the owner who reluctantly had to set her free.

12.47 Harlow, Joan Hiatt. **Star in the Storm.** Aladdin, 2001. 150 pp. ISBN 0-689-84621-5. Fiction

Set in 1912 Newfoundland, this is a story of one dog's bravery in rescuing passengers from a floundering boat in a violent storm. It is also the story of one girl's love for her dog and her courage and devotion to him and her community. This is a story to enthrall all dog lovers, yet its appeal is universal with its themes of courage, devotion, and forgiveness.

12.48 Hiaasen, Carl. **Hoot.** Knopf, 2002. 292 pp. ISBN 0-375-82181-3. Fiction

Roy, a transplant to Florida from Montana, definitely feels like a fish out of water, or perhaps an owl out of its burrow. What starts out as a way to avoid a bully on the school bus quickly draws attention to his cause of rescuing the habitat of burrowing owls. The controversy surrounding the small plot of land these owls nest in brings together the environmental, judicial, political, and personal concerns of all the characters.

12.49 Jennings, Richard W. **The Great Whale of Kansas.** Houghton Mifflin, 2001. 150 pp. ISBN 0-618-10228-0. Fiction

While digging a hole in his backyard, a Kansas boy unearths the fossilized bones of an enormous prehistoric creature. The discovery, though thrilling, brings with it controversy. Told in first person, the unnamed boy fights against the State Museum of Natural History as it attempts to destroy the facts the fossils reveal, facts that may shatter much of what is known about the prehistoric world. He must also contend with his father, who wants to increase the family income through the discovery.

12.50 Kehret, Peg. **Cages.** Puffin, 2001 (Originally published in 1991). 150 pp. ISBN 0-141-31230-0. Fiction

This straightforward narrative tells the story of Kit, a teenage girl who is arrested for shoplifting. As punishment, Kit has to do community service at a local animal shelter. Ashamed, Kit hides her crime and the punishment from her parents—her mother is sick and her father is an alcoholic. At the shelter, Kit learns about how complex life can be and how important honesty is.

12.51 Koja, Kathe. **Straydog.** Frances Foster Books, 2002. 106 pp. ISBN 0-374-37278-0. Fiction

Known for her individuality, Rachel becomes intrigued by a collie she encounters while volunteering at the local animal shelter. Though the animal is feral, Rachel is convinced that if she loves the dog and gains its trust, adoption is possible. As she writes an essay for her English class, Rachel begins to understand the collie, as if through this essay she and the dog have become one. Rachel learns that not all dogs can be tamed, and the collie has to be euthanized.

12.52 Lang, Andrew. **The Animal Story Book.** Illustrated by H. J. Ford. Dover, 2002 (Originally published in 1896). 400 pp. ISBN 0-486-42187-2. Fiction

This reissue of the 1896 book by the same name is an unabridged, unaltered version of short stories, anecdotes, fables, and folktales all involving animals and collected by Lang from various authors and traditions. Lang wanted to give readers stories "about the friends of children and fairies—the beasts," and he presents sixty-six tales ranging from those about very large mammals to those about ants, from those about birds to those about snakes and sea creatures.

12.53 Lawrence, Iain. **Ghost Boy.** Delacorte, 2000. 326 pp. ISBN 0-385-32739-0. Fiction

Weary of the ridicule heaped on him by schoolmates and his parents, Harold "the Ghost," a fourteen-year-old albino boy, leaves home to join the circus. Full of colorful, sometimes freakish people, the circus offers Harold the opportunity to blend in and even seem normal. His success working with the elephants brings him fame in the circus as he searches for love and acceptance.

12.54 London, Jack. **White Fang.** Atheneum, 2000 (Originally published in 1906). Illustrated by Ed Young. 261 pp. ISBN 0-689-82431-9. Fiction

The men who are searching for gold in the Klondike region need good dogs who are strong and can withstand extreme cold. White Fang is such a dog. He learns to fight, to survive, and to mistrust "man-animals." In a brutal world in which only the fittest survive, White Fang comes to glory. Only after being befriended by young Weedon Scott does White Fang realize that humans can be compassionate and that life can include love.

12.55 Porte, Barbara Ann. **Beauty and the Serpent: Thirteen Tales of Unnatural Animals.** Illustrated by Rosemary Feit Covey. Simon & Schuster, 2001. 117 pp. ISBN 0-689-84147-7. Fiction

A collection of fictional, short, and somewhat scary stories describes the events of animals with abnormal interests. Domesticated animals such as cats and dogs along with snakes serve as mysterious and sometimes murderous characters. Combined, these tales might cause the reader to rethink previous ideas of animal "cuddliness" and steer clear of these sometimes dangerous, definitely strange animals.

12.56 Price, Reynolds. **A Perfect Friend.** Atheneum, 2000. 168 pp. ISBN 0-689-83029-7. Fiction

Ben's mother died a year earlier, and he encounters life's dangers and comforts, happiness and sorrow, as he moves toward regaining the sense of safety he lost when his mother died. Through his uncanny ability to communicate with animals and his love of elephants, he finally is able to acknowledge his grief and look to the future. Ben's encounters with Sala, a traveling circus elephant, enable him to deal with his feelings and move on.

12.57 Rawlings, Marjorie Kinnan. **The Yearling.** Aladdin, 2001 (Originally published in 1938). 513 pp. ISBN 0-689-84623-1. Fiction

In this timeless story, Jody is growing up in the isolated, swampy backwoods of Florida. His loneliness is lessened when he adopts an orphaned fawn whom he names Flag. Jody loves the deer, and it becomes his best friend; but as Flag grows, he destroys crops and makes the family's life more difficult. When he must give up his pet, Jody is heartbroken.

12.58 Savage, Deborah. **Summer Hawk.** Puffin, 2001. 298 pp. ISBN 0-14-131220-3. Fiction

Fifteen-year-old Taylor rescues an orphaned baby hawk and, wanting to save the animal's life, finds herself at an animal rehabilitation center in rural Pennsylvania. There she lands a summer public relations job for the center that awakens her deep desire to become a journalist. Fueled by friendship with a special boy and admiration for the skilled doctor at the animal shelter, Taylor senses emotions inside herself that she is just beginning to understand.

12.59 Smith, Roland. **The Last Lobo.** Hyperion, 2001. 178 pp. ISBN 0-786-81564-7. Fiction

Jake is in Brazil with his research biologist father when he hears that his grandfather, Taw, has left his retirement home and returned to the Hopi reservation in Arizona. When Jake goes in search of Taw, he finds not only his grandfather but also a mystery. Livestock on the reservation is being killed, and there is speculation that the culprit may be a Mexican lobo, a wolf species that has long disappeared from Arizona. Jake stays to help solve this environmental issue.

12.60 Taylor, Theodore. **Lord of the Kill.** Blue Sky, 2002. 246 pp. ISBN 0-439-33725-9. Fiction

Sixteen-year-old Ben enjoys his job caring for exotic big cats in the Los Coyotes Preserve. A typical day turns into frightening suspense, however, when he discovers a human body in the habitat of two blood-covered jaguars. In an intriguing turn of events, Lord of the Kill, a valuable Siberian tiger, is kidnapped and held for ransom. This book effectively blends mystery with ethical issues related to poaching of endangered species and canned hunts, or the killing of exotic animals for sport.

Poetry

12.61 Fletcher, Ralph. **Have You Been to the Beach Lately?** Photographs by Andrea Sperling. Orchard, 2001. 48 pp. ISBN 0-531-30330-6. Poetry

These poems, narrated by an eleven-year-old, evoke days at the ocean beach with family, including a little brother, and young teen girls as well as clams, waves, sand in hair and teeth, bonfires at night, and other wonderful beach experiences. The more than thirty poems are enhanced by photographs that help recreate the sights, sounds, and smells of the seashore.

12.62 Levy, Constance. **Splash! Poems of Our Watery World.** Illustrated by David Soman. Orchard, 2002. 40 pp. ISBN 0-439-29318-9. Poetry

This collection of brief poems—none more than twenty-five lines long—explores various aspects of water in our world. Topics range from everyday life (doing laundry, making tea) to the wonders of nature (fog, icebergs, salmon spawning). In addition to creating mind pictures and rhythm, Levy's language is often playful and fun.

12.63 Singer, Marilyn. **Footprints on the Roof: Poems about the Earth.** Illustrated by Meilo So. Knopf, 2002. 40 pp. ISBN 0-375-81094-3. Poetry

A meditative collection of poetry, Singer's *Footprints on the Roof* includes nineteen poems focused on the many seasons, moods, and phenomena of the earth. Sparse language lets readers focus on the element of nature at the heart of each poem. Illustrations by Meilo So accompany each poem and add to the simplistic back-to-nature feel of the collection. Basic themes and patterns help beginning poetry readers understand and appreciate the art form.

V Challenges of Today's World

13 Diversity

13.1 Abelove, Joan. **Go and Come Back.** Puffin, 2000. 177 pp. ISBN 0-14-130694-7. Fiction

Narrated by Alicia, a young woman from a Peruvian jungle village, this episodic novel gives the reader a unique view of culture through two American women, Joanna and Margarita, who have come to Peru's jungle to study Alicia's Isabo culture. Eventually they all learn "how to be" with one another, and the Americans come to understand the logic and richness of the Isabo culture, as does Alicia of the American culture.

13.2 Alvarez, Julia. **How Tía Lola Came to ~~Visit~~ Stay.** Knopf, 2000. 145 pp. ISBN 0-375-90215-0. Fiction

This entertaining novel describes a Dominican American family in Vermont and what happens when their irrepressible aunt, Tía Lola, comes to visit from the Dominican Republic. Follow along as Tía Lola brings laughter and excitement into her nephew Miguel's life. This is a warm and humorous book that will have readers wishing for a Tía Lola of their own.

13.3 Banks, Jacqueline Turner. **A Day for Vincent Chin and Me.** Houghton Mifflin, 2001. 112 pp. ISBN 0-618-13199-X. Fiction

In 1982 Vincent Chin, a Chinese American, was killed in Detroit because his tormentors thought he was Japanese, and they hated the auto industry's competition from Japan. These real events are the catalyst for this novel about Tommy, a Japanese American living in Kentucky who hopes that his mother won't take up Chin's cause because Tommy wants to blend in. When Tommy and his friends take up a cause of their own, Tommy learns to value his mother's activism and his own background.

13.4 Belton, Sandra. **McKendree.** Greenwillow, 2000. 262 pp. ISBN 0-688-15950-8. Fiction

In 1948, Tilara Haynes spends a memorable summer with her Aunt Cloelle in West Virginia. She was sent by her father, a Boston minister, to learn more about her African American roots. During her stay, Tilara and her friends spend time doing odd jobs at a nursing home called McKendree. Tilara finds a new confidence and self-esteem by the end of the summer.

13.5 Bode, Janet. **The Colors of Freedom: Immigrant Stories.** Franklin Watts, 1999. 144 pp. ISBN 0-531-11530-5. Nonfiction

This book is a mosaic of the hopes, dreams, and fears of high school students throughout the United States as they talk about their roots. Included are memories of their homelands through their words, photos, and recipes. Building on a framework that explores the varied composition of those who immigrated here, Janet Bode examines the diversity of American society.

13.6 Bolden, Tonya. **Rock of Ages: A Tribute to the Black Church.** Illustrated by R. Gregory Christie. Knopf, 2002. Unpaged. ISBN 0-679-89485-3. Poetry

This boldly illustrated prose poem powerfully personifies the black church in its many denominations from her "invisible" incarnation during slavery to the present day. The few but precise words convey the history, music, biographies, events, deeds, locations, and inspiration of the church. In addition, the notes and author's note at the end are helpful additions to the information in the main text.

13.7 Bruchac, Joseph. **The Heart of a Chief.** Puffin, 2001. 153 pp. ISBN 0-141-31236-X. Fiction

Should schools use Native American names for sports teams? This is the topic Chris Nicola and his friend choose for their language arts project at Rangerville Junior High. The issue divides his school, just as the question of opening a casino on the Penacook Indian Reservation, where Chris lives, divides his tribe. Chris's developing leadership skills enable him to influence decisions about the questions facing his school and reservation.

13.8 Canales, Viola. **Orange Candy Slices and Other Secret Tales.** Piñata, 2001. 122 pp. ISBN 1-55885-332-4. Fiction

This collection of short stories invites readers into the lives of Mexican Americans. At times the tales are humorous as the narrator attempts to make sense of her life and her place in her family. Other times it is filled with sadness as she loses loved ones. The important role that religion plays in the narrator's life is presented in a lighthearted manner. All of the stories are warm and welcoming.

13.9 Carmi, Daniella. **Samir and Yonatan.** Translation by Yael Lotan. Arthur A. Levine Books, 2000. 183 pp. ISBN 0-439-13504-4. Fiction

Samir, a Palestinian boy, is in an Israeli hospital with four children, all Israelis. He is frightened by the hate he feels for a fellow patient whose brother is an Israeli soldier. Through Samir's dreams and thoughts, the reader learns his family's story. Another patient, Yonatan, befriends Samir, and they share the realization that there is a context for life and hope larger than the current conflict as well as a smaller one—knowing others as individuals rather than as groups.

13.10 Danticat, Edwidge. **Behind the Mountains.** Orchard, 2002. 153 pp. ISBN 0-439-37299-2. Fiction

Celiane loves her home in the Haitian mountains but still longs for her father, who moved to New York City over five years ago and has never returned. When her long-awaited visa finally arrives, Celiane and her family reunite with their father in Brooklyn, New York, but it does not turn out to be the blissful reunion they had hoped for. In this intriguing story, we learn of the modern-day immigrant experience through the eyes of one lonely, loving teen.

13.11 Ellis, Deborah. **The Breadwinner.** Douglas & McIntyre, 2001. 170 pp. ISBN 0-88899-416-8. Fiction

When Parvana's father is taken away by the Taliban, the family has no son old enough to earn a living. The responsibility falls to eleven-year-old Parvana to disguise herself as a boy in order to work as her father did as a translator. As a boy, she experiences a whole new world and sees her homeland suffering from the repression of the Taliban regime.

13.12 Ferreira, Anton. **Zulu Dog.** Farrar, Straus and Giroux, 2002. 195 pp. ISBN 0-374-39223-4. Fiction

Finding Gillette, a bush dog, and adopting him gives eleven-year-old Vusi a sense of purpose as he struggles with his life of poverty in rural, postapartheid South Africa. Together they hunt, and the bond between them grows even stronger after the puppy loses a leg in a battle with a leopard. They meet the daughter of a white farmer, and the unlikely friendship between Vusi, a Zulu, and Shirley not only challenges their own preconceptions but also eventually alters the future for the communities they represent.

13.13 Ho, Minfong. **Gathering the Dew.** Orchard, 2003. 199 pp. ISBN 0-439-38197-5. Fiction

When the communists take over Cambodia in the 1980s, Nakri and her siblings are torn from city life and forced to work in countryside labor camps. Their arduous struggle to survive deplorable conditions finds liberation on the day the Khmer Rouge are overthrown, and Nakri and her family are reunited. Eventually they make their way from refugee camps to the streets of New York, where they create a new life while still preserving their time-honored and precious traditions and memories.

13.14 Hoyt-Goldsmith, Diane. **Buffalo Days.** Photographs by Lawrence Migdale. Holiday House, 1997. 32 pp. ISBN 0-82341-3276. Nonfiction

This book profiles ten-year-old Clarence Tree Irons Jr., a member of the Crow Indian tribe, as he and his family attend the Crow Fair and Rodeo. This multiday festival, which includes dance contests, drumming, rodeo competitions, and horse races, celebrates the Buffalo Days, the time when the buffalo were plentiful. Colorful photographs of all aspects of the festival are included, and present-day buffalo management strategies are described.

13.15 Jiménez, Francisco. **Breaking Through.** Houghton Mifflin, 2001. 193 pp. ISBN 0-618-01173-0. Nonfiction

Jiménez presents a collection of vignettes that chronicle the lives of young Panchito and his family as the young boy works his way through middle school and high school. Each chapter describes a particular hardship or small victory as the young man and his family struggle with poverty, prejudice, and illness in the late fifties and early sixties in southern California. Panchito and his older brother Roberto endure to support their family as they negotiate between their Mexican culture and American culture.

13.16 Johnston, Tony. **Any Small Goodness: A Novel of the Barrio.** Illustrated by Raul Colon. Blue Sky, 2001. 128 pp. ISBN 0-439-18936-5. Fiction

Arturo Rodriguez is trying to find his niche in the world. He loves his family and enjoys hanging out with friends. Proud of his Mexican heritage, Arturo knows the importance of remembering who he is and where he comes from. He knows too the importance of recognizing that any small goodness is important. Living in the barrio of East Los Angeles, Arturo must remind himself of this fact often and create good when he does not find enough of it.

13.17 Lachtman, Ofelia Dumas. **The Summer of El Pintor.** Arte Público, 2001. 235 pp. ISBN 1-55885-327-8. Fiction

Monica's father has resigned his important government job in Washington, D.C. That means she must leave her boarding school in Virginia and move with him to Los Angeles. What she is not prepared for is living in a barrio in a house once owned by her mother. New experiences include a new friend named Toni and a cat named Sopa.

13.18 Lanier, Shannon, and Jane Feldman. **Jefferson's Children: The Story of One American Family.** Photographs by Jane Feldman. Random House, 2000. 144 pp. ISBN 0-375-80597-4. Nonfiction

One of the enduring rumors of American history proclaims the relationship between Thomas Jefferson and Sally Hemings, the African American slave who was the half-sister of Jefferson's wife. Verification of the story occurred with the results of DNA testing in 1998. Lanier, a descendent of this union, traveled throughout the country interviewing members of the extended family.

13.19 Lu, Chi Fa, with Becky White. **Double Luck: Memoirs of a Chinese Orphan.** Holiday House, 2001. 212 pp. ISBN 0-8234-1560-0. Nonfiction

Orphaned at age three in 1944, Chi Fa was shuttled from relative to relative to stranger, often hungry and mistreated but always strong and resourceful as he—and China—went through tumultuous changes. In 1969, Chi Fa was able to immigrate to the United States but returned to China in 1996 to visit the older sister who had, when she was able, taken care of him. This remarkable memoir of resilience and determination and the power of kindness includes photographs, a map, and a time line.

13.20 Mantell, Paul. **Cool as Ice.** Little, Brown, 2001. 148 pp. ISBN 0-316-13489-9. Fiction

Twelve-year-old Chris, a former figure skater, is chosen to be on the traveling ice hockey team. Together with his friend Derek, who happens to be the only African American in the league, they must prove to the other players that it is what is in one's heart and mind that makes a true champion. This is one in the series of Matt Christopher sports novels.

13.21 Mendelsohn, James. **Barbara Jordan: Getting Things Done.** Twenty-First Century Books, 2000. 192 pp. ISBN 0-7613-1467-9. Nonfiction

Life for Barbara Jordan was never easy. Try as she might, she was never like the girls she grew up with. She was tall, big, and very dark skinned. Beyond the physical differences, she was strong spirited and independent, two qualities that would later aid her in becoming the first black woman elected from a southern state to the U.S. Congress. Among her accomplishments were her fight for civil rights and her stand in favor of the impeachment of President Nixon.

13.22 Mendoza, Patrick M. **Between Midnight and Morning: Historic Hauntings and Ghost Tales from the Frontier, Hispanic, and Native American Traditions.** August House, 2000. 128 pp. ISBN 0-87483-607-7. Fiction

This collection of fifteen ghost stories brings together traditional stories of Hispanic and Native American cultures, many of which are hundreds of years old and have been passed down orally. All stories have been extensively researched and are guaranteed to be culturally authentic and historically accurate. Each story is followed by further information about it. Stories combine the scary with the humorous and are sure to entertain readers.

13.23 Myers, Walter Dean. **Malcolm X: A Fire Burning Brightly.** Illustrated by Leonard Jenkins. HarperCollins, 2000. 30 pp. ISBN 0-06-027707-6. Nonfiction

This beautifully illustrated picture book narrative is a biography of the black leader Malcolm X. Born in 1925, he was introduced to the idea of equality by his father. Malcolm faced difficult times in his youth. While in jail, he discovered the writings and philosophy of Elijah Muhammad and the Nation of Islam. The book chronicles Malcolm's rise to fame as a black leader in the struggle for equal rights.

13.24 Na, An. **A Step from Heaven.** Front Street, 2001. 160 pp. ISBN 1-886910-58-8. Fiction

Young Ju narrates her family's emigration experience when they move from Korea to the United States. As Young Ju grows up, her outlook and voice change as she reveals the incredible obstacles to success in her family's adopted country. After enduring years of abuse from her alcoholic father, Young Ju takes a stand and helps her mother and brother realize that they have choices and can succeed through education and determination. In addition, her mother gives Young Ju more insight into their family.

13.25 Namioka, Lensey. **An Ocean Apart, a World Away.** Delacorte, 2002. 197 pp. ISBN 0-385-73002-0. Fiction

In 1921, sixteen-year-old Yanyan meets Baoshu, a young revolutionary intent on restoring the Manchu dynasty in China. When Baoshu asks her to marry him, a choice that would require Yanyan to give up her dream of becoming a doctor, she chooses her career, traveling to the United States to enroll at Cornell University. There, she faces prejudice because of her cultural background and gender, but she also makes new friends, including the brilliant and attentive Chinese student L. H.

13.26 Nava, Julian. **Julian Nava: My Mexican-American Journey.** Piñata/Arte Público, 2002. 233 pp. ISBN 1-55885-364-2. Nonfiction

Like many immigrant children, Julian Nava grew up feeling that he was neither American nor Mexican. But Nava did not let prejudice and discrimination overwhelm his ambition. In this autobiography, Nava reminisces about his journey from boyhood in a Los Angeles barrio to doctoral studies at Harvard University, leadership of the Los Angeles school board, and eventually a position as President Carter's ambassador to Mexico.

13.27 Nye, Naomi Shihab. **Habibi.** Simon Pulse, 1999. 271 pp. ISBN 0-689-80149-1. Fiction

Moving from St. Louis to Jerusalem makes life interesting for Liyana Abboud, who believes in looking for the silver lining even in the midst of age-old troubled race relations between Arabs and Jews. She basks in her Arab grandmother's stories and falls in love with a peacemaking Jewish boy. Old and young learn from each other in this exceptional novel that joyously embraces religious and ethnic diversity through the beauty of the author's language and the breadth of her spirit.

13.28 Placide, Jaira. **Fresh Girl.** Wendy Lamb Books, 2002. 213 pp. ISBN 0-385-32753-6. Fiction

At age twelve, Brooklyn-born Mardi Desravines, raised in Haiti by her grandmother and forced to leave Haiti during a coup, returns to her parents in New York. Now, two years later, after repressing her memories of fleeing Haiti, hiding in a cornfield, and being raped by a soldier, Mardi is eventually able to confide in her supportive family. The novel is ultimately about the healing power of loving families and the emotional dangers of keeping secrets.

13.29 Saldaña, René Jr. **The Jumping Tree.** Delacorte, 2001. 181 pp. ISBN 0-385-32725-0. Fiction

Rey Castaneda is a devoted American and a devoted Mexican. Balancing the two heritages is surprisingly easy for him. He respects the freedom he has in his Texas hometown as well as the Chicano bloodline that races through his veins. As Rey travels between the two countries, he learns a great deal about who he is and the world in which he lives. Crossing the border between childhood and adulthood, Rey learns that people are just people.

13.30 Salisbury, Graham. **Island Boyz: Short Stories.** Wendy Lamb Books, 2002. 260 pp. ISBN 0-385-72970-7. Fiction

This collection of one poem and ten short stories, some previously published, vividly evokes the unique qualities of the Hawaiian Islands as well as the common concerns and experiences of teens of varied backgrounds everywhere: peer pressure, love, the effects of war, rebellion, group dynamics, difficult choices, and family situations. Salisbury reveals the teens' realities with humor, suspense, authentic voices, and rich description. In addition, many conclusions are unexpected and offer interesting surprises.

13.31 San Souci, Robert D., reteller. **A Terrifying Taste of Short and Shivery: Thirty Creepy Tales.** Illustrated by Lenny Wooden. Delacorte, 2000. 160 pp. ISBN 0-385-32255-0. Fiction

These thirty chilling ghost stories have been gathered from countries around the world, including Australia, Germany, India, El Salvador, Japan, the British Isles, Canada, China, Poland, and the United States. Retold by Robert D. San Souci, each story is just a few pages long—perfect for reading around a campfire or by flashlight in a dark room. This is a good book to share story by story as the authors bring us spine-tingling tales from faraway places.

13.32 Schneider, Mical. **Annie Quinn in America.** Carolrhoda, 2001. 246 pp. ISBN 1-57505-510-4. Fiction

Annie Quinn and her brother Thomas leave Ireland in the 1840s, in the midst of the potato famine, to join their sister Bridget in New York City in the domestic service of the Fairchilds of Gramercy Park. In the United States, they find a different set of hardships; instead of hunger, they find discrimination and deception.

13.33 Veciana-Suarez, Ana. **The Flight to Freedom.** Orchard, 2002. 197 pp. ISBN 0-439-38199-1. Fiction

Writing in the diary her father had once given her, thirteen-year-old Yara describes life with her family in Havana, Cuba, in 1967, as well as their forced flight from the communist regime of Fidel Castro to Miami, Florida. There, she experiences a strange new world—a place where freedom is a relative word. Yara's descriptions of a strange land and foreign customs create an intriguing exploration of what freedom really means, especially to those who consider it a precious gift.

13.34 Velásquez, Gloria. **Ankiza.** Piñata, 2000. 144 pp. ISBN 1-55885-309-X. Fiction

Told in the form of two narratives, one from the viewpoint of Ankiza, a high school junior of African American and Native American ancestry, and one from the viewpoint of Professor Sonia Gonzales, the Hispanic mother of one of Ankiza's friends, this novel presents issues of race and interracial dating. The flashpoint event is hate mail Ankiza receives when Hunter, of Italian and Dutch ancestry, asks her to the senior prom.

13.35 Welch, Catherine A. **Ida B. Wells-Barnett: Powerhouse with a Pen.** Carolrhoda, 2000. 104 pp. ISBN 1-57505-352-7. Nonfiction

Born a slave but freed at the age of three when the Civil War ended, Ida B. Wells grew to be a leader in the fight against racial intolerance in the late 1800s. When her friend was lynched by a mob of white men, Wells, a journalist, traveled, gave speeches, wrote for newspapers, and helped to organize the NAACP.

13.36 Whelan, Gloria. **Homeless Bird.** HarperCollins, 2000. 216 pp. ISBN 0-06-028454-4. Fiction

This novel of life in contemporary India relates the story of thirteen-year-old Koly whose parents arrange her marriage to an ill boy. Soon she is widowed and deserted in a holy city where many widows congregate. Koly refuses to allow tradition to tie her to a life of begging. She is able to use her talent for embroidery to make a living and a new life for herself.

13.37 Whitesel, Cheryl Aylward. **Rebel: A Tibetan Odyssey.** HarperCollins, 2000. 190 pp. ISBN 0-688-16735-7. Fiction

Thunder is a fourteen-year-old Tibetan farm boy who longs to travel, but as a Tibetan, he is forbidden contact with the outside world. Then Thunder meets a foreign explorer, and despite persistent warnings by his parents, he agrees to keep meeting this person. The result: banishment from Tibet. Thunder is sent to live in a monastery to spend his days in quiet study and contemplation. But Thunder learns that the outside world is anything but quiet.

13.38 Woodson, Jacqueline. **If You Come Softly.** Puffin, 2000. 192 pp. ISBN 0-698-11862-6. Fiction

Jeremiah, an African American teenager whose wealthy and famous parents have just separated, is caught off guard when he falls in love with Ellie, a white Jewish girl who goes to the same prep school he does in New York City. The couple discovers just how difficult an interracial relationship can be when they face the disapproving stares of people on the streets and at school and find out how painful it is to be stereotyped.

13.39 Yep, Laurence. **Dream Soul.** HarperCollins, 2000. 245 pp. ISBN 0-06-028389-0. Fiction

In 1927 West Virginia, fifteen-year-old Joan Lee struggles with her responsibilities to her family, her Chinese heritage, her American life, and her desire to fit in with her peers. The cultural and generational conflicts climax when Joan and her younger siblings wish to celebrate Christmas. Interactions among neighbors, peers, and the mysterious Barringtons who have recently arrived in town contribute to Joan's emerging understanding of her parents, her heritage, and herself.

13.40 Yumoto, Kazumi. **The Letters.** Translated by Cathy Hirano. Farrar, Straus and Giroux, 2002. 165 pp. ISBN 0-374-34383-7. Fiction

Chiaki, a young Japanese American woman, flies across the United States to attend the funeral of her former landlady and friend. She remembers conversations and events shared with the landlady that helped Chiaki cope with her father's death. A devout Buddhist, the landlady suggested that Chiaki write letters to her father. At the funeral, Chiaki is able to read the letters she and her mother wrote. Published in Japan in 1997, this novel has been translated into English for U.S. publication.

14 Problems and Issues

14.1 Andryszewski, Tricia. **Kosovo: The Splintering of Yugoslavia.** Millbrook, 2000. 63 pp. ISBN 0-7613-1750-3. Nonfiction

This book places the recent crisis in the Serbian province of Kosovo in the context of a long history of conflict in the Balkan states. Tracing the turbulent history of the region over centuries through the breakup of Yugoslavia in the 1980s and culminating in the conflict and crisis in Kosovo in the 1990s, this book provides readers with an in depth understanding of recent world events.

14.2 Andryszewski, Tricia. **The Reform Party: Ross Perot and Pat Buchanan.** Millbrook, 2000. 64 pp. ISBN 0-7613-1906-9. Nonfiction

The Reform Party is part of a series by Millbrook Press called Headliners that offers an in-depth exploration of some of today's most pressing world issues. This book explains how the Reform Party started and what it and Pat Buchanan have stood for, especially in the 1992 and 1996 presidential campaigns. It also offers some informed guesses about how the Reform Party will likely fare in future election campaigns.

14.3 Bode, Janet, and Stan Mack. **For Better, for Worse: A Guide to Surviving Divorce for Preteens and Their Families.** Simon & Schuster, 2001. 160 pp. ISBN 0-689-81945-5.

Divided in two parts, this book presents an honest and often painful look at the effects of divorce on preteens. In the first part, seven preteens describe their experiences and discuss various issues in their own words, using a variety of formats to express themselves, including poetry, cartoons, art, and advice. Each narrative is followed by brief comments and insights from therapists. Part two provides information and resources for parents.

14.4 Bodnarchuk, Kari J. **Kurdistan: Region under Siege.** Lerner, 2000. 104 pp. ISBN 0-8225-3556-4. Nonfiction

Living in Turkey, Iraq, Iran, and Syria, the Kurds are the largest ethnic group in the world without a country. They have been denied the right to speak their own language and govern themselves, and the news often includes stories about their slaughter and haunting pictures of survivors in refugee camps. This book explains the origins of the Kurds' plight, reveals their complicated relationships with one another, and discusses how the conflicts might be resolved.

14.5 Boyers, Sara Jane. **Teen Power Politics: Make Yourself Heard.** Twenty-First Century Books, 2000. 120 pp. ISBN 0-7613-1307-9. Nonfiction

This book addresses the issue of politics but specifically in the interest of teens, providing information on the importance of voting, how to understand what the media is telling you, and how your actions in your community affect the global community. The author mixes quotes from a variety of famous people and stories from ordinary teens who have made a difference by exercising their political voice. The last chapter provides a resource appendix.

14.6 Cameron, Sara. **Out of War: True Stories from the Front Lines of the Children's Movement for Peace in Colombia.** Scholastic, 2001. 188 pp. ISBN 0-439-29721-4. Nonfiction

Civil war has raged in Colombia, South America, for more than forty years, leaving children who have lost their parents and homes, their schools, and security. Yet today young Colombians are leading the efforts to end the fighting. Together with the International Children's Movement for Peace organization, these young people have formed a coalition designed to build a better future. This haunting work tells their individual stories with grit, despair, and eternal hope.

14.7 Cohen, Daniel. **George W. Bush: The Family Business.** Millbrook, 2000. 48 pp. ISBN 0-7613-1851-8. Nonfiction

Throughout history, politics has been the focus for many families. Cohen explores the legacy of the Bush family, concentrating on George W. Bush, then governor of Texas and U.S. presidential candidate. Although teeming with interesting personal details of George W. Bush's evolution as a political figure, the book is dominated by the Bush family's business interests. And though generally informative, the book's tone often takes on that of a political campaign.

14.8 Cohen, Daniel. **The Impeachment of William Jefferson Clinton.** Twenty-First Century Books, 2000. 112 pp. ISBN 0-7613-1711-2. Nonfiction

In 1998 the U.S. House of Representatives voted for two articles of impeachment against William Jefferson Clinton, president of the United States of America. The charges were committing perjury and obstructing justice. Only one other president has been impeached: Andrew Johnson in 1868. And like Andrew Johnson, President Clinton was acquitted by the U.S. Senate after a brief trial. Author Cohen takes a controversial topic and outlines it in clear and easy-to-read language.

14.9 Farish, Leah. **Lemon v. Kurtzman: The Religion and Public Funds Case.** Enslow, 2000. 128 pp. ISBN 0-7660-1339-1. Nonfiction

Separation of church and state has been an issue much debated in the funding of public schools. Since the establishment of the First Amendment, many cases have tested founding fathers' intent, and *Lemon v. Kurtzman,* handed down in 1971, attempted to establish guidelines for determining cause. Beginning with a history of the case, the author examines the reasons for the Supreme Court's decision and how this decision has affected the issue since.

14.10 Fridell, Ron. **Spying: The Modern World of Espionage.** Twenty-First Century Books, 2002. 144 pp. ISBN 0-7613-1662-0. Nonfiction

Through pictures and exceptional detail, this book allows us to gaze into the secret world of the United States' intelligence communities as it describes the modern world of espionage, with agents and agencies shifting gears to deal with new technologies and new problems. Readers will learn about the government's efforts to gather secrets, process information, and develop new technologies designed to provide information about what's happening in the world and our communities.

14.11 Gay, Kathlyn. **Leaving Cuba: From Operation Pedro Pan to Elian.** Twenty-First Century Books, 2000. 144 pp. ISBN 0-7613-1466-0. Nonfiction

In 1959, Fidel Castro took over the government of Cuba. In the ensuing years, Castro's dictatorship caused thousands of frightened parents to send their children to the United States in Operation Pedro Pan and the Mariel boatlift. Thousands more have risked their lives over the years to reach American soil and freedom. This book documents the experiences of these exiled Cubans, from the children of Operation Pedro Pan to the poignant story of Elian Gonzalez.

14.12 Gay, Kathlyn. **Silent Death: The Threat of Chemical and Biological Terrorism.** Twenty-First Century Books, 2001. 128 pp. ISBN 0-7613-1401-6. Nonfiction

Biochemical weapons present a significant threat that can cause death and debilitating illness for large numbers of people only seconds after exposure. Easy production and lethal power make these weapons appealing to terrorist groups. The book presents a candid picture of how such weapons are made, their potential effects, and efforts to control access and production. Infowar is also discussed as a future threat that could cripple countries dependent on information technology. Additional resources include appendixes of biochemical agents and foreign terrorist organizations.

14.13 Gellman, Marc, and Thomas Hartman. **Bad Stuff in the News: A Guide to Handling the Headlines.** SeaStar, 2002. 120 pp. ISBN 1-58717-132-5. Nonfiction

Covering many issues of modern life, this handbook helps preteens and teens handle the negative and frightening news that surrounds us every day. By discussing issues such as gang violence, poverty, environmental assaults, abuse, terrorism, and others, the authors give readers insight into the causes of these problems. They also provide concrete actions for dealing with these realities and show ways to make a difference and combat them. Sensitive and positive, this book provides both humor and compassion throughout.

14.14 Gottfried, Ted. **The Death Penalty: Justice or Legalized Murder?** Twenty-First Century Books, 2002. 144 pp. ISBN 0-7613-2155-1. Nonfiction

Gottfried presents a thought-provoking examination of capital punishment in the United States, bringing passion and politics to this ongoing debate. He provides readers with a chronology and history of the death penalty and dives into moral and constitutional dilemmas surrounding capital punishment, challenging readers to examine deep beliefs about democracy, civilization, and justice. A list of additional resources, index, and glossary are included.

14.15 Gottfried, Ted. **Northern Ireland: Peace in Our Time?** Millbrook, 2002. 63 pp. ISBN 0-7613-2252-3. Nonfiction

For many centuries there has been civil unrest throughout Ireland. Peace talks have come and gone with little resolution throughout the years. This book chronicles Ireland's violent history, including information about leaders such as William of Orange and present-day leader David Trimble. Issues such as nationality and religion are discussed as important factors in the turmoil. Photographs and illustrations enrich the basic text.

14.16 Gottfried, Ted. **The 2000 Election.** Millbrook, 2002. 59 pp. ISBN 0-7613-2406-2. Nonfiction

The 2000 U.S. presidential election between George W. Bush and Albert Gore Jr. was filled with controversy. An error in the Florida machines resulted in hand counting. But what started as a Florida debate over voting procedures grew into a nationwide reformation of the voting process. Along with an in-depth description of this election, related topics such as the history of the Electoral College and accounts of previous controversial elections are included.

14.17 Hoobler, Dorothy, and Tom Hoobler. **The 1980s: Earthsong.** Millbrook, 2002. 147 pp. ISBN 0-7613-1608-6. Fiction

Hoobler, Dorothy, and Tom Hoobler. **The 1990s: Families.** Millbrook, 2002. 148 pp. ISBN 0-7613-1609-4. Fiction

In these ninth and tenth volumes of The Century Kids series, different generations of the Aldrich, Vivanti, and Dixon families are highlighted as they confront environmental issues in the 1980s and issues of family, computers, and Y2K in the 1990s. Photographs from the highlighted decade and appendixes of family trees, historical notes, and Things That Really Happened add to an appreciation of how events of the time affected these families.

14.18 Kowalski, Kathiann M. **Campaign Politics: What's Fair? What's Foul?** Lerner, 2000. 97 pp. ISBN 0-8225-2630-1. Nonfiction

The opening quote by Thomas Jefferson, "If a nation expects to be ignorant and free . . . it expects what was and never will be," sets the stage for this book about politics in the United States. Written in an easy-to-read format, it begins with a look at campaign ads and candidates' mudslinging and concludes with how policymakers are attempting to "clean up the game." Various points of view are presented.

14.19 Landau, Elaine. **The New Nuclear Reality.** Twenty-First Century Books, 2000. 128 pp. ISBN 0-7613-1555-1. Nonfiction

Post–cold war threats of nuclear weapons are explored without presenting sensational visions of nuclear annihilation. Political instability and the acquisition of nuclear capabilities in countries such as India and Pakistan, along with the dismantling of the former Soviet Union's nuclear arsenal, have created concerns over nuclear proliferation. World powers such as the United States play vital roles in controlling and discouraging nuclear weapon development and enhancing world safety. The book includes additional readings and a list of organizations concerned with nuclear proliferation.

14.20 Landau, Elaine. **Osama bin Laden: A War against the West.** Twenty-First Century Books, 2002. 142 pp. ISBN 0-7613-1709-0. Nonfiction

Born in 1957 to a wealthy and powerful family in Saudi Arabia, Osama bin Laden has become one of the most hated or revered men in the world, depending on your perspective. As a young man, he lived a fast-paced, glamorous lifestyle until he experienced a spiritual rebirth that resulted in him adopting Islamic extremism. His mission became to wage jihad or holy war against the Western culture he now hated.

14.21 Lunger, Norman L. **Big Bang: The Loud Debate over Gun Control.** Twenty-First Century Books, 2002. 160 pp. ISBN 0-7613-2260-4. Nonfiction.

Without showing partiality toward either side, the arguments of the gun control debate are presented and discussed. The American sense of identity with the right to bear arms is noted, validated, and encouraged. Legislation, both historic and current, regarding gun control is intensively explained, as are the events that brought the legislation into existence. This emotive book concludes by presenting means of compromise and ways to satisfy all parties.

14.22 Meltzer, Milton. **Ain't Gonna Study War No More: The Story of America's Peace Seekers.** Random House, 2002. 290 pp. ISBN 0-375-82260-7. Nonfiction

This nonfictional time line discusses those who have chosen throughout history not to fight. Also known as pacifists, early Christians, Quakers, and Vietnam draft dodgers are discussed in a context that promotes understanding diversity and differing beliefs as beneficial to any member of a democratic society. Author Meltzer's overall argument is that a nation molded by religious freedom and tolerance should accept those who choose peace over war.

14.23 Meltzer, Milton. **The Day the Sky Fell: A History of Terrorism.** Random House, 2002. 290 pp. ISBN 0-375-82250-X. Nonfiction

Spurred by the events of September 11, 2001, this story serves as a revamped edition of a book about the history of terrorism. Various aspects of terrorism are examined, including those cultures that teach terrorism and those that have declared war against it. Terrorism used for the "greater good" is also debated, along with the question of whether terrorism is ever acceptable. Discussions of areas such as Ireland and the Middle East are also included.

14.24 New Moon Books Girls Editorial Board. **New Moon Friendship: How to Make, Keep, and Grow Your Friendships.** Crown, 1999. 90 pp. ISBN 0-517-88581-6. Nonfiction

Authored by ten- to fourteen-year-old girls who also serve on the editorial board for the magazine *New Moon,* this series takes on topics that are important to young people, especially girls. This title focuses on friendship. Highlights include lists of additional resources, interviews with prominent women, and Point of View boxes sharing individual girls' experiences in their own voices. Each title is practical and reader-friendly, with a down-to-earth tone.

14.25 New Moon Books Girls Editorial Board. **New Moon Money: How to Get It, Spend It, and Save It.** Crown, 2000. 90 pp. ISBN 0-517-88585-9. Nonfiction

Authored by ten- to fourteen-year-old girls who also serve on the editorial board for the magazine *New Moon,* this series takes on topics that are important to young people, especially girls. This title focuses on money and money management. Highlights include lists of additional resources, interviews with prominent women, and Point of View boxes sharing individual girls' experiences in their own voices. Each title is practical and reader-friendly, with a down-to-earth tone.

14.26 New Moon Books Girls Editorial Board. **New Moon Sports: What Sports Can Do for You and What You Can Do for Sports.** Crown, 1999. 90 pp. ISBN 0-517-88583-2. Nonfiction

Authored by ten- to fourteen-year-old girls who also serve on the editorial board for the magazine *New Moon,* this series takes on topics that are important to young people, especially girls. This title focuses on sports. Highlights include lists of additional resources, interviews with prominent women, and Point of View boxes sharing individual girls' experiences in their own voices. Each title is practical and reader-friendly, with a down-to-earth tone.

14.27 New Moon Books Girls Editorial Board. **New Moon Writing: How to Express Yourself with Passion and Practice.** Crown, 2000. 90 pp. ISBN 0-517-88587-5. Nonfiction

Authored by ten- to fourteen-year-old girls who also serve on the editorial board for the magazine *New Moon,* this series takes on topics that are important to young people, especially girls. This title focuses on writing. Highlights include lists of additional resources, interviews with prominent women, and Point of View boxes sharing individual girls' experiences in their own voices. Each title is practical and reader-friendly, with a down-to-earth tone.

14.28 Spencer, William. **Iraq: Old Land, New Nation in Conflict.** Twenty-First Century Books, 2000. 144 pp. ISBN 0-7613-1356-7. Nonfiction

This book traces the history of Iraq, from its Mesopotamian origins nearly eight thousand years ago to its current political and economic crisis. Although often known for its interactions with other nations and its mistreatment of its own people, Iraq has made significant contributions to the world, such as a written language. The author provides readers with an understanding of how this country, known as the "world center for Islam," ended up at war with the world.

14.29 Spencer, William. **The United States and Iran.** Twenty-First Century Books, 2000. 128 pp. ISBN 0-7613-1554-3. Nonfiction

Present-day conflicts with Middle Eastern countries can be confusing without some understanding of their historical contexts. This accessible book provides an overview of U.S.-Iran relations from the 1800s to the present, discussing the impact of Islam on Iran's governments, the fall of the last shah, the rise of Ayatollah Khomeini, the American hostage crisis, and the United States' current trade embargo on Iran. A detailed index and well-organized chapters with subheadings make this an ideal book for research.

14.30 Stewart, Whitney. **The 14th Dalai Lama.** Lerner, 2000. 128 pp. ISBN 0-8225-9691-1. Nonfiction

From a humble birth on a Tibetan farm rose the current spiritual leader of Buddhism believed to be the living embodiment of the deity of compassion. Raised from childhood to be the political and spiritual leader of his people, he was forced into exile when China invaded Tibet. Devoting his life to human rights and nonviolence, he garnered the 1989 Nobel Prize for Peace. Through such efforts and numerous books, the fourteenth Dalai Lama is recognized and respected throughout the world.

14.31 Vanderwarker, Peter. **The Big Dig: Reshaping an American City.** Little, Brown, 2001. 56 pp. ISBN 0-316-60598-0. Nonfiction

Urban growth and traffic congestion have created problems in most major cities. This book focuses on the massive construction project to solve the problem in Boston. The Central Artery/Tunnel Project—The Big Dig—was begun in 1991 and is the largest public construction project in the history of this country. Vanderwarker presents a historical perspective on the problem while using his photographs to illustrate the changes that are designed to be its remedy.

14.32 Whitney, Brooks. **School Smarts: All the Right Answers to Homework, Teachers, Popularity, and More!** Illustrated by Tracy McGuinness. Pleasant Company, 2000. 96 pp. ISBN 1-58485-165-1. Nonfiction

Conveniently hole-punched to fit into a notebook, *School Smarts* provides excellent and specific advice on all the essential school issues, from organization to talking to the teacher to reading, listening, note taking, group work, homework, taking tests, making presentations, popularity issues, and studying. Interspersed throughout with Big Truths, this handbook includes colorful and creative graphics and photos geared to upper elementary and middle grade girls, although the advice is useful for most grade levels.

15 Geography and Cultures

15.1 Bartlett, Anne. **The Aboriginal Peoples of Australia.** Lerner, 2002. 48 pp. ISBN 0-8225-4854-2. Nonfiction

Useful for research as well as for pleasure reading, each title in this series profiles indigenous peoples from around the world, including the Mohawk, the Masai, and Aboriginal Australians. Balancing attention to the past with consideration of the present, the books include interesting details about each group's language, customs, and family structure. Numerous paintings, maps, and photographs with lively captions make the stories come to life.

15.2 Batten, Mary. **Anthropologist: Scientist of the People.** Photographs by A. Magdalena Hurtado and Kim Hill. Houghton Mifflin, 2001. 64 pp. ISBN 0-618-08368-5. Nonfiction

If you thought moving to a new school or neighborhood is hard, imagine the feelings of anthropologist Magdalena Hurtado, who faces the challenge of stepping back in time and fitting in with the South American Ache hunter-gatherer tribe. To learn more about these people, the anthropologist leaves behind her modern ways and participates in the Ache work, meals, play, and special rituals. Hurtado hopes to understand how the tribe can preserve its identity as modern housing, farming, medicine, and other conveniences are introduced.

15.3 Fleischman, Paul, editor. **Cannibal in the Mirror.** Photographs by John Whalen. Twenty-First Century Books, 2000. 64 pp. ISBN 0-7613-0968-3. Nonfiction

The editor uses an interesting combination of quotations from explorers and missionaries and photographs to draw comparisons between the customs of primitive cultures and those of modern society. Parallels are made between courtship rituals, families, appearance, and beliefs. Modern humans may not be as postmodern as they believe since many modern rituals have ancient origins.

15.4 Gay, Kathlyn, and Christine Whittington. **Body Marks: Tattooing, Piercing, and Scarification.** Millbrook, 2002. 112 pp. ISBN 0-7613-2352-X. Nonfiction

"What is wrong with this generation?" is a question often asked by adults shocked by the recent trend among younger people of tattooing and body piercing. But tattooing, piercing, and scarification are not unique to the current younger generation. These practices have existed across many cultures throughout history. Body marks have been used to brand slaves and criminals and also to indicate nobility. The authors describe body marking purposes and procedures throughout history, along with contemporary health and safety concerns.

15.5 Gutman, Bill. **The Look-It-Up Book of the 50 States.** Illustrated by Anne Wertheim. Random House, 2002. 160 pp. ISBN 0-375-81213-X. Nonfiction

This resource book provides colorful illustrations, photographs, and informative sidebars to accompany interesting and informative narratives about how each state became part of the United States, how each contributes to the country, places to visit, and resources. The inclusion of unique facts and trivia about each state makes this book a frequent source of information.

15.6 Hopkins, Lee Bennett, selector. **My America: A Poetry Atlas of the United States.** Illustrated by Stephen Alcorn. Simon & Schuster, 2000. 83 pp. ISBN 0-689-81247-7. Poetry

In celebration of America, Hopkins has collected poems that capture the diversity of our country and our people. The book, a poetic trip across the United States, is organized into eight regional sections with maps and factual profiles of each state. The volume has vivid illustrations, each poem accompanied by a Stephen Alcorn painting.

15.7 Kirk, Connie Ann. **The Mohawks of North America.** Lerner, 2002. 48 pp. ISBN 0-8225-4853-4. Nonfiction

Useful for research as well as for pleasure reading, each title in this series profiles indigenous peoples from around the world, including the Mohawk, the Masai, and Aboriginal Australians. Balancing attention to the past with consideration of the present, the books include interesting details about each group's language, customs, and family structure. Numerous paintings, maps, and photographs with lively captions make the stories come to life.

15.8 Kizilos, Peter. **Tibet: Disputed Land.** Lerner, 2000. 80 pp. ISBN 0-8225-3563-7. Nonfiction

Written at the early adolescent level, this book offers a detailed overview of Tibet's history. Issues such as its changing relationships with China, India, and Britain are thoroughly discussed, and reasons for each nation's interest in Tibet are explained. Important treaties, people, and events are highlighted, with special emphasis on Tibetan culture. A glossary of key terms and a chronology of important dates are also provided to enhance the reader's learning.

15.9 Kort, Michael G. **The Handbook of the Middle East.** Twenty-First Century Books, 2002. 303 pp. ISBN 0-7613-1611-6. Nonfiction

Its ongoing political disputes and ownership of two-thirds of the world's petroleum reserves give prominence to the Middle East in everyday news. This handbook provides current information on the history, geography, politics, and people of this important region. Information is included on North Africa; Israel, the Palestinian Authority, and Jordan; Lebanon, Syria, and Iraq; Turkey and Iran; and the countries of the Arabian Peninsula. Sections containing maps and flags, a chronology, and an encyclopedia containing summaries of important people, places, and events make this a useful resource for students.

15.10 Kort, Michael G. **The Handbook of the New Eastern Europe.** Twenty-First Century Books, 2001. 256 pp. ISBN 0-7613-1362-1. Nonfiction

Along with outlining the histories of the countries that constitute the 450,000 square miles that make up the area known as eastern Europe, the author has included maps and photographs that vividly illustrate this region's people and land. This handbook includes political and geographical maps of the region, flags of the countries, and a chronology of significant historical events. Over fifty pages are devoted to an encyclopedia that provides details about significant people and places of eastern Europe.

15.11 McQuail, Lisa. **The Masai of Africa.** Lerner, 2002. 48 pp. ISBN 0-8225-4855-0. Nonfiction

Useful for research as well as for pleasure reading, each title in this series profiles indigenous peoples from around the world, including the Mohawks, the Masai, and Aboriginal Australians. Balancing attention to the past with consideration of the present, the books include interesting details about each group's language, customs, and family structure. Numerous paintings, maps, and photographs with lively captions make the stories come to life.

15.12 Pelta, Kathy. **Rediscovering Easter Island.** Lerner, 2001. 112 pp. ISBN 0-8225-4890-9. Nonfiction

Easter Island is like a small dot in the vast Pacific Ocean, yet the island is well known because of the massive, mysterious stone figures that adorn the land. The author gives an interesting history of the island, including stories of the sightings made by explorers in the early 1700s. This book recounts what visitors over the ages have learned about the island and the mysteries that it holds.

15.13 Perl, Lila. **Dying to Know about Death, Funeral Customs, and Final Resting Places.** Twenty-First Century Books, 2001. 95 pp. ISBN 0-7613-1564-0. Nonfiction

Life after death is a central mystery in many cultures, but some groups embrace death. The ancient Egyptians, for example, mummified their loved ones because they believed that the existence of the body guaranteed eternal life of the soul. This book discusses funeral customs among prehistoric and ancient peoples and customs among world religions. The history of disposing of the dead is explained, as well as the history of carved headstones.

15.14 Steele, Philip. **The Atlas of People and Places.** Copper Beech, 2002. 88 pp. ISBN 0-7613-2719-3. Nonfiction

This work is a comprehensive guide to people and places throughout the world, including North America, South America, Europe, Asia, Africa, and Oceania. An introductory section provides an overview of the history of the human world, including its people, languages, economies, and governments. The second part includes maps, photographs, and diagrams along with facts and descriptions of the landscapes and peoples of the world's regions and countries. A glossary and index round out the book.

Series Books

Hello U.S.A. Series

15.15 Bratvold, Gretchen. **Wisconsin.** Lerner, 2002. 84 pp. ISBN 0-8225-4052-5. Nonfiction

Di Piazza, Domenica. **Arkansas.** Lerner, 2002. 84 pp. ISBN 0-8225-4073-8. Nonfiction

Fredeen, Charles. **New Jersey.** Lerner, 2002. 84 pp. ISBN 0-8225-4060-6. Nonfiction

Johnston, Joyce. **Alaska.** Lerner, 2002. 84 pp. ISBN 0-8225-4051-7. Nonfiction

Johnston, Joyce. **Hawaii.** Lerner, 2002. 84 pp. ISBN 0-8225-4056-8. Nonfiction

Schulz, Andrea. **North Carolina.** Lerner, 2002. 84 pp. ISBN 0-8225-4072-X. Nonfiction

Warner, J. F. **Massachusetts.** Lerner, 2002. 84 pp. ISBN 0-8225-4050-9. Nonfiction

If you are researching a state for a social studies report, begin reading from the back of these books. Each book contains narrative chapters on the state's land, history, people, economy, and environment. The last part of the book consists of a digest of facts about the state. Information in this last section includes facts-at-a-glance, fun facts, a historical time line, a list of fiction and nonfiction books related to the state, and much more. Each book is indexed and contains many colorful photographs, maps, and diagrams.

The Lands, Peoples, and Cultures Series

15.16 Banting, Erinn. **Ireland: The Culture.** Crabtree, 2002. 32 pp. ISBN 0-7787-9719-8. Nonfiction

This book combines text and photographs to describe the culture of Ireland with its rich tradition of the arts, music, and literature, as well as its religious heritage. The importance of religion and the many holidays and festivals, castles, tombs, and ruins are some of the topics featured in this cultural overview. Also of interest are discussions of the English and Gaelic languages and

Ireland's folktales and legends. This is one of a trio of books focused on the country of Ireland.

15.17 Banting, Erinn. **Ireland: The Land.** Crabtree, 2002. 32 pp. ISBN 0-7787-9717-1. Nonfiction

Using maps and many color photographs, the author describes this divided country. The Emerald Isle is known for its beautiful, lush countryside and its farming and fishing, but this country's cities and industries are also highlighted. Other sections of the book examine climate, geography, and wildlife. This is one of a trio of books focused on the country of Ireland.

15.18 Banting, Erinn. **Ireland: The People.** Crabtree, 2002. 32 pp. ISBN 0-7787-9718-X. Nonfiction

Using illustrations and many photographs, the author describes the heritage of the Irish people and their struggles for independence. The Republic of Ireland won independence from Britain, while Northern Ireland is still battling. The book also explores the importance of family and friends, city life and country life, as well as language, food, school, work, and leisure activities. This is one of a trio of books focused on the country of Ireland.

15.19 Kalman, Bobbie. **China: The Culture.** Crabtree, 2001. 32 pp. ISBN 0-7787-9380-X. Nonfiction

Photographs abound in this book that describes the culture of China, including modern and traditional activities and customs. Appreciation of tradition and a combination of the old and new are characteristic of the Chinese culture. Art and theater, Chinese cuisine, symbolic writing, the horoscope, dress, and ceremony are some of the topics featured in this cultural overview. This is one of a trio of books focused on the country of China.

15.20 Kalman, Bobbie. **China: The Land.** Crabtree, 2001. 32 pp. ISBN 0-7787-9378-8. Nonfiction

Using maps and many color photographs, the author describes the variety of geography, topography, and climate in China, the world's third largest country. China's history is related through many of its political changes and social difficulties. Along with shortages of food, housing, and transportation come the tradeoffs of magnificent natural and historic wonders. This is one of a trio of books focused on the country of China.

15.21 Kalman, Bobbie. **China: The People.** Crabtree, 2001. 32 pp. ISBN 0-7787-9379-6. Nonfiction

Using illustrations and many photographs, the author describes the people of China and aspects of their lives, including family life, language, food, school, work, and leisure activities. China has the largest population in the world; how does the country deal with issues of overpopulation? How does rural life reconcile with urban life? This is one of a trio of books focused on the country of China.

15.22 Kalman, Bobbie. **India: The Culture.** Crabtree, 2001. 32 pp. ISBN 0-7787-9383-4. Nonfiction

Photographs abound in this book that describes the culture of India, including the important role that religion plays in traditional activities and customs. Religion and faith also influence the art of the country, and the crafts, dress, festivals, and celebrations all reflect various religions. Highlighted are the important roles of the performing arts and food. This is one of a trio of books focused on the country of India.

15.23 Kalman, Bobbie. **India: The Land.** Crabtree, 2001. ISBN 0-7787-9381-8. Nonfiction

Using maps and many color photographs, the author describes the variety of geography, topography, animals, weather, farming and industry, and problems found in the various settings of rural and urban life in India. This is one of a trio of books focused on the country of India.

15.24 Kalman, Bobbie. **India: The People.** Crabtree, 2001. ISBN 0-7787-9382-6. Nonfiction

Using illustrations and many photographs, the author describes the people of India who, numbering over a billion, constitute the second largest population in the world. The vast geography, various customs and religions, and social issues all make for serious challenges for India's people to overcome. The book includes interactive activities for the reader and calls to action. This is one of a trio of books focused on the country of India.

15.25 Kalman, Bobbie. **Japan: The Culture.** Crabtree, 2001. 32 pp. ISBN 0-7787-9377-X. Nonfiction

Photographs abound in this book that describes the culture of Japan, including both the modern and traditional activities and customs celebrated by the Japanese. Appreciation of nature, art and theater, religion, dress, and ceremony are some of the topics featured in this cultural overview. This is one of a trio of books focused on the country of Japan.

15.26 Kalman, Bobbie. **Japan: The Land.** Crabtree, 2001. 32 pp. ISBN 0-7787-9381-8. Nonfiction.

Using maps and many color photographs, the author describes the variety of geography, topography, animals, weather, farming and industry, and problems found in the various settings of rural and urban life in Japan. This is one of a trio of books focused on the country of Japan.

15.27 Kalman, Bobbie. **Japan: The People.** Crabtree, 2001. 32 pp. ISBN 0-7787-9376-1. Nonfiction

Using illustrations and many photographs, the author describes the people of Japan and elements that make up their lives, including family life, language, food, school, work, and leisure activities. This is one of a trio of books focused on the country of Japan.

15.28 Nickles, Greg. **Argentina: The Culture.** Crabtree, 2001. 32 pp. ISBN 0-86505-246-8. Nonfiction

This book combines text and photographs to describe the culture of Argentina, including both historic and contemporary activities and customs. The importance of religion, the many holidays and festivals, art, dress, food, music, and dance are some of the topics featured in this cultural overview. Also of interest is a discussion of Argentina's favorite folktales and literature. This is one of a trio of books focused on the country of Argentina.

15.29 Nickles, Greg. **Argentina: The Land.** Crabtree, 2001. 32 pp. ISBN 0-86505-244-1. Nonfiction

Using maps and many color photographs, the author describes the variety of geography, topography, animals, weather, and farming and industry in Argentina. He also discusses the vast differences found in the settings of rural and of urban life. From the tropical rain forests of the north to the mountains of the south, Argentina's weather is as varied as its terrain. This is one of a trio of books focused on the country of Argentina.

15.30 Nickles, Greg. **Argentina: The People.** Crabtree, 2001. ISBN 0-86505-245-X. Nonfiction

Using illustrations and many photographs, the author describes the varied backgrounds of the people of Argentina and the difficulties they have had to deal with throughout their country's troubled history. Topics included reflect the importance of family and friends, city life and country life, as well as language, food, school, work, and leisure activities. This is one of a trio of books focused on the country of Argentina.

15.31 Nickles, Greg. **Russia: The Culture.** Crabtree, 2000. 32 pp. ISBN 0-86505-320-0 Nonfiction.

Russian social life and customs are captured in illustrations and photographs. The cultural history is as varied as the geography and the people. Russia has long been one of the world's greatest centers for the ballet; yet it is also a country that cherishes its history as represented through folk dance. This is one of a trio of books focused on the country of Russia.

15.32 Nickles, Greg. **Russia: The Land.** Crabtree, 2000. 32 pp. ISBN 0-86505-318-9. Nonfiction.

Russia, as the largest country in the world, has a varied landscape, from rolling plains to striking mountain ranges to great frozen wilderness. The rich farmland of the plains is irrigated by the Volga River, the longest river in Europe. This beautifully illustrated volume captures many of the facets of this varied country. This is one of a trio of books focused on the country of Russia. A glossary at the end of each volume contributes to the value of the series.

15.33 Nickles, Greg. **Russia: The People.** Crabtree, 2000. 32 pp. ISBN 0-86505-319-7. Nonfiction

The people of Russia are richly portrayed in the photographs in this volume. Their backgrounds are as varied as the geography of this diverse country. Most of the Russian people live in the major cities of Moscow or St. Petersburg or in areas near these cities. This book presents pictures of the many aspects of their lives, including family, language, food, school, work, and leisure activities. This is one of a trio of books focused on the country of Russia.

15.34 Rosenberg, Anne. **Nigeria: The Culture.** Crabtree, 2001. 32 pp. ISBN 0-86505-249-2. Nonfiction

Photographs abound in this book that describes the mixed cultures of Nigeria, including both the modern and traditional activities and customs celebrated by the Nigerian people. Family tradition, colorful dress, arts and crafts, music, dance, and ceremony are some of the topics featured in this cultural overview. This is one of a trio of books focused on the country of Nigeria.

15.35 Rosenberg, Anne. **Nigeria: The Land.** Crabtree, 2001. 32 pp. ISBN 0-86505-247-6. Nonfiction

Maps and many color photographs assist the author in describing the most populated country of the African continent. Topics include geography, topography, animals and plant life, weather, travel, and farming and industry. The author also details the great variety found in the many settings of rural and urban life in Nigeria. This is one of a trio of books focused on the country of Nigeria.

15.36 Rosenberg, Anne. **Nigeria: The People.** Crabtree, 2001. 32 pp. ISBN 0-86505-328-6. Nonfiction

Using illustrations and many photographs, the author describes the people of Nigeria and their varied histories. The book focuses on the primary ethnic groups from thousands of years ago to the present and elements that make up the daily lives of contemporary Nigerians, including village and city life, languages, foods, school, work, and sports and leisure activities. This is one of a trio of books focused on the country of Nigeria.

We Came to North America Series

15.37 Fahey, Kathleen. **The Italians.** Crabtree, 2000. 32 pp. ISBN 0-7787-0189-1. Nonfiction

Fahey describes the colorful heritage of Italian immigrants in the United States, including language, foods, and music. The book also looks at the lives of several well-known Italian Americans. Fahey uses illustrations, maps, personal stories, and many photographs to chronicle the five-hundred-year history of Italian culture in North America.

15.38 Green, Jen. **The Africans.** Crabtree, 2000. 32 pp. ISBN 0-7787-0198-0. Nonfiction

This book chronicles the history of African Americans from the days of slavery, nearly five hundred years ago, up to the present. Using posters, photographs, maps, and diary excerpts, the author brings to life the horrible conditions imposed by a life of slavery as well as the prejudice faced and the progress made since the end of the Civil War.

15.39 Horton, Casey. **The French.** Crabtree, 2000. 32 pp. ISBN 0-7787-0199-9. Nonfiction

Since the French first traveled to North America some 450 years ago, they have made important contributions to U.S. culture. Using photographs, illustrations, maps, and diary excerpts, the author catalogs the influence of the French from northern Canada to the southern United States. Beginning with the early explorers and fur traders and then the priests and missionaries, the impact of the French can be noted all through our culture.

15.40 Horton, Casey. **The Jews.** Crabtree, 2000. 32 pp. ISBN 0-7787-0201-4. Nonfiction

Using photographs, illustrations, maps, and personal accounts, the author describes how Jews traveled to North America to escape persecution in Europe. Cataloging a long history, the author focuses on the flight of Jewish peoples from Russia, Poland, and Germany to the United States and Canada, detailing the horrific conditions that necessitated their immigration and the prejudices faced since. Included are brief backgrounds of the Jewish religion and people, highlighting the contributions of famous Jewish Americans and Jewish culture.

15.41 Kite, Lorien. **The Chinese.** Crabtree, 2000. 32 pp. ISBN 0-7787-0202-2. Nonfiction

For the last 150 years, Chinese immigrants have struggled to make a better life for themselves in North America. Detailing the rich heritage of China, the author traces through photographs, illustrations, maps, and diary excerpts the important contributions made and the prejudice faced by Chinese immigrants.

15.42 Nickles, Greg. **The Hispanics.** Crabtree, 2001. 32 pp. ISBN 0-7787-0186-7. Nonfiction

This book describes the diverse backgrounds of the different Hispanic immigrant groups and their religious, cultural, and social contributions to North American culture. Using illustrations, maps, personal stories, and many photographs, this book looks at the variety of Spanish-speaking cultures from Europe, South America, and Central America that contribute to our rich heritage.

The World in Maps Series

15.43 Bramwell, Martyn. **Africa.** Lerner, 2000. 56 pp. ISBN 0-8225-2914-9. Nonfiction

Bramwell, Martyn. **Australia, the Pacific, and Antarctica.** Lerner, 2000. 40 pp. ISBN 0-8225-2917-3. Nonfiction

Bramwell, Martyn. **Central and South America.** Lerner, 2000. 40 pp. ISBN 0-8225-2912-2. Nonfiction

Bramwell, Martyn. **Europe.** Lerner, 2000. 48 pp. ISBN 0-8225-2913-0. Nonfiction

Bramwell, Martyn. **North America and the Caribbean.** Lerner, 2000. 48 pp. ISBN 0-8225-2911-4. Nonfiction

Bramwell, Martyn. **Northern and Western Asia.** Lerner, 2000. 40 pp. ISBN 0-8225-2915-7. Nonfiction

Bramwell, Martyn. **Southern and Eastern Asia.** Lerner, 2000. 48 pp. ISBN 0-8225-2916-5. Nonfiction

The seven books in the World in Maps series provide both maps and background information about the countries in every region of the world. Each country's entry begins with a picture of its flag and information about governmental status, area, population, capital, languages, and currency. The entry explores the country's geography, natural resources, and other significant information.

VI Challenges of Yesterday

16 Historical Fiction

16.1 Alder, Elizabeth. **Crossing the Panther's Path.** Farrar, Straus and Giroux, 2002. 272 pp. ISBN 0-374-31662-7. Fiction

Billy Calder lives in a world of uncertainty. Torn between his Irish and Mohawk ancestries, Billy strives to make sense of the violence around him. Concerned about the treatment the Native Americans receive from the European Americans, Billy befriends Tecumseh and prepares to engage in battle against the United States. The War of 1812 unfolds in this novel, which is based on a true story, and readers gain insights into Tecumseh's life and the bravery exhibited by Billy Calder.

16.2 Anderson, Laurie Halse. **Fever, 1793.** Aladdin, 2002. 252 pp. ISBN 0-689-84891-9. Fiction

The 1793 epidemic of yellow fever has infected Philadelphia. Sixteen-year-old Mattie Cook, whose family owns a popular coffeehouse on High Street, is sent away to escape the epidemic, but she is stricken with the disease. When she survives, she returns to Philadelphia. As the disease ravages her family, it is up to Mattie to keep the family business alive. Although her life is disrupted by the epidemic, Mattie grows into a responsible young woman.

16.3 Ayres, Katherine. **Stealing South: A Story of the Underground Railroad.** Delacorte, 2001. 197 pp. ISBN 0-385-72912-X. Fiction

Life has never been dull for Will Spencer. Living in Atwater, Ohio, the Spencer family has always helped runaway slaves pass through the Underground Railroad. While he prides himself on his involvement with this important passage, Will wants to experience life on his own. Bound for independence as a peddler, Will discovers that people are not always what they seem to be and that it's not always easy to tell wrong from right.

16.4 Bat-Ami, Miriam.**Two Suns in the Sky.** Puffin, 2001. 213 pp. ISBN 0-14-230036-5. Fiction

Chris Cook, age fifteen, a Christian resident of Oswego, New York, and Adam Bornstein, a Jewish refugee from Yugoslavia now living in a refugee camp in Oswego, meet and fall in love. Adam's mother and Chris's parents are opposed to the relationship. The town of Oswego exhibits complex reactions to the refugees, who live behind fences and whose movements are limited. Chris and Adam alternately narrate the novel. The author's note includes details about the camp, which was built in 1944.

16.5 Bennett, Cherie, and Jeff Gottesfeld. **Anne Frank and Me.** Putnam, 2001. 288 pp. ISBN 0-399-23329-6. Fiction

Nicole Burns is very much a twenty-first-century girl. She lives in the suburbs and navigates the Internet with ease. When she is knocked unconscious during a museum field trip to the Anne Frank exhibit, Nicole finds herself transported back in time to 1942 Paris where she discovers the horrors of being Jewish in that Nazi-occupied city. On a transport to a concentration camp, Nicole meets young Anne Frank, whose diary she has just studied in school.

16.6 Blackwood, Gary L. **Moonshine.** Marshall Cavendish, 1999. 158 pp. ISBN 0-7614-5056-4. Fiction

Moonshine has a double meaning for thirteen-year-old Thad McCune: liquor made illegally and stories he makes up about selling moonshine as well as the stories his mother makes up to explain his dad's absence. This Depression-era tale takes place in rural Missouri. A startling confrontation at a moonshine still forces Thad to come out of his isolation.

16.7 Blakeslee, Ann R. **Summer Battles.** Marshall Cavendish, 2000. 127 pp. ISBN 0-7614-5064-5. Fiction

In 1926, eleven-year-old Kath and her sister are visiting with their grandfather in Indiana where Grando is a minister confronting activities of the Ku Klux Klan. He is the target of escalating attacks because Serena, an African American woman, works for him. In Kath's struggle to understand events and prove that she is grown up, she gets into trouble, acts bravely, and learns about the insidiousness of prejudice.

16.8 Blos, Joan W. **Brooklyn Doesn't Rhyme.** Illustrated by Paul Birling. Aladdin, 2000. 86 pp. ISBN 0-689-83557-4. Fiction

When Rosey's sixth-grade teacher invites the class to write about their lives and their families, Rosey begins to capture memories in a composition book. In a clear, distinctive voice, she recounts a number of stories—some funny, some sad—about her Jewish immigrant parents, her extended family members, and her friends, all of whom live in Brooklyn at the turn of the twentieth century.

16.9 Bradley, Kimberly Brubaker. **Weaver's Daughter.** Delacorte, 2000. 166 pp. ISBN 0-385-32769-2. Fiction

Set in the late 1700s in the "Southwest Territory" of Tennessee, this is the story of a young girl plagued by asthma. The book paints a vivid portrait of the hardships of pioneer life. With the support of her family, Lizzie survives the struggle against her illness.

16.10 Brooke, Peggy. **Jake's Orphan.** Aladdin, 2001. 266 pp. ISBN 0-7434-2703-3. Fiction

Tree lives in an orphanage but is offered the chance to live and work on a farm in North Dakota. If the family likes his work, they might adopt him. His younger brother runs away from the orphanage and comes to join him. Together they find a way to make a home on the farm and learn the meaning of family. This story gives an accurate account of the difficulties of farm life in the early 1900s. Historical notes are included.

16.11 Cadnum, Michael. **Raven of the Waves.** Orchard, 2001. 200 pp. ISBN 0-531-30334-9. Fiction

On his first Viking raid, seventeen-year-old Lismond is horrified and amazed at the brutality of his shipmates, men he has known his entire life. Searching for gold and treasure, the Vikings travel to a small Anglo-Saxon village. While there, the raiders capture Wiglaf, a boy only a few years younger than Lismond. As much as he can, Lismond befriends Wiglaf and risks his own life to free his new friend.

16.12 Carbone, Elisa. **Storm Warriors.** Knopf, 2001. 168 pp. ISBN 0-375-80664-4. Fiction

Set on Pea Island off the coast of North Carolina in the 1890s, this story is about Nathan, who desperately wants to become a member of the United States Life-Saving Service. Nathan's grandfather tells him to set his goals high but not be discouraged if things don't work out. Nathan's father is more abrupt and warns him that even though the black man believed things would be different after the Civil War, things have not changed; there will never be a black surfman on the Carolina coast.

16.13 Cheng, Andrea. **Marika.** Front Street, 2002. 160 pp. ISBN 1-886910-78-2. Fiction.

Marika, a Jew, is growing up in Budapest during the Nazi occupation of Hungary. Marika's family changes her name to Maria and tries to hide the fact that they are Jewish by obtaining forged documents, baptizing her, and sending her to Catholic school. Their efforts are unsuccessful, and the family is captured and sent to the concentration camps. The family is reunited when the Russians capture the city from the Germans.

16.14 Clarke, Breena. **River, Cross My Heart.** Little, Brown, 2000. 272 pp. ISBN 0-316-89816-3. Fiction

Johnnie Mae and her younger sister Clara like living near the banks of the Potomac in Washington, D.C. But the seduction of the river causes great sadness when young Clara drowns in its murky waters. Devastated by the loss of her sister, Johnnie Mae has to face the guilt of being responsible for her sister's death and at the same time grapple with the injustice and inequities faced by African Americans in post–World War I United States.

16.15 Coleman, Evelyn. **Circle of Fire.** Pleasant Company, 2001. 146 pp. ISBN 1-58485-340-9. Fiction

Mendy, a young African American girl, discovers that her secret hiding place is being vandalized by trespassers. When she attempts to scare them away, Mendy finds out that the intruders are members of the Klu Klux Klan who are filled with hate for her and her family. Mendy receives help from her best friend and his father, who are both white, and together they stop the Klan from bombing a school that Eleanor Roosevelt is visiting.

16.16 Cushman, Karen. **Matilda Bone.** Clarion, 2000. 167 pp. ISBN 0-395-88156-0. Fiction

Like other of Cushman's adolescent female protagonists, Matilda lives in the Middle Ages. Unlike them, she has been shaped by an excessively pious childhood. When Matilda is apprenticed to Red Peg the Bonesetter, she is exposed to a truer, deeper sort of goodness, but conflicted Matilda takes a long time to recognize the warmth and depth of Peg's charity.

16.17 Dadey, Debbie. **Cherokee Sister.** Delacorte, 2000. 119 pp. ISBN 0-385-32703-X. Fiction

A clear account of the events of the Trail of Tears with a surprise ending, *Cherokee Sister* is told from the viewpoint of twelve-year-old Allie, a white settler in 1838 Georgia. Her best friend Leaf, a Cherokee, is forcibly removed with other Cherokee to Oklahoma. Because Allie has dark hair and tan skin, she is taken with the Cherokee while she is visiting Leaf. Throughout the story, the author includes examples of both unreasonable hatred and reassuring love from Cherokee and whites alike.

16.18 Dahlberg, Maurine F. **The Spirit and Gilly Bucket.** Farrar, Straus and Giroux, 2002. 234 pp. ISBN 0-374-31677-5. Fiction

Gilly Bucket knows that slavery is wrong; her father told her so. Too bad her aunt and uncle don't realize it. Faced with living on her relatives' farm, which uses slave labor, Gilly discovers much about life and about the Underground Railroad. Growing up without her mother and searching for a father who has gone in search of gold, Gilly learns that growing up is not always easy. She learns too that friends make it easier and that life does get better.

16.19 Demas, Corinne. **If Ever I Return Again.** HarperCollins, 2000. 197 pp. ISBN 0-06-028717-9. Fiction

In 1856, twelve-year-old Celia Snow sets sail with her parents on her father's whaling ship. She chronicles her ensuing adventures on the more than two-year voyage in a series of letters written to her cousin Abigail. Life aboard ship is not easy for Celia, but she learns everything she can about being a captain's daughter. When disaster strikes, she must gather all her courage, strength, and newfound knowledge to save the expedition and the lives of those she loves.

16.20 Disher, Garry. **The Divine Wind: A Love Story.** Arthur A. Levine Books, 2002. 153 pp. ISBN 0-439-36915-0. Fiction

In the northern Australia town of Broome, Hart's life is turned upside down by the coming of World War II. He is in love with a Japanese immigrant and has to face the fact that many people see her as the enemy, despite the fact that she was born and raised in Australia. The tensions of living during wartime are almost unbearable.

16.21 Easton, Richard. **A Real American.** Clarion, 2002. 155 pp. ISBN 0-618-13339-9. Fiction

In 1881 the longtime Pennsylvania farmers are being displaced by the immigrant coal miners, mostly from Italy, after coal is discovered in the region. Nathan, a farmer's son, befriends Arturo, a coal miner his own age. The resentment and hatred between the adult farmers and miners affect the boys' relationship until they find a way to be themselves and show the adults how friendship should work. Nathan realizes that to be a "real" American, Arturo doesn't have to be just like Nathan.

16.22 Ernst, Kathleen. **Whistler in the Dark.** Pleasant Company, 2002. 155 pp. ISBN 1-58485-486-3. Fiction

Emma Henderson comes home from school one day and is shocked to find her mother wearing pants. In 1867, women do not normally wear pants. When her mother is offered a job writing for a newspaper in the wilderness of the Colorado Territory, Emma learns what a strong and capable person her mother really is. Together they fight the prejudice of the town against women in the workplace. Information about the women's movement is included in an author's note.

16.23 Fletcher, Susan. **Walk across the Sea.** Atheneum, 2001. 214 pp. IBSN 0-689-84133-7. Fiction

Eliza begins her account of why her family no longer tends the lighthouse in Crescent City with a quasi apology to her brother, whose childhood will be spent on a midwestern farm instead of the rocky Pacific coast. Eliza's actions cost her father his lighthouse keeper's job, but Eliza's refusal to accept her father's antipathy for the Chinese immigrants should not cause her shame. Racial tensions of post–gold rush California are honestly depicted, but Eliza's conflict of loyalties gives this novel energy and particular relevance.

16.24 Forrester, Sandra. **Wheel of the Moon.** HarperCollins, 2000. 165 pp. ISBN 0-688-17149-4. Fiction

In the seventeenth and eighteenth centuries, many people were kidnapped from cities in the British Isles and sent as indentured servants to work on the Virginian tobacco plantations. Fourteen-year-old Pen Downing, an orphan, travels from a rural village in England to London in 1627 and joins a group of orphans. Kidnapped and sent to Virginia, she must make a new life for herself after her owner's sister-in-law buys what's left of her seven-year indenture and sets her free.

16.25 Galloway, Priscilla. **The Courtesan's Daughter.** Delacorte, 2002. 250 pp. ISBN 0-385-72907-3. Fiction.

Phano has a mortal enemy who will stop at nothing to destroy her life. This man claims that she is his property and that she does not come from a respectable family—a serious threat in ancient Athenian culture. Even after she is married to the most influential man in Athens and is herself named the Savior of Athens, Phano feels threatened by this man's power. To defeat him, she must discover who she is and who she wants to be.

16.26 Garland, Sherry. **In the Shadow of the Alamo.** Harcourt, 2001. 282 pp. ISBN 0-15-201744-5. Fiction

Drafted into the Mexican army at fifteen, Lorenzo Bonifacio learns rapidly the pain and sorrow of growing up in the heat of battle. As the Mexican troops move near the Battle of the Alamo in Texas, Lorenzo begins to question the authority of his Mexican leader, General Santa Anna, and his own alliances with his fellow soldiers. Forced to behave older than he is, Lorenzo learns to cope with few friends, an inability to speak English, and a ruthless enemy.

16.27 Giff, Patricia Reilly. **Nory Ryan's Song.** Delacorte, 2000. 176 pp. ISBN 0-385-32141-4. Fiction

Nory Ryan, like most twelve-year-olds, enjoys the outdoors and music and has friends and family who love her. And, although growing up in 1845 on Maiden Bay on the West coast of Ireland where her family has lived for generations has never been easy, it is home. When the potato famine strikes, Nory soon realizes that home is much more than a place and that love often requires sacrifice.

16.28 Greene, Jacqueline Dembar. **One Foot Ashore.** Walker, 2000. 196 pp. ISBN 0-8027-7601-9. Fiction

In this sequel to *Out of Many Waters,* Maria Ben Lazar and her sister Isobel, kidnapped by Catholic monks, escape from the monastery where they have been held for six years during the Portuguese Inquisition. Forced to separate during their escape, sixteen-year-old Maria arrives alone in Amsterdam. She is welcomed into the home of her new friend, Dutch painter Rembrandt, who helps her find her family.

16.29 Gregory, Kristiana. **Jenny of the Tetons.** Harcourt, 2002 (Originally published in 1989). 164 pp. ISBN 0-15-216770-6. Fiction

This Great Episodes series novel effectively weaves together fiction and nonfiction in a history of pioneers and Native Americans in the Idaho Territory of the 1870s. Real people and events are the catalysts for this intriguing novel of fifteen-year-old Carrie Hill, orphaned in an attack by Native Americans and subsequently cared for by an English trapper and his Shoshoni wife, Jenny. Carrie overcomes her enmity toward Native Americans as a group through her relationship with Jenny. Additional resources include a map and brief Shoshoni glossary.

16.30 Gregory, Kristiana. **The Legend of Jimmy Spoon.** Harcourt, 2002 (Originally published in 1990). 197 pp. ISBN 0-15-216776-5. Fiction

The story of Jimmy Spoon was inspired by Elijah Nicholas Wilson's memoirs describing being taken from his family in Utah in 1854 to become a son to Old Mother of the Shoshoni. Encountering prejudice within the tribe, Jimmy is caught between two cultures even as he questions why the Crow and Shoshoni are unable to overcome their age-old enmity to make peace with each other. The novel includes a brief Shoshoni glossary, an epilogue, and an author's note.

16.31 Hahn, Mary Downing. **Promises to the Dead.** Clarion, 2000. 202 pp. ISBN 0-395-96394-X. Fiction

During the early Civil War years in Maryland, thirteen-year-old Jesse Sherman, out of a sense of responsibility and a desire to make ethical choices, makes two promises to the dead. Because of these promises, he starts on a journey to Baltimore as well as on an exploration of his sense of right and wrong and of current events. The author has provided an interesting afterword.

16.32 Harlow, Joan Hiatt. **Joshua's Song.** Margaret K. McElderry Books, 2002. 176 pp. ISBN 0-689-84119-1. Fiction

World War I has ended but an influenza epidemic has hit Boston, killing Joshua Harper's father, who leaves his family in debt. When the family falls on hard times, Joshua takes a job as a newspaper boy, where he gains an education on the streets and finds a reporter who pays for the stories Joshua gives him. The climax of the story relates a real event, the explosion of a tanker full of molasses that exploded in Boston's North End, killing twenty-one people.

16.33 Hausman, Gerald. **Tom Cringle: Battle on the High Seas.** Illustrated by Tad Hills. Simon & Schuster, 2000. 185 pp. ISBN 0-689-82810-1. Fiction

Thirteen-year-old Tom Cringle leaves England for sea duty near Jamaica and Cuba during the War of 1812. While enduring sea battles, deaths of friends, illnesses, earthquake, kidnapping, and storms, Tom forms friendships and develops self-confidence, eventually rising to the rank of lieutenant. Tom's eagle eye and loyalty serve him well, and Tad Hills's illustrations and the authentic details of the era bring to life the characters and events recounted in Tom's log.

16.34 Heisel, Sharon. **Precious Gold, Precious Jade.** Holiday House, 2000. 186 pp. ISBN 0-8234-1432-9. Fiction

Angelena and her sister Evangeline make friends with a newcomer to their western mining town. This friendship concerns their family and friends because their new friend, Leeana, is a young Chinese girl from the immigrant part of town called China Shacks. Through their friendship, the girls learn many new things about the very different Chinese culture; they also, however, discover the bad side of their own culture as they witness the destruction that hate and bigotry can cause.

16.35 Heneghan, James. **The Grave.** Farrar, Straus and Giroux, 2000. 256 pp. ISBN 0-374-32765-3. Fiction

In 1974 Liverpool, Tom Mullen has spent all thirteen years of his life being shifted from foster home to foster home. When he and his best mate Brian explore a construction site, Tom slips into a hole and finds himself in 1847 Ireland during the potato famine. On this journey, he connects with the Monaghans and learns what it means to be a family during this difficult and historic time.

16.36 Herschler, Mildred Barger. **The Darkest Corner.** Front Street, 2000. 240 pp. ISBN 1-886910-54-5. Fiction

Teddy discovers that her father, a bank president and a Klansman, participated in the lynching of her best friend's father.

Teddy loves her father but hates what he has done. During the next five years, her social consciousness emerges as she witnesses the events of the 1960s' civil rights movement. Teddy's growing sense of right and wrong alienates her from her father as he struggles to protect his reputation.

16.37 Hesse, Karen. **A Time of Angels.** Hyperion, 2000. 276 pp. ISBN 0-7868-2534-0. Fiction

When the 1918 flu epidemic strikes, Hannah Gold, age fourteen, must flee Boston, leaving her ill sisters and Tanta Rose behind. Ill herself, Hannah slowly recovers under the care of an old German farmer in Vermont, whom the townspeople view suspiciously. Confused by her visions of angels and worried about her family, Hannah is torn between her life in Boston and country life. Lyrically written and full of earthly and heavenly angels, this book evokes the historical era of World War I.

16.38 Hesse, Karen. **Witness.** Scholastic, 2001. 161 pp. ISBN 0-439-27199-1. Fiction

Witness tells the story of how the Ku Klux Klan, with its racist propaganda hidden under the guise of American patriotism, disrupts life in a quiet Vermont town in 1924. The blank verse narrative is told in sixteen different voices and centers on two children, twelve-year-old African American Leonora Sutter and six-year-old Jewish Esther Hirsch. Their presence in the town creates dissent among local inhabitants as they wrestle with their own prejudices and beliefs.

16.39 Hill, Pamela Smith. **A Voice from the Border.** HarperTrophy, 2000. 244 pp. ISBN 0-380-73231-9. Fiction

Margaret is trying to understand her father's loyal southerner decision regarding slavery. Living in the border state of Missouri, her father has left to join the Confederacy. At home, Margaret's neighbors are bitterly divided—some support the North and others the South—and Margaret must decide whose side she is on. Caught between a sense of justice and familial duty, young Margaret finally comes to terms with what it means for all people—regardless of color—to be free.

16.40 Holm, Jennifer L. **Our Only May Amelia.** HarperCollins, 1999. 253 pp. ISBN 0-06-027822-6. Fiction

May Amelia is a twelve-year-old girl growing up in Nasel, Washington, in 1899 in a family with seven brothers. The adults think she should behave like a proper young lady, but May Amelia just wants to do whatever the boys do. And what do they do besides have adventures of their own? They tease her, teach her, look after her, defend her, comfort her, and rescue her. All this makes for entertaining reading about life in the wilderness one hundred years ago.

16.41 Horowitz, Anthony. **The Devil and His Boy.** Puffin, 2001. 178 pp. ISBN 0-698-11913-4. Fiction

Horowitz's character Tom is a matter of historical conjecture. The young Elizabeth Tudor was rumored to have had a child by Thomas Seymour; in this novel, that child was Tom's father. But Tom is caught up in a plot to assassinate the queen while ostensibly performing in a period melodrama. The Elizabeth in this novel is an old woman, full of what-ifs; her promise to sponsor Tom's application to work with Master Shakespeare becomes a symbol of redemption for both her and her secret grandson.

16.42 Hughes, Dean. **Soldier Boys.** Atheneum, 2001. 162 pp. ISBN 0-689-81748-7. Fiction

Spencer, an American, wants to be a paratrooper and prove himself to his town, his father, and, most of all, to himself. Dieter, a member of Hitler Youth, has actually met Hitler himself and wants desperately to fight for the honor of his homeland. During the Battle of the Bulge, these two lives intersect, and both young men have to confront the realities of war. Through their stories, readers are forced to think about what courage really means.

16.43 Hurst, Carol Otis. **In Plain Sight.** Houghton Mifflin, 2002. 154 pp. ISBN 0-618-19699-4. Fiction

Sarah is dismayed when her charming, storytelling father leaves their Massachusetts farm in search of gold in California. Her mother, a serious woman, must go to work in the local mill to pay their creditors and keep the farm going. As the family faces a series of hardships, Sarah longs for her father's warmth and resents her mother's distant coolness. As time goes by, Sarah learns important lessons about family, responsibility, and what constitutes parental love.

16.44 Ingold, Jeanette. **The Big Burn.** Harcourt, 2002. 295 pp. ISBN 0-15-216470-7. Fiction

It is the hot, dry summer of 1910, and wildfires are breaking out in the mountainous forests of Montana and Idaho. Lizbeth and her sister Ceclia stay on their land until it is almost too late to escape the fire. Jarrett loses his job but tries to prove himself fighting the fires. Seth, a black soldier, joins the battle against the fires hoping to find respect and acceptance. These young peoples' lives become intertwined as the fires burn out of control and consume everything in their path.

16.45 Isaacs, Anne. **Torn Thread.** Scholastic, 2000. 188 pp. ISBN 0-590-60363-9. Fiction

During the two years she and her sister are enslaved in a Nazi prison camp, twelve-year-old Eva Buchbinder often remembers their father's words of encouragement: "If we can't find a way around, God will teach us to fly" and "Try to stay alive just one more hour." The author has conducted meticulous research to accurately convey her mother-in-law's horrendous Holocaust experience within the context of the love, courage, and fortitude that enabled her to survive.

16.46 Kimball, K. M. **The Star-Spangled Secret.** Aladdin, 2001. 234 pp. ISBN 0-689-84550-2. Fiction

Caroline can't accept what she's told by the captain of the ship on which her brother served: that Charlie fell from the dock and drowned. Caroline's quest to learn the truth, set against the backdrop of the War of 1812, takes her from her family's plantation in Maryland to the White House to the docks of Baltimore and shows a young woman who's got the grit, determination, and strength of character to serve her family and follow her own heart.

16.47 Kochenderfer, Lee. **The Victory Garden.** Delacorte, 2002.164 pp. ISBN 0-385-32788-9. Fiction

Irrepressible Teresa discovers the power of one (or a few) to make a difference in people's lives and in the war effort in 1943 Kansas. Struggling with her brother's absence through enlistment as a pilot, a classmate's erratic behavior, her neighbor's inability to tend his huge victory garden, and the tomato contest, Teresa discovers the value of organization, helping others, and setting goals and experiences the confusion of sometimes becoming the adult in a situation. The book includes a world map and an author's note.

16.48 Koller, Jackie French. **Someday.** Orchard, 2002. 215 pp. ISBN 0-439-29317-0. Fiction

Set in the Great Depression, this coming-of-age novel is based on real events in 1930s Massachusetts. Celie's life is about to change radically. Her family's home, which dates back to the American Revolution, like all the rest of the homes in their valley is scheduled to be destroyed when the area is flooded to create a reservoir. Celie must come to terms with the loss of friends, her town, her home, and her heritage.

16.49 Lawrence, Iain. **Lord of the Nutcracker Men.** Delacorte, 2001. 210 pp. ISBN 0-385-72924-3. Fiction

Through ten-year-old Johnny's war games with soldiers carved by his father and his father's letters from the front, the realities of war are revealed as they affect those at home and those in battle. The letters and carved soldiers reflect reality, but Johnny's fears grow as his pretend battles seem to foreshadow real events. Set in 1914 England, this novel makes connections between the *Iliad* and all wars. Author Lawrence provides an illuminating map and author's note.

16.50 Levitin, Sonia. **Clem's Chances.** Orchard, 2001. 208 pp. ISBN 0-439-29314-6. Fiction

In 1860, Clem Fontayne loses his mother and sister to fever and decides to find his educated French father in the California gold fields. From Missouri over the Great Plains to San Francisco, Clem endures hardship but also bonds with people along the way. He perseveres, using examples from his favorite book, *Oliver Twist*, as inspiration. The story contains many historical references such as the Mormon migration, free blacks working in the West, the Pony Express, and the Lincoln-Douglas election.

16.51 Lisle, Janet Taylor. **The Art of Keeping Cool.** Aladdin, 2002. 250 pp. ISBN 0-689-83788-7. Fiction

Robert, his mother, and his sister leave their farm in Ohio to spend the war years in Rhode Island with his father's family while his father is overseas. Along with his cousin Elliot, Robert watches as heavy artillery is delivered to the nearby fort. Elliot is a talented artist who befriends and becomes the student of a famous German artist who has moved to their community. The artist evokes suspicions that trigger a chain of events that change the cousins and their community.

16.52 Lisle, Janet Taylor. **Sirens and Spies.** Aladdin, 2002 (Originally published in 1985). 207 pp. ISBN 0-689-84457-3. Fiction.

Elsie, a talented young violinist, turns against Miss Fitch, her teacher, and even refuses to visit her when the older woman is brutally attacked and hospitalized. What has happened to make Elsie turn on her teacher and call her "the old fraud"? Her disenchantment with Miss Fitch is based on information Elsie discovered about the past and on her willingness to judge without checking the facts.

16.53 Little, Kimberley Griffiths. **The Last Snake Runner.** Knopf, 2002. 202 pp. ISBN 0-375-81539-2. Fiction

After his mom dies, Kendall, half European American and half Acoma Indian, is incensed when his dad remarries a descendant of the Spanish conquistadors, the ancestral enemy of his mother's people. To clear his head, Kendall, the last surviving male member of the Snake Clan, runs to the desert where he is transported back in time to the Snake Clan's battle at Acoma. While the true events presented are horrific, their descriptions are taken from first-person accounts written by a Spanish soldier.

16.54 Love, D. Anne. **A Year without Rain.** Holiday House, 2000. 118 pp. ISBN 0-8234-1488-4. Fiction

Rachel and her brother are close to their father, particularly since their mother's death. But the worst drought in years forces Pa to send them away from their home in the Dakota Territory to stay with their aunt in Savannah, Georgia. Their excitement when Pa comes to take them back home is short lived when they find out he is planning to marry their schoolteacher. Rachel's determination to keep that from happening causes more problems than the drought.

16.55 Lurie, April. **Dancing in the Streets of Brooklyn.** Delacorte, 2002. 195 pp. ISBN 0-385-72942-1. Fiction

It is 1944, and thirteen-year-old Judy lives in Bay Bridge enjoying games of stickball and the pleasures of Coney Island. When secrets from her family's past emerge, she feels mixed up and confused. But as Judy and her friends and family face a series of problems, she begins to learn about the importance of friendship and forgiveness—especially of oneself. This book celebrates the life of the Norwegians who immigrated to Brooklyn in the early 1900s.

16.56 Lyons, Mary E., and Muriel M. Branch. **Dear Ellen Bee: A Civil War Scrapbook of Two Union Spies.** Atheneum, 2000. 155 pp. ISBN 0-689-82379-7. Fiction

Though fictional, *Dear Ellen Bee* is based on the real lives of two women abolitionists. Liza, a freed slave, and Miss Bet, a Richmond socialite, join forces to spy on the Confederates. Through their efforts, lives are saved and the Union cause is advanced. The two learn valuable lessons about human nature, the ugliness of war, and what it means to be free. They learn too that they are strong and that love is a powerful emotion.

16.57 Matas, Carol. **The War Within: A Novel of the Civil War.** Simon & Schuster, 2001. 151 pp. ISBN 0-689-82935-3. Fiction

In her diary, thirteen-year-old Hannah Green reveals the conflicts experienced by a southern Jewish family in 1862. Her account reflects the civil strife of the times and internal battles as people reexamine their thoughts and beliefs concerning slavery in light of discrimination against themselves. Based on fact, this novel deals with the discrimination and prejudice toward two groups of people—southern Jews by the Union and black slaves by the Confederates.

16.58 Mazer, Harry. **A Boy at War: A Novel of Pearl Harbor.** Simon & Schuster, 2001. 104 pp. ISBN 0-689-84161-2. Fiction

December 7, 1941, often referred to as a Day of Infamy, was the day Japan attacked Pearl Harbor in Hawaii, launching the entry of the United States into World War II. The day begins like any other for Adam, who is fishing with friends. The attack changes everything, however, as he tries to find his missing military father and adjust to life during wartime.

16.59 Murphy, Rita. **Black Angels.** Delacorte, 2001. 163 pp. ISBN 0-385-32776-5. Fiction

In 1961 Georgia, eleven-year-old Celli Jenkins witnesses events involving the civil rights movement and the Freedom Riders. Through her African American caretaker Sophie, her long-lost grandmother from the north, and her mother, Celli comes to more complete intergenerational and interracial understandings, and her view of her place in the world and her family changes. She sees black angels, who wordlessly help her, in her white neighborhood. The unusual and interesting events of this story are written in a captivating, lyrical style.

16.60 Napoli, Donna Jo. **Daughter of Venice.** Delacorte, 2002. 271 pp. ISBN 0-385-32780-3. Fiction

Although she lives in one of the most romantic and beautiful cities in the world, Donata has never seen most of her enchanting city. Set in 1592, this book tells the story of a noble girl who is destined for seclusion in a convent. Donata's daring plan to escape captivity dressed as a boy and explore her surroundings helps bring alive the beauty and history of Venice in this captivating tale of adventure.

16.61 Osborne, Mary Pope. **Adaline Falling Star.** Scholastic, 2000. 169 pp. ISBN 0-439-05947-X. Fiction

In the late 1800s, explorer Kit Carson lost his wife to cholera. Forced to return to a mapping expedition, Kit leaves his daughter Adaline with cousins in St. Louis, a couple whose treatment of her turns cruel. Because Adaline's mother was Arapaho Indian, Adaline must endure not only a new lifestyle but also racial taunts about her half-breed status. She isn't even allowed to go to school but must work as the schoolhouse servant. Desperate, she flees in search of her father.

16.62 Park, Linda Sue. **The Kite Fighters.** Decorations by Eung Won Park. Clarion, 2000. 136 pp. ISBN 0-395-94041-9. Fiction

In 1473, two brothers bound by tradition and their love for each other combine their talents to compete in the most important competition in Seoul, Korea. The eldest brother, Kee-sup, is heir to all the privileges of the House of Lee. Young-sup, the second born, regardless of his wants or wishes, must do whatever he can to help his brother fulfill his role as the eldest. This inequality creates tension but, working together during the kite-flying festival, the brothers overcome their rivalry.

16.63 Park, Linda Sue. **When My Name Was Keoko.** Clarion, 2002. 192 pp. ISBN 0-618-13335-6. Fiction

This richly delineated novel of one family's resilience as it struggles to preserve its culture and family is based on fact, describing Sun-hee/Keoko's growth in understanding her brother, parents, uncle, and herself during part of the long Japanese occupation of Korea. The compromises, risks, escalating Japanese oppression, and daily life are revealed through Sun-hee's journals and her older brother Tae-yul's journals and letters, which provide two fascinating points of view of the same events.

16.64 Pearsall, Shelley. **Trouble Don't Last.** Random House, 2002. 231 pp. ISBN 0-375-81490-6. Fiction

In 1859, eleven-year-old Samuel flees slavery in Kentucky with another slave, Harrison, who he later discovers is his grandfather. The process of the Underground Railroad will fascinate readers, and Samuel and Harrison's meeting on the route from Kentucky to Canada may remind them of Huck and Jim's adventures on the Mississippi as they reveal the contrasting good and evil impulses of people. Pearsall's map and endnote help set this novel in its historical context.

16.65 Pressler, Mirjam. **Shylock's Daughter.** Translated by Brian Murdoch. Phyllis Fogelman Books, 2001. 266 pp. ISBN 0-8037-2667-8. Fiction

Pressler has taken the character Jessica from *The Merchant of Venice* and given her context and depth. It is easy to sympathize with a sixteen-year-old caught up in adult hatreds and clashes and in love with Christian Lorenzo. But—and this is a tribute to Pressler's complex narrative—it is also easy to find sympathy for her scorned and beleaguered father. Venice in 1568, with its merchant princes, its opulence, and its ghettoes, beckons mature readers to undertake an exploration of loyalties and betrayals that they will find oddly contemporary.

16.66 Pryor, Bonnie. **Joseph's Choice: 1861.** Illustrated by Bert Dodson. HarperCollins, 2000. 168 pp. ISBN 0-688-17633-X. Fiction

Joseph's and his family's lives are changed dramatically with the beginning of the Civil War. When Joseph sees how his good friend is mistreated because of the color of her skin, he makes the choice to oppose slavery. Joseph's relationship with his stepfather is reaffirmed when they both stand up for the abolitionist movement in their town.

16.67 Pullman, Philip. **The Ruby in the Smoke.** Dell Laurel-Leaf, 2000. 230 pp. ISBN 0-394-89589-4. Fiction

Sally Lockhart penetrates London's Victorian underworld in search of the Seven Blessings. The Indian Meeting, the opium trade, and the despair of the poor all influence Sally's fate, but it is the single-minded viciousness of Mrs. Holland that will drive this absorbing novel to its conclusion.

16.68 Radin, Ruth Yaffe. **Escape to the Forest: Based on a True Story of the Holocaust.** Illustrated by Janet Hamlin. HarperCollins, 2000. 85 pp. ISBN 0-06-028520-6. Fiction

Sarah recognizes the name Adolf Hitler, but he and his soldiers are not a threat. The Russians have taken over her community, and she is safe. But this safety evaporates when Sarah and her family are forced to move into a Jewish ghetto where they learn all about fear, hunger, and cold. When the family is sent to an extermination camp, Sarah's parents encourage her to escape to the forest, where she struggles to survive.

16.69 Rees, Celia. **Witch Child.** Candlewick, 2002. 261 pp. ISBN 0-7636-1829-2. Fiction

When her grandmother is accused of witchcraft, it is obvious that fourteen-year-old Mary Newbury is in danger. She escapes from England by joining a group of Puritan colonists, around whom she must hide her special talents. Mary travels to Salem with the group and then into the wilderness, where they seek to establish a new community. Soon suspicions arise and accusations necessitate flight once again. Mary's story is told in diary form.

16.70 Reit, Seymour. **Behind Rebel Lines: The Incredible Story of Emma Edmonds, Civil War Spy.** Illustrated by Patrick B. Whelan. Harcourt, 2001 (Originally published in 1988). 144 pp. ISBN 0-152-16427-8. Fiction

Emma Edmonds wanted to fight for the Union Army during the Civil War, but being a woman, she was banned from serving. So she cut her hair short, lowered her voice, and joined the army. During her career, she became a master at disguising herself, pretending at times to be a laundry woman, a slave, and a soldier. She also was a spy who went behind enemy lines. This fictionalized account was based on the memoirs of the real Emma Edmonds.

16.71 Reit, Seymour. **Guns for General Washington: A Story of the American Revolution.** Harcourt, 2001 (Originally published in 1990). 142 pp. ISBN 0-15-216435-9. Fiction

Frustrated with the lack of progress of General Washington's army, which is at a standstill due to bitter winter conditions and a lack of artillery, Henry Knox and his brother Will lead a group of brave comrades across three hundred miles of dangerous terrain to Fort Ticonderoga. There, they gather close to two hundred cannons and bring them back to Boston to help the army defend itself against the British navy in the face of rumors about a new British offensive.

16.72 Rinaldi, Ann. **The Coffin Quilt: The Feud between the Hatfields and the McCoys.** Harcourt, 2001. 228 pp. ISBN 0-15-216450-2. Fiction

Feuding with the Hatfields has always been a part of Fanny McCoy's life, but things take a definite turn for the worse when her sister Roseanna falls in love with Johnse Hatfield and runs away with him. The violence, kidnapping, and killing escalate until it seems there is no way to stop it. Amid the terror and heartbreak, Fanny searches for a way out of the evil and hatred to make a life for herself.

16.73 Rinaldi, Ann. **The Education of Mary: A Little Miss of Color, 1832.** Jump at the Sun/Hyperion, 2000. 252 pp. ISBN 0-7868-0532-3. Fiction

In this story set in 1832, Mary Harris is a young "nigra girl" in Canterbury, Connecticut, with the skin color of a white girl and a father who longs for his children to have the education he never had. When Mary's older sister asks the headmistress of the Canterbury Female Academy, where Mary works and gets lessons in secret, if she can attend in the same classrooms as the white students, the value of education and human rights are tested like never before in that town.

16.74 Rinaldi, Ann. **Girl in Blue.** Scholastic, 2001. 310 pp. ISBN 0-439-07336-7. Fiction

Sarah Wheelock runs away when her father tries to marry her to the older farmer next door. Disguised as a man, she enlists in the Union Army, where she fights in the battle of Manassas and witnesses the horrors of war firsthand. When Sarah's officers discover she is not a man, they are so impressed by her ruse that they offer her a position in Pinkerton's Secret Service. Sarah accepts and is placed in the household of a notorious Confederate spy.

16.75 Robinet, Harriette Gillem. **Missing from Haymarket Square.** Atheneum, 2001. 137 pp. ISBN 0-689-83895-6. Fiction

Dinah Bell is the daughter of a union organizer in 1886 Chicago, but her father has been taken away by the Pinkertons. As the unions step up their campaign for an eight-hour day (Dinah, at twelve, works twelve hours a day; grown men and women work sixteen hours), the opposition becomes more personal and more life threatening. Dinah's best friends are Austrian immigrants; together the children steal and scheme to survive as events move inexorably to what history now calls the Haymarket Riot.

16.76 Rubalcaba, Jill. **The Wadjet Eye.** Clarion, 2000. 133 pp. ISBN 0-395-68942-2. Fiction

Set in 45 B.C., the story opens with Damon's mother's death in Alexandria and ends with his reconciliation with his Roman legionnaire father in Spain. Narrated by seventeen-year-old Damon, a medical student, the novel demonstrates how Damon's and his friend Artemas's different personalities complement each other. During the course of their journey, we see the comparison of Alexandria and Rome through encounters with Cleopatra, Cicero, and Caesar. An excellent glossary, afterword, and bibliography are included.

16.77 Ryan, Pam Muñoz. **Esperanza Rising.** Scholastic, 2000. 262 pp. ISBN 0-439-12041-1. Fiction

When she was a little girl, Esperanza lived like a princess. In Mexico her family owned a large plantation, and until her father's death she had everything she desired. After a fire destroys the plantation, she and her family are forced to move to California's Depression-era labor camps, where Esperanza learns how hard life can be. But as the title suggests, Esperanza rises, no matter what hardships she faces.

16.78 Schultz, Jan Neubert. **Horse Sense: The Story of Will Sasse, His Horse Star, and the Outlaw Jesse James.** Carolrhoda, 2001. 177 pp. ISBN 1-57505-998-3. Fiction

Will Sasse, a boy from Minnesota, decides to try his hand at horse breeding. What he doesn't know is that the man who owns the stud horse is really the famous outlaw Jesse James. Will joins the town's posse to help bring the James gang to justice and recapture his prize horse, which has been stolen by the outlaw gang.

16.79 Severance, John B. **Braving the Fire.** Clarion, 2002. 148 pp. ISBN 0-618-22999-X. Fiction

At age fifteen, Jem is torn between his grandfather's loyalty to the Confederacy and his father's belief in the preservation of the Union. After his father goes to war and his grandfather leaves for supplies, Jem and his lifelong friend Hank enlist in the Union Army. The two friends stay together through training and fight together until, in the middle of battle, they are separated. A battlefield accident and a leg wound change Jem's life.

16.80 Skurzynski, Gloria. **Rockbuster.** Atheneum, 2001. 253 pp. ISBN 0-689-83991-X. Fiction

Set in the early part of the twentieth century, this historical novel tells the story of Tommy Quinlan, a gifted musician forced to work in a Utah coal mine by his family's poverty. When Joe Hill, the songwriter for the miners' union, is convicted of murder under questionable circumstances, Tommy must decide whether to carry on Hill's dangerous work or walk away from the union—a decision with important consequences for his new romance with the mine owner's daughter.

16.81 Slate, Joseph. **Crossing the Trestle.** Marshall Cavendish, 1999. 144 pp. ISBN 0-7614-5053-X. Fiction

Narrated by eleven-year-old Petey, this novel set in post–World War II West Virginia describes Petey's fear of heights when crossing the railroad trestle to school. All of the main characters have figurative trestles to cross. Fourteen-year-old Loni is afraid of her eye surgery to replace the eye lost in the accident that killed her father, and Stone is dealing with postwar trauma. All is resolved in a richly drawn historical context.

16.82 Smith, Roland. **The Captain's Dog: My Journey with the Louis and Clark Tribe.** Harcourt, 2000. 287 pp. ISBN 0-15-202696-7. Fiction

This delightful book chronicles the adventures of the historical Louis and Clark expedition down the Missouri River and across the Rocky Mountains in their search for the Northwest Passage to the Pacific Ocean. The story unfolds through a unique combination of excerpts from Lewis's personal journey and a narrative told from the viewpoint of the explorer's faithful (and insightful) dog, Seaman.

16.83 Speare, Elizabeth George. **The Witch of Blackbird Pond.** Illustrated by Barry Moser. Houghton Mifflin, 2001 (Originally published in 1958). 205 pp. ISBN 0-395-91367-5. Fiction

In 1678, Katherine (Kit) Tyler arrives unexpectedly in the Puritan colony of Connecticut from the island of Barbados after her grandfather dies. With no other family left, Kit's aunt and uncle include her in their family. But Kit finds everything about this strict Puritan home and community harsh and unsettling. Lonely and confused, she becomes friends with a woman who the community believes is a witch. Kit is accused of witchcraft and must make difficult decisions about her future.

16.84 Sturtevant, Katherine. **At the Sign of the Star.** Farrar, Straus and Giroux, 2000. 137 pp. ISBN 0-374-30449-1. Fiction

Set in London in 1677, this is the story of Meg Moore, the daughter of an English bookseller. This well-read and outspoken young lady spends her days discussing books with the customers and dreams of inheriting the bookstore. When her widowed father decides to remarry, Meg becomes concerned about her future and losing her inheritance. Author Sturtevant provides a fascinating view of seventeenth-century life from a young girl's perspective.

16.85 Tate, Eleanora E. **The Minstrel's Melody.** Pleasant Company, 2001. 163 pp. ISBN 1-58485-310-7. Fiction

Orphelia, a gifted musician, is forbidden by her parents to perform at the nearby St. Louis World's Fair. When she runs away with a minstrel show, she solves a family mystery by discovering some family history and learning the reasons for her parents' apprehension about her performing. Set against the backdrop of the 1904 World's Fair, minstrel shows, lynchings, and Missouri history, this novel includes a map and a brief history of the times.

16.86 Tingle, Rebecca. **The Edge on the Sword.** Putnam, 2001. 277 pp. ISBN 0-399-23580-9. Fiction

Aethelflaed, a fifteen-year-old girl living in ninth-century Britain, is betrothed to Ethelred of Merciato to strengthen the alliance between West Saxony and Mercia. Flaed is taught to read and write, to wield a sword and fight, and to understand the tactics of warfare. The fictional Aethelflaed is as vivid and magnificent as the historical personage she portrays. This is a story of one young girl's transition to adulthood and her acceptance of all its responsibilities.

16.87 Wallace, Barbara Brooks. **Secret in St. Something.** Atheneum, 2001. 149 pp. ISBN 0-689-83464-0. Fiction

Robin is determined to escape with his baby brother Danny from the beatings and cruelty of his brutal stepfather. But New York City in the late 1800s is a dangerous, dirty place for two children on their own. Life on the streets is harsh and scary until four other boys share their home in a church cellar and Robin uncovers a secret that changes their lives.

16.88 Whelan, Gloria. **Return to the Island.** HarperCollins, 2000. 185 pp. ISBN 0-06-028253-3. Fiction

The third in The Island Trilogy and set on Mackinac Island, Michigan, the story follows Mary O'Shea's life after she returns from England in 1818. Mary faces a difficult choice between marrying James and returning to England or marrying White Hawk/Gavin Sinclair and staying on the island where her father left her a farm. If she stays, she can continue her girls' school and White Hawk can continue to help his tribe, the L'Arbre Croche. Accurate historical references frame the story events.

16.89 Willis, Patricia. **The Barn Burner.** Clarion, 2000. 196 pp. ISBN 0-395-98409-2. Fiction

In Depression-era Ohio, fourteen-year-old Ross Cooper leaves his family after a confrontation with his newly unemployed father. When he is seen fleeing a barn fire set by a barn burner, Ross begins two journeys: one to the Warfield family and their warm support and one to an understanding of his parents and the stresses of the Great Depression, including the difficulty of providing for one's family.

16.90 Wolff, Virginia Euwer. **Bat 6.** Scholastic, 1999. 230 pp. ISBN 0-59089-800-0. Fiction

In local Oregon tradition, each year the sixth-grade girls from Barlow play the sixth-grade girls from Bear Creek Ridge in a softball game known as Bat 6. Through the voices of twenty-one girls who play in the 1949 game, this book explores the conflict between Aki, a Japanese American girl who spent part of the war years in an internment camp, and Shazam, a girl on the opposing team whose father was killed by the Japanese during the war.

16.91 Wood, Frances M. **Daughter of Madrugada.** Delacorte, 2002. 159 pp. ISBN 0-385-32719-6. Fiction

When Mexico lost California to the United States in 1846, the Californios suddenly became foreigners in their own land. The subsequent encroachment of settlers onto the huge ranchos during the gold rush forced thirteen-year-old Cesa de Haro and her extended family to accept their sudden loss of wealth and land. They also had to cope with the patronizing attitudes and prejudice of the newcomers. Cesa, strong-willed yet reflective about her life, eventually discovers her identity as a Californio woman and as the link between the generations.

16.92 Yolen, Jane, and Robert J. Harris. **Queen's Own Fool: A Novel of Mary Queen of Scots.** Philomel, 2000. 388 pp. ISBN 0-399-23380-6. Fiction

Traveling through Paris with her uncle's troupe of players, Nicola Ambruzzi is included in the summons to play before the queen, Mary of Scotland. Thus begins a long and often sad relationship as Mary brings Nicola into the circle of four Maries and ultimately home to Scotland and exile. Nicola's clear-eyed appraisal of Mary, which never mistakes applause for love, helps the reader grasp the plots, conflicts, and multiple personalities who surround and manipulate the young queen.

Historical Series

In the two series of historical novels written in diary (Dear America) or journal (My Name Is America) formats, the authors create a protagonist (an adolescent girl in Dear America and an adolescent boy in My Name Is America) who encounters circumstances that were significant in the context of the time. Both series put a human and youthful face on major times in the history of the United States. In addition to the narrative, the diary or journal is placed in an interesting context through the epilogue, historical notes, photographs, illustrations, and maps.

Each book in the Dear Mr. President series asks readers to imagine an event during a presidential administration and to assume that a young person would write to the president about it and that the president would respond. The books center on a series of fictional letters between U.S. presidents and the young people about political and daily events of the time. Interactive footnotes send readers to the Winslow Press Web site, where photographs, primary sources, and links to other resources on the period can be found. Each book also includes a historical note from the author, suggestions for further reading, and information about the U.S. Postal Service at the time the book is set.

All of the books in the Royal Diaries series include the diary narrative as well as an informative epilogue, historical note, family tree, glossary of characters, and photos, drawings, and maps. These "diaries" are meticulously researched accounts of strong young women who by their royal heritage are on the threshold of great power and responsibility. The series gives readers a perspective on the historical role of monarchy and women throughout history.

Dear America Series

16.93 Deneberg, Barry. **Mirror, Mirror on the Wall: The Diary of Bess Brennan.** Scholastic, 2002. 139 pp. ISBN 0-439-19446-6. Fiction

Bess Brennan, a twelve-year-old girl, has gone blind as a result of an accident. She describes how she slowly adjusts to the loss of her sight—just as she and her twin Elin, who helps her keep the diary, have had to adjust to life after the death of their father. We also learn much about the history of the Perkins School for the Blind, which, opening in 1832, changed forever the way blind individuals live in U.S. society.

16.94 Denenberg, Barry. **One Eye Laughing, The Other Weeping: The Diary of Julie Weiss.** Scholastic, 2000. 243 pp. ISBN 0-439-09518-2. Fiction

Julie Weiss is an average girl. She adores her father, tolerates her older brother, and shares secrets with her best friend. She lives a privileged life in her Vienna, Austria, home; Adolf Hitler and his hatred of Jews are a world away. It seems that none of the problems plaguing Germany can harm Julie or her family. Her father is a respected doctor and the family has many friends. Julie soon learns, however, how quickly peace can evaporate and friends turn into enemies.

16.95 Garland, Sherry. **Valley of the Moon: The Diary of Maria Rosalia de Milagros.** Scholastic, 2001. 224 pp. ISBN 0-439-08820-8. Fiction

In the midst of the war between Mexico and the United States, Maria Rosalia finally learns about her mother and father and embraces the identity she had been missing. Recording her thoughts in a discarded diary, Maria Rosalia comments on the people, surroundings, cultures, and events she encounters growing up as a half-Indian orphan.

16.96 Hansen, Joyce. **I Thought My Soul Would Rise and Fly: The Diary of Patsy, a Freed Girl.** Scholastic, 1997. 202 pp. ISBN 0-590-84913-1. Fiction

Patsy limps when she walks and stammers when she speaks, but she is not slow of mind. Having secretly learned to read and write, she records the events that take place immediately before and after the freeing of the slaves in December 1865. Patsy also reads the newspaper to the other freed men and women and teaches the plantation children their letters. She eventually becomes a teacher and administers to the educational needs of her people.

16.97 Janke, Katelan. **Survival in the Storm: The Dust Bowl Diary of Grace Edwards.** Scholastic, 2002. 190 pp. ISBN 0-439-21599-4. Fiction

Grace Edwards lives in Dalhart, Texas, in 1935 when dust begins to swirl, and the lives of Grace and her family and friends are changed forever as they try to survive in the consequent "dust bowl." The author, a fifteen-year-old from Dalhart, won the 1998 Dear America Student Writing Contest and was inspired to write Grace's story by the rich history of her hometown and interviews with dust bowl survivors who still live there. The book includes photographs and historical notes.

16.98 McKissack, Patricia C. **Color Me Dark: The Diary of Nellie Lee Love, the Great Migration North.** Scholastic, 2000. 224 pp. ISBN 0-590-51159-9. Fiction

This is a compelling account of one family's migration from Tennessee to Chicago in "Red Summer, 1919," so named because of the many lynchings that occurred at that time. Undercurrents of Klan activities, lynchings, color prejudice among African Americans, and information about African history, major figures in the new civil rights movement after World War I, and publications and organizations are revealed through eleven-year-old Nellie Lee's diary and experiences. Included are historical background, photos, and a map.

16.99 Murphy, Jim. **My Face to the Wind: The Diary of Sarah Jane Price, a Prairie Teacher.** Scholastic, 2001. 182 pp. ISBN 0-590-43810-7. Fiction

After her father's death in 1881 in Broken Bow, Nebraska, fourteen-year-old Sarah Jane convinces the school board to replace the previous teacher, her father, with her as she tries to avoid being sent to an orphan asylum. The young teacher gains confidence despite her lack of experience, a rundown schoolhouse without books and other supplies, and a life-threatening snowstorm that destroys the school. Additional resources include an epilogue, a historical note, and photos.

16.100 White, Ellen Emerson.**Where Have All the Flowers Gone? The Diary of Molly MacKenzie Flaherty.** Scholastic, 2002. 188 pp. ISBN 0-439-14889-8. Fiction

This book follows Molly MacKenzie Flaherty through the turbulent year of 1968. A high school junior, Molly struggles through her allegiances to various causes. Patrick, her beloved brother, volunteered to fight in Vietnam. Now Molly is forced on a daily basis to reconsider where she stands on the issue of the war. Classroom discussions, parties, volunteer opportunities, and days out with her friends are no longer easy situations for her. Being privy to Molly's thoughts in this diary format helps readers capture the ambiguity of this period in U.S. history.

Dear Mr. President Series

16.101 Armstrong, Jennifer. **Theodore Roosevelt: Letters from a Young Coal Miner.** Winslow, 2000. 118 pp. ISBN 1-890817-27-9. Fiction

Frank Kovacs, a teenage coal miner, writes a letter to President Roosevelt. In their correspondence, they discuss the plight of workers, the movement toward child labor laws, strikes, and unionization.

16.102 Armstrong, Jennifer. **Thomas Jefferson: Letters from a Philadelphia Bookworm.** Winslow, 2000. 117 pp. ISBN 1-890817-30-9. Fiction

It is 1803, and twelve-year-old schoolgirl Amelia Hornsby from Philadelphia writes to President Jefferson about the Lewis and Clark Expedition. As their correspondence continues, she and the president discuss the duel between Aaron Burr and Alexander Hamilton and the death of Jefferson's daughter.

16.103 Kroll, Steven. **John Quincy Adams: Letters from a Southern Planter's Son.** Winslow, 2001. 121 pp. ISBN 1-890-81793-7. Fiction

William Pratt, a twelve-year-old planter's son from Georgia, writes to President John Quincy Adams. They discuss the struggle between white settlers and the Creek tribes over possession of Georgia farmland. The treatment of Native Americans had emerged in that period as a significant problem.

16.104 Pinkney, Andrea Davis. **Abraham Lincoln: Letters from a Slave Girl.** Winslow, 2001. 136 pp. ISBN 1-890817-60-0. Fiction

Although it was illegal for slaves to learn to read and write, a number of them did. Lettie Tucker, a slave girl on a Charleston, South Carolina, plantation, not only learned to write but also wrote to President Lincoln, urging him to free the slaves. The president's letters show his evolving position against slavery.

16.105 Winthrop, Elizabeth. **Franklin D. Roosevelt: Letters from a Mill Town Girl.** Winslow Press, 2001.153 pp. ISBN 1-890817-61-9. Fiction

In 1933 the country was mired in the Great Depression. Twelve-year-old Emma Bartoletti, daughter of Italian immigrants, writes a letter to President Franklin Delano Roosevelt. Their correspondence examines the conditions of joblessness, homelessness, and hunger. Emma wonders how the president's New Deal will help solve these problems.

My Name Is America Series

16.106 Bruchac, Joseph. **The Journal of Jesse Smoke: A Cherokee Boy.** Scholastic, 2001. 208 pp. ISBN 0-439-12197-3. Fiction

In his journal, Jesse Smoke, a sixteen-year-old Cherokee, relates the difficulties and cruelties that members of his tribe experience when they are driven from their homes in southeastern United States. The governmental policy of moving all the Cherokee and other tribes to west of the Mississippi River leads to the brutal Trail of Tears, which Jesse recounts.

16.107 Levine, Ellen. **The Journal of Jedediah Barstow, an Emigrant on the Oregon Trail.** Scholastic, 2002. 172 pp. ISBN 0-439-06310-8. Fiction

This is the fictional journal of thirteen-year-old orphan Jedediah Barstow as he makes a wagon train journey to Oregon. His description of his experiences brings that period of history and all the trials associated with such an intense journey (bears, rattlesnakes, raging rivers, wide open plains, difficult fellow travelers) come to life for contemporary readers.

16.108 Myers, Walter Dean. **The Journal of Joshua Loper: A Black Cowboy.** Scholastic, 1999. 158 pp. ISBN 0-590-02691-7. Fiction

On his first cattle drive, sixteen-year-old Joshua provides innocent yet discerning commentary on the attitudes, people, and events of the post–Civil War West through his journal. The white trail boss and Joshua develop an understanding of each other as well as a wary respect, gradually becoming people to one another instead of stereotypes.

16.109 Philbrick, Rodman. **The Journal of Douglas Allen Deeds: The Donner Party Expedition.** Scholastic, 2001. 138 pp. ISBN 0-439-21600-1. Fiction

Through his journal, Douglas Allen Deeds tells the story of his journey across the United States as part of the Donner expedition in 1846. Over two hundred wagons began the journey in Independence, Missouri, but eight months later there were no wagons left, and fewer than one hundred of the original travelers reached California. Douglas details the trials of the wagon journey and the extreme conditions that eventually led some of the members of the party to resort to cannibalism.

16.110 White, Ellen Emerson.**The Journal of Patrick Seamus Flaherty, United States Marine Corps.** Scholastic, 2002. 192 pp. ISBN 0-439-14890-1. Fiction

The wartime journal of Patrick Seamus Flaherty provides a personal view of the still-controversial Vietnam War that is thrilling and heartbreaking right up to the very last page. Patrick, a grunt from Boston, joins the Marines on the morning of his eighteenth birthday but soon realizes that volunteering might not have been such a good idea. Patrick shares his personal thoughts and gruesome details of the war but omits obscenities in his journal as a promise to his father.

The Royal Diaries Series

16.111 Gregory, Kristiana. **Eleanor, Crown Jewel of Aquitaine.** Scholastic, 2002. 187 pp. ISBN 0-439-16484-2. Fiction

In 1136, Eleanor was the fourteen-year-old daughter and oldest surviving child of one of the most powerful and feared landowners in France. Eleanor lived a privileged life, but that life ended the following year when her father died while on a pilgrimage to Spain. Although bright and remarkably well educated for a young woman of her time, Eleanor was no match for her father's enemies. Her marriage to Louis VII was quickly arranged, and the merger of their lands created a powerful alliance.

16.112 Holman, Sheri. **Sondok: Princess of the Moon and Stars.** Scholastic, 2002. 192 pp. ISBN 0-439-16586-5. Fiction

Because little is actually known about the childhood of Princess Sondok, Holman supposes what her life was like. We do know that as queen, Sondok built Asia's oldest standing astronomical observatory. She also tried to maintain a balance between the traditional beliefs of shamanism and the conflicting views of Buddhism and of Confucianism, representing the ever-increasing influence of China on Korean culture.

16.113 Kirwan, Anna. **Victoria, May Blossom of Brittania.** Scholastic, 2001. 219 pp. ISBN 0-439-21598-6. Fiction

This is the diary of Victoria, an intelligent, witty, and opinionated young lady who finds growing up in a castle with her mother and stepfather difficult, especially when there is so much strife between her royal relatives. Soon after Victoria learns that she is heiress to the throne of England, she is forced to leave behind her childhood and look toward the good of the country she will rule.

16.114 Lasky, Kathryn. **Jahanara: Princess of Princesses.** Scholastic, 2002. 187 pp. ISBN 0-439-22350-4. Fiction

The diary of Jahanara, great-granddaughter of Akbar, the greatest Moghul ruler of India, takes us into a distant and fascinating world. We learn about the jewels and elephants and servants at Jahanara's disposal. We also learn about her family and the intrigues and ways in which family members plot against one another, about the tensions between Muslims and Hindus, and about the history of the Moghul empire—of which Jahanara served as the empress until she almost died in a terrible fire.

16.115 Lasky, Kathryn. **Mary, Queen of Scots: Queen without a Country.** Scholastic, 2002. 202 pp. ISBN 0-439-19404-0. Fiction

Crowned queen of Scotland at the age of nine months after her father, King James V, dies, Mary's life is always embroiled in politics. At five she was sent to France to live under the protection of King Henry II until she was old enough to marry his son Francis. This arranged marriage was a political alliance. Mary and Francis are friends and playmates who go to dances and hawking together. Author Lasky's epilogue, historical note with a quick history of the Renaissance and Reformation, Stuart-DeGuise family tree, illustrations, and maps all set the story of the young Queen Mary in its interesting historical context.

16.116 Meyer, Carolyn. **Isabel: Jewel of Castilla.** Scholastic, 2000. 204 pp. ISBN 0-439-07805-9. Fiction

In the midst of political unrest, young Isabel of Castilla is sent away to Segovia by her half brother, King Enrique of Castilla, who claims the throne. He also tries to arrange a marriage for Isabel that would benefit him politically, but Isabel has her own ideas. She is determined to marry Fernando, Prince of Aragon and King of Sicily. She schemes until she is successful. Together, she and Fernando form the royal partnership that financed Columbus's travels to the New World.

16.117 White, Ellen Emerson. **Kaiulani: The People's Princess.** Scholastic, 2001. 240 pp. ISBN 0-439-12909-5. Fiction

This story relates the life of a valiant young woman and the shame of blatant American imperialism. A constitution was forced on the Hawaiian people that gave most of the real power to U.S. nationals; most native islanders were not allowed to vote. It became Kaiulani's mission to travel in order to intercede for her people. Although she was Queen Liliuokalani's heir, she never ruled. Raised to duty and obligation, Kaiulani tried to keep faith with a vanishing culture.

16.118 Yep, Laurence. **Lady of Ch'iao Kuo: Warrior of the South.** Scholastic, 2001. 300 pp. ISBN 0-439-16483-4. Fiction

Princess Redbird is a member of the royal family of the Hsien people, who have been invaded by China. When she is sixteen, her father sends her to study Chinese customs and language so that she will be an appropriate spokesperson for her people. While she enjoys her schooling, Redbird must soon embark on a more serious task. China and Hsien are both attacked by a warring tribe, and it is Redbird's responsibility to unite the two in order to defeat their common foe. Her talent for diplomacy, her intelligence, and her resilience help her make the decisions that will benefit her people.

17 Historical Nonfiction

17.1 Aaseng, Nathan. **Navaho Code Talkers.** Walker, 2000. 105 pp. ISBN 0-8027-7589-6. Nonfiction

During World War II, the United States was frustrated that the Japanese were able to break whatever code our armed forces used. The Marines proposed using a code based on the oral language of the Navaho tribe. A special platoon was formed with Navaho volunteers whose efforts were instrumental in helping the United States win the war in the Pacific. Including photographs, this book is a fascinating explanation of a Native American contribution that is often overlooked in histories of World War II.

17.2 Ambrose, Stephen E. **The Good Fight: How World War II Was Won.** Atheneum, 2001. 96 pp. ISBN 0-689-84361-5. Nonfiction

This book chronicles World War II from the tragic bombing of Pearl Harbor to the Marshall Plan in a very readable format for young historians. In addition to the descriptions of major events, personal anecdotes from soldiers add useful detail. Highlighting the book are color and black-and-white photographs, as well as detailed maps. Each topic discussed includes a Quick Facts section, and the lists of Web sites are also useful.

17.3 Armstrong, Jennifer. **Shipwreck at the Bottom of the World: The Extraordinary True Story of Shackleton and the *Endurance*.** Crown, 2000. 134 pp. ISBN 0-375-81049-8. Nonfiction

This recipient of the Orbis Pictus Award for Outstanding Nonfiction for Children recounts the adventure of Ernest Shackleton and his crew of twenty-seven explorers who attempted, unsuccessfully, to cross Antarctica in 1914 to 1915. Armstrong captures the brutal character of Antarctica and its ever-changing face. The text also captures the characters of Shackleton and his crew. Remarkably, all twenty-eight members of the ill-fated expedition survived their ordeal. Journal entries by Shackleton and other team members as well as photographs by expedition photographer Frank Hurley add interest and immediacy to the account.

17.4 Armstrong, Jennifer. **Spirit of Endurance.** Illustrated by William Maughan. Crown, 2000. 32 pp. ISBN 0-517-80091-8. Nonfiction

This picture book is an excellent accompaniment to Armstrong's *Shipwreck at the Bottom of the World.* This shortened account of the 1914–1915 Ernest Shackleton–led expedition to cross Antarctica chronicles the troubled journey of the failed expedition and the courage of the crew. This story of unbelievable challenges and remarkable survival is complemented by the photographs of expedition photographer Frank Hurley. It is the paintings by Maughan, however, that here add interest and color to the account.

17.5 Aronson, Marc. **Sir Walter Ralegh and the Quest for El Dorado.** Clarion, 2000. 222 pp. ISBN 0-395-84827-X. Nonfiction

One of the most dramatic figures of the sixteenth century, Sir Walter Ralegh was an explorer and courtier whose exploits include searching for El Dorado, the legendary golden city; sponsoring a settlement on Roanoke Island that has come to be known as the Lost Colony; and fighting off the Spanish Armada. The book also discusses Ralegh's intimate relationship with Queen Elizabeth I, his longtime patron, and the intrigue around his fall from favor and eventual execution by beheading.

17.6 Bachrach, Susan D. **The Nazi Olympics: Berlin 1936.** Little, Brown, 2000. 136 pp. ISBN 0-316-07087-4. Nonfiction

Covering the period from 1931, when Berlin was chosen as the site for the 1936 Olympics, to the end of World War II in 1945, this carefully researched book explores the intersection between Nazism and sports in Germany. Athletes who boycotted the Olympics are profiled as well as those who lost their lives in the Holocaust. Numerous photographs and examples of propaganda from the period make this dark but fascinating moment in history come to life.

17.7 Bartoletti, Susan Campbell. **Kids on Strike!** Houghton Mifflin, 1999. 208 pp. ISBN 0-395-88892-1. Nonfiction

Anyone who has ever complained about a part-time job should read this book to see what working conditions for young people used to be like in the United States. Bartoletti describes a number of child labor strikes during the nineteenth and early twentieth centuries. Personal stories and striking photographs make the times come alive and create respect for young people who were brave enough to stand up to powerful industry leaders and spark change for future workers.

17.8 Beller, Susan Provost. **Billy Yank & Johnny Reb: Soldiering in the Civil War.** Twenty-First Century Books, 2000. 93 pp. ISBN 0-7613-1869-0. Nonfiction

Using photographs and excerpts from actual letters and diaries, Beller represents the Civil War as experienced by the average soldier. This well-researched story is told from the point of view of two young soldiers, one from the North and one from the South. Combined with the writings of others, their accounts offer a moving picture of the horrors and realities of that conflict.

17.9 Bolden, Tonya, editor. **33 Things Every Girl Should Know about Women's History: From Suffragettes to Skirt Lengths to the E.R.A.** Crown, 2002. 240 pp. ISBN 0-375-81122-2. Nonfiction

In thirty-three chapters by different authors, U.S. history and the women who have shaped and influenced it are presented in various formats. Photographs, sketches, and charts illustrate the many aspects and contributions to American life women have made. From Abigail Adams to Charlotte Woodward, Emma Lazarus, Mary Harris "Mother" Jones, Jeannette Rankin, and Hilary Clinton, among others, the stories of achievement and commitment put these women's times in perspective.

17.10 Bridges, Ruby. **Through My Eyes.** Scholastic, 1999. 64 pp. ISBN 0-590-18923-9. Nonfiction

"When I was six years old, the civil rights movement came knocking at the door." So begins Ruby Bridges's powerful first-person narrative of being the first black child to attend an integrated elementary school in Louisiana in 1960. The book is illustrated with numerous photographs from the period and also includes excerpts from interviews with Ruby's teacher and parents. Ruby's honest and brave voice comes through on every page.

17.11 Calvert, Patricia. **Standoff at Standing Rock: The Story of Sitting Bull and James McLaughlin.** Twenty-First Century Books, 2001. 143 pp. ISBN 0-7613-1360-5. Nonfiction

This is a dual biography of Chief Sitting Bull and James McLaughlin, whose lives are depicted through parallel time lines. Chief Sitting Bull lived by the Sioux code and was well respected among his people, and James McLaughlin was well known as an idealistic Indian agent. This historical narrative demonstrates each of their leadership qualities, how and why their paths crossed, and how as a consequence history changed.

17.12 Clinton, Catherine. **The Black Soldier: 1492 to the Present.** Houghton Mifflin, 2000. 116 pp. ISBN 0-395-67722-X. Nonfiction

This book provides insight into the military accomplishments of the African American soldier from the early 1500s to the present, recognizing the contributions made by this group despite their hardships and discrimination against them as they fought for the independence and ideals of the United States. Recounted are the achievements of many African American individuals who were not recognized at the time, such as Prince Whipple, who rowed across the river with George Washington at the Battle of Trenton.

17.13 Cohen, Daniel. **Yellow Journalism: Scandal, Sensationalism, and Gossip in the Media.** Twenty-First Century Books, 2000. 126 pp. ISBN 0-7613-1502-0. Nonfiction

In a clear, concise narrative, author Daniel Cohen writes about the history of "yellow journalism" czars such as Pulitzer and Hearst, as well as many infamous figures highlighted by the media, such as Sam Shepard and O. J. Simpson. Filling the chapters with lively anecdotes and colorful tales, Cohen traces the origins of scandalous journalism from its turn-of-the-century heyday (when a comic strip *The Yellow Kid* spawned the generic term for all sensationalist press) to current media trends.

17.14 Colman, Penny. **Girls: A History of Growing Up Female in America.** Scholastic, 2000. 192 pp. ISBN 0-590-37129-0. Nonfiction

Ever wonder what it was like to immigrate to the New World on a sailing ship, live in a pueblo, or work in the Lowell mills? Relying on photographs, firsthand accounts, and other primary sources, this information-packed book is the place to answer your questions or satisfy your curiosity. The lives of everyday

American girls from throughout history are profiled, including those from various backgrounds and cultures. Learn about the Casket Girls, the flappers, and the all-girl singing groups of the 1960s, among others.

17.15 Cooper, Michael L. **Fighting for Honor: Japanese Americans and World War II.** Clarion, 2000. 118 pp. ISBN 0-395-91375-6. Nonfiction

After Japan's attack on Pearl Harbor in 1941, the U.S. government sent American citizens of Japanese descent to live in internment camps—essentially makeshift homes set up behind barbed wire fences. Determined to prove their patriotism, twelve hundred young Japanese from these camps joined the army. Using excerpts from diaries, military records, and archival photos, this book describes the remarkable and brave people who faced both humiliation and danger honorably.

17.16 Cooper, Michael L. **Remembering Manzanar: Life in a Japanese Relocation Camp.** Clarion, 2002. 68 pp. ISBN 0-618-06778-7. Nonfiction.

Manzanar was the site of a relocation camp for Japanese Americans during World War II. Replete with archival photographs, this account relates the experiences of those forced to live in the camp and of Japanese Americans who were so eager to prove their loyalty to the United States that they endured their incarceration with dignity and courage. While in the camps, they attempted to establish a sense of normal life with dances, church services, and baseball games.

17.17 Coulter, Laurie. **Secrets in Stone: All about Maya Hieroglyphs.** Illustrated by Sarah Jane English. Little, Brown, 2001. 48 pp. ISBN 0-316-15883-6. Nonfiction

When the Spanish invaded the Maya in the sixteenth century, they ordered all Mayan books destroyed. Lost along with the books were important clues to deciphering the Mayan hieroglyphics found throughout ruins unearthed three centuries later by archaeologists. This book includes information about the Maya civilization and how the hieroglyphics have been deciphered. The Glyphmaster and Web links included in the book help readers create their own messages in Mayan hieroglyphics.

17.18 Cunningham, Chet. **Chief Crazy Horse.** Lerner, 2000. 112 pp. ISBN 0-8225-4978-6. Nonfiction

A vision quest, broken treaties, and the death of his best friend in a battle with U.S. Army troops over Native American lands all help to develop the legendary fighting spirit of Chief Crazy Horse, the great Sioux warrior who defeated Custer at the Battle of Little Big Horn. Never taking personal benefit from his many visions, Crazy Horse spent fifteen years fighting on behalf of Native Americans, only to be killed by his own people.

17.19 Dahl, Roald. **The Mildenhall Treasure.** Illustrated by Ralph Steadman. Knopf, 2000. 79 pp. ISBN 0-375-81035-8. Nonfiction

This is the true story of Gordon Butcher, a plowman who in 1942 accidentally discovered the greatest buried Roman treasure in British history. Butcher's trusting nature allowed him to be cheated out of a sizable fortune. Never one to look for riches, however, Butcher accepted his loss with grace. Dahl originally wrote about this discovery as an article for *The Saturday Evening Post* in 1946. After World War II, the treasure was recovered and placed in the British Museum, where it remains today.

17.20 Doherty, Kieran. **To Conquer Is to Live: The Life of Captain John Smith of Jamestown.** Twenty-First Century Books, 2001. 144 pp. ISBN 0-7613-1820-8. Nonfiction

Illustrated with black-and-white drawings, maps, reproductions, and nautical charts, this biography looks at Smith's role in early colonial history. The author provides a context for Smith's own, often questioned, account of his relationship with Pochahontas and for his feud with other colonists that finally drove him from the New World, which, Doherty assures us, Smith had come to love. This will be a valuable text for examining seventeenth-century exploration and colonization.

17.21 Downs, Sandra Friend. **Florida in the Civil War: A State in Turmoil.** Twenty-First Century Books, 2001. 80 pp. ISBN 0-7613-1973-5. Nonfiction

This work contains first-person accounts of Florida's participation in the Civil War. Written especially for young readers, it provides a historically accurate account of Florida's unique place in the history of this war. A state with an indefensible coastline and filled with many transplanted northerners and Confederate deserters, Florida's diminished role within the Confederacy receives a thorough explanation.

17.22 Eldridge, Jim. **Warriors! True Stories of Combat, Skill and Courage.** Scholastic, 2001. 128 pp. ISBN 0-439-29650-1. Nonfiction

Eldridge traces the concept of the warrior over time, from the gladiators, known for brute strength, to the samurai, known for their honor code, to the skill of the knights in armor, to the spirit of rebellion evident in those who defended the Alamo against the Mexican army. He includes a chapter on U.S. Special Forces, has separate sections on various weapons used by various warriors, and provides overviews of certain time periods and facts about historical events.

17.23 Erickson, Paul. **Daily Life in the Pilgrim Colony, 1636.** Clarion, 2001. 48 pp. ISBN 0-618-05846-X. Nonfiction

This richly illustrated volume presents a broadly based view of life in colonial America in 1636, sixteen years after the initial settlement in Plymouth. Erickson examines life in the colony, from meals and clothing to games the young people played and the work families did to maintain their homes. Photographs of the National historic site in Plymouth and of artifacts from the period complement the description of colonial life.

17.24 Farbman, Melinda, and Frye Gaillard. **Spacechimp: NASA's Ape in Space.** Enslow, 2000. 48 pp. ISBN 0-7660-1478-9. Nonfiction

Most of us remember Alan Shepard Jr. as the first American in space. Perhaps less famous but no less important is Chimp 65, known as Ham, America's first chimp in space, who paved the way for Shepard's flight and future space explorers. The authors focus on Ham's life, from his capture in Africa, through his space service, to his retirement in a North Carolina zoo. The book incorporates history with many photographs.

17.25 Feinberg, Barbara Silberdick. **Abraham Lincoln's Gettysburg Address: Four Score and More.** Twenty-First Century Books, 2000. 79 pp. ISBN 0-7613-1610-8. Nonfiction

"Four score and seven years ago" is one of the best-known phrases in the world, and many have read Lincoln's Gettysburg Address. Fewer people, however, have taken the time to look at the history behind the words. This book provides insight into President Lincoln's positions on the Constitution, the Declaration of Independence, and slavery when he wrote the address. Firsthand accounts, well-placed quotations, and color illustrations describe Lincoln's struggle while writing his speech for a tired and war-torn nation.

17.26 Feinberg, Barbara Silberdick. **The Articles of Confederation: The First Constitution of the United States.** Twenty-First Century Books, 2002. 110 pp. ISBN 0-7613-2114-4. Nonfiction

Unfair treatment angers even the most peaceful person. The colonists of the 1700s were no different. Great Britain made it difficult for them to survive by imposing high taxes and cutting off their trade with the rest of the world. Seeing no other way, the colonists sought separation from their homeland. After much deliberation and a recommendation by Richard Henry Lee that the colonies should be free and independent states, the Articles of Confederation were adopted. America had become self-governing.

17.27 Feinstein, Stephen. **The 1980s: From Ronald Reagan to MTV.** Enslow, 2000. 64 pp. ISBN 0-7660-1424-X. Nonfiction

Feinstein tackles the 1980s, describing events from the release of *E.T.*, to the Iran-Contra scandal and the *Challenger* tragedy, to fashion trends such as pastel T-shirts and sports jackets for men and the yuppie look. The introduction to popular culture of Cabbage Patch Kids, CDs, break dancing, rap music, Margaret Thatcher, and Chernobyl are just a few of the topics explored in the effort to define the decade of the 1980s and to demonstrate its unique place in the history of the United States.

17.28 Feldman, Ruth Tenzer. **Don't Whistle in School: The History of America's Public Schools.** Lerner, 2001. 88 pp. ISBN 0-8225-1745-0. Nonfiction

The author provides an interesting and comprehensive account of the history of education and schooling in the United States. From one teacher and one-room schoolhouses to the global classroom, schooling over the last four hundred years is recounted in vivid detail with illustrations and photographs. Helpful extras include early school rules and lessons, a list of historic schools open for visits, and a selected bibliography.

17.29 Feldman, Ruth Tenzer. **Thurgood Marshall.** Lerner, 2001. 112 pp. ISBN 0-8225-4989-1. Nonfiction

Feldman presents a spellbinding account of the journey of Thurgood Marshall from lawyer, judge, and U.S. solicitor general to wearing the black robe of a Supreme Court justice. The story chronicles the strength and passion that drove young Thurgood in his fight for equality, particularly for black Americans seeking equal educational opportunities. The work gives insight into his role in such landmark cases as *Brown v. Board of Education* and his legacy as a champion for civil rights.

17.30 Ferrie, Richard. **The World Turned Upside Down: George Washington and the Battle of Yorktown.** Holiday House, 1999. 168 pp. ISBN 0-8234-1402-7. Nonfiction

In this account of the decisive battle of the American Revolution, Ferrie presents an insightful view of George Washington and the events of the final campaign of the war. The joint effort of the American and French forces on land and sea allowed the unlikely defeat of the British troops in spite of their superior training and numbers. The book's title, based on a nursery rhyme, is from the song the British band played as it marched out of Yorktown in defeat.

17.31 Fradin, Dennis Brindell. **Bound for the North Star: True Stories of Fugitive Slaves.** Houghton Mifflin, 2000. 198 pp. ISBN 0-395-97017-2. Nonfiction

This anthology of fugitive slave tales documents their struggles and fight for emancipation. Despite the threat of slave hunters, the Fugitive Slave Law, and countless dangers, many slaves used the North Star to navigate their way to freedom. The stories of those courageous slaves who successfully escaped to freedom serve as an inspiration to us all.

17.32 Freedman, Russell. **Give Me Liberty! The Story of the Declaration of Independence.** Holiday House, 2000. 90 pp. ISBN 0-8234-1448-5. Nonfiction

In this wonderfully illustrated book, Freedman details the events leading up to the writing of the Declaration beginning with the Boston Tea Party in 1773 and tracing the major actions of the patriots. At the Continental Congress, which met in Philadelphia to respond to the British, Thomas Paine, Richard Henry Lee, John Adams, and other leaders advocated dissolving all relationships with Britain. The committee that was appointed to draft the statement included the young Thomas Jefferson, who helped draft the document that delegates from all thirteen colonies agreed on.

17.33 Freedman, Russell. **In the Days of the Vaqueros: America's First True Cowboys.** Clarion, 2001. 70 pp. ISBN 0-395-96788-0. Nonfiction

Illustrated with paintings and drawings, Freedman's history of the cowboy begins with the sixteenth century and the Native American vaqueros and ends with the modern American West cowboys. Freedman credits the vaqueros with introducing the typical dress and speech of the cowboy. He also describes the origin of rodeos, the development of haciendas and ranchos, and the creation of horsemanship games. Historical tidbits are offered as well. The word *buckaroo,* for example, resulted from American cowboys' pronunciation of *vaquero.*

17.34 Galt, Margot Fortunato. **Stop This War! American Protest of the Conflict in Vietnam.** Lerner, 2000. 88 pp. ISBN 0-8225-1740-X. Nonfiction

Through a collection of first-person interviews, newspaper accounts, and other primary sources, the author tells the story of the continually growing wave of protest against U.S. involvement in the conflict in Vietnam during the turbulent 1960s and early 1970s. The book calls for Americans to remember this tumultuous time in our past and to resolve that a war like the one in Vietnam never happen again.

17.35 Giblin, James Cross. **The Life and Death of Adolf Hitler.** Clarion, 2002. 246 pp. ISBN 0-395-90371-8. Nonfiction

Did you ever wonder how Adolf Hitler became so powerful? Hitler was a loner who experienced frequent rejection during his youth. By age eighteen, he had lost both parents and his younger brother to disease and been rejected by art schools. In 1914, Hitler joined the German army and emerged ready to provide hope to a Germany in the throes of economic and cultural decline. Little did the world realize the direction Hitler's leadership would take.

17.36 Gold, Alison Leslie. **A Special Fate: Chiune Sugihara, Hero of the Holocaust.** Scholastic, 2000. 176 pp. ISBN 0-590-39525-4. Nonfiction

As vice consul for the Japanese government in Lithuania during World War II, Chiune Sugihara saved the lives of thousands of Jews. Acting against the orders of his superiors, he issued transit visas allowing Jews to travel through the Soviet Union in order to escape the Nazis. Vignettes of people whom Chiune assisted supplement his story and show the gratitude felt for him by the Jewish community. This inspirational story of personal conviction and heroism provides another perspective on the Holocaust.

17.37 Goldsmith, Connie. **Lost in Death Valley: The True Story of Four Families in California's Gold Rush.** Twenty-First Century Books, 2001. 144 pp. ISBN 0-7613-1915-8. Nonfiction

This illustrated biography tells the true story of four families of brave pioneers who were lured across California's Death Valley by hopes of striking it rich during the gold rush. Each person who made the trip endured great hardship, and no family survived intact. The author uses primary texts and historical research to recreate this harrowing tale of exploration and heroism.

17.38 Gottfried, Ted. **Children of the Slaughter: Young People of the Holocaust.** Illustrated by Stephen Alcorn. Twenty-First Century Books, 2001. 112 pp. ISBN 0-761-31716-3. Nonfiction

Gottfried, Ted. **Deniers of the Holocaust: Who They Are, What They Do, Why They Do It.** Illustrated by Stephen Alcorn. Twenty-First Century Books, 2001. 112 pp. ISBN 0-761-31950-6. Nonfiction

Gottfried, Ted. **Displaced Persons: The Liberation and Abuse of Holocaust Survivors.** Illustrated by Stephen Alcorn. Twenty-First Century Books, 2001. 112 pp. ISBN 0-761-31924-7. Nonfiction

Gottfried, Ted. **Heroes of the Holocaust.** Illustrated by Stephen Alcorn. Twenty-First Century Books, 2001. 112 pp. ISBN 0-761-31717-1. Nonfiction

Gottfried, Ted. **Martyrs to Madness: The Victims of the Holocaust.** Illustrated by Stephen Alcorn. Twenty-First Century Books, 2000. 128 pp. ISBN 0-761-31715-5. Nonfiction

Gottfried, Ted. **Nazi Germany: The Face of Tyranny.** Illustrated by Stephen Alcorn. Twenty-First Century Books, 2000. 128 pp. ISBN 0-761-31714-7. Nonfiction

In this series of books on the Holocaust, Gottfried explores many topics ranging from the rise of Nazism in Germany to the liberation of the death camps at the end of World War II and the birth of the nation of Israel. This book presents the Holocaust in a personal way rather than relying on mind-numbing numbers and statistics. The graphic design of the series, with its rich illustrations and many photographs, makes these books attractive to readers.

17.39 Gottfried, Ted. **The Road to Communism.** Illustrated by Melanie Reim. Twenty-First Century Books, 2002. 144 pp. ISBN 0-7613-2557-3. Nonfiction

Beginning as early as the nineteenth century, Russian revolutionaries were determined to end capitalism and the monarchy in favor of a socialist government. The revolution changed the atmosphere of international relations. Gottfried discusses the major characters in the revolution and the events that made them famous. While younger readers will appreciate the style and readability of the book, more mature audiences will benefit from the rich vocabulary.

17.40 Gottfried, Ted. **The Stalinist Empire.** Illustrated by Melanie Reim. Twenty-First Century Books, 2002. 127 pp. ISBN 0-7613-2558-1. Nonfiction

In Gottfried's account of Soviet Russia, Joseph Stalin and his role in communism are presented through text and revealing illustrations. A detailed discussion about how one person can influence a nation and the course of history includes facts about Stalin's tyranny and ability to retain power, and Gottfried isn't afraid to ask some hard questions.

17.41 Hansen, Joyce. **"Bury Me Not in a Land of Slaves": African-Americans in the Time of Reconstruction.** Franklin Watts, 2000. 160 pp. ISBN 0-531-11539-9. Nonfiction

Reconstruction began as a time of hope and opportunity with the promise of education and equal rights for the freed African American men and women. These expectations were brutally smashed by the creation of black codes and Jim Crow laws and the willful perpetuation of oppression and violence against African Americans and any whites supporting their cause. These tragic times come alive through the experiences of ordinary people and brief biographical sketches of black leaders, accompanied by quotes, illustrations, and photographs.

17.42 Haskins, Jim, and Kathleen Benson. **Conjure Times: Black Magicians in America.** Walker, 2001. 174 pp. ISBN 0-802-78762-2. Nonfiction

On the surface, this book is about black magicians such as Richard Potter, billed as "America's First Negro Magician." The authors use personal accounts, snippets of journals and news stories, photographs, and handbills to tell the story of an overlooked part of our country's past. Beneath the surface, this is also a compelling story of racial segregation and bigotry in theater, in vaudeville, and in general.

17.43 Hipperson, Carol Edgemon, compiler. **The Belly Gunner.** Twenty-First Century Books, 2001. 160 pp. ISBN 0-7613-1873-9. Nonfiction

Dale Aldrich was a gunner on a B-17 bomber during World War II. His story begins at the time he is drafted and continues through training and actual performance as a gunner. He is later shot down and becomes a prisoner of war for over a year. Side notes and a time line help the reader put Dale's story into the historical context of World War II and the Holocaust.

17.44 Hoobler, Dorothy, and Thomas Hoobler. **Vanity Rules: A History of American Fashion and Beauty.** Twenty-First Century Books, 2000. 160 pp. ISBN 0-7613-1258-7. Nonfiction

Imagine a man squeezing into pants so tight that he needed to hang them on special hooks and lower himself into them from a stepladder! A woman in this same Revolutionary War era might wear a hairdo so high she couldn't pass through doorways. This book traces fashion trends among American men and women from colonial times through the 1990s. The authors describe how factors ranging from the sewing machine to modern cosmetic surgery have helped shape notions of beauty.

17.45 Kendall, Martha E. **Failure Is Impossible! The History of American Women's Rights.** Lerner, 2001. 96 pp. ISBN 0-8225-1744-2. Nonfiction

This book provides a fast-paced overview of the history of women's quest for equality, from a discussion of individuals who defied the Puritan church to a brief introduction to the United Nations' Fourth International Conference on Women in 1995. Details, such as the origin of the word *spinster* and excerpts from leaders in the women's movement throughout history, keep the reader engaged. A time line of major events from 1607 through 2000 and brief biographies of "remarkable women" in American history also provide insight and interest.

17.46 Ketchum, Liza. **Into a New Country: Eight Remarkable Women of the West.** Little, Brown, 2000. 135 pp. ISBN 0-316-49597-2. Nonfiction

These eight extraordinary women made major contributions to western settlement. From slave Biddy Mason, who went to court in California to win her freedom and then spent the rest of her life helping others, to Bethenia Owens-Adair, who graduated from medical school at forty and became the first woman physician in the Pacific Northwest, these eight women all made lasting marks.

17.47 Krohn, Katherine. **Women of the Wild West.** Lerner, 2000. 112 pp. ISBN 0-8225-4980-8. Nonfiction

This work features countless courageous women who played an important role in the development of the American West. Calamity Jane, Annie Oakley, and Molly Brown became folk legends as they challenged traditional roles and stereotypes. Others, such as Esther Morris, Laura Ingalls Wilder, Clara Brown, and Virginia Reed, are lesser known but were no less important in paving the way for women to be able to exhibit their individuality as well as their more adventurous spirit.

17.48 Krull, Kathleen. **Lives of Extraordinary Women: Rulers, Rebels (and What the Neighbors Thought).** Illustrated by Kathryn Hewitt. Harcourt, 2000. ISBN 0-15-2008070-1. Nonfiction

Rich with eye-catching illustrations, this book provides brief but fascinating descriptions of twenty of the most influential women in history. These biographical sketches include a wide range of women from around the world, some loved, some hated, but each a leader who had an impact on history. Following each entry is a short section titled "Ever After" noting what occurred after the woman's death.

17.49 Lalicki, Tom. **Spellbinder: The Life of Harry Houdini.** Holiday House, 2000. 88 pp. ISBN 0-8234-1499-X. Nonfiction

For those who want to know more about the most famous magician in history, this fascinating biography of Ehrich Weiss, better known as Harry Houdini, will satisfy their curiosity. The famous magician stunned audiences with his awe-inspiring illusions and magic tricks. Original photos and primary source documents from Houdini's life make this an engaging text.

17.50 Landau, Elaine. **Heroine of the *Titanic:* The Real Unsinkable Molly Brown.** Clarion, 2001. 132 pp. ISBN 0-395-93912-7. Nonfiction

Myths and legends abound about Molly Brown as a heroine of the *Titanic* disaster, but the real story of Margaret Tobin Brown's life is even more fascinating. Born to Irish immigrant parents in Hannibal, Missouri, shortly after the Civil War, she later followed her brother to a rough mining town in Colorado where few women lived. There, Margaret demonstrated traits that followed her throughout her life: courage, determination, and compassion for those in need.

17.51 Landau, Elaine. **John F. Kennedy, Jr.** Twenty-First Century Books, 2000. 128 pp. ISBN 0-7613-1857-7. Nonfiction

This book chronicles the life of the son of the thirty-fifth president of the United States. Showing how John Kennedy Jr. was shaped by family tragedies, including the assassination of his father, the book gives readers a rare glimpse into the events that influenced the life of this young lawyer-turned-publisher and leaves us wondering what his future might have held if he had not met an untimely death at the age of thirty-eight. Numerous photographs help personalize the life of one of the most famous members of America's "Camelot."

17.52 Levine, Ellen. **Darkness over Denmark: The Danish Resistance and the Rescue of the Jews.** Holiday House, 2000. 164 pp. ISBN 0-8234-1447-7. Nonfiction

The role of the Danish people during World War II was unique. Denmark was the only occupied country to resist the Nazis' attempts to destroy the Jewish population, helping the majority of the eight thousand Danish Jews escape certain death in the concentration camps. Levine relates the events by interspersing the stories of rescuers, the rescued, and resisters based on interviews she conducted.

17.53 Levinson, Nancy Smiler. **Magellan and the First Voyage around the World.** Clarion, 2001. 132 pp. ISBN 0-395-98773-3. Nonfiction

This narrative of Magellan's life and voyage around the world is easy to read and enhanced with numerous pictures. Everything from the selection of the sailors to the dangers encountered as they circumnavigated the globe is discussed. Clips from their logs, lists of provisions, and maps augment the historical facts. Readers may be surprised to learn that Magellan never completed the trip. His dedication to the task inspired his crew to continue their voyage even after his death.

17.54 McGowen, Tom. **Air Raid! Bombing Campaigns of World War II.** Twenty-First Century Books, 2001. 64 pp. ISBN 0-7613-1810-0. Nonfiction

McGowen, Tom. **Carrier War: Aircraft Carriers in World War II.** Twenty-First Century Books, 2001. 64 pp. ISBN 0-7613-1808-9. Nonfiction

The Military Might series traces the development of modern warfare in the sky and on the seas using World War II as a backdrop to describe the technological innovations that led to weapons of mass destruction. The author describes key battles and explains how planes and ships on both sides of the war were deployed with strategic purpose to devastate cities and military installations. Not for the faint of heart, these books document the horrors of war in graphic detail.

17.55 McGowen, Tom. **Assault from the Sea: Amphibious Invasions in the Twentieth Century.** Twenty-First Century Books, 2002. 64 pp. ISBN 0-7613-1811-9. Nonfiction

The author details military amphibious operations, with special attention given to Gallipoli, Norway, and the Pacific Islands; North Africa and Sicily; Europe; and Korea. Generous use of photographs adds to a meticulous account of the events and the geography of significant military battles waged on the water during the twentieth century. Additional resources include two illustrated maps showing locations of European and Pacific amphibious invasions.

17.56 McGowen, Tom. **Assault from the Sky: Airborne Infantry of World War II.** Twenty-First Century Books, 2002. 64 pp. ISBN 0-7613-1809-7. Nonfiction

The author provides an illustrated chronology of the use of airborne infantry in World War II, starting with the first use of airborne troops by the Germans in the invasion of the Netherlands in 1940. McGowen captures the urgency of Allied forces as they successfully implemented several air assaults that changed the tide of the war. The book includes an illustrated map showing locations of airborne infantry attacks in Europe.

17.57 McKissack, Patricia C., and Fredrick L. McKissack. **Days of Jubilee: The End of Slavery in the United States.** Scholastic, 2003. 134 pp. ISBN 0-590-10764-X. Nonfiction

On January 1, 1863, President Abraham Lincoln's Emancipation Proclamation officially took effect. Since, however, there was no television or radio broadcasting the proclamation throughout the southern states, much less any uniform enforcement, there was no single day on which all slaves were released from bondage. This book, based on slave narratives collected during the 1930s, recounts varied jubilee days experienced by African Americans. The book includes a time line and many excerpts from primary documents.

17.58 Meltzer, Milton. **There Comes a Time: The Struggle for Civil Rights.** Random House, 2001. 193 pp. ISBN 0-375-80407-2. Nonfiction

Including a time line and photographs, this thorough, interesting, evenhanded, and well-researched history of the civil rights movement in the United States starts three hundred years ago with the forced mass migration from Africa, concentrates on the 1960s, and ends with the need to find common ground in order to continue making progress regarding civil rights. Meltzer demonstrates causes and effects and puts events in a compelling context for young readers.

17.59 Miller, William. **Richard Wright and the Library Card.** Illustrated by Gregory Christie. Lee & Low, 2000. 28 pp. ISBN 1-880000-88-1. Nonfiction

This picture book recounts an episode in the life of noted author Richard Wright. Readers discover Wright's fascination with words as they follow him through his quest to learn to read and to obtain a library card, something relatively unheard of for an African American of his time. His quest becomes a reality and provides Wright with "a ticket to freedom" that can be found only between the pages of a book. Illustrations provide a visual representation of the text.

17.60 Monceaux, Morgan, and Ruth Katcher. **My Heroes, My People: African Americans and Native Americans in the West.** Illustrated by Morgan Monceaux. Frances Foster Books, 1999. 61 pp. ISBN 0-374-30770-9. Nonfiction

Illustrated with Monceaux's bold mixed-media portraits, this collection of biographies narrates the stories of the famous and the infamous, the well known and the little known, in such categories as "the fur trade," "women," buffalo soldiers," "criminals and lawmen," and "legends," among others. The introduction to the American West, the authors' notes, and suggestions for further reading are informative and create an overview of the West and the settlers' and explorers' search for freedom.

17.61 Monroe, Judy. **The Sacco and Vanzetti Controversial Murder Trial: A Headline Court Case.** Enslow, 2000. 112 pp. ISBN 0-7660-1387-1. Nonfiction

In 1921, Nicola Sacco and Bartolomeo Vanzetti were convicted and executed for the murder of two fellow workers. Eighty years later their guilt remains a topic of debate. The author chronicles the case's history, the trial, and many social and political elements that contributed to this famous event using photographs and actual transcripts from the court records. Readers are left to reach their own conclusions regarding the validity of the trial and its remaining unanswered questions.

17.62 Mora, Pat. **A Library for Juana: The World of Sor Juana Inés.** Illustrated by Beatriz Vidal. Knopf, 2002. Unpaged. ISBN 0-375-80643-1. Nonfiction

Beautifully illustrated, this engaging picture book history of Sor Juana Inés de la Cruz (Juana Ramirez de Asbaje), 1648–1695, relates her love of words and her persistence in learning to read. Juana moves from her home to the palace in Mexico City and finally to the convent. She challenges the traditional roles for women regarding education and becomes a famous poet, scholar, nun, and voracious reader with an avid curiosity about her world.

17.63 Myers, Walter Dean. ***Amistad:* A Long Road to Freedom.** Puffin, 2001. 99 pp. ISBN 0-14-130004-3. Nonfiction

A time line of events from 1839 to 1842 and maps, photos, and illustrations add important information to this narrative of the uprising of illegally captured Africans against the captain and crew of the slave ship *Amistad.* Sengbe Pieh instigated the revolt and learned some English in order to lead the enslaved people in their court fight to return to Africa. John Quincy Adams was one of the defenders of the slaves as their complicated case resulted in a landmark Supreme Court ruling.

17.64 Nelson, Marilyn. **Carver: A Life in Poems.** Front Street, 2001. 112 pp. ISBN 1-886910-53-7. Poetry

Nelson's short but pithy poems, as well as the accompanying photographs and historical footnotes, reveal in great detail George Washington Carver's complicated and fascinating life and his many contributions to science, society, and education. The shifting viewpoints in the fifty-nine poems enable readers to see the mosaic of Carver's world, making his achievements all the more impressive. Interestingly, the final photograph is of the author's father, one of the Tuskegee Airmen.

17.65 Nelson, Pete. **Left for Dead: A Young Man's Search for Justice for the USS *Indianapolis.*** Delacorte, 2002. 201 pp. ISBN 0-385-90033-3. Nonfiction

This is a true story about a fourteen-year-old boy named Hunter Scott who uncovered pertinent facts about the sinking of the USS *Indianapolis* through a history project at school. Hunter became so intrigued that he began interviewing survivors and running down obscure pieces of information. Hunter's obsession to clear the captain who was held responsible for the tragedy lasted many years, but in 2001 the captain was exonerated.

17.66 Nir, Yehuda. **The Lost Childhood: A World War II Memoir.** Scholastic, 2002. 283 pp. ISBN 0-439-16389-7. Nonfiction

This moving and vivid memoir tells the horrific story of a young boy who lived through and survived the Holocaust in Poland during World War II. The young Jewish boy, disguising himself as a Catholic, faces the constant fear of being discovered by the Nazis. This is a story of survival in the midst of constant fear and deprivation.

17.67 Oertelt, Henry A., with Stephanie Oertelt Samuels. **An Unbroken Chain: My Journey through the Nazi Holocaust.** Lerner, 2000. 160 pp. ISBN 0-822-52952-1. Nonfiction

When twenty-two-year-old Henry Oertelt was sent to a Nazi concentration camp, the odds were against his ever returning to his home in Berlin. Oertelt describes his amazing survival by exploring eighteen events that linked to form his chain of life. Just one weak or broken link would have resulted in his death. This book exposes the Nazis' cruelty and shows how one man was able to thwart their plans for his destruction.

17.68 Philip, Neil, editor. **A Braid of Lives: Native American Childhood.** Clarion, 2000. 77 pp. ISBN 0-395-64528-X. Nonfiction

Accompanied by many wonderful photos, this volume of first-hand accounts from adult Native Americans from twenty-one different tribes is an effective history as they remember their childhoods in the nineteenth and twentieth centuries. Their memories reveal similarities, striking differences, and hardships—including abuse and teasing—as well as happy events. Readers of all ethnicities will be able to connect with the typical childhood memories of mischief and fun.

17.69 Pressler, Mirjam. **Anne Frank: A Hidden Life.** Translated by Anthea Bell. Puffin, 2001. 176 pp. ISBN 0-14-131226-2. Nonfiction

Told with balance and poignancy, this descriptive account of Anne Frank's life before her family was discovered and transported to the death camps succeeds in conveying Anne's remarkable courage and voice and the enormity of the tragedy that consumed her. This latest work is filled with new information from interviews with surviving friends and neighbors and previously unpublished excerpts from her famous diary.

17.70 Rau, Margaret. **The Wells Fargo Book of the Gold Rush.** Atheneum, 2001. 143 pp. ISBN 0-689-83019-X. Nonfiction

What was life like on the frontier for the early gold miners? They lived in small, cramped mining towns, dug for gold during the day, and dreamed of their families back home. And there were many who were lured west by the promise of gold from 1848 through 1855. This book chronicles the rise of the Wells Fargo system to meet the growing demands of handling money in these mining towns. Excellent illustrations and a detailed bibliography are included.

17.71 Roberts, Jeremy. **King Arthur: How History Is Invented.** Lerner, 2001. 104 pp. ISBN 0-8225-4891-7. Nonfiction

In the fifteen hundred years since Arthur probably reigned, stories of his life and legend have grown. The Arthurian story begs the question of whether it is fact or fiction. Roberts explores different theories and seeks evidence and historical consistency to sort factual probability from fiction. The volume is replete with illustrations, many of which first appeared in early Arthurian manuscripts.

17.72 Roberts, Jeremy. **Saint Joan of Arc.** Lerner, 2000. 112 pp. ISBN 0-8225-4981-6. Nonfiction

Filled with extraordinary courage and the belief that she was a tool of God, Joan of Arc, a devoutly Catholic peasant girl, inspired a king and a country to follow her into battle to reclaim France from England. After defeating the British in many battles, Joan was captured, convicted of heresy by the Catholic Church, and put to death. Two hundred years later sainthood was bestowed on Joan in an effort to boost the morale of the French people.

17.73 Robertson, James I. **Standing Like a Stone Wall: The Life of General Thomas J. Jackson.** Atheneum, 2001. 185 pp. ISBN 0-689-82419-X. Nonfiction

General Thomas "Stonewall" Jackson grew up an orphan in Virginia. A graduate of West Point and a professor at Virginia Military Institute when the Civil War began, he joined the Confederate Army and became known as a courageous, dedicated, and tireless leader. This biography describes the several different sides to his character and includes photographs and an index.

17.74 Rosenburg, John. **Alexander Hamilton: America's Bold Lion.** Twenty-First Century Books, 2000. 188 pp. ISBN 0-7613-1617-5. Nonfiction

This biography of Alexander Hamilton shows how he rose from a humble background to become an instrumental member of George Washington's staff during the American Revolution. As one of our founding fathers, his later contributions to the design of government were balanced by controversy and scandal in his private life. From the framing of the Constitution to his famous duel with Aaron Burr, Hamilton remains a colorful character who some claim was the real genius behind the creation of our government.

17.75 Rubin, Susan Goldman. **Fireflies in the Dark: The Story of Friedl Dicker-Brandeis and the Children of Terezin.** Holiday House, 2000. 47 pp. ISBN 0-8234-1461-2. Nonfiction

This is the compelling and poignant story of one Jewish woman, Friedl Dicker-Brandeis, and her years at Terezin concentration camp during which she taught art to the children imprisoned there. Through her selfless efforts, she used art to inspire and sustain hope in a horrible and horrifying situation. With an emphasis on hope, this book draws on interviews with survivors, diaries, and the artwork of the children of Terezin to make life in a concentration camp accessible to young readers.

17.76 Salisbury, Cynthia. **Elizabeth Cady Stanton: Leader of the Fight for Women's Rights.** Enslow, 2002. 128 pp. ISBN 0-7660-1616-1. Nonfiction

Elizabeth Cady Stanton was born in 1815 into a life of privilege. From early experiences in her father's law office, Elizabeth learned that laws governing men and women were different and unfair. Armed with this belief, she promoted women's right to vote. Considered to be a radical, Elizabeth Cady Stanton laid the groundwork for the ratification of the Nineteenth Amendment.

17.77 Schmidt, Gary D. **William Bradford: Plymouth's Faithful Pilgrim.** Eerdmanns, 1999. 200 pp. ISBN 0-8028-5148-7. Nonfiction

Orphaned at an early age, young William Bradford defied his uncles when he started attending a church that became a part of the Separatist movement in England. This involvement was the foundation of a faith that eventually led Bradford to Holland and then to a role as a founding member of the Plymouth Colony. This biography traces the evolution of Bradford, who was the leader of and inspiration for the colony in its difficult days.

17.78 Stanley, Jerry. **Hurry Freedom: African Americans in Gold Rush California.** Crown, 2000. 86 pp. ISBN 0-517-80094-2. Nonfiction

Many African Americans were among the thousands of fortune seekers drawn west by the California gold rush of 1849. In this wild rush for riches, some African Americans found fortune—discovering gold and becoming successful merchants and businessmen. Others, however, suffered hardship, disappointment, and discrimination. Jerry Stanley tells young readers the story of the gold rush through the voice of one African American who became rich and an early leader in the struggle for civil rights. The book includes vivid black-and-white photographs.

17.79 Stewart, Whitney. **Deng Xiaoping: Leader in a Changing China.** Lerner, 2001. 128 pp. ISBN 0-8225-4962-X. Nonfiction

This book traces the life of Deng Xiaoping, one of the most influential leaders of modern China, from his early days as a student of communism in China, France, and Russia through his military and political careers. Numerous photographs take the reader on a journey through Deng's China, from the rural, rice-growing province in which he grew up to Tiananmen Square, the site of the famous 1989 student uprising.

17.80 Stolley, Richard B., editor. **LIFE: Our Century in Pictures for Young People.** Little, Brown, 2000. 232 pp. ISBN 0-316-81589-6. Nonfiction

Using photographs from *LIFE* magazine, editor Stolley presents a pictorial chronology of the twentieth century. Many of the photos capture the indelible images of the times. Photographs are accompanied by nine chapters written by highly respected authors of adolescent literature, including Katherine Paterson, Jane Yolan, Avi, Robert Cormier, Lois Lowry, Patricia McKissack and Fredrick McKissack, Jerry Spinelli, Gary Paulsen, and Cynthia Rylant.

17.81 Streissguth, Tom. **Queen Cleopatra.** Lerner, 2000. 112 pp. ISBN 0-8225-4946-8. Nonfiction

Ambitious, alluring, and *powerful* are all words to describe the subject of this A&E biography: Cleopatra. This informative read presents the life of the Egyptian queen who lived from 69 B.C.E. to 30 B.C.E. Detailed and illustrative, this is a smart reference for both youngsters and adults who are eager to learn more about this famous queen of ancient and regal Egypt.

17.82 Sullivan, George. **The Civil War at Sea.** Twenty-First Century Books, 2001. 80 pp. ISBN 0-7613-1553-5. Nonfiction

The graphics and photographs in this history of the Civil War help illustrate the importance of sea battles during this conflict. In an effort to give readers a visual as well as textual account of major activities of the Confederate and Union navies, the author provides glimpses into how the war was engaged on the seas, on inland rivers, and in bays and harbors. The stories provide powerful details demonstrating the importance of water battles in determining the course of the war.

17.83 Sundel, Al. **Christopher Columbus and the Age of Exploration.** Enslow, 2002. 128 pp. ISBN 0-7660-1820-2. Nonfiction

Readers board ship and journey with Christopher Columbus from his childhood onward into adulthood, getting glimpses into the past that are easily visualized as the author chronicles the ideas and beliefs of the late 1400s. As a new century dawns, readers witness much change, including the discovery of America. A time line provides information about Columbus's birth and voyages. The book also discusses two opposing views concerning Columbus and the conquistadors: one sees them as heroic and the other as cruel.

17.84 Taylor, Theodore. **Air Raid—Pearl Harbor! The Story of December 7, 1941.** Harcourt, 2001 (Originally published in 1971). 192 pp. ISBN 0-15-216421-9. Nonfiction

This book explores both the Japanese and American points of view of the events leading up to and through the attack on Pearl Harbor on December 7, 1941. Military and political perspectives are described using journalistic material and material gathered through interviews with both Japanese and American leaders. The narrative flows quickly and readers become absorbed in the history as it unfolds in almost novel-like fashion.

17.85 Tibbitts, Alison Davis. **John Paul Jones: Father of the American Navy.** Enslow, 2002. 128 pp. ISBN 0-7660-1448-7. Nonfiction

This biography of the life and times of John Paul Jones incorporates varied anecdotal accounts, illustrations, and photographs. Using an easy-to-read format, it notes the career of an American naval hero during the American Revolution. The book also includes some information about other historical figures such as George Washington and France's King Louis XVI.

17.86 Vogt, Gregory. **John Glenn's Return to Space.** Millbrook, 2000. 72 pp. ISBN 0-7613-1614-0. Nonfiction

John Glenn, the first American to orbit the earth, made history again by returning to space at the age of seventy-seven. This book gives detailed accounts of both the 1962 and 1998 missions. John Glenn's first flight lasted four hours, fifty-five minutes, and twenty-three seconds from liftoff to splashdown. *Discovery*'s flight lasted nearly nine days. Photographs capture the training, equipment, and responsibilities of both flights.

17.87 Waldman, Neil. **Wounded Knee.** Atheneum, 2001. 54 pp. ISBN 0-689-82559-5. Nonfiction

In this stirring historical account, Neal Waldman uses simple pictures and words to convey the background events that led to the massacre at Wounded Knee Creek on December 28, 1890, in South Dakota. There, the last free remnants of the proud nomadic hunters—the Lakota—faced the might of the United States Army. Forced to cast aside their ancient ways, the Lakota, as told in vivid language and pictures, fell prey to the European intruders.

17.88 Warren, Andrea. **We Rode the Orphan Trains.** Houghton Mifflin, 2001. 132 pp. ISBN 0-618-11712-1. Nonfiction

Between 1854 and 1929, close to 200,000 children were sent by the Children's Aid Society from New York City and other eastern cities by train to find homes in the West and Midwest. This extraordinary book tells the life stories of some of these children, accompanied by photographs showing them as both children and adults. This resource puts a human face on a little-known aspect of our nation's history and includes a description of other sources that provide information about the Orphan Train.

17.89 Washington, George. **George-isms: The 100 Rules George Washington Wrote When He Was 14—and Lived by All His Life.** Atheneum, 2000. 80 pp. ISBN 0-689-84082-9. Nonfiction

This slim volume contains 110 ethical rules of behavior that a young George Washington wrote out and kept by his side throughout his life. The rules are presented here as quotations (updated for contemporary audiences by the publishers). Rule 50, for example, cautions the reader not to believe rumors.

17.90 Watkins, Richard. **Slavery: Bondage throughout History.** Illustrated by Richard Watkins. Houghton Mifflin, 2001. 125 pp. ISBN 0-395-92289-5. Nonfiction

Whether religious, political, or social in origin, slavery has always existed in parts of the world to benefit those in power. Starting with the earliest known accounts some five thousand years ago, Watkins chronicles the many forms and locations of slavery. In addition, this book provides an interesting overview of specific people who fought against this form of human oppression.

17.91 Winget, Mary. **Eleanor Roosevelt.** Lerner, 2001. 105 pp. ISBN 0-8225-4985-9. Nonfiction

The life and times of a much-loved first lady are detailed in this biography of Eleanor Roosevelt. From the early, sad life of this American icon to her rich, fulfilling adult years, readers discover who she was and how she lived her life. The contributions Roosevelt made to the women's movement are chronicled as well as the role she played during World War II. Her dedication to helping the less fortunate is also showcased.

17.92 Woods, Geraldine. **The Salem Witchcraft Trials: A Headline Court Case.** Enslow, 2000. 104 pp. ISBN 0-7660-1383-9. Nonfiction

Salem, Massachusetts, was a dangerous place to live in 1692. Nearly 150 people were held in prison and 19 were actually convicted of witchcraft and hanged. Using excerpts from historical documents, maps, illustrations, and photographs, the author examines the period in history that experienced this widespread fear and paranoia and shares with us the reasons why this time continues to be of such interest today.

17.93 Woods, Michael, and Mary B. Woods. **Ancient Communication: From Grunts to Graffiti.** Runestone, 2000. 88 pp. ISBN 0-8225-2996-3. Nonfiction

Communication is perhaps the form of technology that makes other technologies possible and is presented as the basis for civilization. From the earliest communication through grunts and growls, humans developed more complex and efficient ways to convey messages. As this technology evolved, the alphabet replaced cuneiform, and paper media replaced the use of clay and animal skins. This book traces that development of communication technologies through the ancient cultures of the Middle East, Egypt, China, Mesoamerica, Greece, Rome, and India.

17.94 Woods, Michael, and Mary B. Woods. **Ancient Computing: From Counting to Calendars.** Runestone, 2000. 88 pp. ISBN 0-8225-2997-1. Nonfiction

The technology of computing initially provided a means for ancient humans to count. Advances in farming created a need to count crops, measure land, track length of seasons, and provide a uniform system for conducting trade. The development of number systems provided a way to perform basic math operations. Such progress led to more formalized studies of mathematics and its applications. By highlighting such advancements in mathematical thinking, the authors validate the contribution of these ideas to modern mathematics.

17.95 Woods, Michael, and Mary B. Woods. **Ancient Construction: From Tents to Towers.** Runestone, 2000. 88 pp. ISBN 0-8225-2998-X. Nonfiction

Advances in the technology of construction led to more sophisticated buildings for shelter as well as monuments, dams, roads and bridges, canals, tunnels, sewage systems, and other structures. The authors trace the development of construction from the structures of the earliest humans during the Stone Age to the magnificent wonders of ancient civilizations including the Greeks, Romans, Chinese, and Mayans. Advances in construction led to improved building materials and methods such as town planning. These influences are still evident in modern construction.

17.96 Woods, Michael, and Mary B. Woods. **Ancient Warfare: From Clubs to Catapults.** Runestone, 2000. 96 pp. ISBN 0-8225-2999-8. Nonfiction

Through descriptive accounts of ancient weaponry, from those of the first humans to those in use during the fall of the western Roman Empire in A.D. 476, the authors create an appreciation for the genius of ancient civilizations in advancing military technology, including plans for using weapons and soldiers in battle. Illustrations and photographs enhance the stories of how ancient warriors fought.

17.97 Worth, Richard. **Pizarro and the Conquest of the Incan Empire in World History.** Enslow, 2000. 128 pp. ISBN 0-7660-1396-0. Nonfiction

Spaniard Francisco Pizarro led his first expedition in quest of the glory and wealth of the New World in 1524. Within a few short years, Pizarro had taken control of the Incan empire. Through easy-to-follow prose spiced with passages from letters and diaries and other historical documents, the reader follows the conflict of two cultures and witnesses the devastating effects of Pizarro's personal ambitions and ruthless nature on a once proud and unique culture.

17.98 Worth, Richard. **Stanley and Livingstone and the Exploration of Africa in World History.** Enslow, 2000. 128 pp. ISBN 0-7660-1400-2. Nonfiction

Dr. David Livingstone left England in 1866 on an expedition to find the source of the Nile River. Five years later journalist Henry Morton Stanley went into the heart of Africa to find the now-missing Livingstone. In the wake of the meeting of these two explorers, the "scramble for Africa" began, and European countries sought to colonize the vast continent based on the attention Stanley and Livingstone brought to bear on it. This book includes excerpts from letters and diaries.

Historical Nonfiction Series

Cities through Time Series:

17.99 Kotapish, Dawn. **Daily Life in Ancient and Modern Athens.** Illustrated by Bob Moulder. Runestone, 2001. 64 pp. ISBN 0-8225-3216-6. Nonfiction

Slavik, Diane. **Daily Life in Ancient and Modern Jerusalem.** Illustrated by Ray Webb. Runestone, 2001. 64 pp. ISBN 0-8225-3218-2. Nonfiction

Toht, Patricia. **Daily Life in Ancient and Modern Moscow.** Illustrated by Bob Moulder. Runestone, 2000. 64 pp. ISBN 0-8225-3220-4. Nonfiction

These books present material in a breezy, informative manner, and the paintings, woodcuts, photography, and illustrations help engage the reader's interest as well as present a pictorial history. The layout is easily understood and helps the student research a topic. Each bibliography is substantial. Additional resources include a glossary, time line, and pronunciation key at the end of each book to provide clarification and framework.

Passport to History Series:

17.100 Day, Nancy. **Your Travel Guide to Ancient Egypt.** Runestone, 2001. 96 pp. ISBN 0-8225-3075-9. Nonfiction

Day, Nancy. **Your Travel Guide to Ancient Greece.** Runestone, 2000. 96 pp. ISBN 0-8225-3076-7. Nonfiction

Day, Nancy. **Your Travel Guide to Ancient Maya Civilization.** Runestone, 2001. 96 pp. ISBN 0-8225-3077-5. Nonfiction

Day, Nancy.**Your Travel Guide to Civil War America.** Runestone, 2001. 96 pp. ISBN 0-8225-3078-3. Nonfiction

Day, Nancy. **Your Travel Guide to Colonial America.** Runestone, 2001. 96 pp. ISBN 0-8225-3079-1. Nonfiction

Day, Nancy. **Your Travel Guide to Renaissance Europe.** Runestone, 2001. 96 pp. ISBN 0-8225-3080-5. Nonfiction

Into ninety-six pages Day packs a thorough, informative, and fascinating summary of the history of these time periods. The paintings, woodcuts, photography, and illustrations help engage the reader's interest as well as present a pictorial history. Essential Questions, Helpful Hints, and Tech Tips focus readers on the material and help them explore each page. A glossary, time line, and pronunciation key at the end of each book provide clarification and a framework. A substantial bibliography is included.

18 Folktales, Myths, and Legends

18.1 Aiken, Joan. **A Necklace of Raindrops and Other Stories.** Illustrated by Kevin Hawkes. Knopf, 2001. 85 pp. ISBN 0-375-80584-2. Fiction

This collection of eight short stories will delight and intrigue the imagination. Reminiscent of classic fairy tales and myths, these enchanting stories combine the elements of the traditional with a "Dr. Seussian" twist to create a patchwork quilt of talking mice, flying pies, and dancing elves.

18.2 Aiken, Joan. **The Wolves of Willoughby Chase.** Illustrated by Pat Marriott. Delacorte, 2000 (Originally published in 1962). 181 pp. ISBN 0-385-32790-0. Fiction

Bonnie and her cousin Sylvia are left at Willoughby Chase with the cruel and evil governess Miss Slighcarp. When she takes over, Miss Slighcarp sends Bonnie and Sylvia to a school for orphans. Their friend Simon rescues them, and they all escape to London with Simon's geese. This reprinted classic, the first of the Wolf Chronicles, provides a vivid picture of the triumph of good over evil.

18.3 Baker, E. D. **The Frog Princess.** Bloomsbury, 2002. 214 pp. ISBN 1-58234-799-9. Fiction

Princess Emeralda is *not* a perfect princess; she brays like a donkey when she laughs and can never please her mother. To escape the pressures of the castle, Emeralda goes to the nearby swamp where she meets Eadric, the talking frog and transformed prince. When she tries to change him back to his original form, the spell backfires and Emeralda is turned into a frog as well. What this unlikely pair does next will keep readers enchanted.

18.4 Baum, L. Frank. **The Wizard of Oz.** Illustrated by Charles Santore. Random House, 2000 (Originally published in 1900). 96 pp. ISBN 0-375-81137-0. Fiction

Charles Santore celebrates the 100th anniversary of the publication of *The Wizard of Oz* with this picture book edition, which condenses the original by focusing on key incidents. Santore's vivid, rich watercolor illustrations truly complement the text. Although shortened, this version is faithful to the original.

18.5 Baum, L. Frank. **The Wonderful Wizard of Oz.** Illustrated by W. W. Denslow. Books of Wonder/HarperCollins, 2000 (Originally published in 1900). 267 pp. ISBN 0-06-029323-3. Fiction

This 100th-anniversary edition of L. Frank Baum's enduring classic *The Wonderful Wizard of Oz* is a facsimile of the classic first edition, replete with two-color illustrations as well as all the original color plates by W. W. Denslow. The story relates the journey of Dorothy and Toto after they are swept away from their home in Kansas to the wonderland of Oz. This journey along the Yellow Brick Road retains the charm that has captivated readers since the original edition was published in 1900.

18.6 Buff, Mary, and Conrad Buff. **The Apple and the Arrow.** Houghton Mifflin, 2001 (Originally published in 1952). 80 pp. ISBN 0-618-12807-7. Fiction

In this reissue of the well-loved classic, readers learn about Walter and William Tell's relationship and the important role they played in Switzerland's fight for freedom. Although most people are familiar with the story of William Tell shooting the arrow through the apple placed on his son's head, most are not familiar with Walter's story. In this illustrated book, the story comes to life as we follow the straight shot of the arrow through time.

18.7 Cadnum, Michael. **Forbidden Forest: The Story of Little John and Robin Hood.** Orchard, 2002. 218 pp. ISBN 0-439-31774-6. Fiction

Can anyone imagine Robin Hood without Little John? The second of Michael Cadmun's stories about the legend of Robin Hood, this book chronicles the life of Little John and how he came to join Robin Hood's band of merry men. Romantic and adventurous, Little John proves to be a brave man who follows a code of honor.

18.8 Cooney, Caroline B. **Goddess of Yesterday.** Delacorte, 2002. 264 pp. ISBN 0-385-72945-6. Fiction

Anaxandra is companion to the crippled princess Callisto, daughter of King Nicander. Fate once more intervenes in Anaxandra's life when King Menelaus of Sparta attacks the island of Siphnos, and Anaxandra is the sole survivor. This courageous heroine inspires affection, and readers become enmeshed with the classic tales of the ancient Greeks through Anaxandra's journey to find shelter and a sense of self. In this retelling, author Cooney brings the ancient Greek epics to life.

18.9 Crossley-Holland, Kevin. **At the Crossing-Places.** Arthur A. Levine Books, 2002. 393 pp. ISBN 0-439-26598-3. Fiction

Thirteen-year-old Arthur pursues the mysteries of his birth parents and fights the betrayals of his half sister as he sets off to become a squire to Lord Stephen and journey with him on the Crusades. This sequel to *The Seeing Stone* is woven against the tapestry of classic high fantasy tales of Camelot, and we watch Arthur's quest against the backdrop of the well-known adventures of Merlin, King Arthur, and the Knights of the Round Table.

18.10 Crossley-Holland, Kevin. **The Seeing Stone.** Arthur A. Levine Books, 2001. 338 pp. ISBN 0-439-26326-3. Fiction

Arthur lives in twelfth-century England, and his life parallels that of the ancient King Arthur, who lived so long ago that myth and history are interchangeable. As the twelfth-century Arthur begins to learn about the other, earlier Arthur, he must also integrate into his understanding the conflicting bits of his own cloudy past. His present is not conflict free, either; his best friend Gatly is a servant and often hungry. Arthur is torn by injustices that the others in his world see as the manifestation of God's will.

18.11 Dahl, Roald. **Roald Dahl's Revolting Rhymes.** Illustrated by Quentin Blake. Knopf, 2002 (Originally published in 1982). 43 pp. ISBN 0-375-81556-2. Poetry

This collection of fractured fairy tales, retold in rhyme by master storyteller Roald Dahl, are funny, fiendishly clever, and satisfying to any lover of the old tales who sometimes wished the stories had ended a bit differently. Dahl spices up his narratives with a bit of gore and dark humor. The verse itself is bright and clever, and when paired with the colorful, slightly irreverent illustrations by longtime Dahl illustrator Quentin Blake, the appeal is enormous.

18.12 Ferris, Jean. **Once upon a Marigold.** Harcourt, 2002. 266 pp. ISBN 0-15-216791-9. Fiction

In this modern-day fairy tale, Ferris tells the story of Christian, who has been raised by a troll, as he falls in love and has to rescue not only his princess but also the entire kingdom from a plot to take it over—a plot hatched by the queen against her husband and daughter. A fast-paced read, the novel bubbles with fun, humor, and warmth and offers a fair amount of wisdom about relationships as well.

18.13 Glassman, Peter, editor. **Oz: The Hundredth Anniversary Celebration.** HarperCollins, 2000. 55 pp. ISBN 0-688-15915-X. Nonfiction

Thirty children's authors and illustrators pay tribute in word and picture to Frank Baum and his enduring classic *The Wizard of Oz*. The tributes take many forms but frequently relate the magical impact the book had on the children who would grow up to write and illustrate for other children.

18.14 Grimm, Jacob, and Wilhelm Grimm. **Grimm's Fairy Tales.** Illustrated by Arthur Rackham. SeaStar, 2001 (Illustrations originally published in 1909). 160 pages. ISBN 1-58717-092-2. Fiction

This edition of the Brothers Grimm classic fairy tales returns to the early translations that were illustrated by Arthur Rackham. Twenty-two of these timeless stories have been selected, including "Hansel and Grethel," "Rapunzel," and "Red Riding Hood." Twenty of Rackham's color illustrations and twenty-eight pen-and-ink drawings accompany the tales.

18.15 Hamilton, Virginia, reteller. **The People Could Fly: American Black Folktales.** Illustrated by Leo Dillon and Diane Dillon. Knopf, 2000 (Originally published in 1985). 173 pp. ISBN 0-375-80471-4. Fiction

This reissue of the 1985 edition of twenty-four folktales now includes a CD, narrated by Virginia Hamilton and James Earl Jones, of eleven of the folktales. Interesting background provided in the introduction and following each folktale, as well as the illustrations by Leo and Diane Dillon, add to the impact and enjoyment of each tale. Divided into tales of animals, the fanciful, the supernatural, and freedom, some of which will be familiar, these stories can be understood on several levels.

18.16 Harris, Joel Chandler. **The Complete Tales of Uncle Remus.** Compiled by Richard Chase. Illustrated by Arthur Burdette Frost, Frederick Stuart Church, J. M. Conde, Edward Windsor Kemble, and William Holbrook Beard. Houghton Mifflin, 2002 (Originally published in 1955). 815 pp. ISBN 0-618-15429-9. Fiction

This new edition of the tales first published beginning in 1880 provides readers with traditional folk literature, full of humorous insights. This is a one-volume compilation of all of Harris's stories of Brer Rabbit, Brer Fox, Brer Wolf, and the other woodland creatures. The collection includes some simplified spellings, footnotes, and definitions to make the dialect easier for readers to comprehend.

18.17 Irving, Washington. **Rip Van Winkle.** Illustrated by Arthur Rackman. SeaStar, 2000 (Originally published in 1819). 109 pp. ISBN 1-58717-039-6. Fiction

This classic American tale of Rip Van Winkle, who falls into a deep sleep while wandering in the Catskills and awakens twenty years in the future to discover the world much changed, has been formatted for easy reading and made visually appealing by the additions of black, white, and sepia-toned illustrations. The foreword and afterword by Peter Glassman, owner of a children's bookstore in New York City, provide a valuable historical context for this favorite work.

18.18 Jaffe, Nina. **Tales for the Seventh Day: A Collection of Sabbath Stories.** Illustrated by Kelly Stribling Sutherland. Scholastic, 2000. 73 pp. ISBN 0-590-12054-9. Fiction

The seventh day of the week, the Sabbath, is a sacred day in the Jewish tradition and is the focus of many rituals and stories. The author shares historical traditions in the rabbinical literature and introduces the reader to a collection of rich tales from around the world. A glossary and a pronunciation guide help the reader enjoy the magic of these tales.

18.19 Kindl, Patrice. **Goose Chase.** Houghton Mifflin, 2001. 214 pp. ISBN 0-618-03377-7. Fiction

Ten-year-old Alexandria lived alone in a small house caring for her family's geese, as she promised her dying mother three years ago. When granted three wishes by an old hag, Alexandria becomes beautiful and rich. Now fourteen, she is held captive in a tower. Her only option is to escape and reach freedom. With her quick wit and the help of her gaggle of geese, Alexandria's adventures entertain us, with plenty of twists and turns along the way.

18.20 Levine, Gail Carson. **Cinderellis and the Glass Hill.** Illustrated by Mark Elliott. HarperCollins, 2000. 104 pp. ISBN 0-06-028336-X. Fiction

In this revision of the classic fairy tale, Cinderella is a boy named Ellis. When one of his many inventions leaves him covered in soot, his brothers nickname him Cinderellis. Although Cinderellis creates many useful inventions trying to win his brothers' friendship, they continue to ignore him. In one last attempt to gain their approval, Cinderellis decides to climb the glass hill in the center of the village and win Princess Marigold's hand in marriage.

18.21 Levine, Gail Carson. **Ella Enchanted.** HarperCollins, 1997. 232 pp. ISBN 0-06-027511-1. Fiction

When Ella of Frell is born, a fairy bestows on her a gift that turns out to be more like a curse: she will always be obedient. After the death of her mother, Ella is at the mercy of her nasty stepmother and stepsisters because she can't help being obedient. Eventually she goes on a quest to break the curse. Combining elements of both the Cinderella and Sleeping Beauty tales, this novel is both funny and fast paced.

18.22 Lyons, Mary E. **Knockabeg: A Famine Tale.** Houghton Mifflin, 2001. 118 pp. ISBN 0-618-09283-8. Fiction

In this Celtic tale, "The Trooping Ones" are trying to save the people of Knockabeg from the terrible potato blight brought on by the Nuckelavees, the evil faeries. As a result, a great war ensues—with one catch: the faeries cannot fight without a human with them. This is where Eamon comes in; the faerie

Sticky is in charge of protecting him and his family. The queen asks Sticky to steal Eamon for the battle since he is such a trustworthy boy.

18.23 Malone, Patricia. **The Legend of Lady Ilena.** Delacorte, 2002. 232 pp. ISBN 0-385-72915-4. Fiction

In the days when Arthur ruled Britain, Ilena, daughter of Moren, comes of age in the northern Vale of Enfert surrounded by the strange customs of the Druid farmers and shepherds of the valley. But Ilena, a Christian, is taught by her father to wield a sword and to be a warrior. At his untimely death, she is instructed to set out for Dun Alyn, her birthplace. The road she takes is full of trials, adventures, and opportunities for learning.

18.24 Martin, Rafe. **The World before This One: A Novel Told in Legend.** Illustrated by Calvin Nicholls. Arthur A Levine Books, 2002. 208 pp. ISBN 0-590-37976-3. Fiction

Crow and his grandmother live on the fringes of their Seneca community, blamed by others for the bad things that have happened to their tribe and struggling to find enough food to survive. Crow knows little of his heritage until a boulder begins to speak to him. He learns the great legends of the Seneca people, but his grandmother fears that he has been possessed. Crow has to figure out his own destiny as he gains the power to become a storyteller.

18.25 McKinley, Robin. **Spindle's End.** Putnam, 2000. 422 pp. ISBN 0-399-23466-7. Fiction

Rosie is an unlikely princess, but then again, her upbringing has been vastly irregular. Rescued by the fairy Kutriana just before a malevolent curse can take effect, Rosie grows up in a village, bonds with animals both wild and domestic, and gets apprenticed to the dour Narl. In her latest reworking of a fairy tale, author McKinley raises potent questions about loyalty, identity, and sacrifice.

18.26 Morris, Gerald. **Parsifal's Page.** Houghton Mifflin, 2001. 232 pp. ISBN 0-618-05509-6. Fiction

Parsifal's Page is the story of a search for chivalry, magic, love, and identity. Piers is a young boy who through a twist of fate becomes page to a seemingly unlikely hero. This is the tale of their adventures with knights, fairies, and many other unusual characters.

18.27 Morris, Gerald. **The Savage Damsel and the Dwarf.** Houghton Mifflin, 2000. 210 pp. ISBN 0-395-97126-8. Fiction

Morris continues to make the Arthurian legend fun for kids; here he retells the story of Gareth (a.k.a Beausmains) and the damsel Lynet, but neither the plot nor the theme slavishly adheres to Malory's version of events. Gareth is a prodigious stiff, but Lynet, as the Sulie court concedes, has potential—and the constant help of a mysterious dwarf. Readers of Morris's earlier works will recognize old friends.

18.28 Napoli, Donna Jo. **Beast.** Atheneum, 2000. 260 pp. ISBN 0-689-83589-2. Fiction

For anyone who wants to know how and why the handsome prince became a beast and how he ended up in his castle in the woods, this book provides answers. When Persian Prince Orasmyn is cursed and turned into a beast, he flees his home and wanders until he arrives in France and establishes a home in an abandoned castle. He dreams of being restored to human form and takes solace in the sacred rose garden he plants. He waits for Belle, the "beauty," to rescue him.

18.29 Nesbit, E. **The Book of Dragons.** Illustrated by H. R. Millar. SeaStar, 2001 (Originally published in 1900). 172 pp. ISBN 1-58717-106-6. Fiction

In this collection of eight stories, dragons, princes, and princesses; rescue missions; and villains are woven into every story. As in all good fairy tales, the princes and princesses always come out on top, outsmarting both the villain and the dragon. This reprinted edition of the 1900 original contains a new afterword by Peter Glassman. Though the book asserts that "everyone loves dragons," younger audiences will be most appreciative of its content.

18.30 Newth, Mette. **The Transformation.** Translated by Faith Ingwersen. Farrar, Straus and Giroux, 2000. 195 pp. ISBN 0-374-37752-9. Fiction

Brendan is sent from his fifteenth-century home in Ireland to Greenland to convert heathens to Christianity. There he meets Naravana, who saves his life and teaches him how to survive the treacherous winter in her land. Their friendship grows and both learn to respect the beliefs of others. Each has a spiritual journey, Naravana's to bring back the sun to her homeland and Brendan's to explore his religious faith.

18.31 Philip, Neil. **The Great Mystery: Myths of Native America.** Clarion, 2001. 145 pp. ISBN 0-395-98405-X. Fiction

Most people are familiar with Roman and Greek myths. They recognize the name of Zeus and those of many other gods and goddesses. Perhaps less familiar, however, are the Native American myths, yet, they too provide explanations about the creation of the world. In Philip's account, readers learn that "the Earth was the mother, and the Sky the father" and discover that various Native American tribes held different beliefs concerning the origins of time. Several photographs and illustrations complement the text.

18.32 Pullman, Philip. **Spring-Heeled Jack.** Illustrated by David Mostyn. Knopf, 2002 (Originally published in 1989). 112 pp. ISBN 0-375-81601-1. Fiction

A day in the life of the "original superhero" follows the misadventures of siblings Rose, Lily, and Ned as Spring-Heeled Jack comes to their rescue with the help of an unwitting sailor, his barmaid sweetheart with a heart of gold, and a surprise guest. Comical quotations at the beginning of each chapter and comic strips throughout add humor, drawing on both modern media and the literary canon.

18.33 Schmidt, Gary D. **Straw into Gold.** Clarion, 2001. 172 pp. ISBN 0-618-05601-7. Fiction

When young Tousle's father takes him to see the royal procession, Tousle pleads for mercy for the captured rebels in the procession, specifically for Innes, a blind boy his own age. The king spares Innes's life on one condition: the boys have seven days to solve a riddle or both will be killed. Tousle and his new friend uncover the riddle's answer and much more in this delightful adventure fantasy that weaves the tale of Rumplestiltskin with the boys' journey of discovery.

18.34 Spinner, Stephanie. **Quiver.** Knopf, 2002. 171 pp. ISBN 0-375-81489-2. Fiction

Artemis, goddess of the hunt, rescues Atalanta, an abandoned baby. When Atalanta becomes a teenager, she runs faster than any other human and is able to hunt as well as most men. Life changes drastically, however, when her father, a king, commands her to produce an heir. Atalanta agrees to marry the first man to outrun her, with the stipulation that anyone who cannot outrun her must die.

18.35 Spires, Elizabeth. **I Am Arachne: Fifteen Greek and Roman Myths.** Frances Foster Books, 2001. 98 pp. ISBN 0-374-33525-7. Fiction

In this clever twist on standard storytelling, fifteen classic tales from Roman and Greek mythology come to life when the main characters narrate their own stories. Pandora, Sisyphus, Arachne, Narcissus, and Pan are among those included in this illustrated collection. The characters share their insights with humor, regret, and personality in this completely engaging read.

18.36 Springer, Nancy. **Rowan Hood: Outlaw Girl of Sherwood Forest.** Philomel, 2001. 170 pp. ISBN 0-399-23368-7. Fiction

What if Robin Hood had a daughter? Rowan Hood, left to her own devices when her mother is murdered, decides to seek out her father, and along the way, disguised as a boy, she collects her own band of followers. Rowan sets out through Sherwood Forest on her quest, supported by a runaway princess, an overgrown boy with magical singing powers, and a half-dog/half-wolf. In the process, she proves herself worthy to carry on the family name and makes peace with her heritage.

18.37 Tchana, Katrin. **The Serpent Slayer: And Other Stories of Strong Women.** Illustrated by Trina Schart Hyman. Little, Brown, 2000. 113 pp. ISBN 0 -316-38701-0. Fiction

Legends and folktales are replete with heroes, but this collection is one of the first to tell the feats of heroines. The collection includes eighteen stories from around the world and full-color illustrations by Trina Schart Hyman. The heroines of these stories overcome challenges with intelligence, ingenuity, and common sense. Multicultural stories present universal perspectives of women's courage and resilience.

18.38 Thomson, Sarah L. **The Dragon's Son.** Orchard, 2001. 181 pp. ISBN 0-531-30333-0. Fiction

Through the voices of four different characters, Thomson retells the legend of King Arthur. First, the newborn son of Nimue is sacrificed to save the infant Arthur. Then Arthur meets his half sisters, Morgan and Elen. Morgan marries the young king, and Elen, married to one of Arthur's knights, raises the king's younger son. The book ends with the tale of Medraud, Arthur's oldest son, who rebels against his father but provides an heir to reunite the destroyed kingdom.

18.39 Vande Velde, Vivian. **The Rumpelstiltskin Problem.** Houghton Mifflin, 2000. 116 pp. ISBN 0-618-05523-1. Fiction.

Vande Velde prefaces these six variations on the story of Rumpelstiltskin with her own tongue-in-cheek retelling of the original story, indicating how it raised questions in her mind that served as the springboard for this collection. The stories and characters vary in tone, from the grim, malevolent Rumpelstiltskin who is eager for a "baby roast" to a female Rumpelstiltskin who wants a human baby to raise as her own.

18.40 Yolen, Jane, editor. **Sherwood: Original Stories from the World of Robin Hood.** Illustrated by Dennis Nolan. Philomel, 2000. 134 pp. ISBN 0-399-23182-X. Fiction

This volume includes eight stories that explore new twists on the well-loved legend, from a story of Robin's birth, to a tale of the burden of tradition on Robin's grandson, to a futurist view in which Robin redistributes wealth, including the sheriff's, by computer. In addition to Yolen, other contributors include Anna Kirwan, Nancy Springer, and Robert J. Harris.

Afterword

Nursery rhymes, fairy tales, and my favorite story—*Alice in Wonderland*—were among my first encounters with literature. My earliest and fondest memories are of my mother reading to me, especially *Alice in Wonderland.* When I learned how to read, I reread the Alice story by myself a few more times. There is no accounting for a child's taste.

It didn't matter that Alice was white living in Britain and that I was black living in the Bronx. She was a little girl like me and I was so frightened for her. I empathized with her, for I'd had some scary nightmares myself. When I was ten years old, someone gave me a copy of *Little Women,* and I read all 546 small-print pages at least twice, if not three times. Once again it didn't matter that all of the characters were white. I found the essence of the story—a family that was caring, giving, and willing to sacrifice for those they loved. I could relate it back to my own family experience.

In those years when I grew up—the late 1940s and early '50s—there was little television, no computers, no video games—few distractions for a kid like me who loved to read. I went through periods: I had a Charles Dickens period and suffered with the poor children of London; then when I was a little older, the romantic mysteries of Daphne DuMaurier caught my interest.

Unfortunately, there were few books for young readers back in those days with positive images of people of color. I read anyway, and by the time I was in high school I was able to finally round out my literary life. I discovered Langston Hughes, who remains one of my favorite writers and poets, most likely because his work was the first time I'd been exposed to literature from a black perspective. By the time I graduated from high school in 1960, I was devouring every African American book, article, essay, and poem that I could find, which tells me that though I was able to discover meaning through literature as a youngster, when I saw myself represented in the literature I read, it was even more powerful for me. I have often felt that my self-esteem and confidence level would have been much higher had I seen myself, my peers, and the people I lived with and loved in the literature I read at an earlier age. But, on the other hand, maybe those books where I didn't see myself forced me to really search for the true meaning of the story.

I wonder whether I would've written differently or have been a better writer if I'd had some of the wonderful children's books we have now with African American characters. Suppose I'd read *Mufaro's Beautiful Daughters* along with *Cinderella;* it certainly would have made a difference in terms of how I thought about myself. I remember sharing *Mufaro's Beautiful Daughters* with a group of sixth graders who were definitely reluctant readers. I can still clearly see how the faces of those boys and girls lit up with surprise and delight when I gathered them around me and they saw beautiful images that looked like themselves. Literature is as personal as it is powerful.

Mufaro's Beautiful Daughters helped me to break the ice with that difficult class, thus making them more receptive to some of the other books I read with them. I used Allen Say's *Grandfather's Journey* to generate a wonderful discussion about their own experiences, since many of the students in that class came from immigrant families and understood the narrator's love of two countries and two places.

Cynthia Rylant's book *When I Was Young in the Mountains* was the inspiration for a successful writing project with these same children. They wrote and illustrated their stories about their family memories—When I Was Young in the Bronx, or When I Was Young in Jamaica, or Bermuda or South Carolina or any number of the places my students hailed from. The important element, then, is both seeing yourself affirmed in some way in the literature you read and connecting with the experiences of the characters.

I didn't have books like *Mufaro's Beautiful Daughters,* but the books, poetry, and stories I did read influenced me as a writer pretty much in the same way that my student writers found so much meaning in Cynthia Rylant's book. Those "old school" books I read in my day armed us with lessons: right usually won out over might; goodness was rewarded; there was always a light at the end of the tunnel; it was more blessed to give than to receive. These were essentially the same lessons I learned at home and in the Sunday school Bible stories we read.

My stories and novels, while not ending with "and they lived happily ever after," do end with "and they lived." I try to leave my young readers with a sense of hope and a sense that there is actually justice in this world, though it does not always come from man. I try to show them what is or was while at the same time showing what can be.

Our children need, more than ever, to be exposed to the power of literature as they begin their journey to adulthood; movies and stories on television cannot replace the transforming possibilities of a piece of literature that truly speaks to the heart. When we watch a movie, we are told pretty much what to think. We do not have to imagine how a character looks or what he or she might sound like. When reading or listening to a story or poem, we participate in the process with the writer or storyteller. We bring our imaginations and perceptions to the work. Literature gives us time to think and to return to the work again and again.

There is an African proverb that says, When an elder dies, the village loses a library. In societies that drew on oral traditions to pass down their literature, the storytellers, griots, grandmothers, and grandfathers were the living libraries who passed on the myths and stories that explained natural phenomena, the history of the nation, the exploits of warriors and rulers, and the fables and proverbs that taught people how to act and interact with one another.

Our own literary traditions, reflecting the need that all of us have to affirm our existence and bring order to our lives, are not that far removed from the oral traditions of our ancestors. We no longer sit around the campfire drawing strength from the wisdom of our elders. The wisdom of our "Tribe" is now written. Though youngsters have video games, computer games, and any number of distractions, everyone still loves a tale well told, or a story well written—even those youngsters who think that they do not like books or do not like to read. They have yet to find the book or story that speaks to them, that moves them. As I said before, literature is also personal.

In these dangerous and difficult times when many of our young people wonder whether there will be a world for them to grow up in, we need to expose them to those voices and ideas that can sustain them. We have had in recent years frightening examples of what happens when kids live in a small world of their own making, feeding on violence and mayhem instead of finding the connection they have to the rest of humankind.

Now more than at any other time we all need to return to our literary beginnings. While we cannot sit by a campfire together and listen to a fable or proverb that might keep us from hurting someone else in blind rage and anger, we can communicate as we make use of the rich store of literature available to us. Teachers, librarians, and all of us who care about children and children's literature might be the last line of defense—the new age of griots—connecting children with literature.

We also have to open our own minds, ignore labels, and get to the heart and message of some of these books that seem to be earmarked for a specific population. For example, because a writer like Walter Dean Myers writes a book about a troubled urban (new euphemism for black) youth and all of the boys in our class or group are white and suburban does not mean that Myers's book would not be appropriate for them. No doubt there is more than one troubled boy in a group or class who might benefit from reading *Monster* or *Bad Boy* or *Handbook for Boys: A Novel.*

We really don't know what will strike a child's or a young person's fancy, so we have to expose the youngsters who come before us to as wide a range of literature as we can and let them make the choice. We know that there is no such thing as a book or character that will appeal to all kids—not even Harry Potter. We must gather all of our children around the campfire and find those tales and those voices that strengthen and sustain each and every one of them.

Children enlighten us. I recently received a letter from an eighth-grade student in a New York City school. The young lady is Asian American and the book she is referring to is about African Americans in the South during Reconstruction. Her teacher assigned the book. This eighth grader so eloquently expresses the point I've been trying to make:

> My favorite part of the book was when the old woman in chapter twelve says, "Trouble never over. Just have to learn how to ride it, like you ride a wild horse." I took that quote and locked it in my heart. . . . I can definitely relate to that and I can use it in life. I'm glad you put that quote in the book because it helps me know that I'm still young and am still learning to ride the wild horse—life.

We must help all of our children ride that wild horse.

Joyce Hansen

Author Index

Illustrator Index

Subject Index

Title Index

Editors

Jean E. Brown is a faculty member at Rhode Island College, where she chairs the Alliance for the Study and Teaching of Adolescent Literature. She currently serves on both the executive board of ALAN and *The ALAN Review* editorial board, and she edits the *Review*'s Non-Print Media Connection Column. In addition, she serves on the executive board of the New England Association of Teachers of English. Brown is a former high school English teacher and department chair who served as president of the Michigan Council of Teachers of English. She was a recipient of MCTE's C. C. Fries Award for service to the profession and has received several awards for scholarship and research, including being named distinguished faculty by the Michigan Association of Governing Boards of State Universities. Nationally, Brown has served on the SLATE Steering Committee; chaired the Conference on English Education's Commission on Intellectual Freedom; served as editor of SLATE Starter Sheets; and been a member of the editorial board of *English Journal*. She has written over seventy articles and book chapters and coauthored and edited ten books.

Elaine C. Stephens earned her master's degree and Ph.D. in reading and language arts from Michigan State University and has over thirty-five years of experience as a classroom teacher, reading consultant, professional development specialist, and teacher educator. Stephens speaks at national and state conferences, conducts professional development workshops, and has written more than sixty publications, including coauthoring and editing ten books, among which are *A Handbook of Content Literacy Strategies; United in Diversity: Using Multicultural Young Adult Literature in the Classroom; Learning about the Civil War; Exploring Diversity: Literature Themes and Activities for Grades 4–8; Teaching Young Adult Literature; Learning about the Holocaust; Images from the Holocaust: A Literature Anthology;* and *Toward Literacy: Theory and Applications for Teaching Writing in the Content Areas.* Stephens is the recipient of awards for excellence in teaching, leadership, and scholarly activities and was recognized for "distinguished teaching and extraordinary contributions to higher education" by the Michigan Association of Governing Boards of State Universities. She has served in a leadership capacity for several organizations and is a member of NCTE and IRA.

This book was typeset in Palatino and Helvetica by Precision Graphics.
Typefaces used on the cover were Book Antiqua, CommercialPi BT, and University Roman BT.
The book was printed on 50-lb. Accent Opaque paper by Versa Press.